Honey
So Sweet

4

Story and Art by
Amu Meguro

Contents

Story Thus Far

One day during junior high, the nervous and cowardly Nao comes across a beat-up delinquent in the middle of a downpour. She leaves him her umbrella and a box of bandages before running away. Now in high school, she runs into the very same delinquent, and he unabashedly asks her to date him with marriage in mind.

At first Nao is afraid of Onise, but she soon discovers that he's a gentle soul, and this time the two become a couple.

At the start of the second semester, Onise makes it his mission to befriend more classmates, such as the ever-charming and popular Futami. Futami starts getting to know Nao through Onise and soon falls for her too.

Once Futami sees how much Onise and Nao care for each other, Futami seems to give up his pursuit of Nao—but if that's so, why does he come to see her in the middle of the sports festival...?

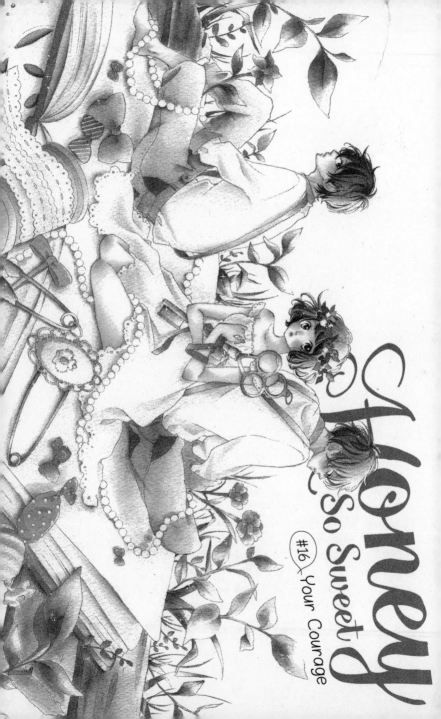

Honey
So Sweet

#16 Your Courage

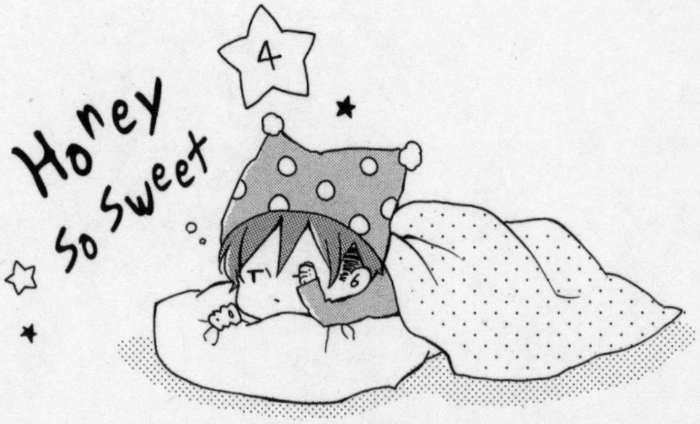
4
Honey So Sweet

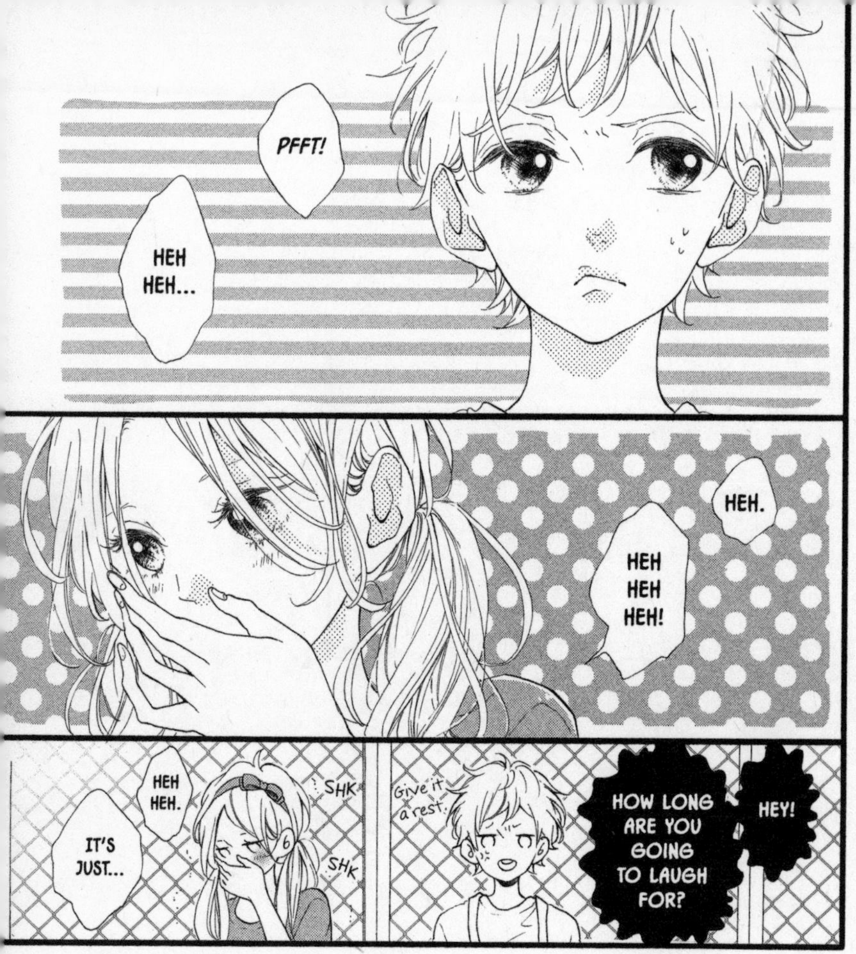
PFFT!
HEH HEH...
HEH.
HEH HEH HEH!
HEY!
HOW LONG ARE YOU GOING TO LAUGH FOR?
Give it a rest.
SHK
HEH HEH.
SHK
IT'S JUST...

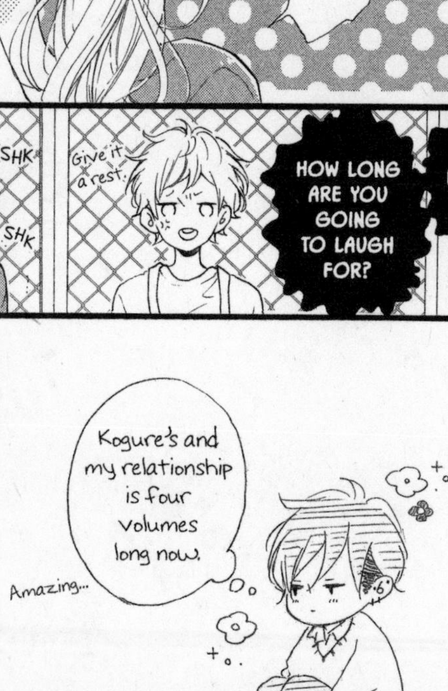
Kogure's and my relationship is four volumes long now.
Amazing...

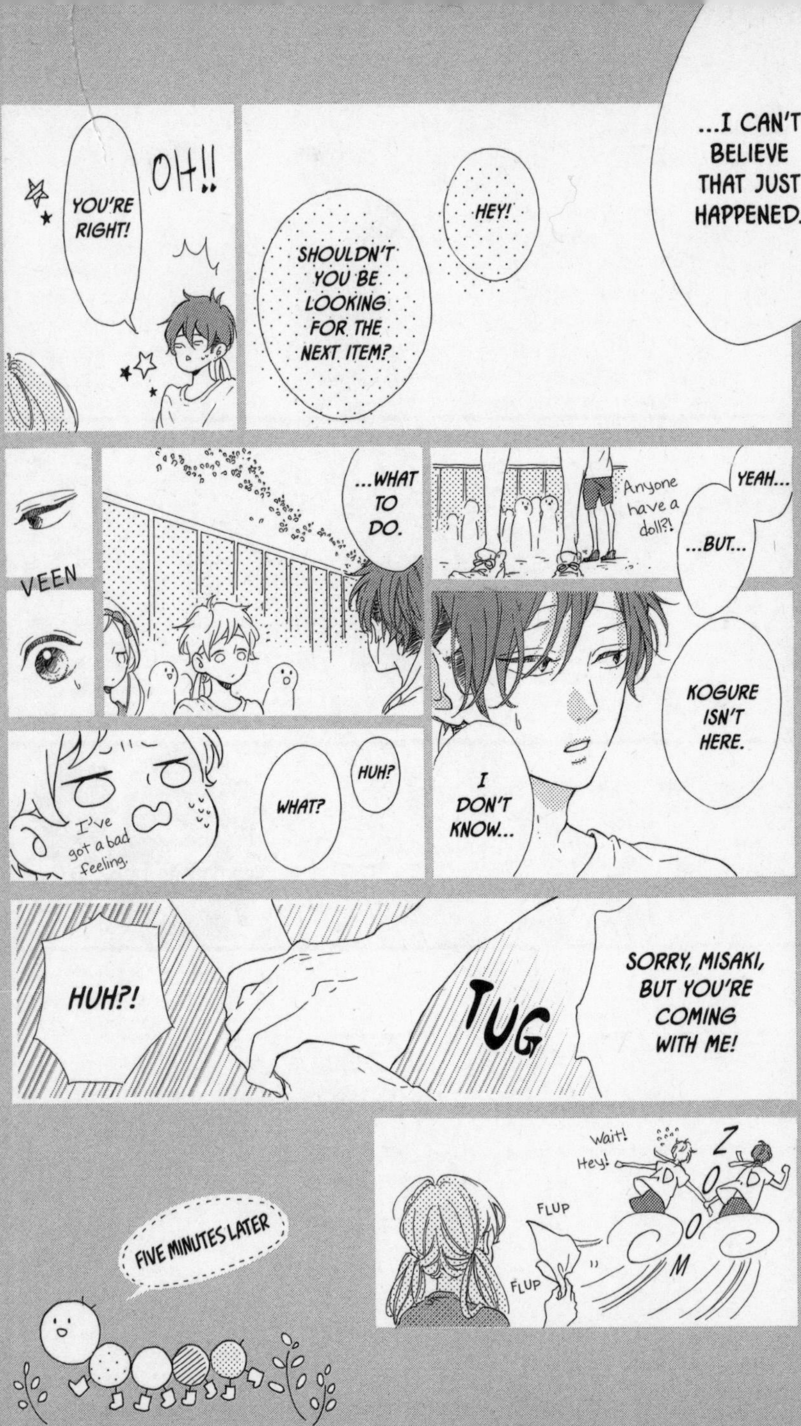
...I CAN'T BELIEVE THAT JUST HAPPENED.
HEY!
SHOULDN'T YOU BE LOOKING FOR THE NEXT ITEM?
OH!!
YOU'RE RIGHT!
YEAH...
...BUT...
Anyone have a doll?!
...WHAT TO DO.
VEEN
KOGURE ISN'T HERE.
I DON'T KNOW...
HUH?
WHAT?
I've got a bad feeling.
SORRY, MISAKI, BUT YOU'RE COMING WITH ME!
TUG
HUH?!
Wait!
Hey!
ZOOM
FLUP
FLUP
FIVE MINUTES LATER

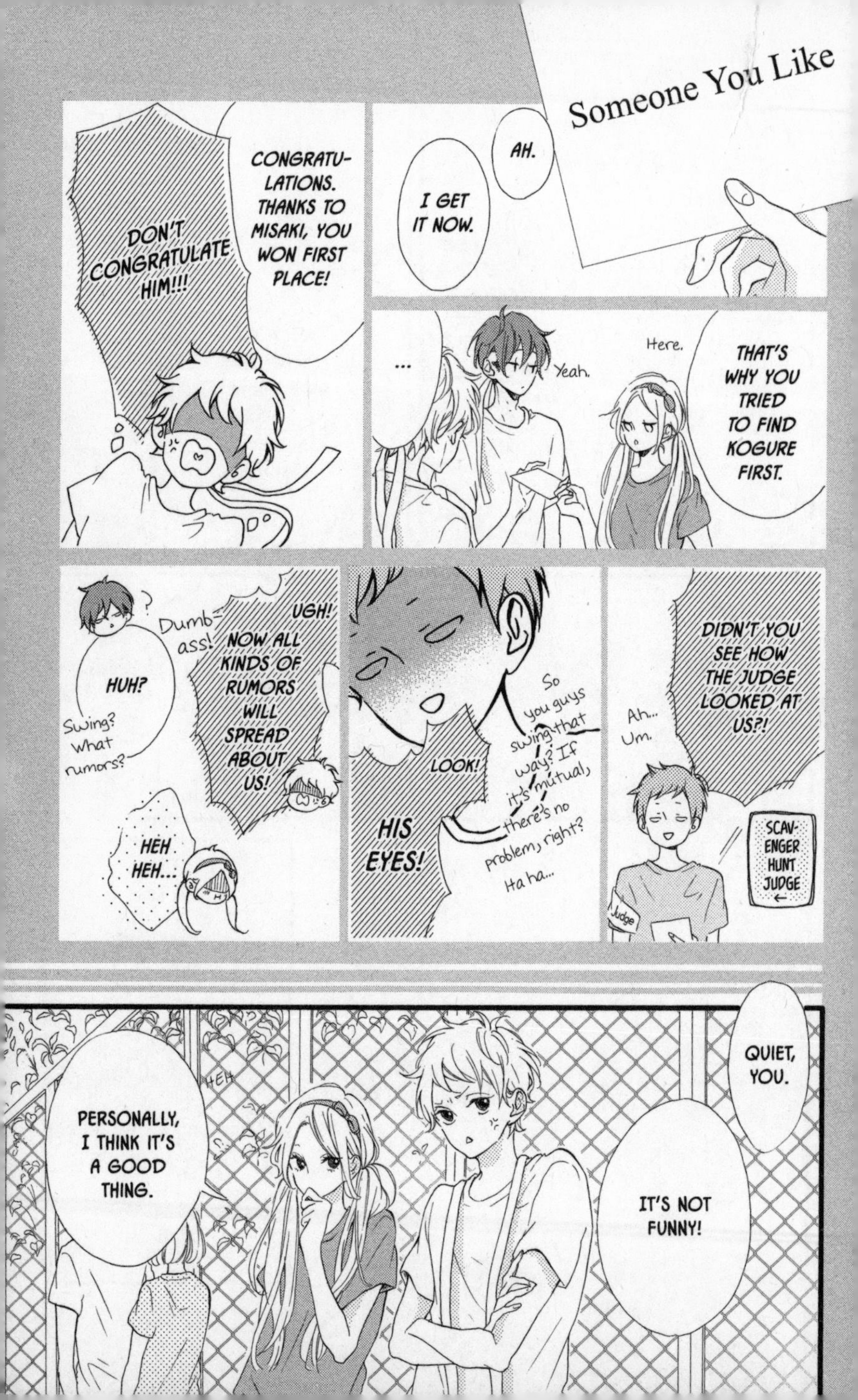
Someone You Like
AH.
I GET IT NOW.
THAT'S WHY YOU TRIED TO FIND KOGURE FIRST.
Here.
Yeah.
...
CONGRATULATIONS. THANKS TO MISAKI, YOU WON FIRST PLACE!
DON'T CONGRATULATE HIM!!!
DIDN'T YOU SEE HOW THE JUDGE LOOKED AT US?!
Ah... Um.
SCAVENGER HUNT JUDGE
Judge
So you guys swing that way? If it's mutual, there's no problem, right? Ha ha...
LOOK! HIS EYES!
UGH! NOW ALL KINDS OF RUMORS WILL SPREAD ABOUT US!
Dumbass!
HUH?
Swing? What rumors?
HEH HEH...
QUIET, YOU.
IT'S NOT FUNNY!
PERSONALLY, I THINK IT'S A GOOD THING.
HEH

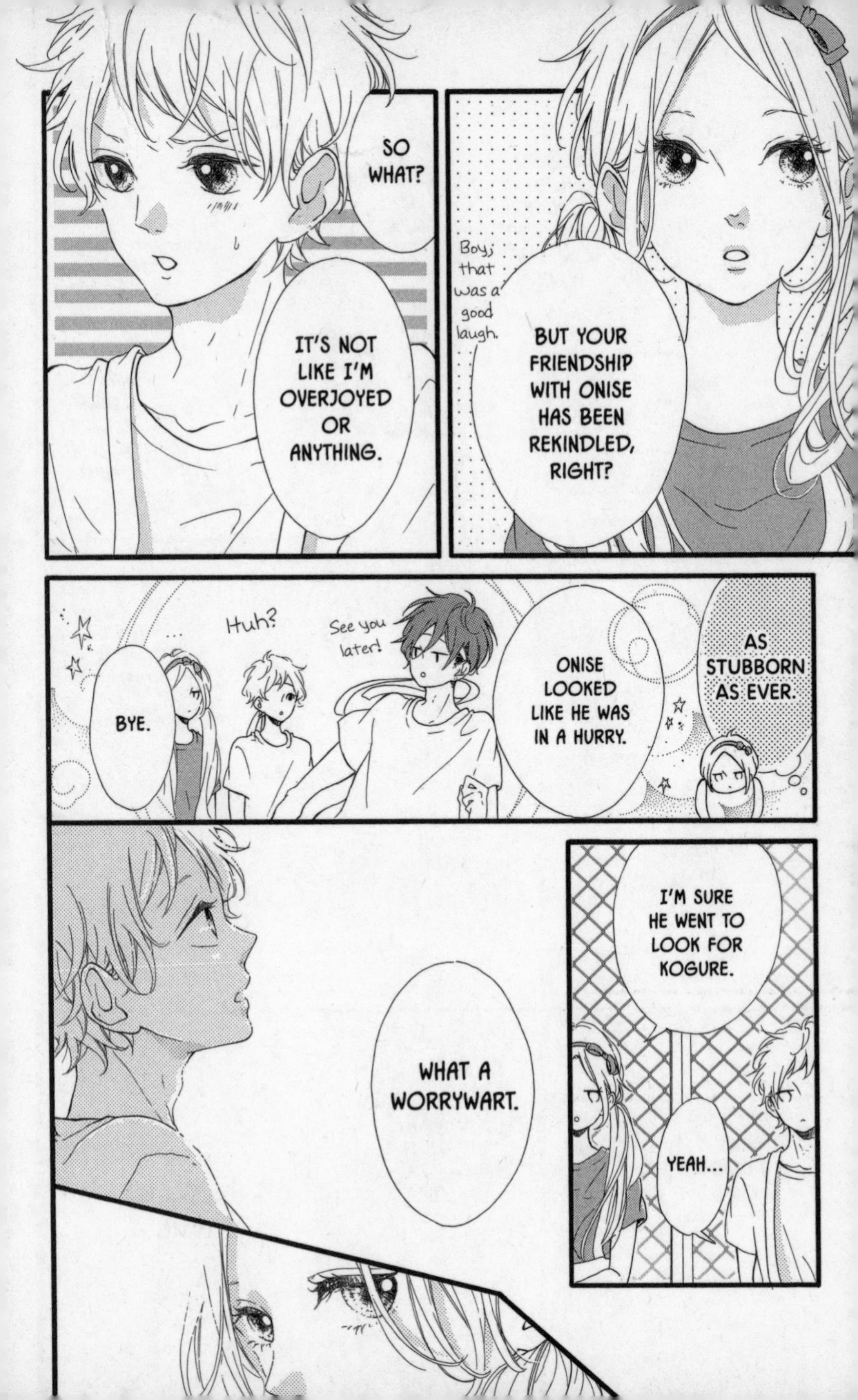
BUT YOUR FRIENDSHIP WITH ONISE HAS BEEN REKINDLED, RIGHT?
Boy, that was a good laugh.
SO WHAT?
IT'S NOT LIKE I'M OVERJOYED OR ANYTHING.
AS STUBBORN AS EVER.
ONISE LOOKED LIKE HE WAS IN A HURRY.
See you later!
Huh?
...
BYE.
I'M SURE HE WENT TO LOOK FOR KOGURE.
YEAH...
WHAT A WORRYWART.

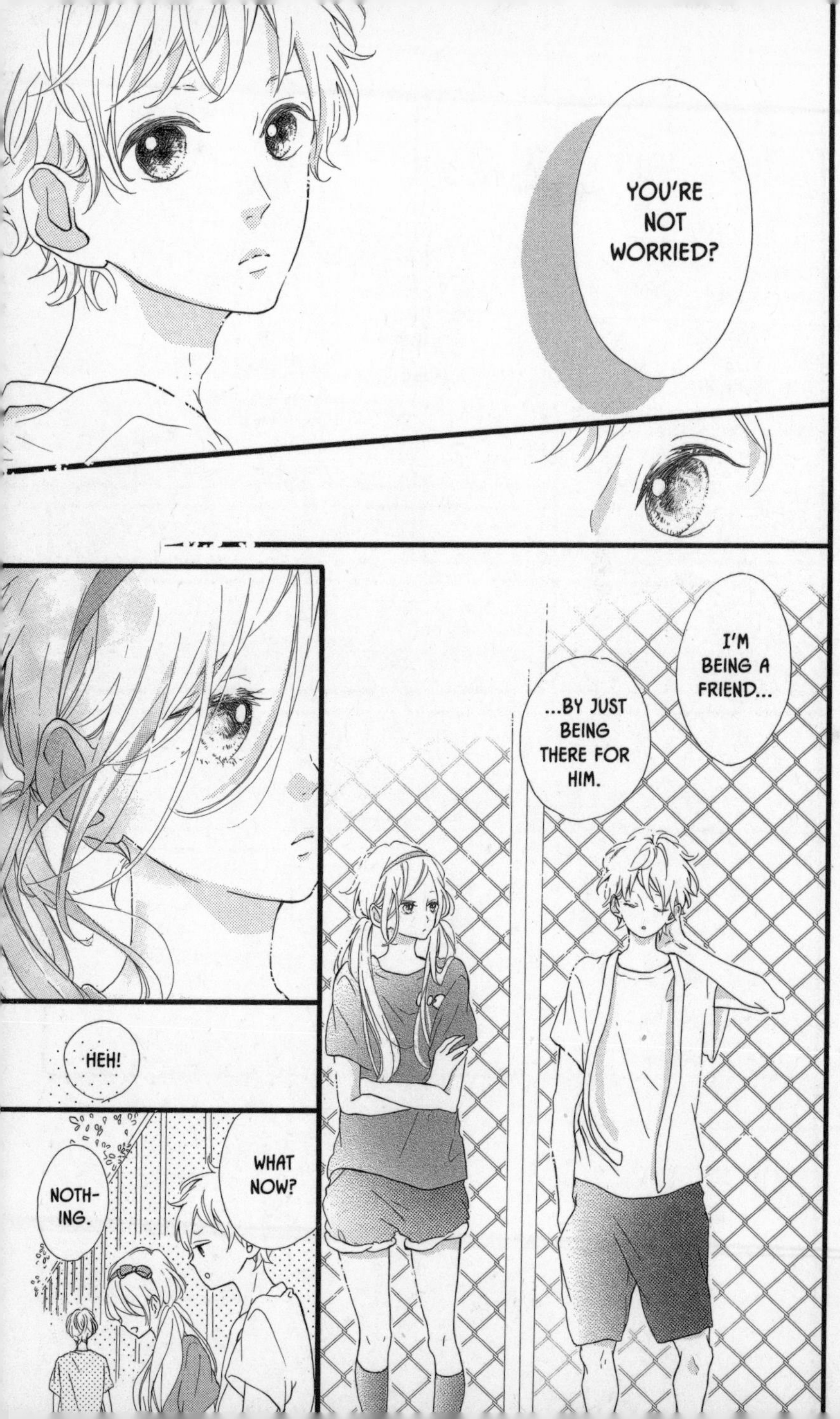
YOU'RE NOT WORRIED?
I'M BEING A FRIEND...
...BY JUST BEING THERE FOR HIM.
HEH!
WHAT NOW?
NOTH-ING.

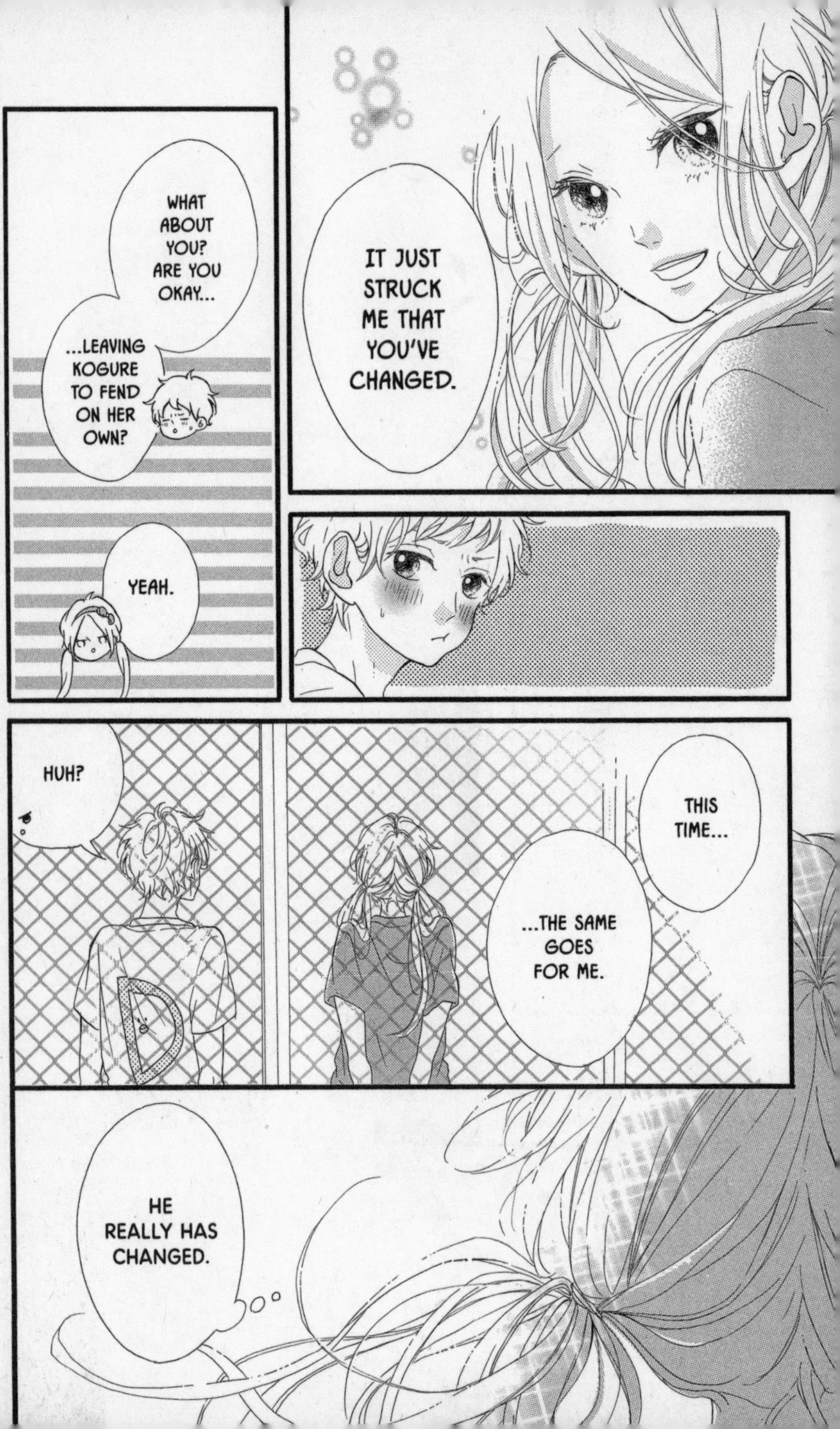
IT JUST STRUCK ME THAT YOU'VE CHANGED.
WHAT ABOUT YOU? ARE YOU OKAY...
...LEAVING KOGURE TO FEND ON HER OWN?
YEAH.
THIS TIME...
...THE SAME GOES FOR ME.
HUH?
HE REALLY HAS CHANGED.

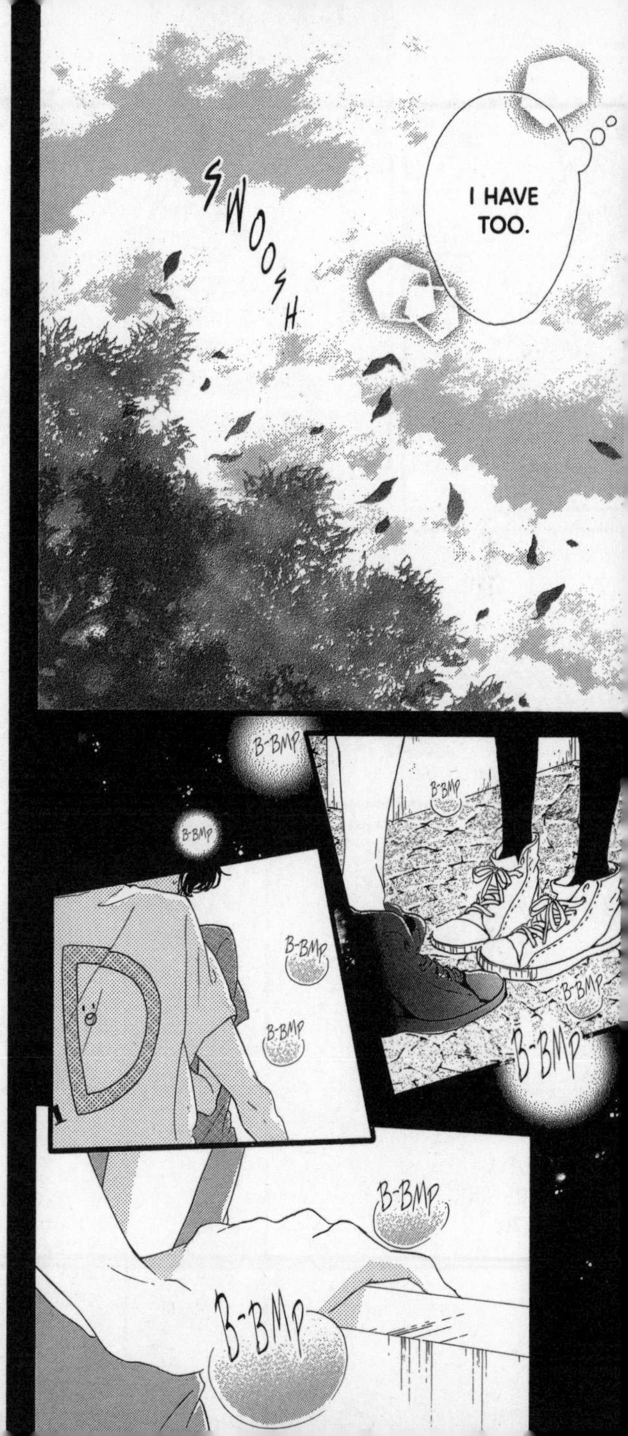
I HAVE TOO.
SWOOSH
B-BMP
B-BMP
B-BMP
B-BMP
B-BMP
B-BMP
B-BMP
B-BMP
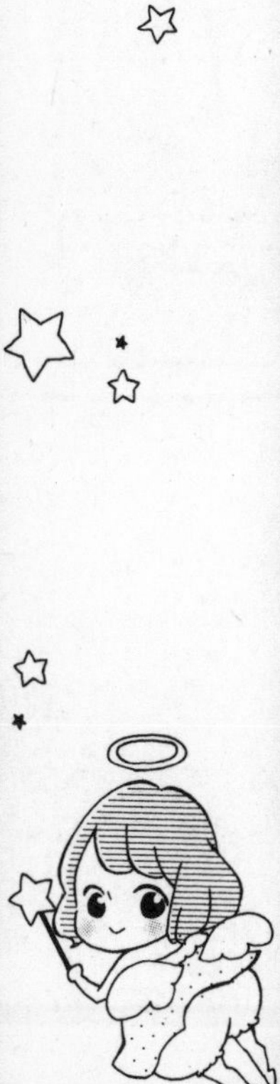

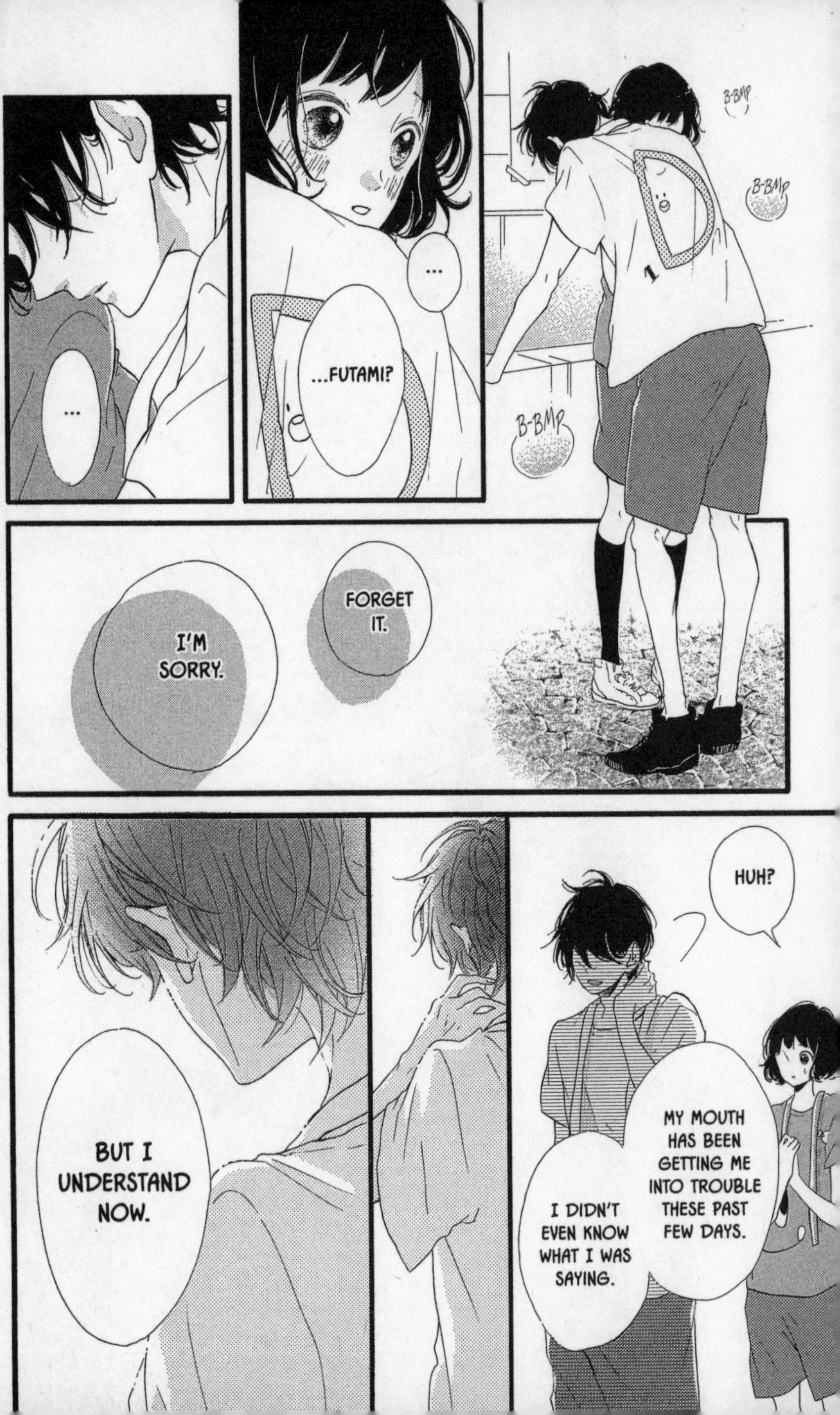
B-BMP
B-BMP
B-BMP
...
...FUTAMI?
...
FORGET IT.
I'M SORRY.
HUH?
MY MOUTH HAS BEEN GETTING ME INTO TROUBLE THESE PAST FEW DAYS.
I DIDN'T EVEN KNOW WHAT I WAS SAYING.
BUT I UNDERSTAND NOW.

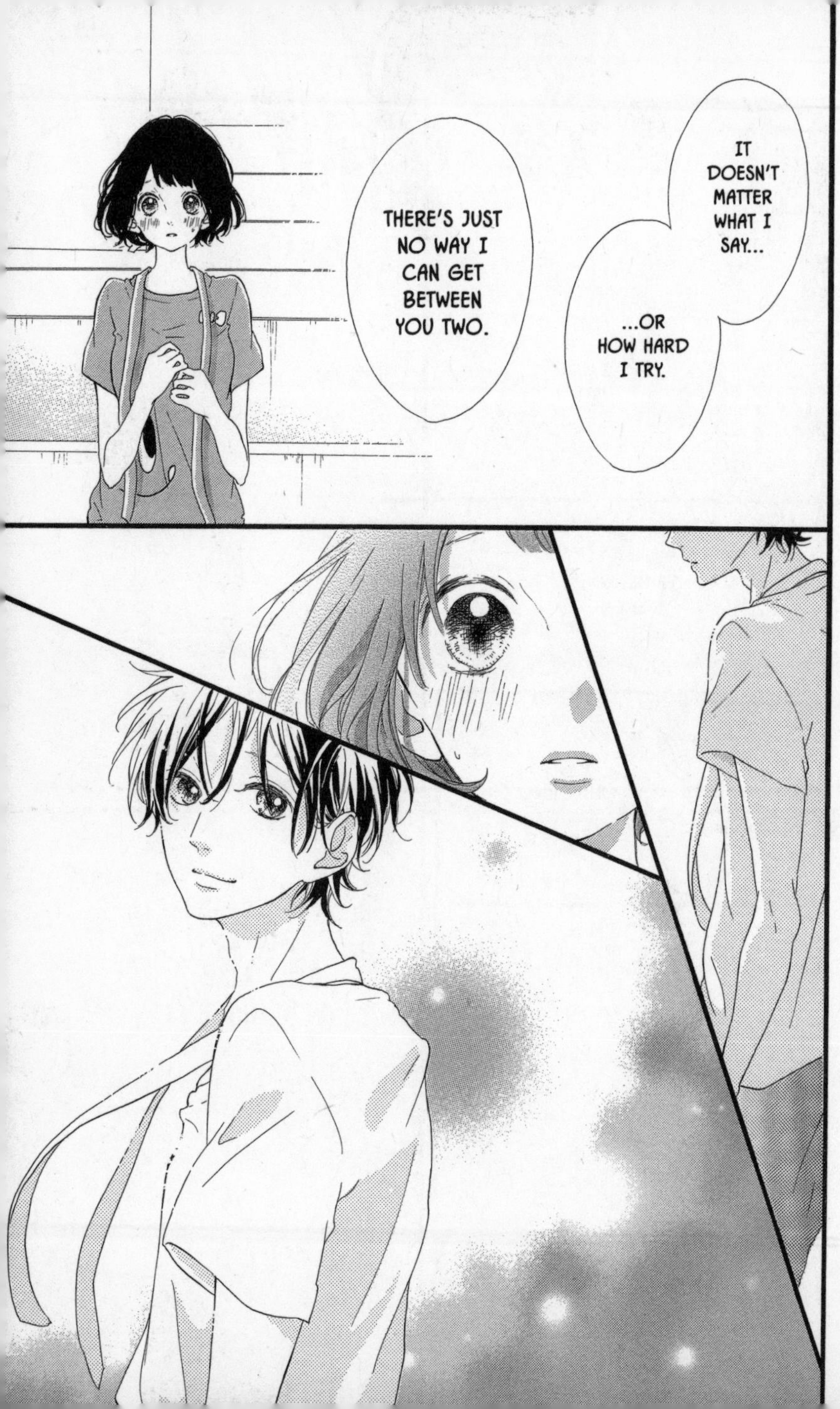
IT DOESN'T MATTER WHAT I SAY...
...OR HOW HARD I TRY.
THERE'S JUST NO WAY I CAN GET BETWEEN YOU TWO.

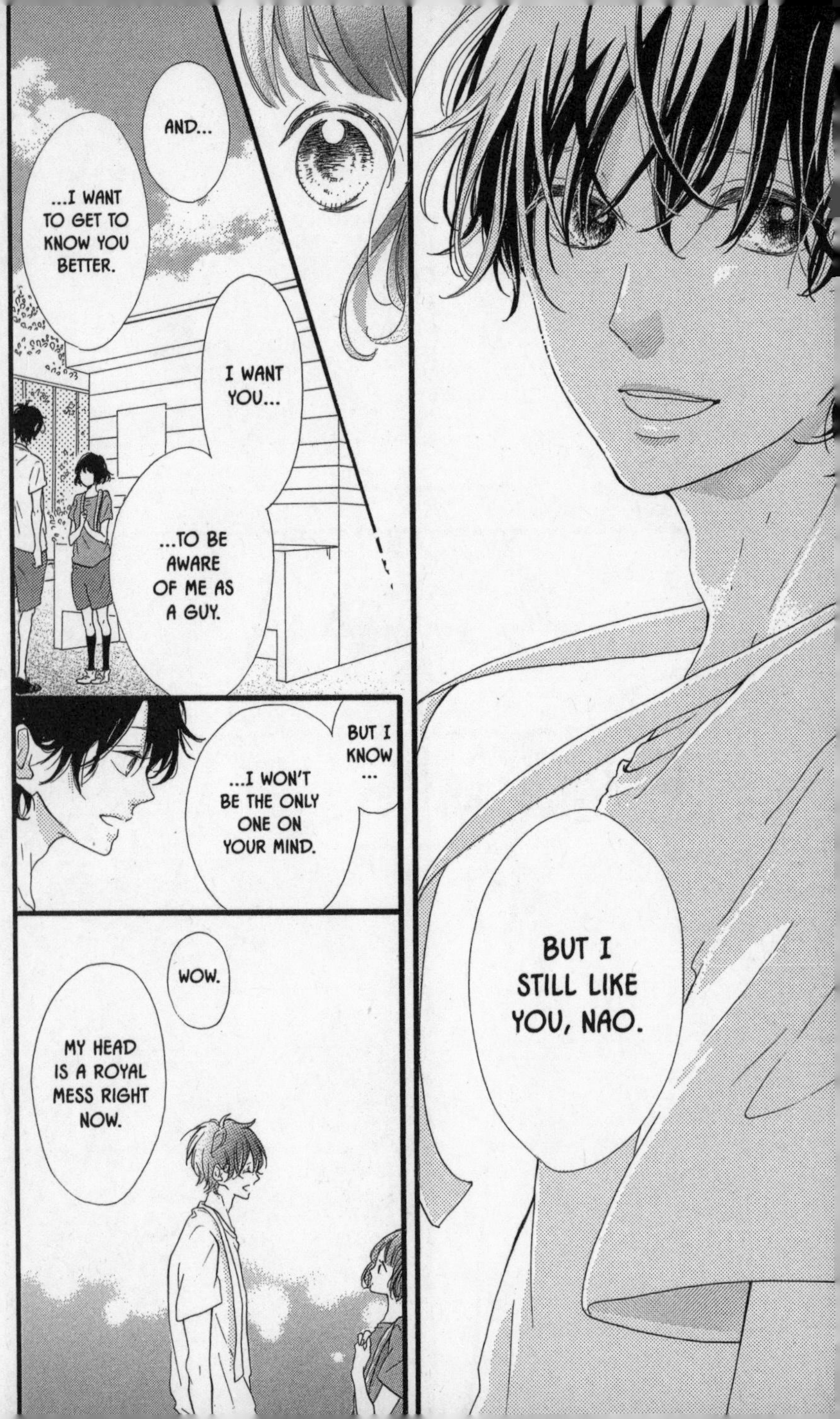
BUT I STILL LIKE YOU, NAO.
AND...
...I WANT TO GET TO KNOW YOU BETTER.
I WANT YOU...
...TO BE AWARE OF ME AS A GUY.
BUT I KNOW...
...I WON'T BE THE ONLY ONE ON YOUR MIND.
WOW.
MY HEAD IS A ROYAL MESS RIGHT NOW.

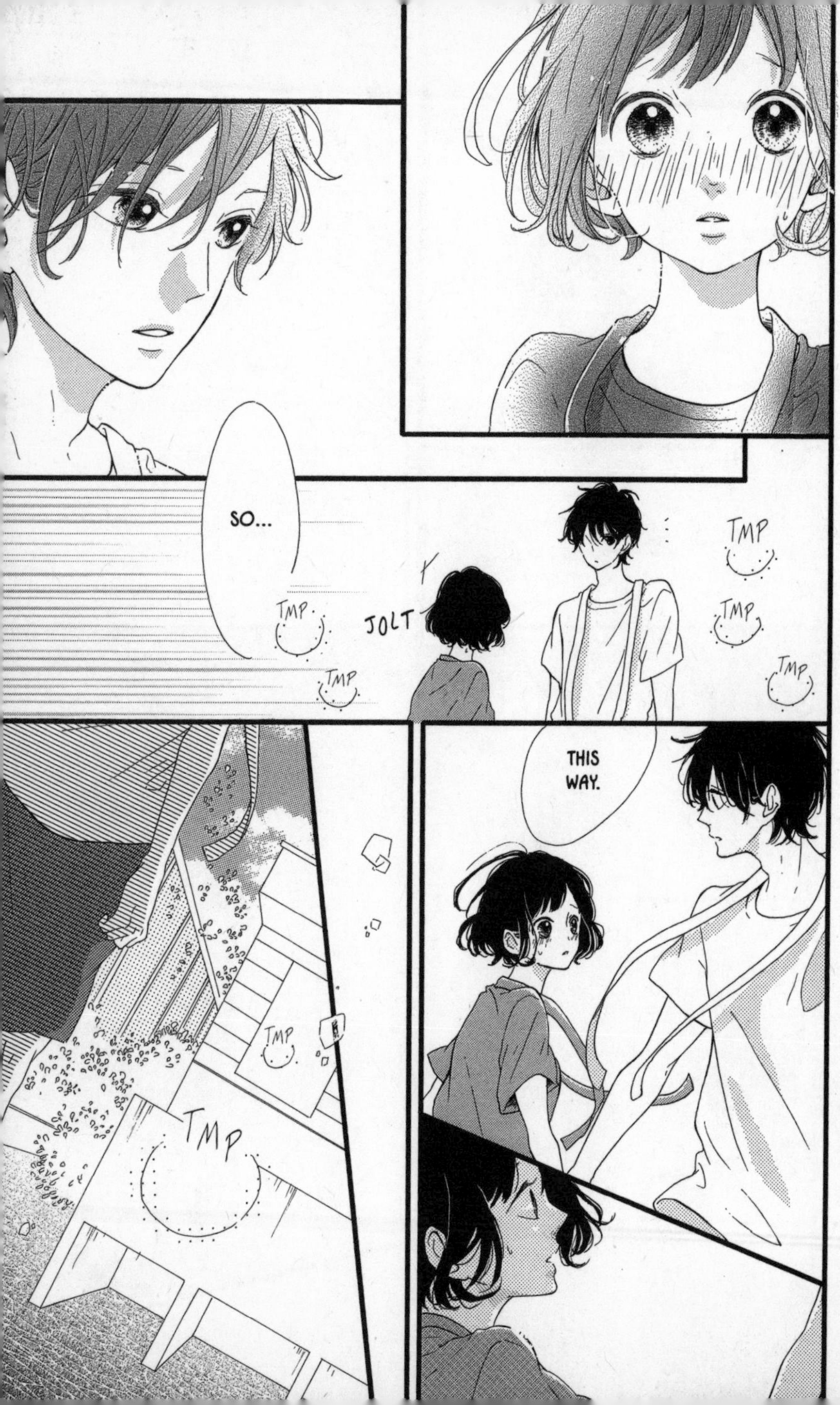
TMP
TMP
TMP
SO...
JOLT
TMP
TMP
THIS WAY.
TMP
TMP

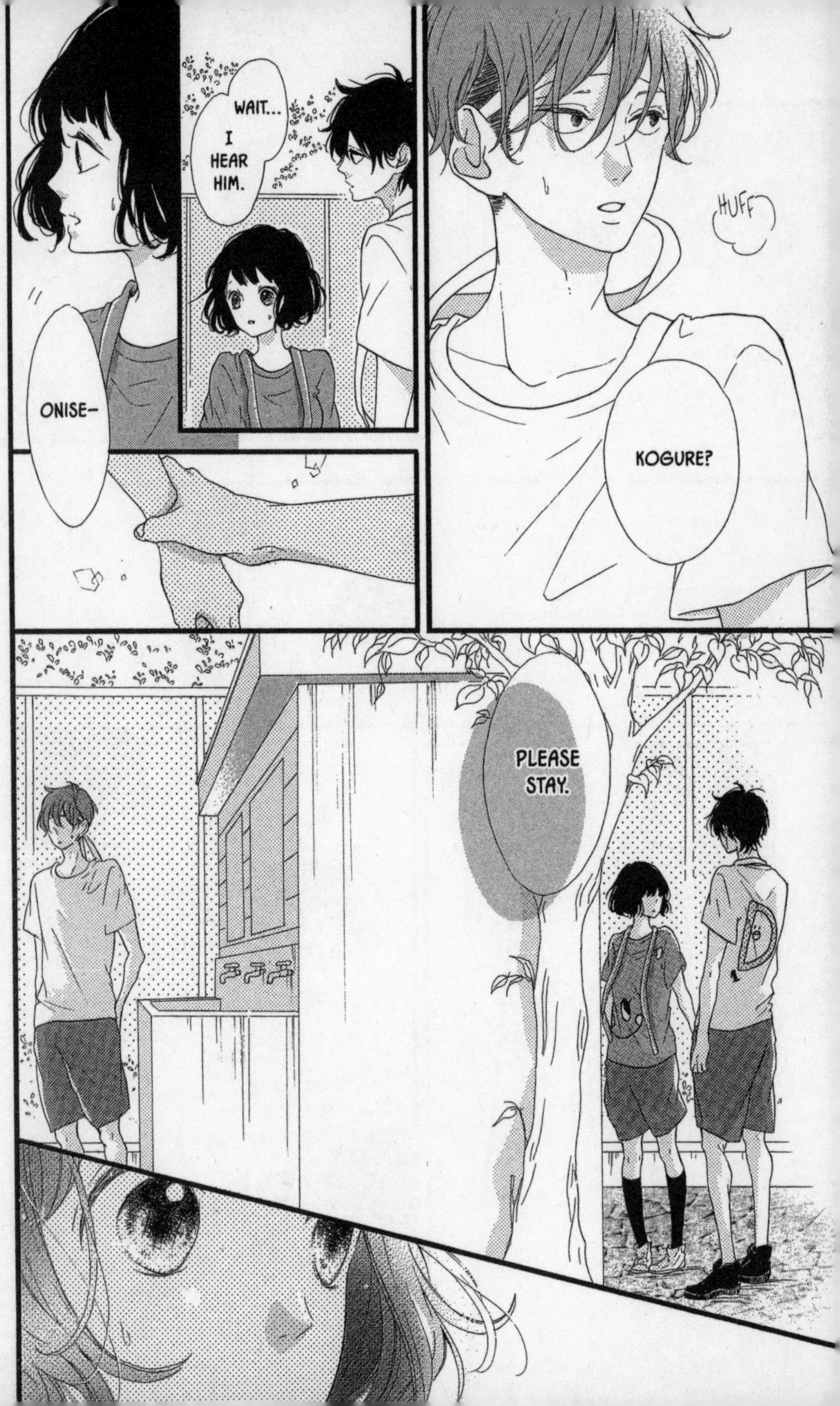
HUFF
KOGURE?
WAIT... I HEAR HIM.
ONISE-
PLEASE STAY.

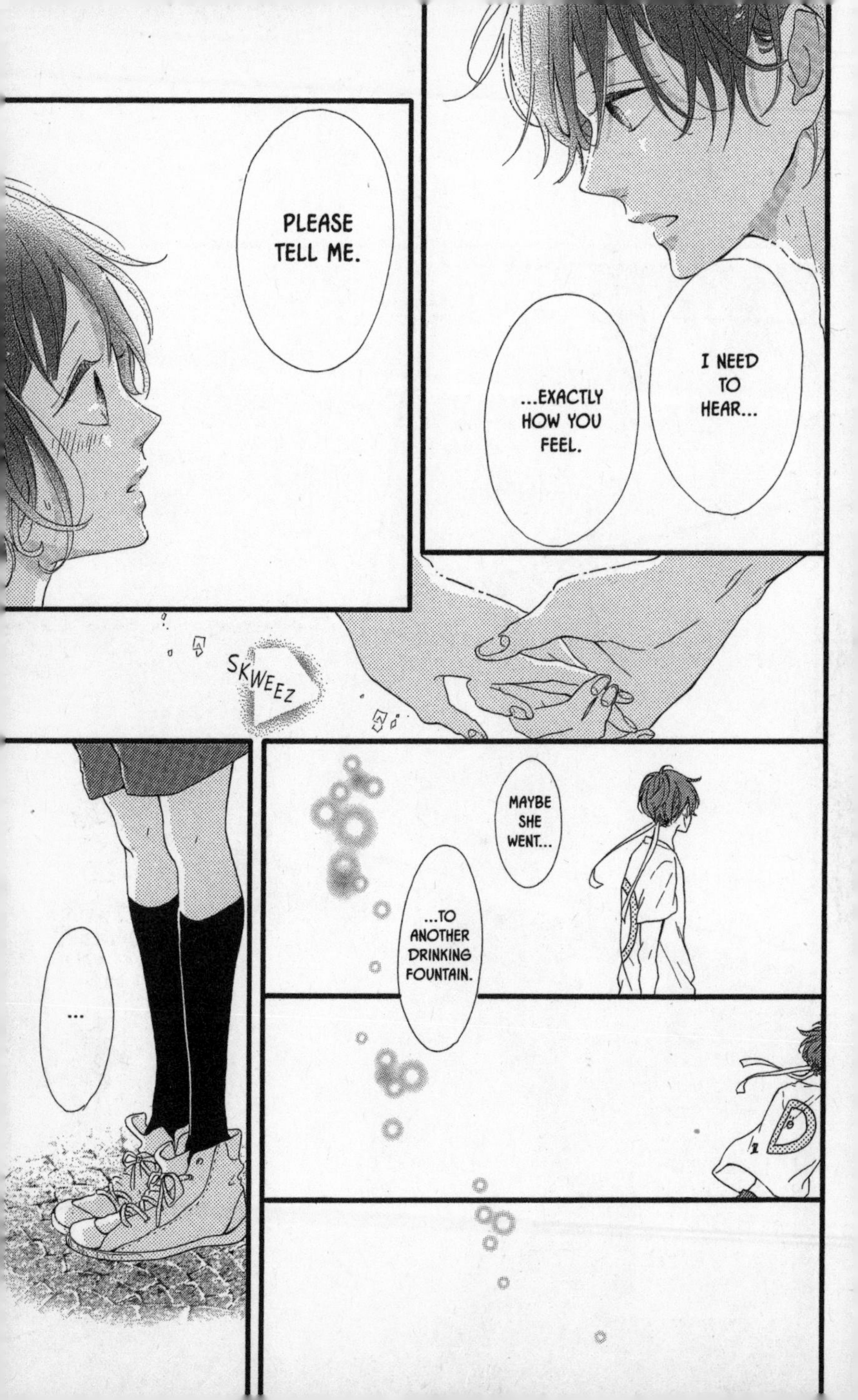
I NEED TO HEAR...
...EXACTLY HOW YOU FEEL.
PLEASE TELL ME.
SKWEEZ
MAYBE SHE WENT...
...TO ANOTHER DRINKING FOUNTAIN.
...

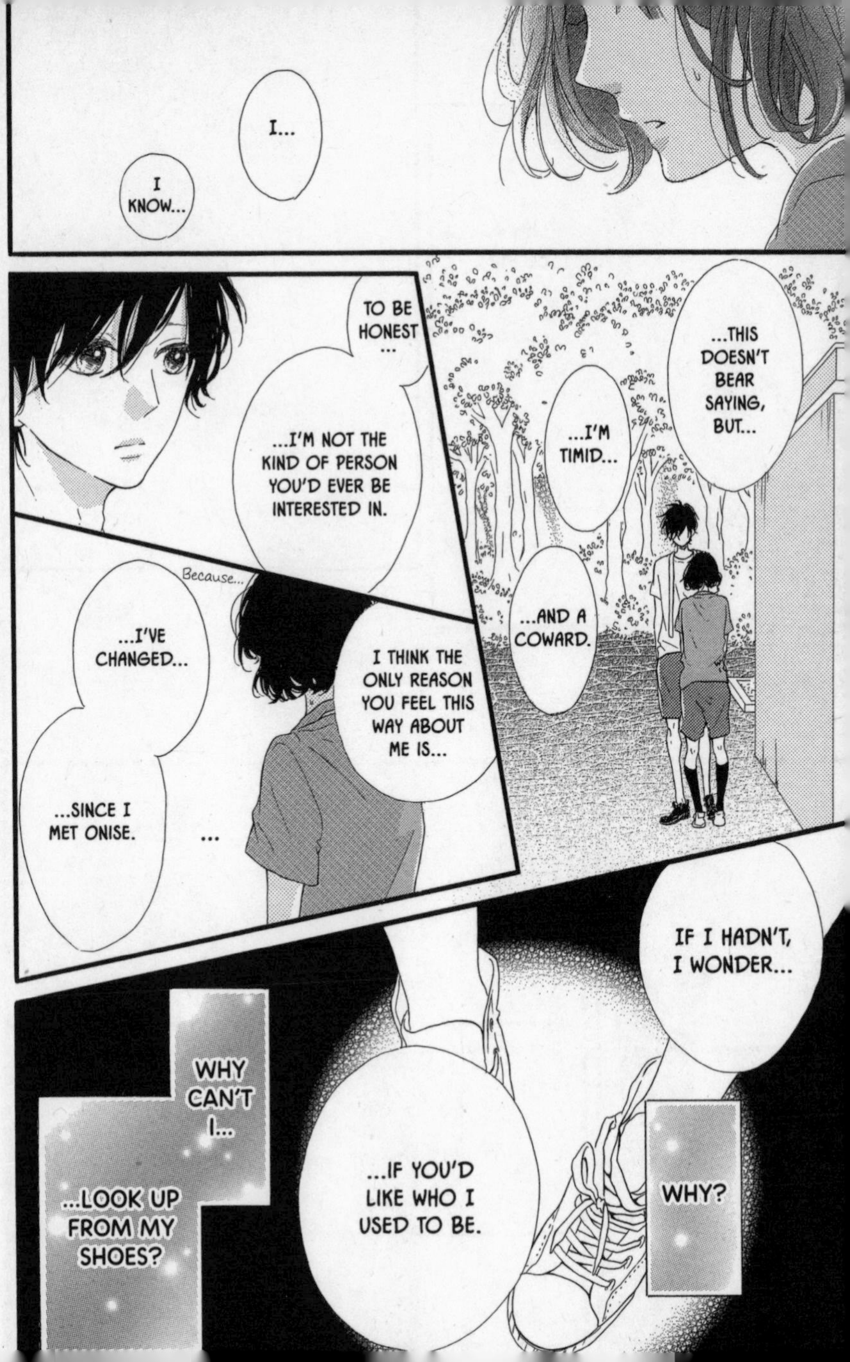
I...
I KNOW...
...THIS DOESN'T BEAR SAYING, BUT...
...I'M TIMID...
...AND A COWARD.
TO BE HONEST ...
...I'M NOT THE KIND OF PERSON YOU'D EVER BE INTERESTED IN.
I THINK THE ONLY REASON YOU FEEL THIS WAY ABOUT ME IS...
Because...
...I'VE CHANGED...
...SINCE I MET ONISE.
...
IF I HADN'T, I WONDER...
...IF YOU'D LIKE WHO I USED TO BE.
WHY?
WHY CAN'T I...
...LOOK UP FROM MY SHOES?

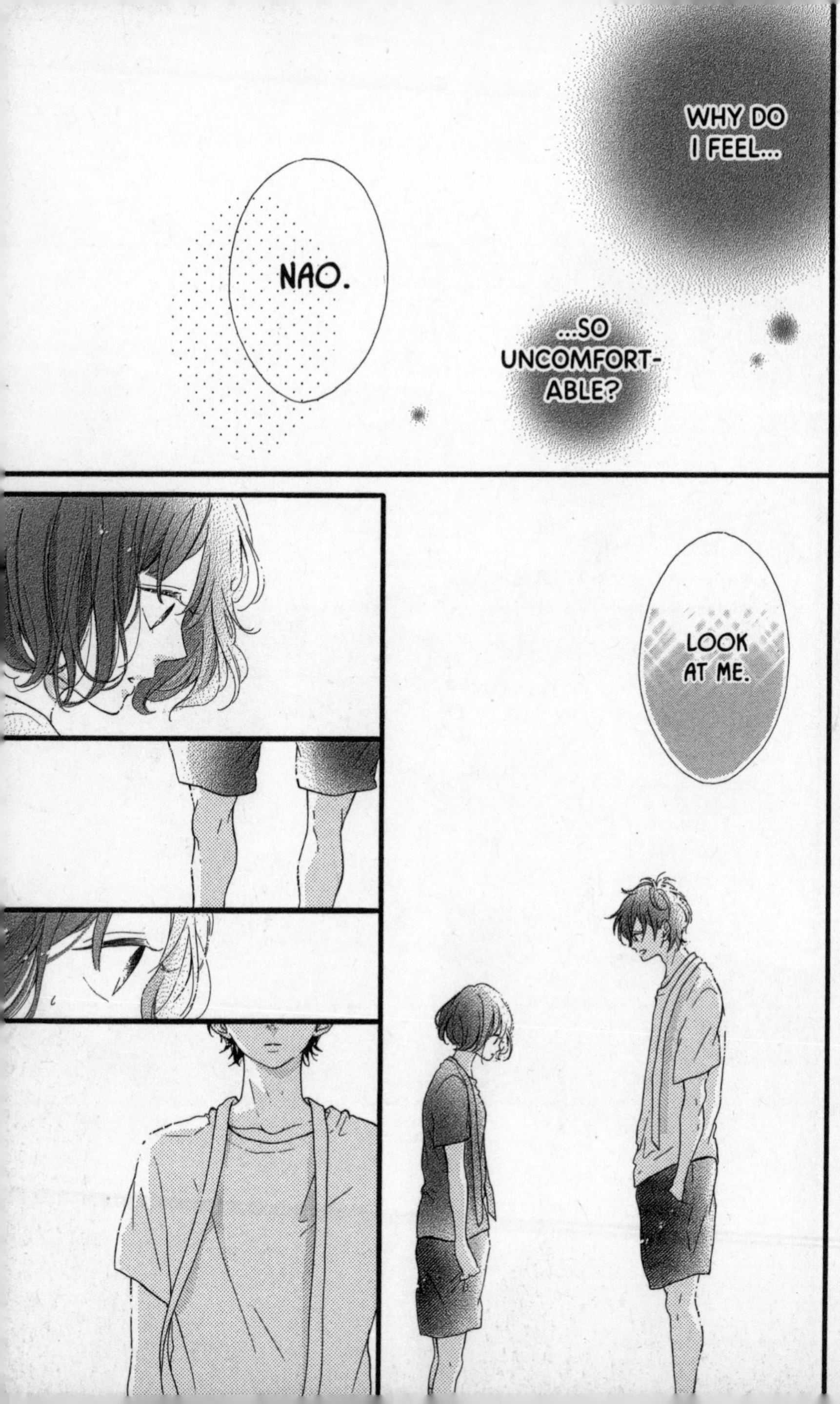
WHY DO I FEEL...
...SO UNCOMFORT-ABLE?
NAO.
LOOK AT ME.

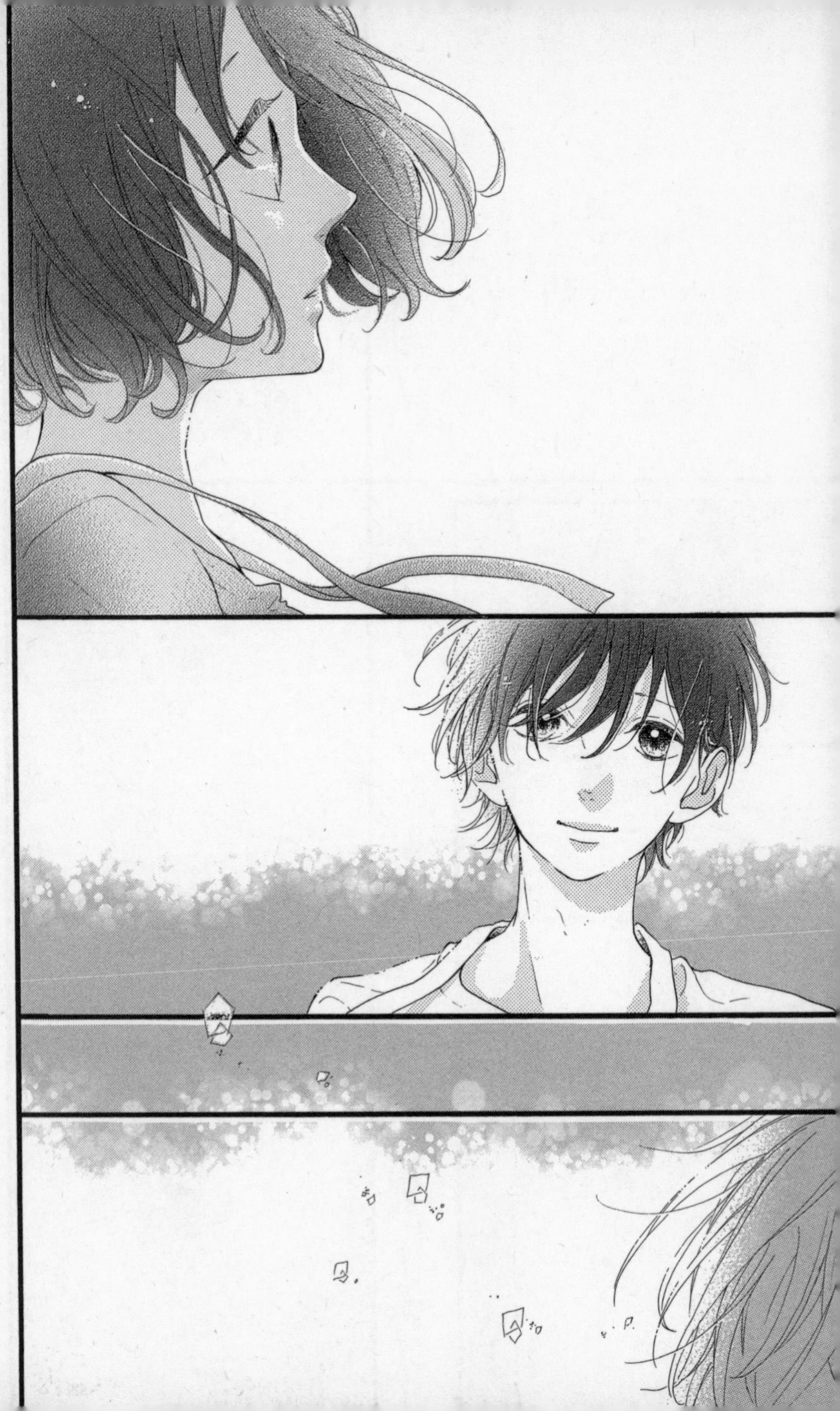

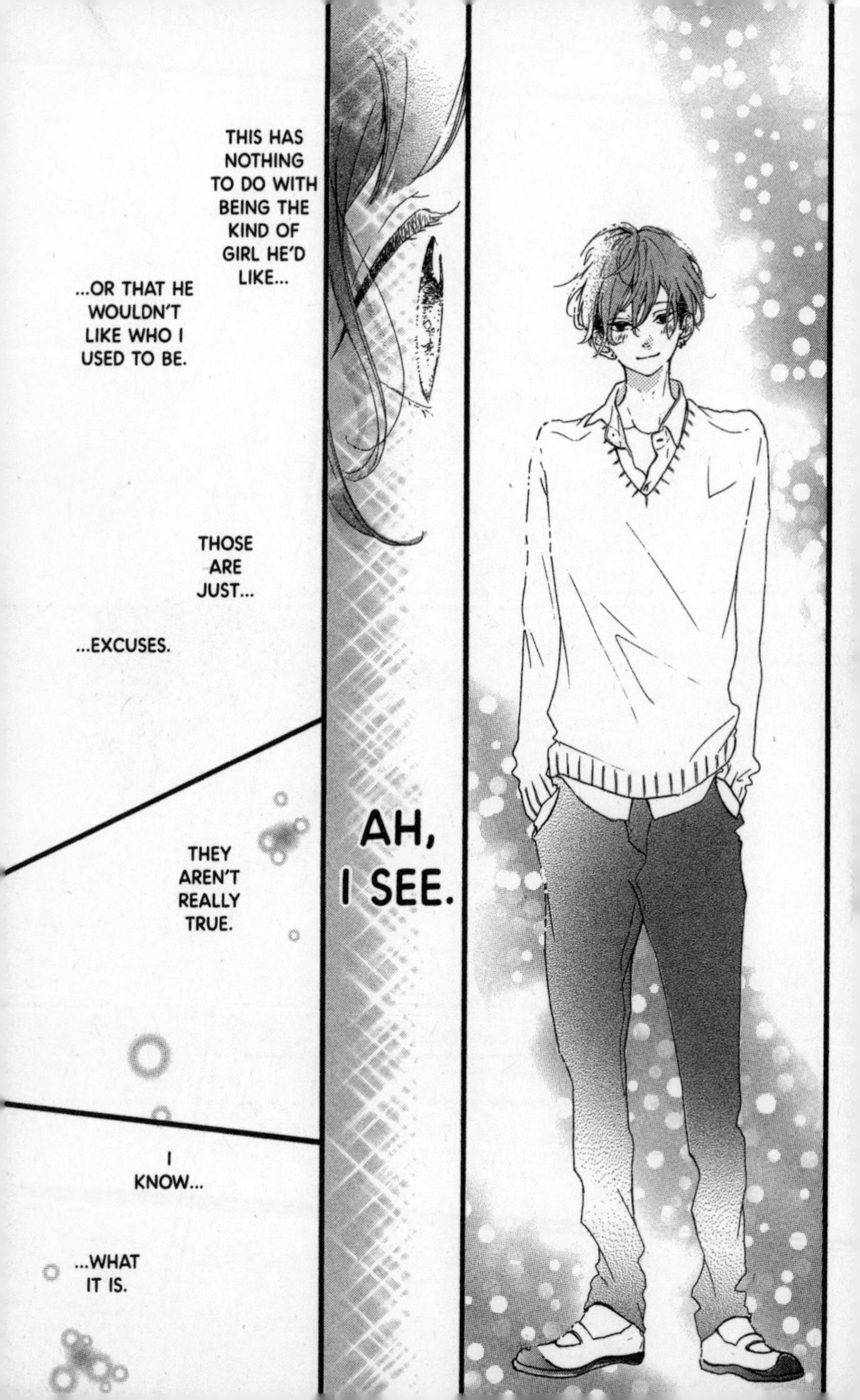
AH, I SEE.
THIS HAS NOTHING TO DO WITH BEING THE KIND OF GIRL HE'D LIKE...
...OR THAT HE WOULDN'T LIKE WHO I USED TO BE.
THOSE ARE JUST...
...EXCUSES.
THEY AREN'T REALLY TRUE.
I KNOW...
...WHAT IT IS.

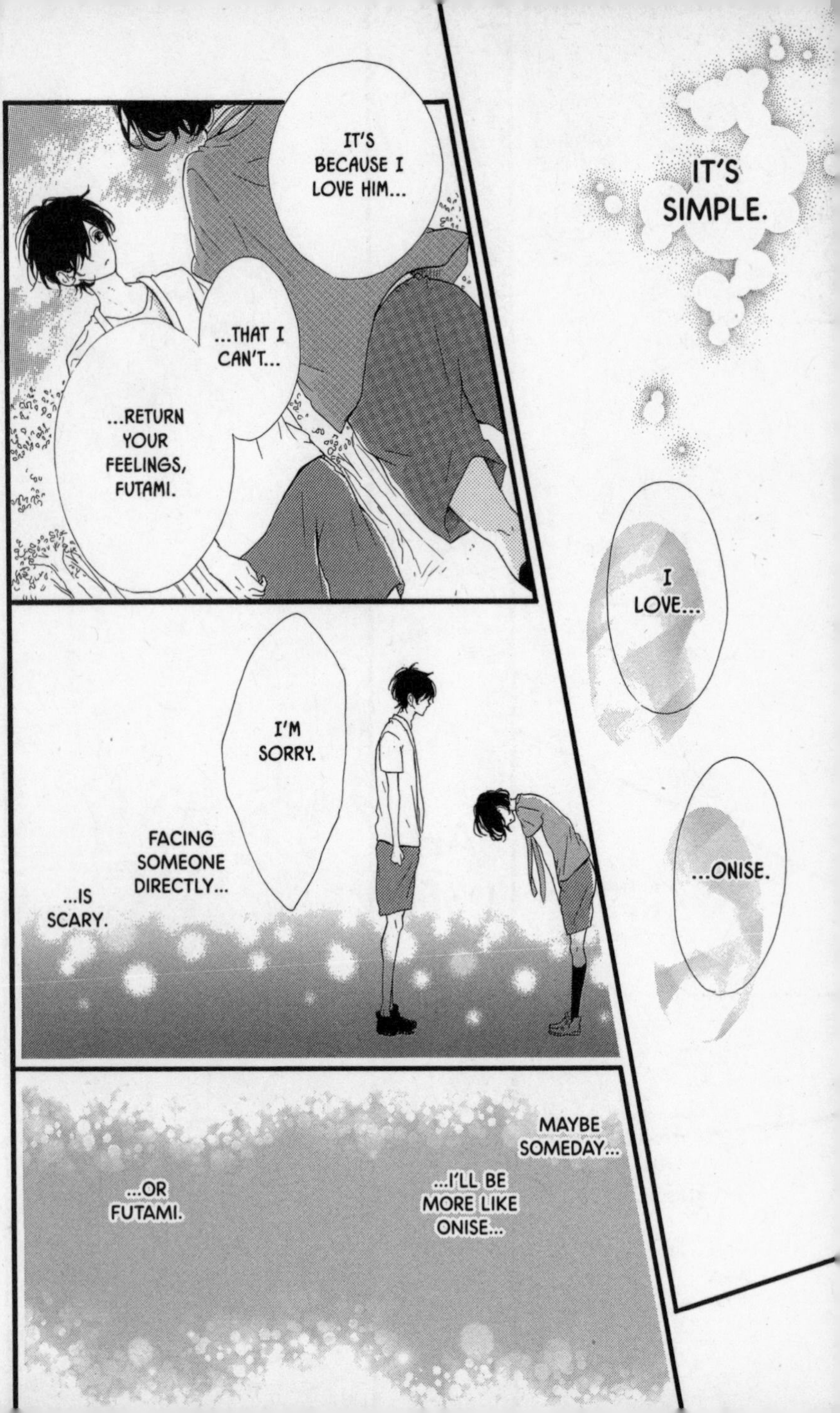
IT'S SIMPLE.
I LOVE...
...ONISE.
IT'S BECAUSE I LOVE HIM...
...THAT I CAN'T...
...RETURN YOUR FEELINGS, FUTAMI.
I'M SORRY.
FACING SOMEONE DIRECTLY...
...IS SCARY.
MAYBE SOMEDAY...
...I'LL BE MORE LIKE ONISE...
...OR FUTAMI.

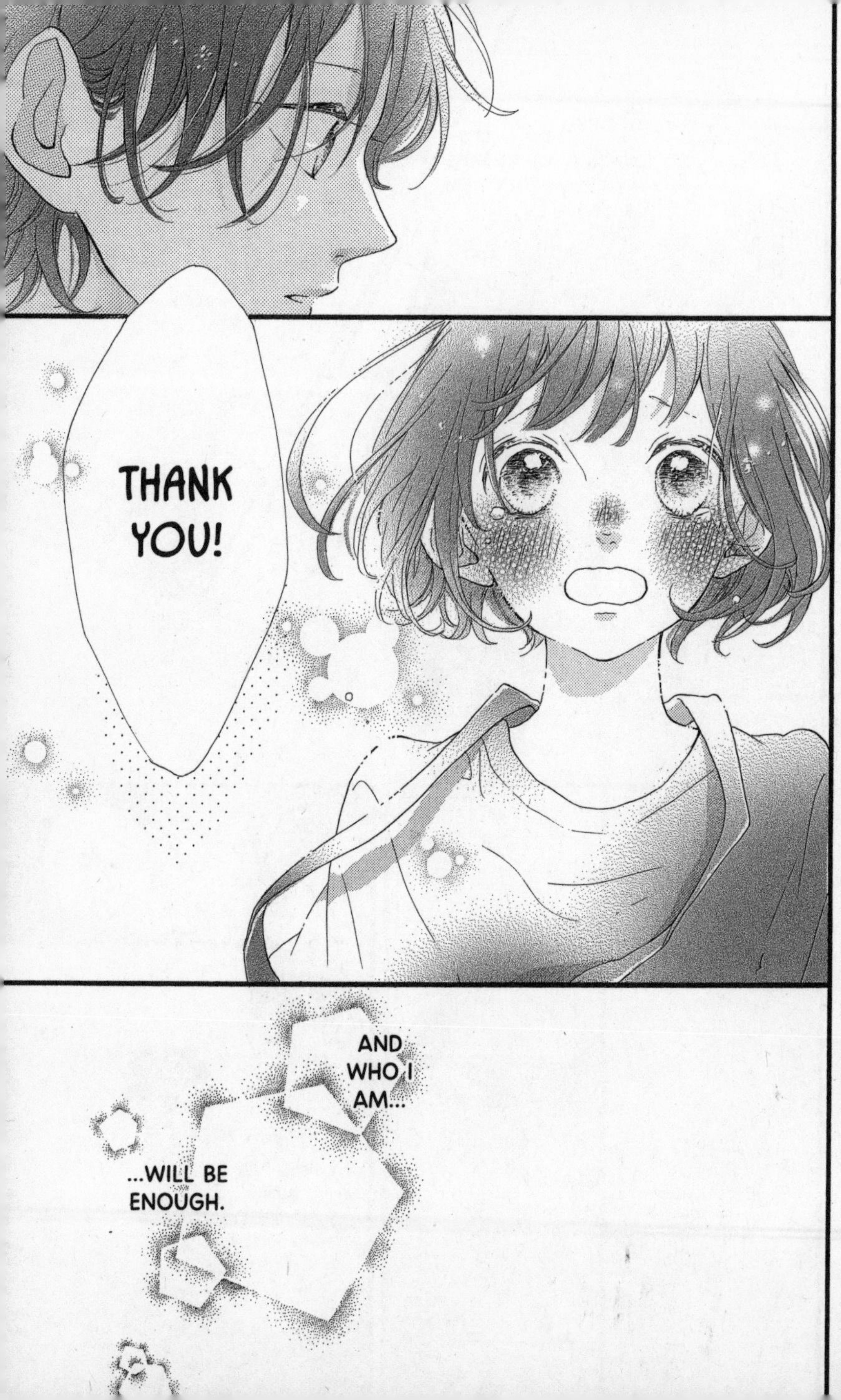
THANK YOU!
AND WHO I AM...
...WILL BE ENOUGH.

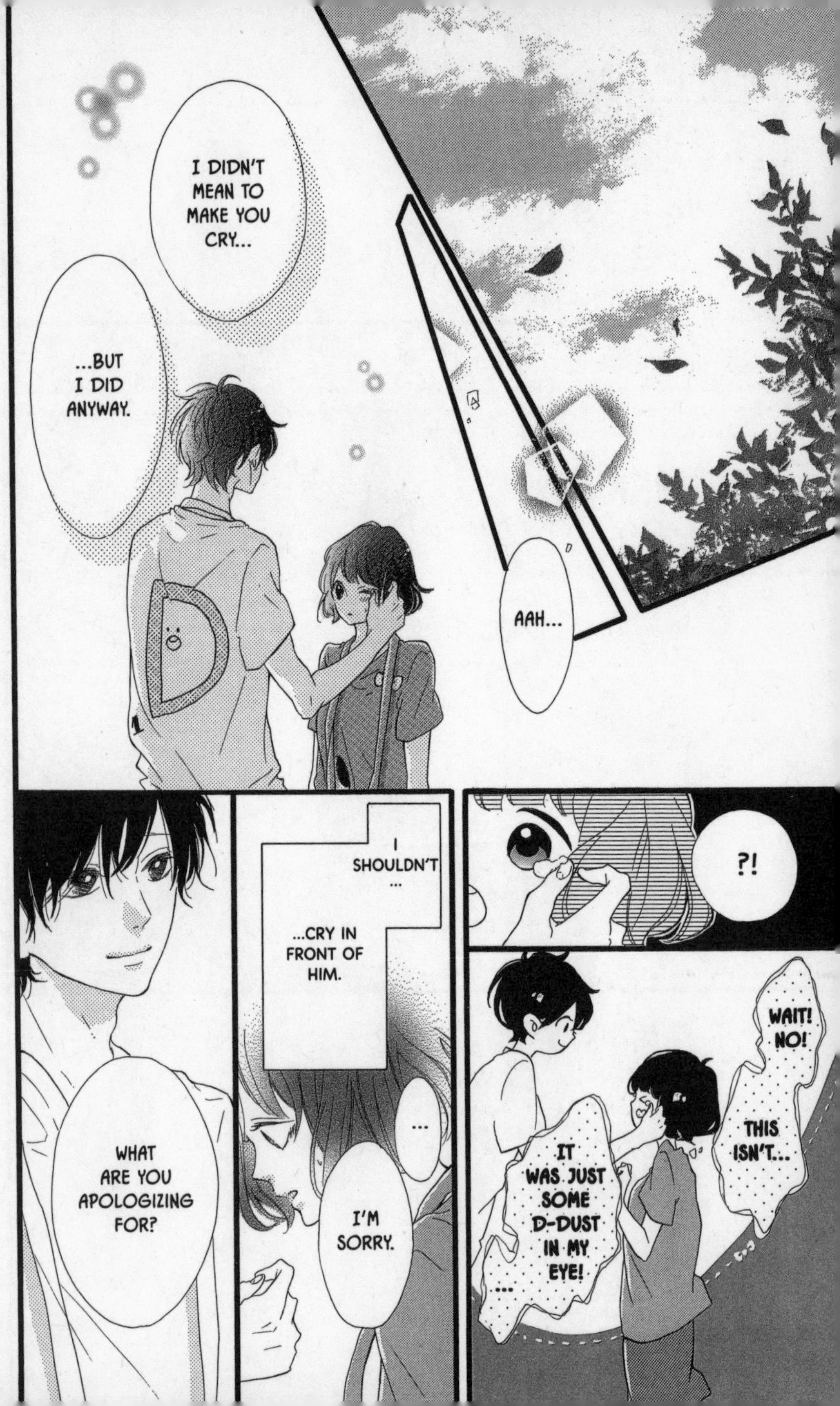
AAH...
I DIDN'T MEAN TO MAKE YOU CRY...
...BUT I DID ANYWAY.
?!
WAIT! NO!
THIS ISN'T...
IT WAS JUST SOME D-DUST IN MY EYE!
...
I SHOULDN'T...
...CRY IN FRONT OF HIM.
...
I'M SORRY.
WHAT ARE YOU APOLOGIZING FOR?

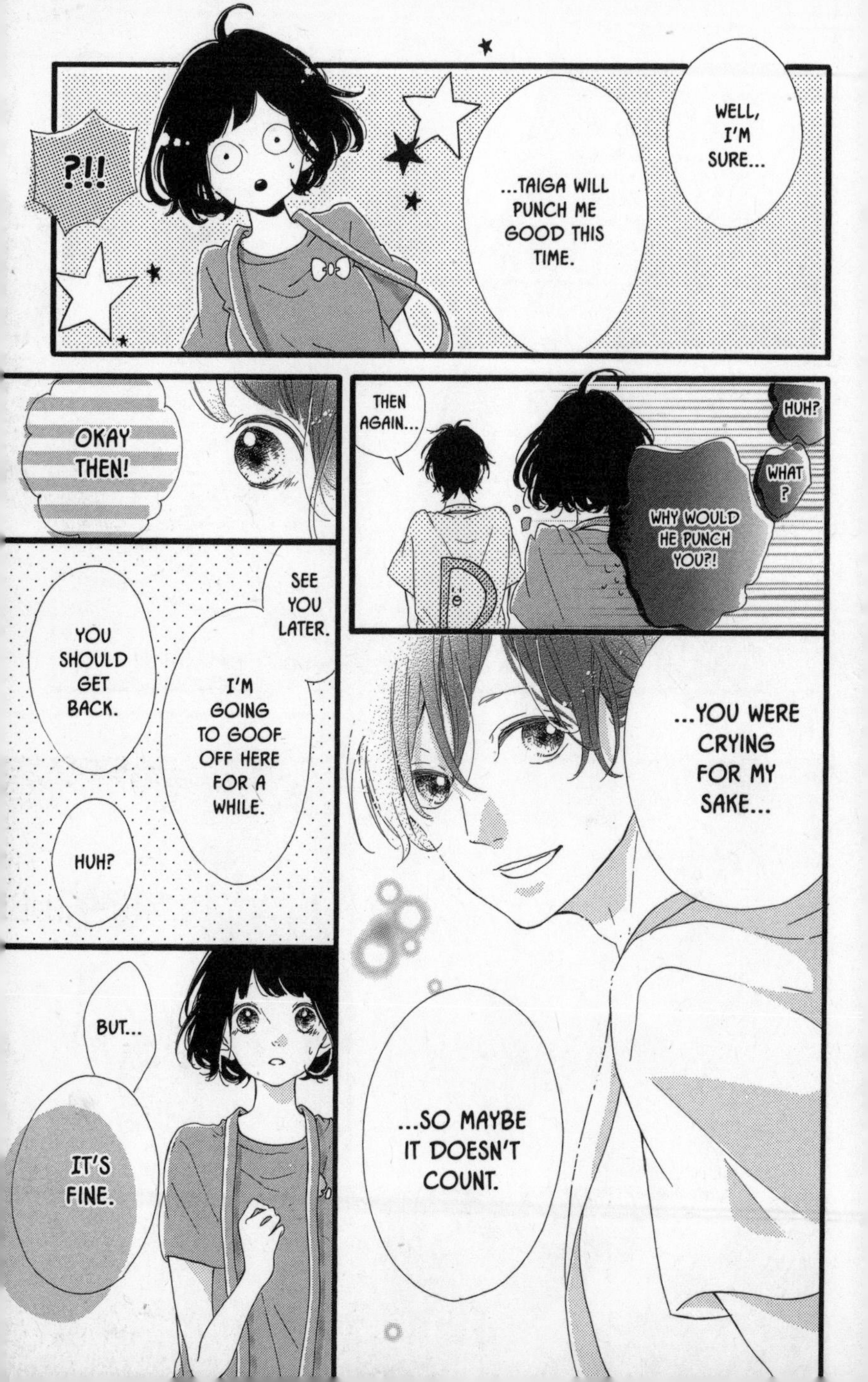
WELL, I'M SURE...
...TAIGA WILL PUNCH ME GOOD THIS TIME.
?!!
HUH?
WHAT?
WHY WOULD HE PUNCH YOU?!
THEN AGAIN...
...YOU WERE CRYING FOR MY SAKE...
...SO MAYBE IT DOESN'T COUNT.
OKAY THEN!
SEE YOU LATER.
I'M GOING TO GOOF OFF HERE FOR A WHILE.
YOU SHOULD GET BACK.
HUH?
BUT...
IT'S FINE.

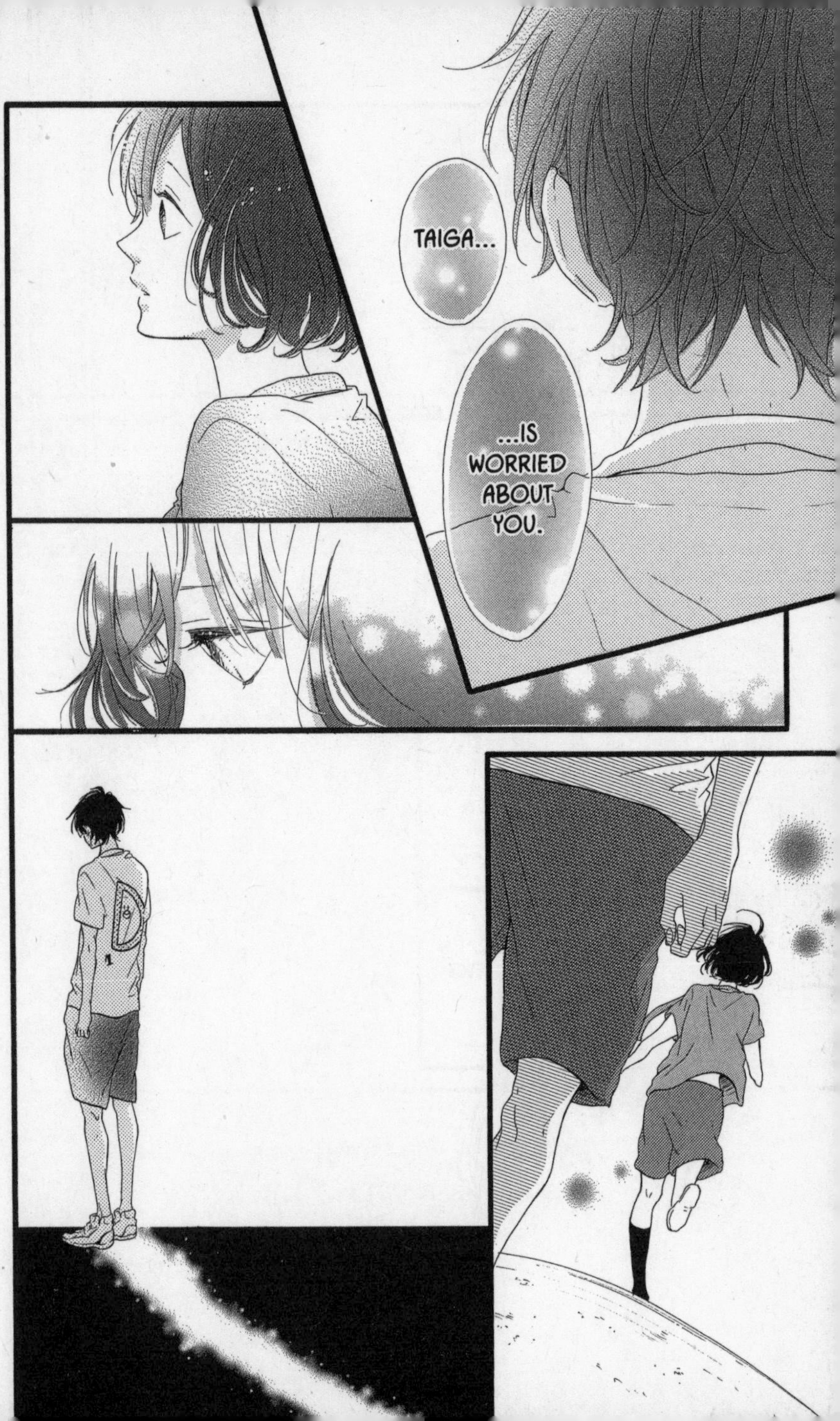
TAIGA...
...IS WORRIED ABOUT YOU.

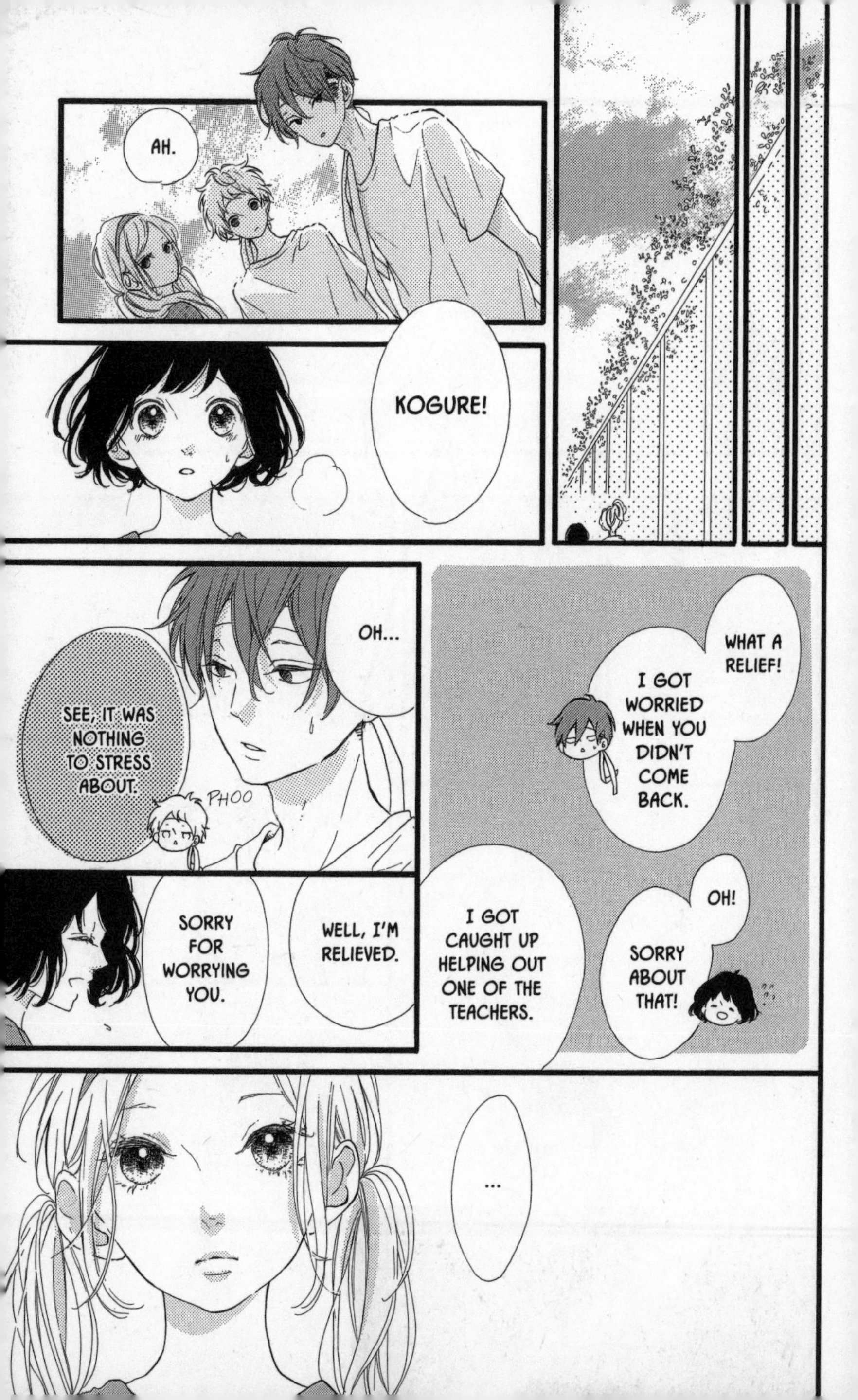
AH.
KOGURE!
WHAT A RELIEF!
I GOT WORRIED WHEN YOU DIDN'T COME BACK.
OH!
SORRY ABOUT THAT!
I GOT CAUGHT UP HELPING OUT ONE OF THE TEACHERS.
OH...
SEE, IT WAS NOTHING TO STRESS ABOUT.
PHOO
WELL, I'M RELIEVED.
SORRY FOR WORRYING YOU.
...

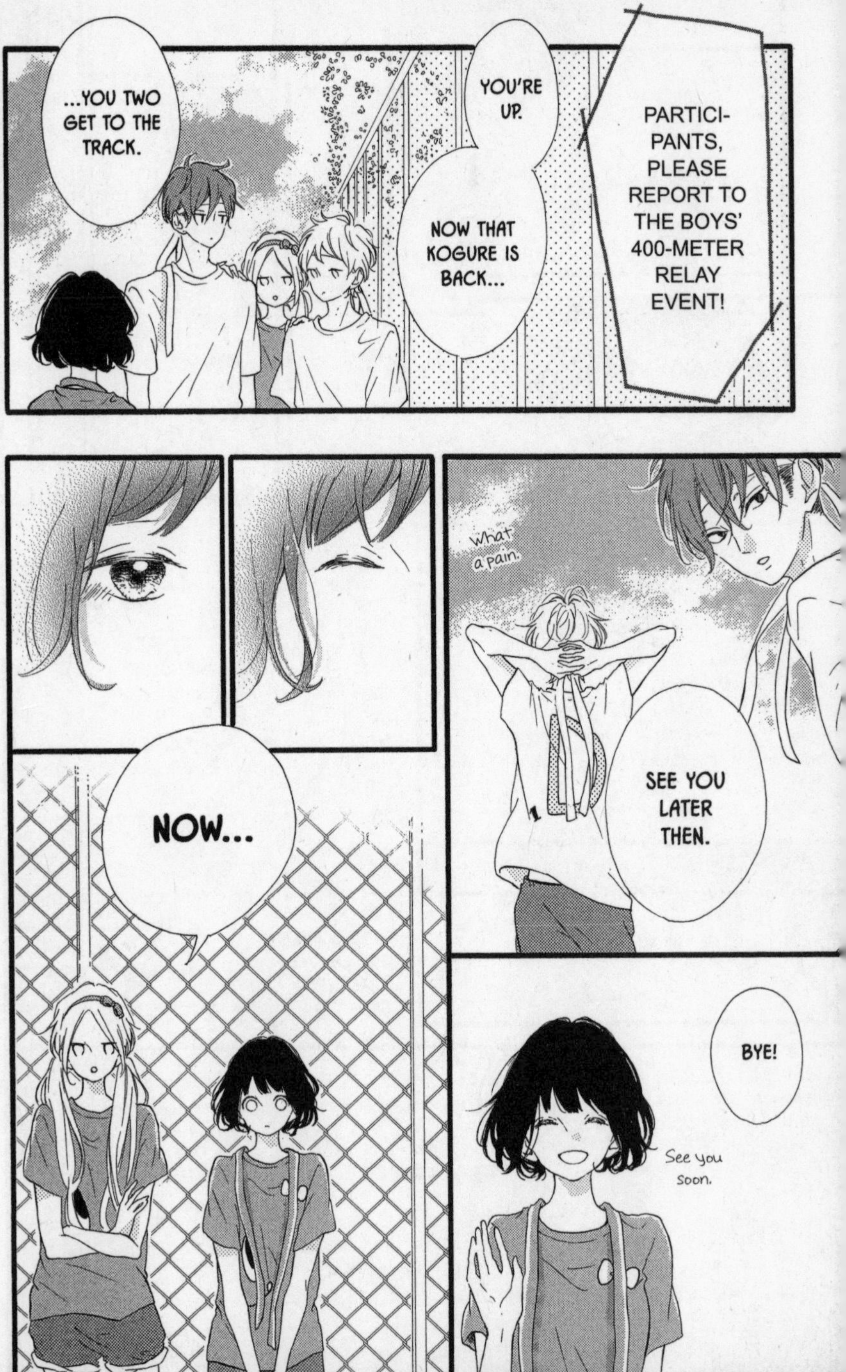
PARTICI-PANTS, PLEASE REPORT TO THE BOYS' 400-METER RELAY EVENT!
YOU'RE UP.
NOW THAT KOGURE IS BACK...
...YOU TWO GET TO THE TRACK.
What a pain.
SEE YOU LATER THEN.
BYE!
See you soon.
NOW...

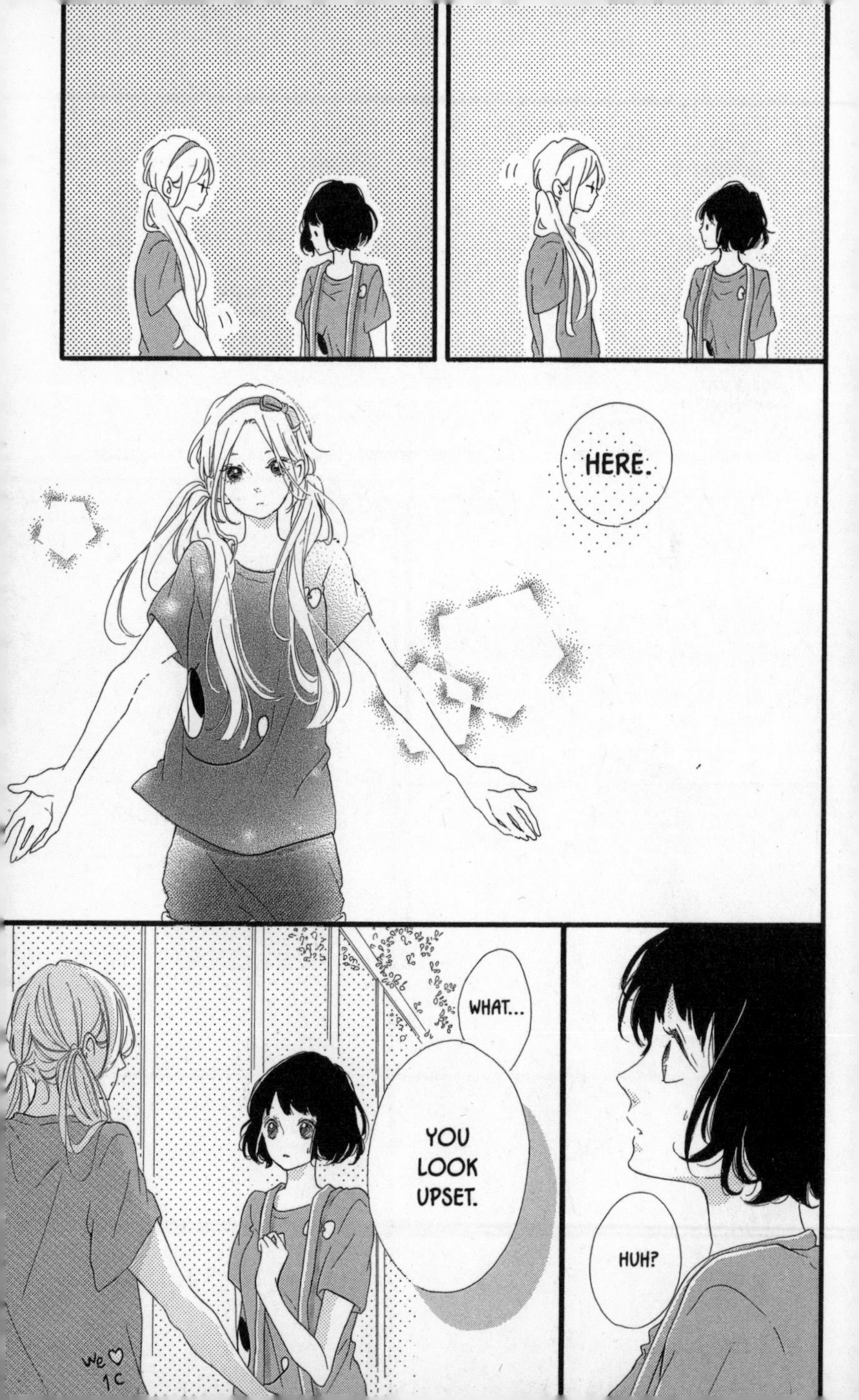
HERE.
HUH?
WHAT...
YOU LOOK UPSET.
We ♡ 1C

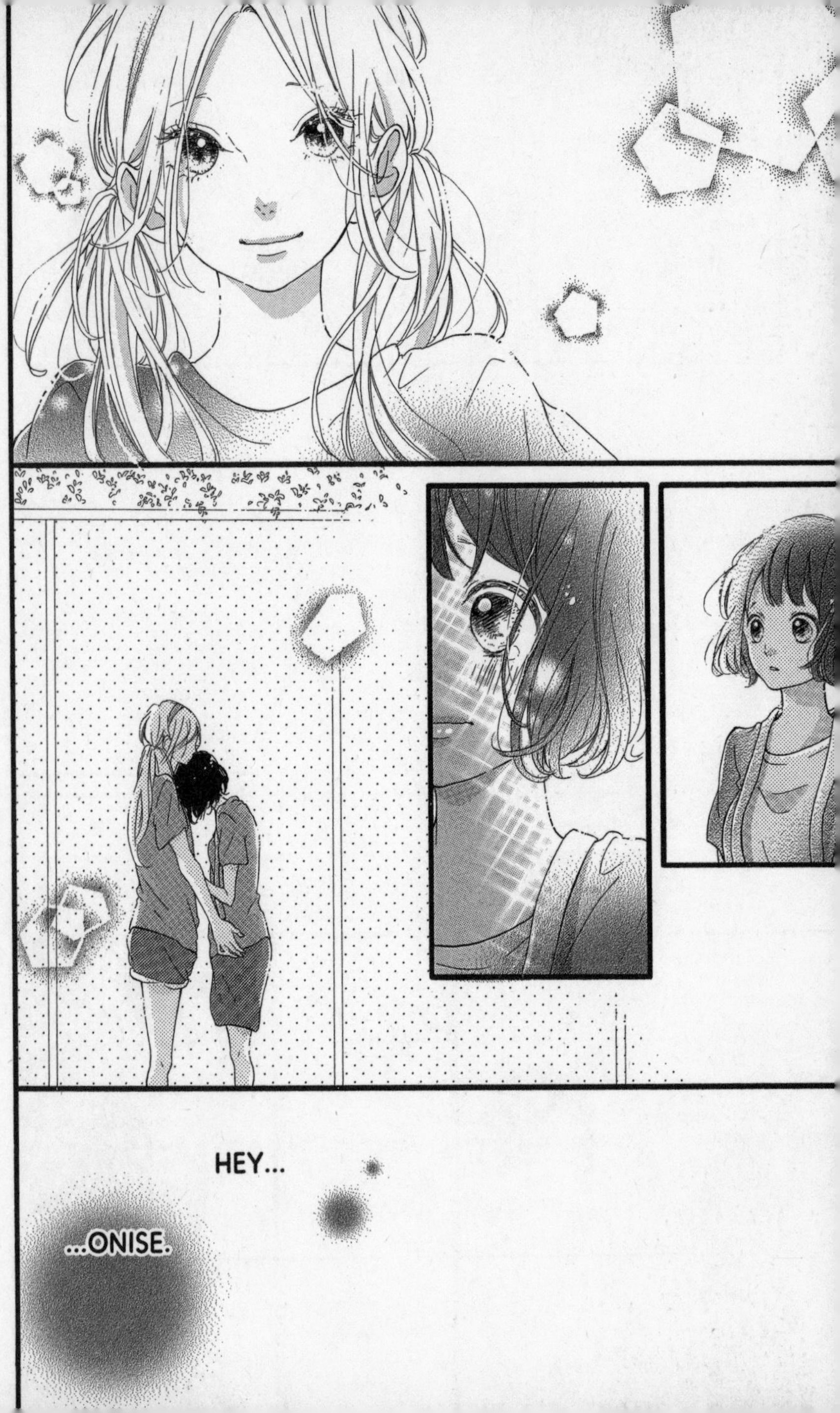
HEY...
...ONISE.

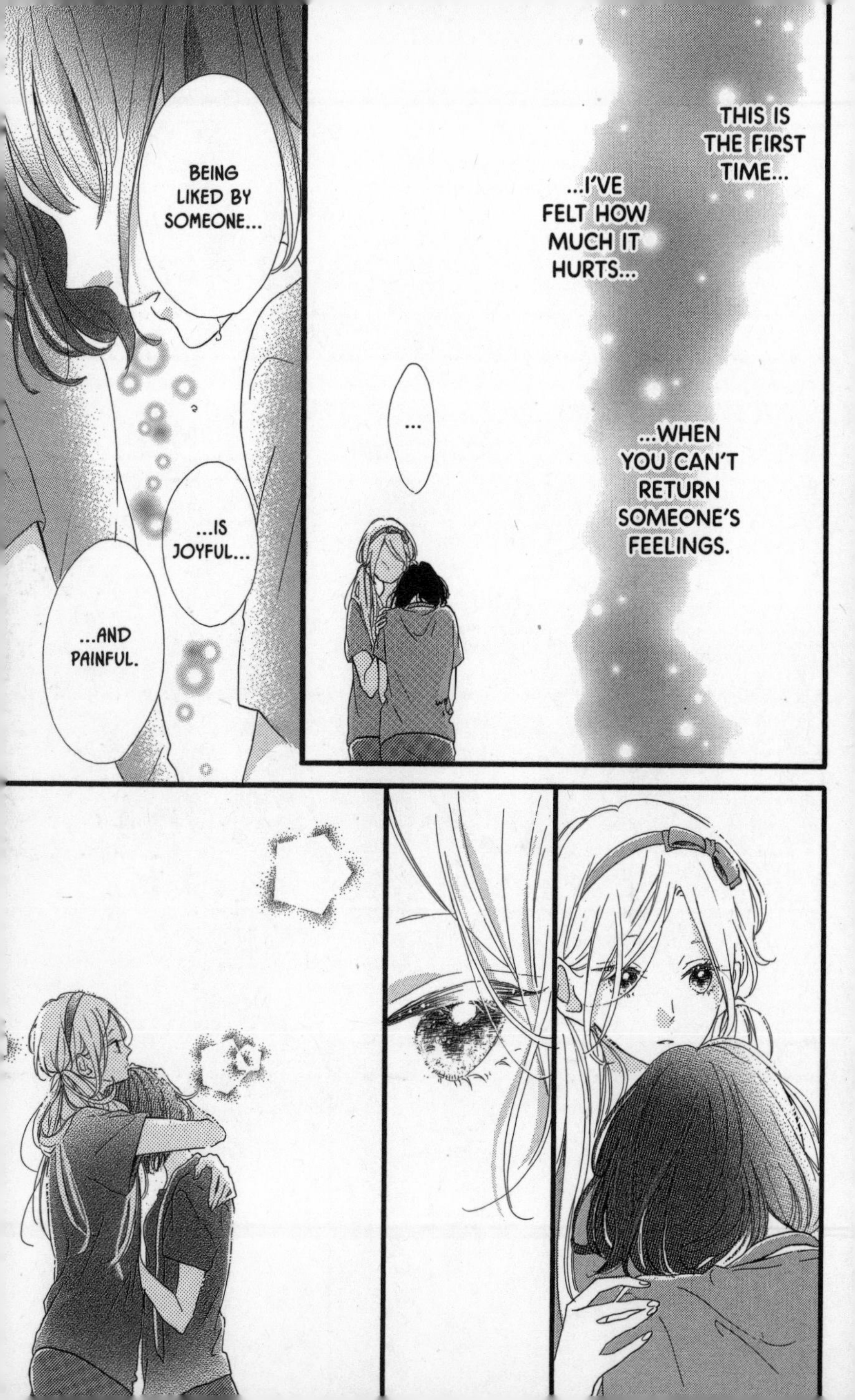
THIS IS THE FIRST TIME...
...I'VE FELT HOW MUCH IT HURTS...
...WHEN YOU CAN'T RETURN SOMEONE'S FEELINGS.
...
BEING LIKED BY SOMEONE...
...IS JOYFUL...
...AND PAINFUL.

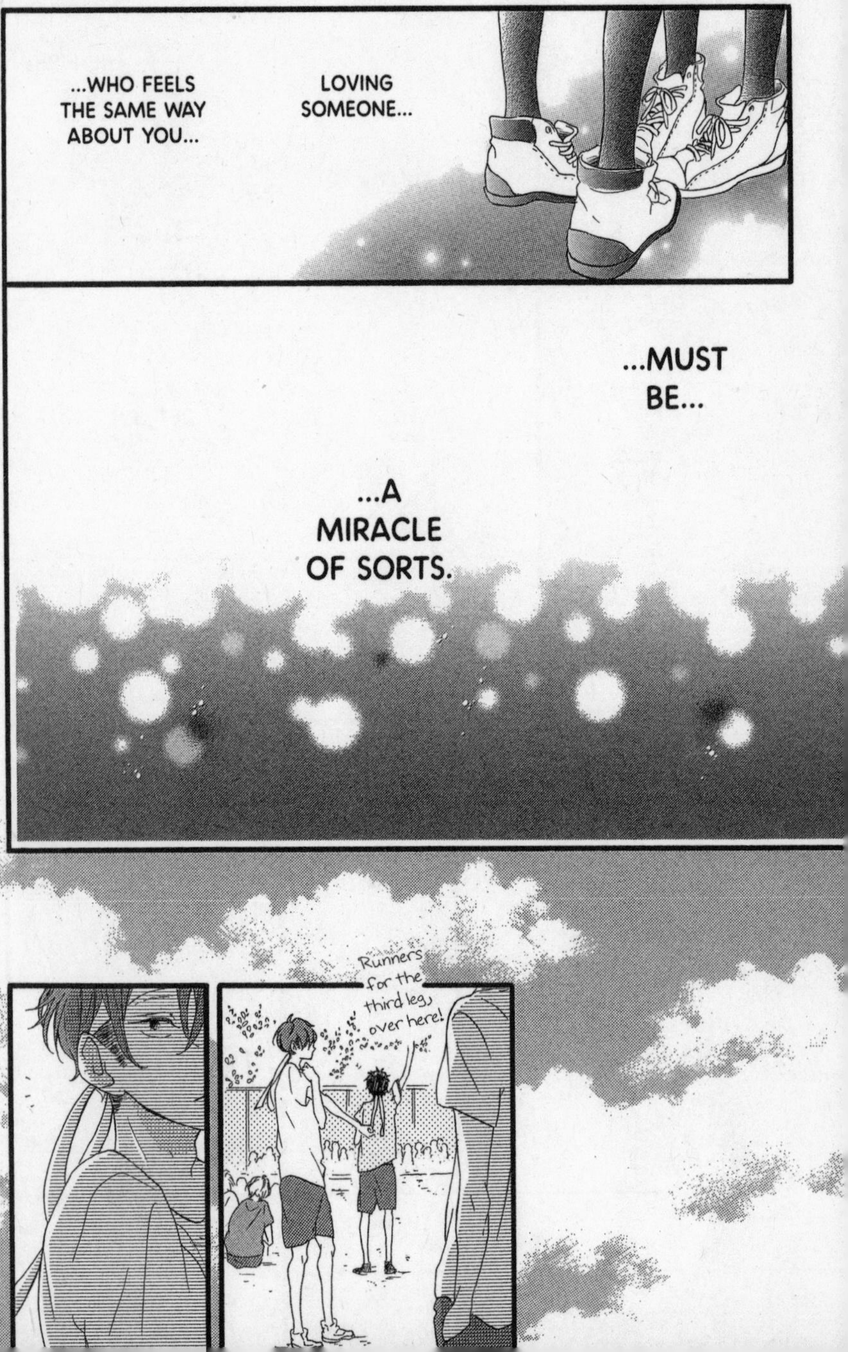
LOVING SOMEONE...
...WHO FEELS THE SAME WAY ABOUT YOU...
...MUST BE...
...A MIRACLE OF SORTS.
Runners for the third leg, over here!

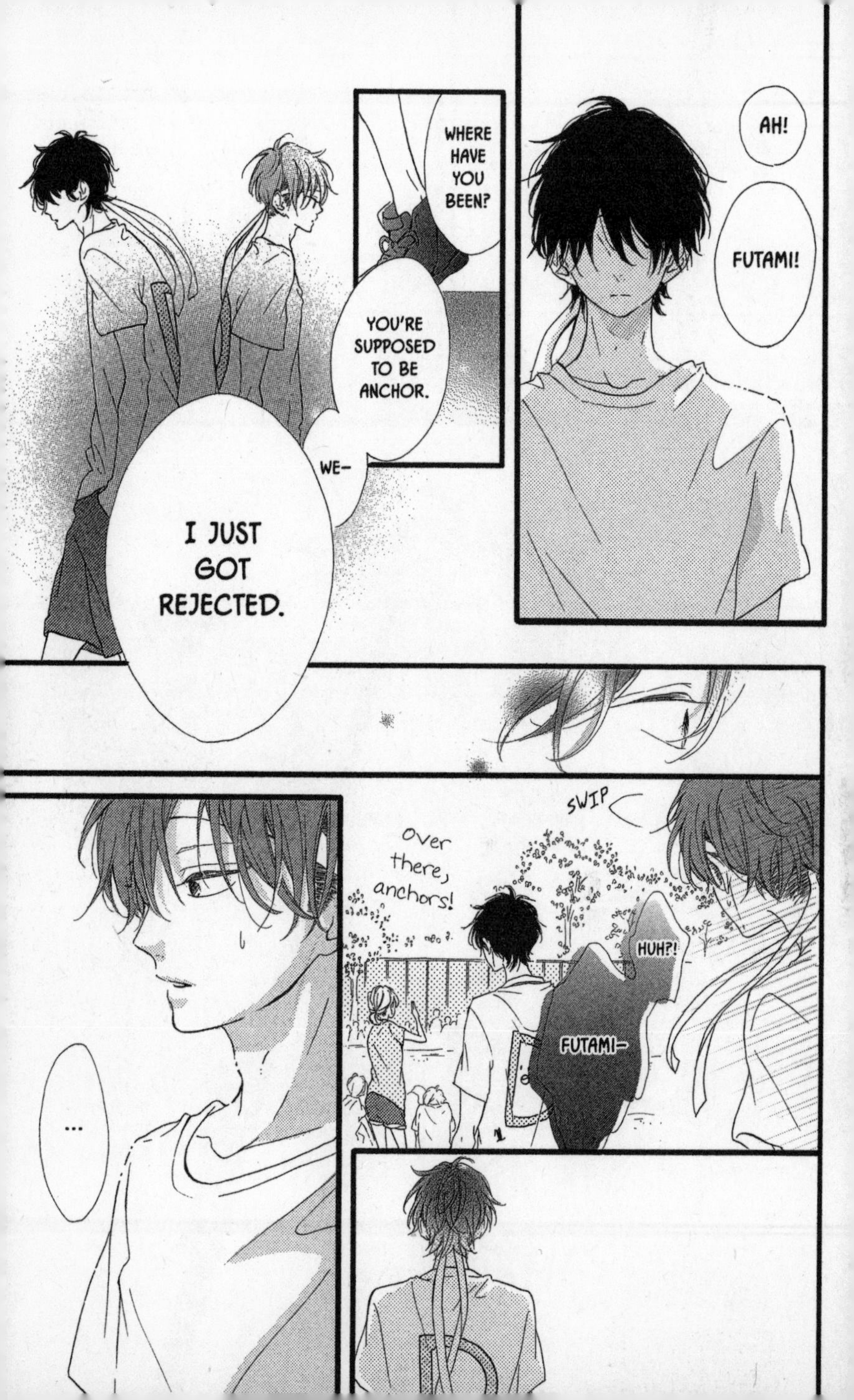
AH!
FUTAMI!
WHERE HAVE YOU BEEN?
YOU'RE SUPPOSED TO BE ANCHOR.
WE-
I JUST GOT REJECTED.
SWIP
Over there, anchors!
HUH?!
FUTAMI-
...

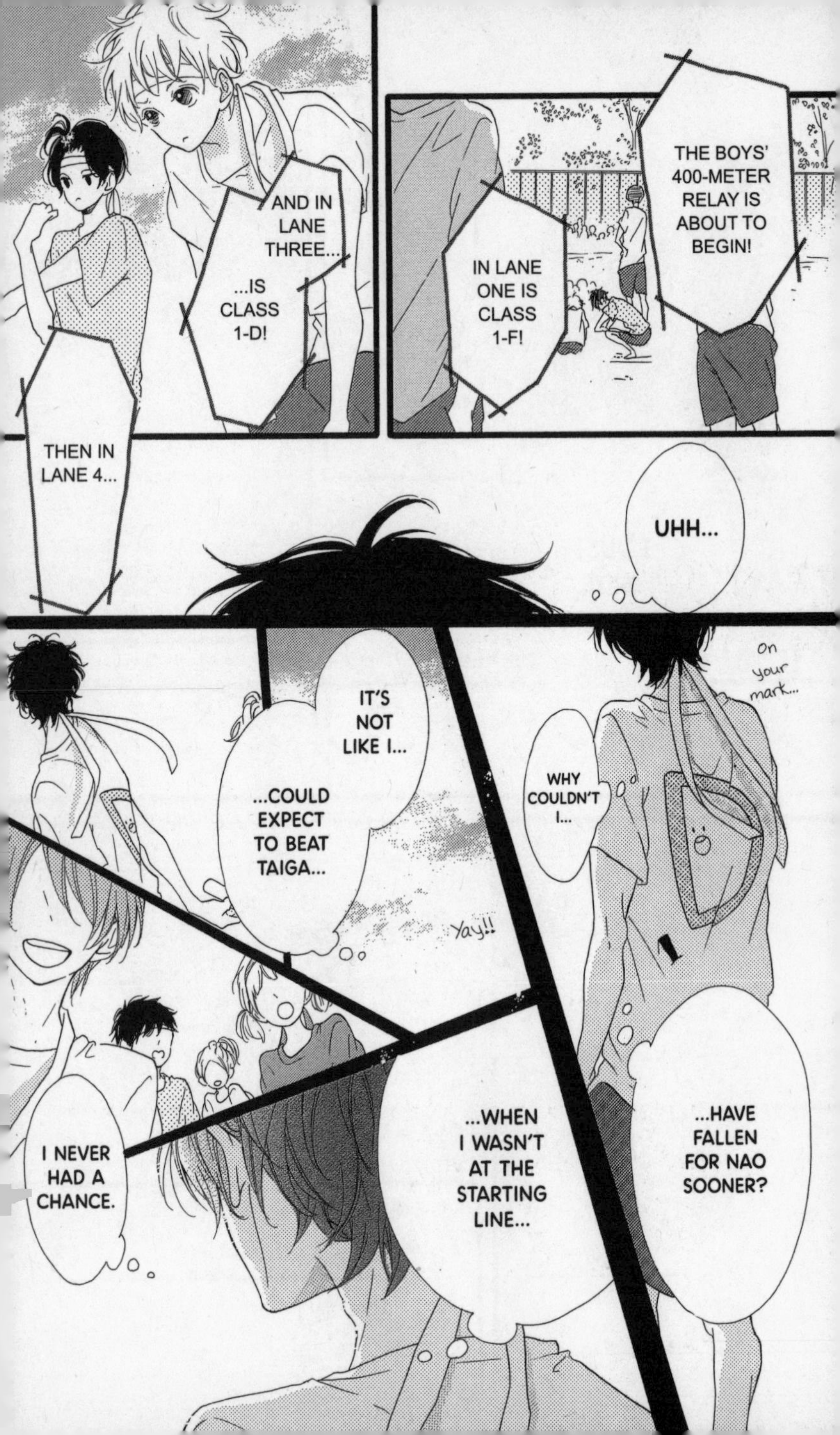
THE BOYS' 400-METER RELAY IS ABOUT TO BEGIN!
IN LANE ONE IS CLASS 1-F!
AND IN LANE THREE...
...IS CLASS 1-D!
THEN IN LANE 4...
UHH...
On your mark...
WHY COULDN'T I...
...HAVE FALLEN FOR NAO SOONER?
...WHEN I WASN'T AT THE STARTING LINE...
IT'S NOT LIKE I...
...COULD EXPECT TO BEAT TAIGA...
Yay!!
I NEVER HAD A CHANCE.

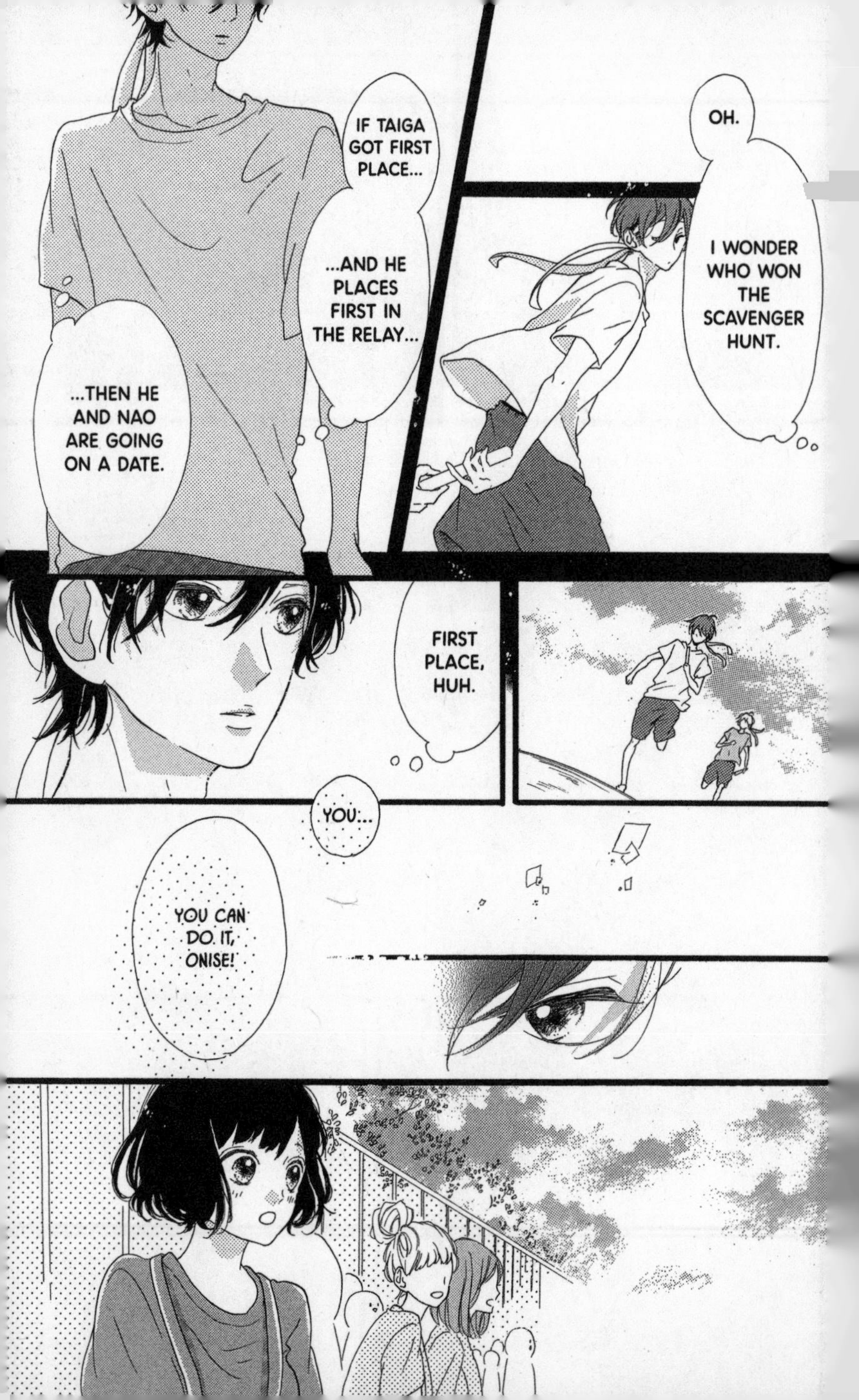
OH.
I WONDER WHO WON THE SCAVENGER HUNT.
IF TAIGA GOT FIRST PLACE...
...AND HE PLACES FIRST IN THE RELAY...
...THEN HE AND NAO ARE GOING ON A DATE.
FIRST PLACE, HUH.
YOU...
YOU CAN DO IT, ONISE!

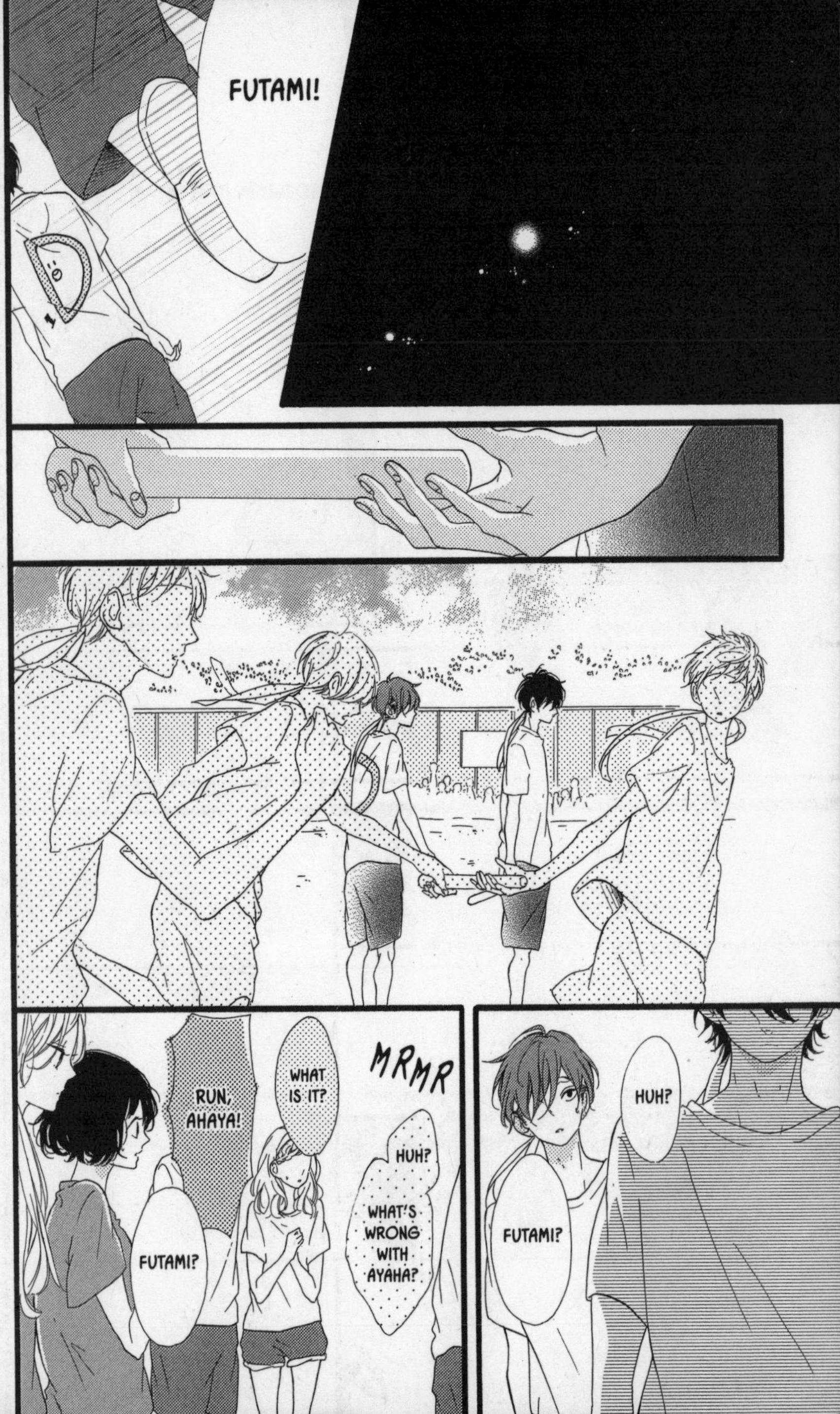
FUTAMI!
HUH?
FUTAMI?
MRMR
WHAT IS IT?
RUN, AHAYA!
HUH?
WHAT'S WRONG WITH AYAHA?
FUTAMI?

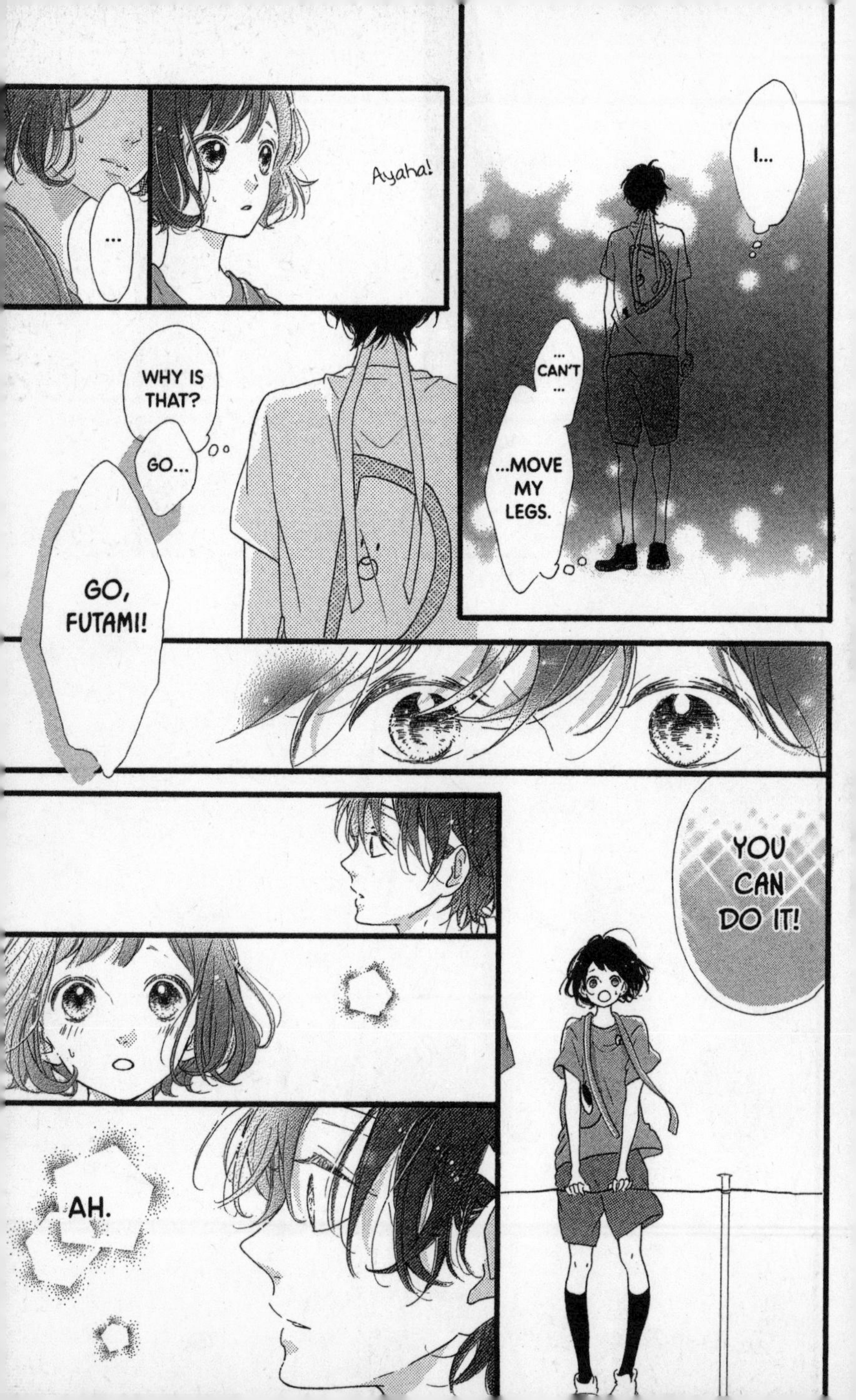
I...
...CAN'T...
...MOVE MY LEGS.
Ayaha!
...
WHY IS THAT?
GO...
GO, FUTAMI!
YOU CAN DO IT!
AH.

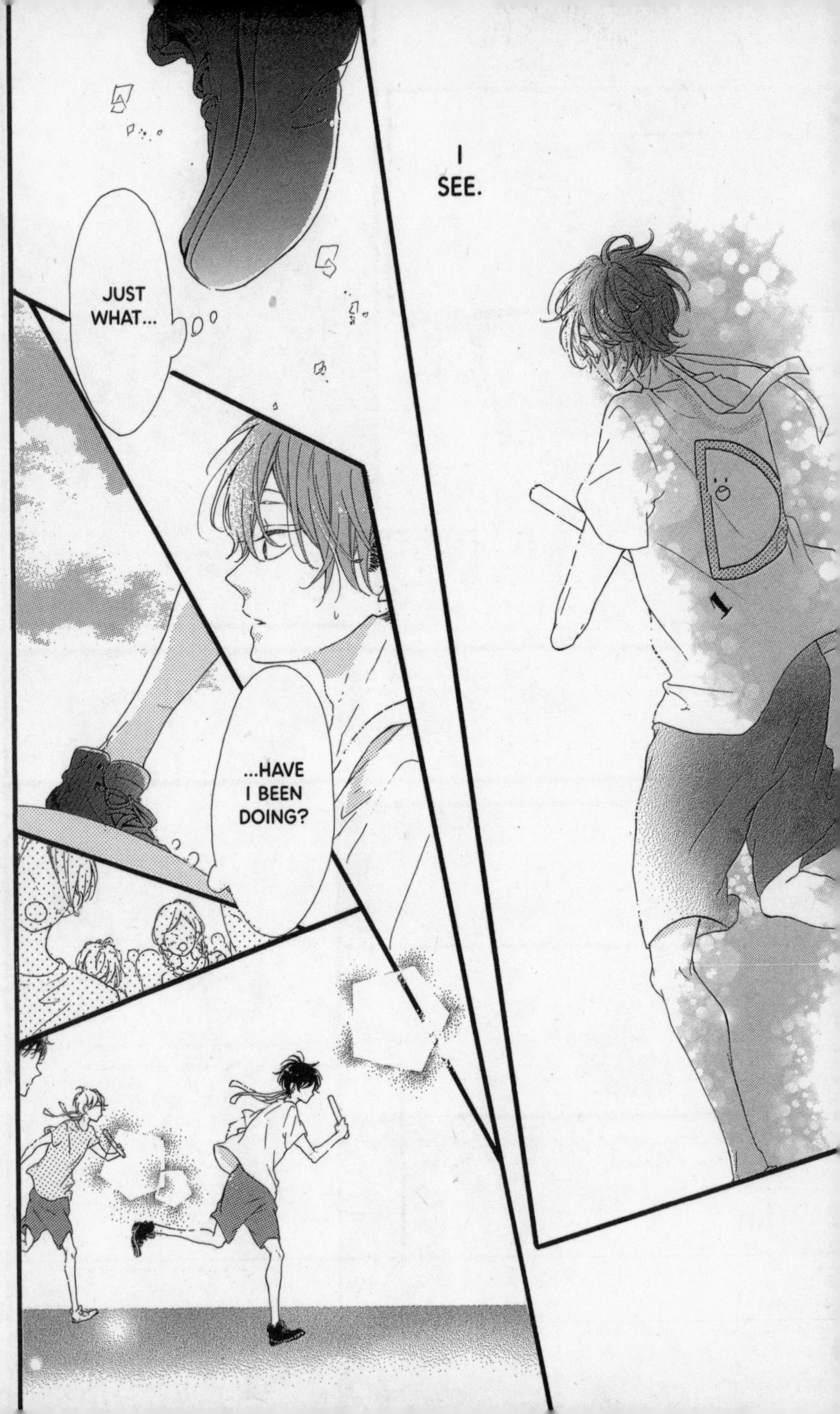
I SEE.
JUST WHAT...
...HAVE I BEEN DOING?

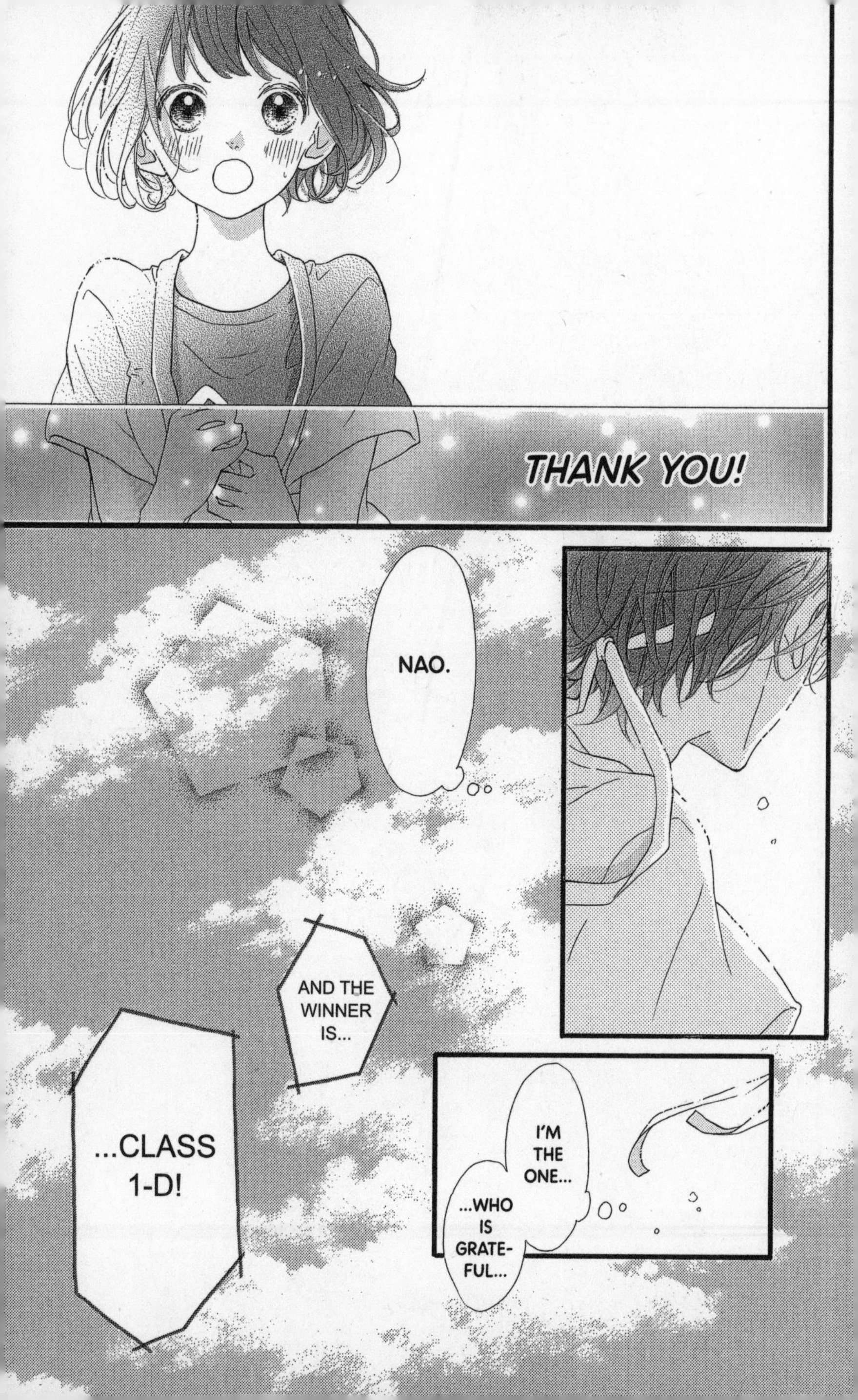

THANK YOU!
NAO.
I'M THE ONE...
...WHO IS GRATEFUL...
AND THE WINNER IS...
...CLASS 1-D!

Honey So Sweet
Character Profile

I made this list based off questions I was asked through Twitter.

Nao Kogure

Age 15

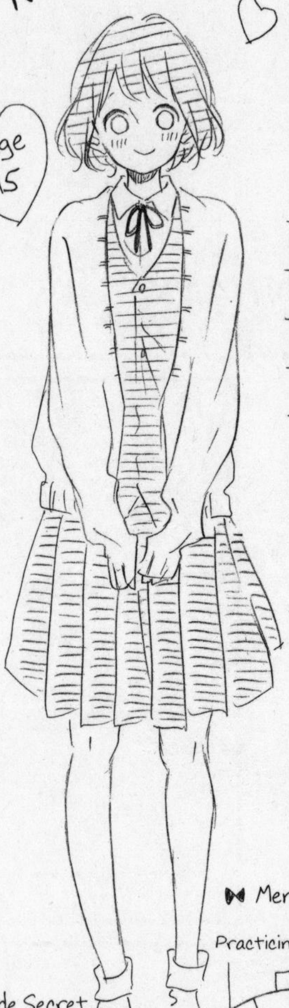

- Birthday: September 25
- Height/Weight: 4'8"/84 lbs
- Blood Type: O
- Hobbies/Skills: Reading/Studying
- Favorite/Least Favorite Food: Rice omelet/Mushrooms
- Favorite Band: Yuzu, Spitz
- Type of Guy: Someone kind
- Personal Mantra: Try your best
- Favorite Thing to Do Before Bed: Good-night text to Onise
- Childhood Dream: Become strong, marry Sou
- Favorite Place: At home with Onise
- Current Obsession: Watching animal videos on YouTube
- Captivated By: Ears
- Stress Reliever: She's not stressed.

Mental Graph

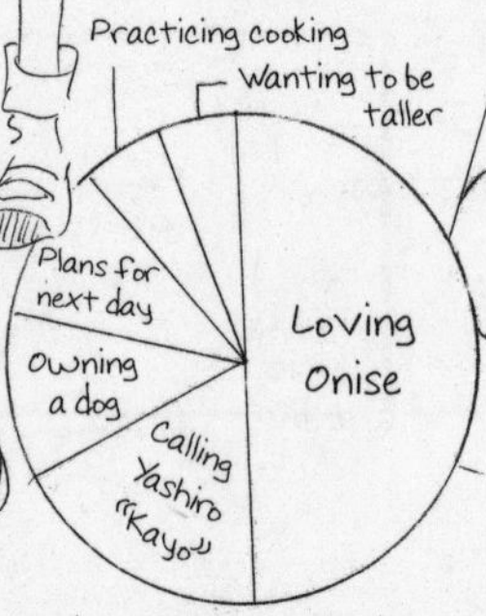

Practicing cooking
Wanting to be taller
Plans for next day
Owning a dog
Calling Yashiro "Kayo"
Loving Onise

Childhood Photo

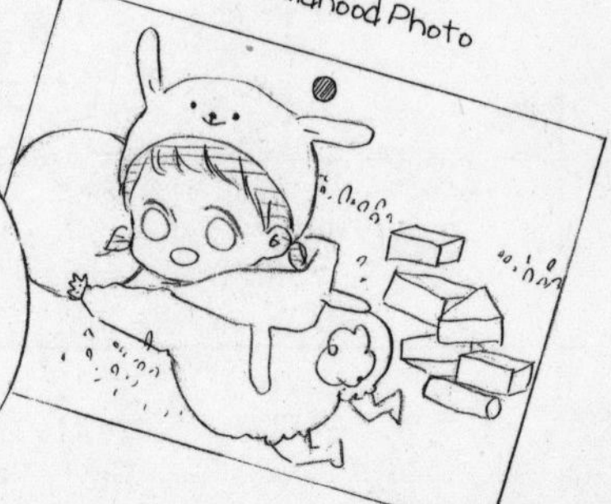

Inside Secret

She's terrible at waking up in the morning and always has bedhead.

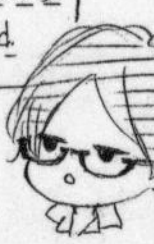

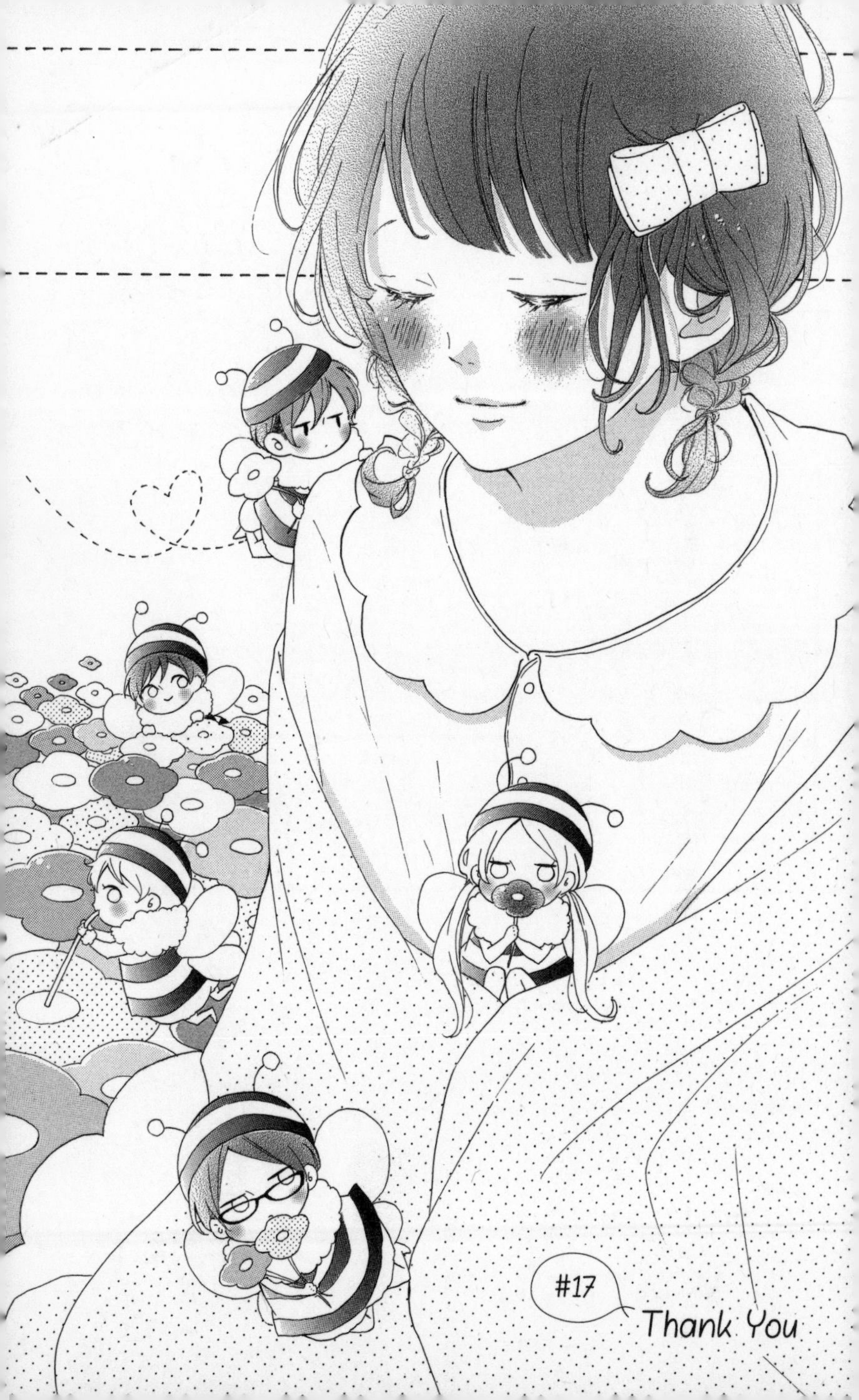
#17
Thank You

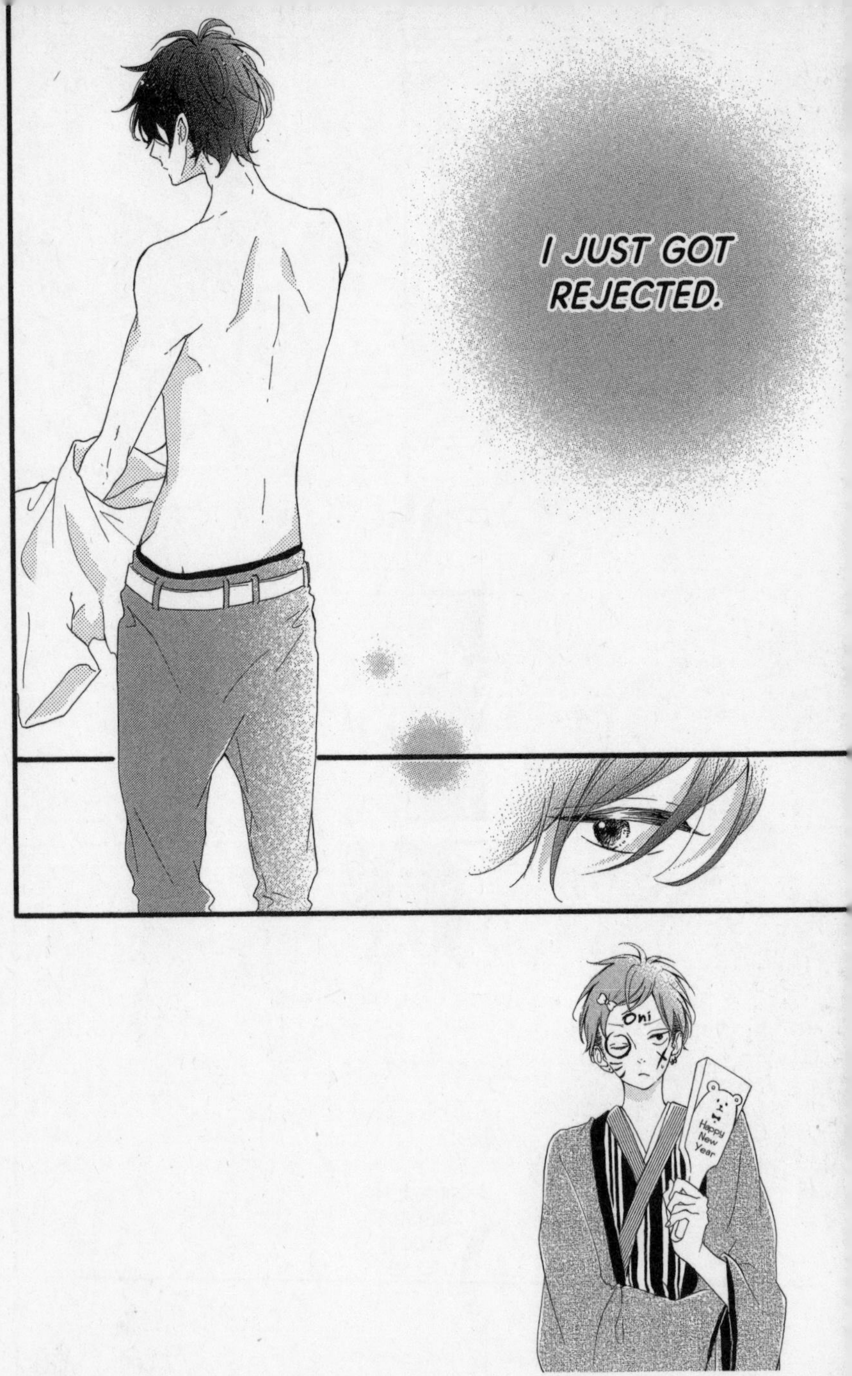
I JUST GOT REJECTED.
Oni
Happy New Year

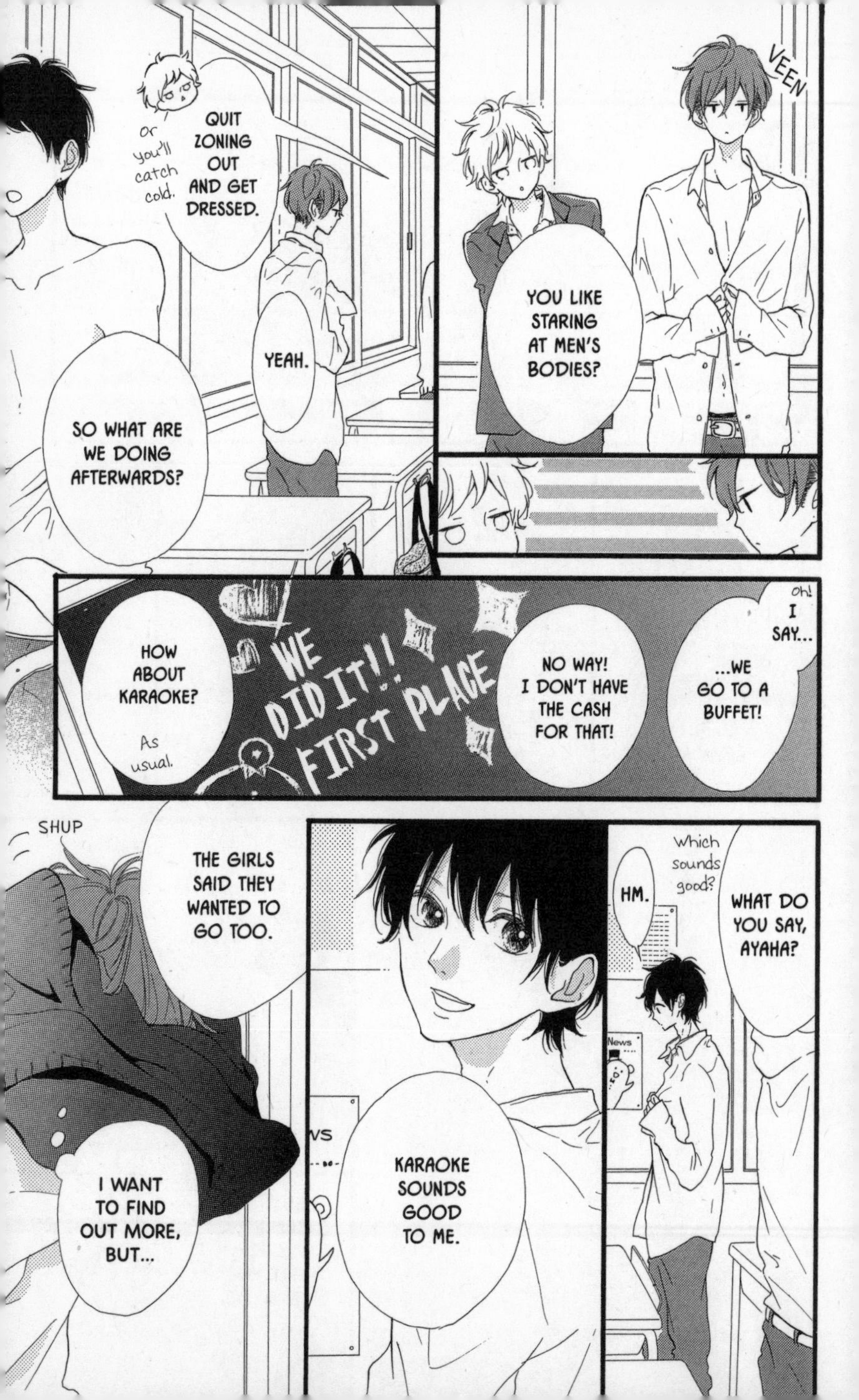
VEEN
YOU LIKE STARING AT MEN'S BODIES?
QUIT ZONING OUT AND GET DRESSED.
Or you'll catch cold.
YEAH.
SO WHAT ARE WE DOING AFTERWARDS?
Oh! I SAY...
...WE GO TO A BUFFET!
NO WAY! I DON'T HAVE THE CASH FOR THAT!
WE DID IT!! FIRST PLACE
HOW ABOUT KARAOKE?
As usual.
WHAT DO YOU SAY, AYAHA?
Which sounds good?
HM.
News
KARAOKE SOUNDS GOOD TO ME.
SHUP
THE GIRLS SAID THEY WANTED TO GO TOO.
I WANT TO FIND OUT MORE, BUT...

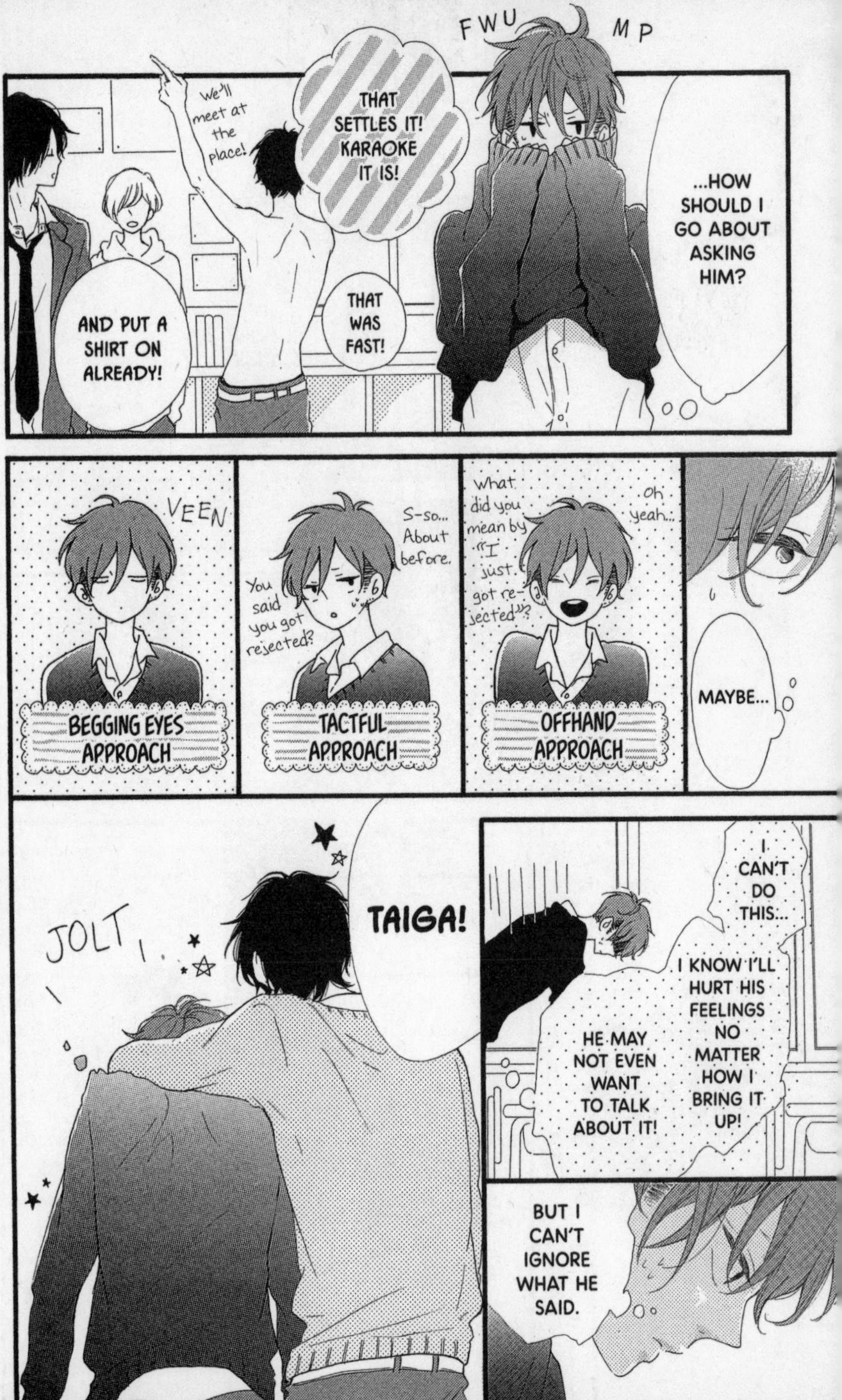
FWUMP
...HOW SHOULD I GO ABOUT ASKING HIM?
THAT SETTLES IT! KARAOKE IT IS!
We'll meet at the place!
THAT WAS FAST!
AND PUT A SHIRT ON ALREADY!
MAYBE...
Oh yeah...
What did you mean by "I just got rejected"?
OFFHAND APPROACH
S-so... About before.
You said you got rejected?
TACTFUL APPROACH
VEEN
BEGGING EYES APPROACH
I CAN'T DO THIS...
I KNOW I'LL HURT HIS FEELINGS NO MATTER HOW I BRING IT UP!
HE MAY NOT EVEN WANT TO TALK ABOUT IT!
BUT I CAN'T IGNORE WHAT HE SAID.
TAIGA!
JOLT

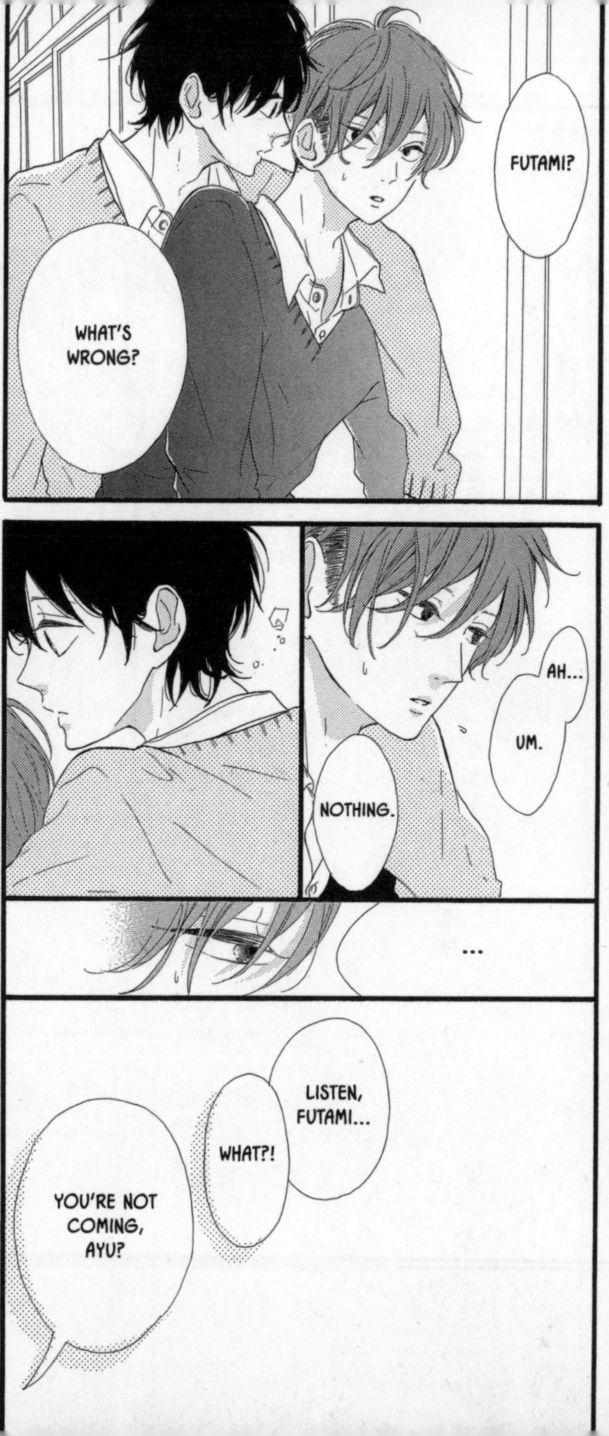
FUTAMI?
WHAT'S WRONG?
AH... UM.
NOTHING.
...
LISTEN, FUTAMI...
WHAT?!
YOU'RE NOT COMING, AYU?

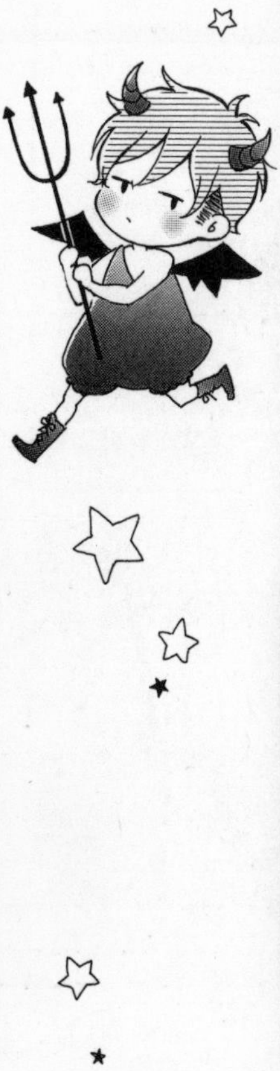

This volume's title page was originally used for the cover of another magazine. I used the fan drawings I received as the basis for it.

Thank you to everyone who submitted something!

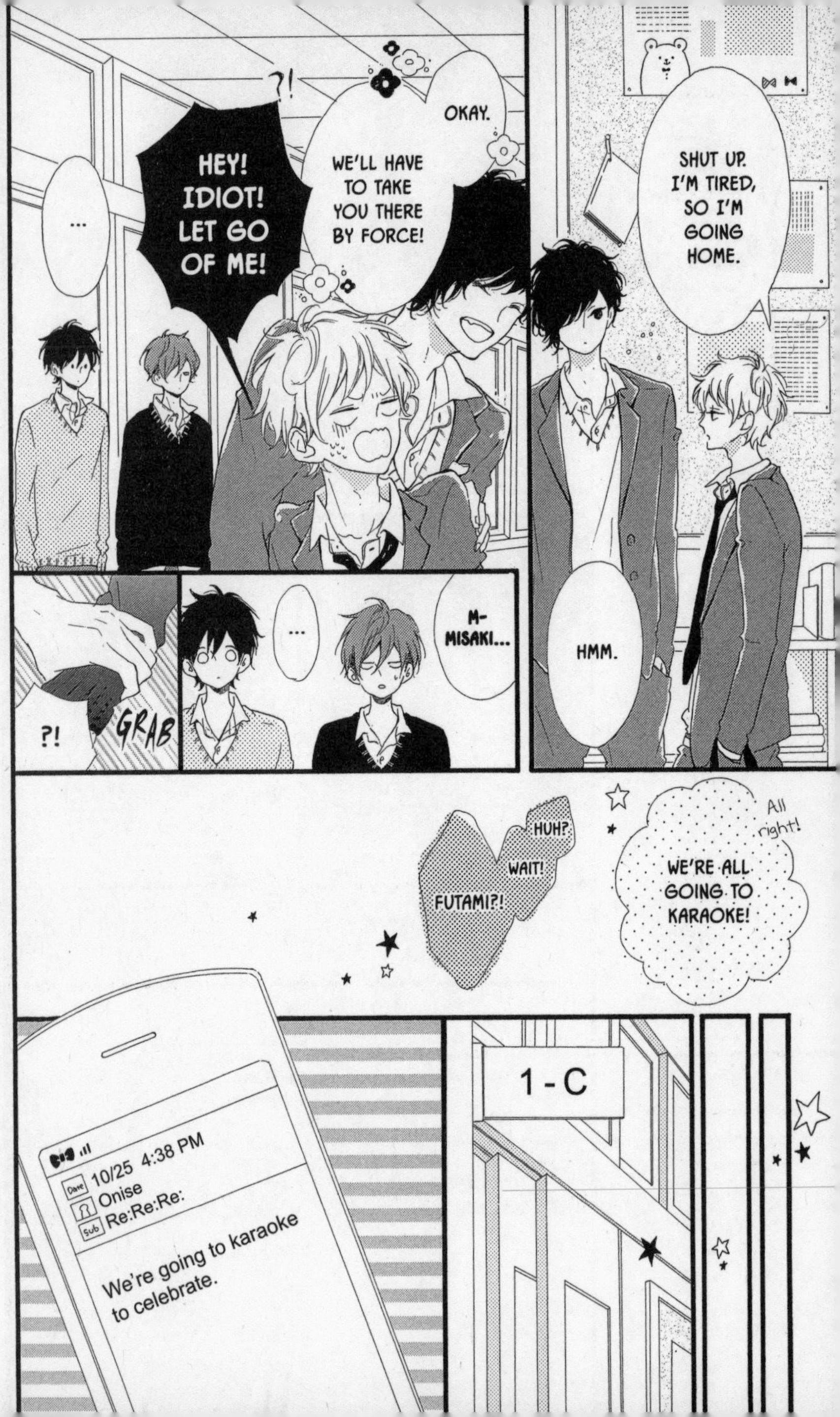
SHUT UP. I'M TIRED, SO I'M GOING HOME.
HMM.
OKAY.
WE'LL HAVE TO TAKE YOU THERE BY FORCE!
?!
HEY! IDIOT! LET GO OF ME!
...
M-MISAKI...
...
?!
GRAB
All right!
WE'RE ALL GOING TO KARAOKE!
HUH?
WAIT!
FUTAMI?!
1 - C
10/25 4:38 PM
Date
Onise
Sub
Re:Re:Re:
We're going to karaoke to celebrate.

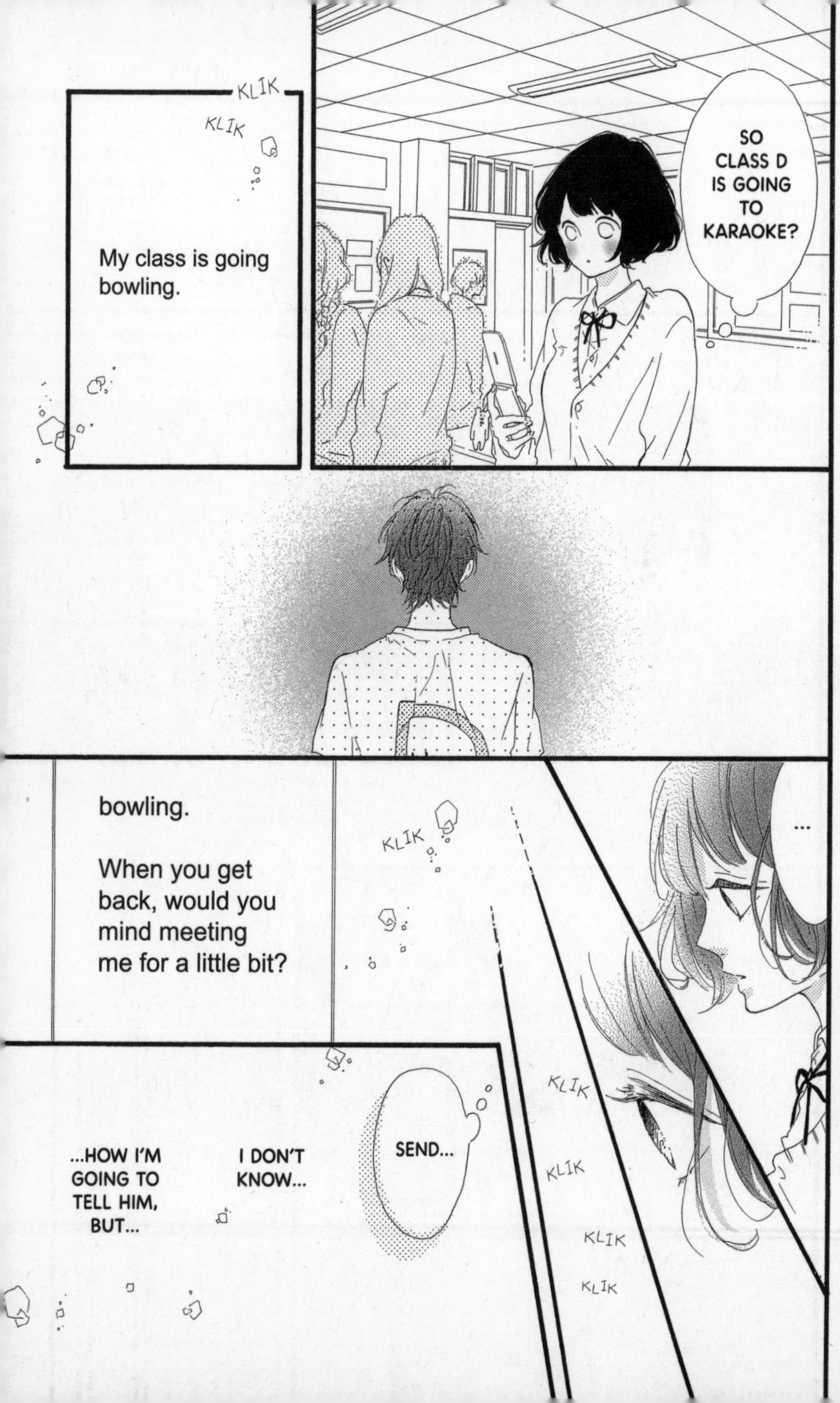
SO CLASS D IS GOING TO KARAOKE?
KLIK
KLIK
My class is going bowling.
...
KLIK
KLIK
KLIK
KLIK
KLIK
bowling.
When you get back, would you mind meeting me for a little bit?
SEND...
I DON'T KNOW...
...HOW I'M GOING TO TELL HIM, BUT...

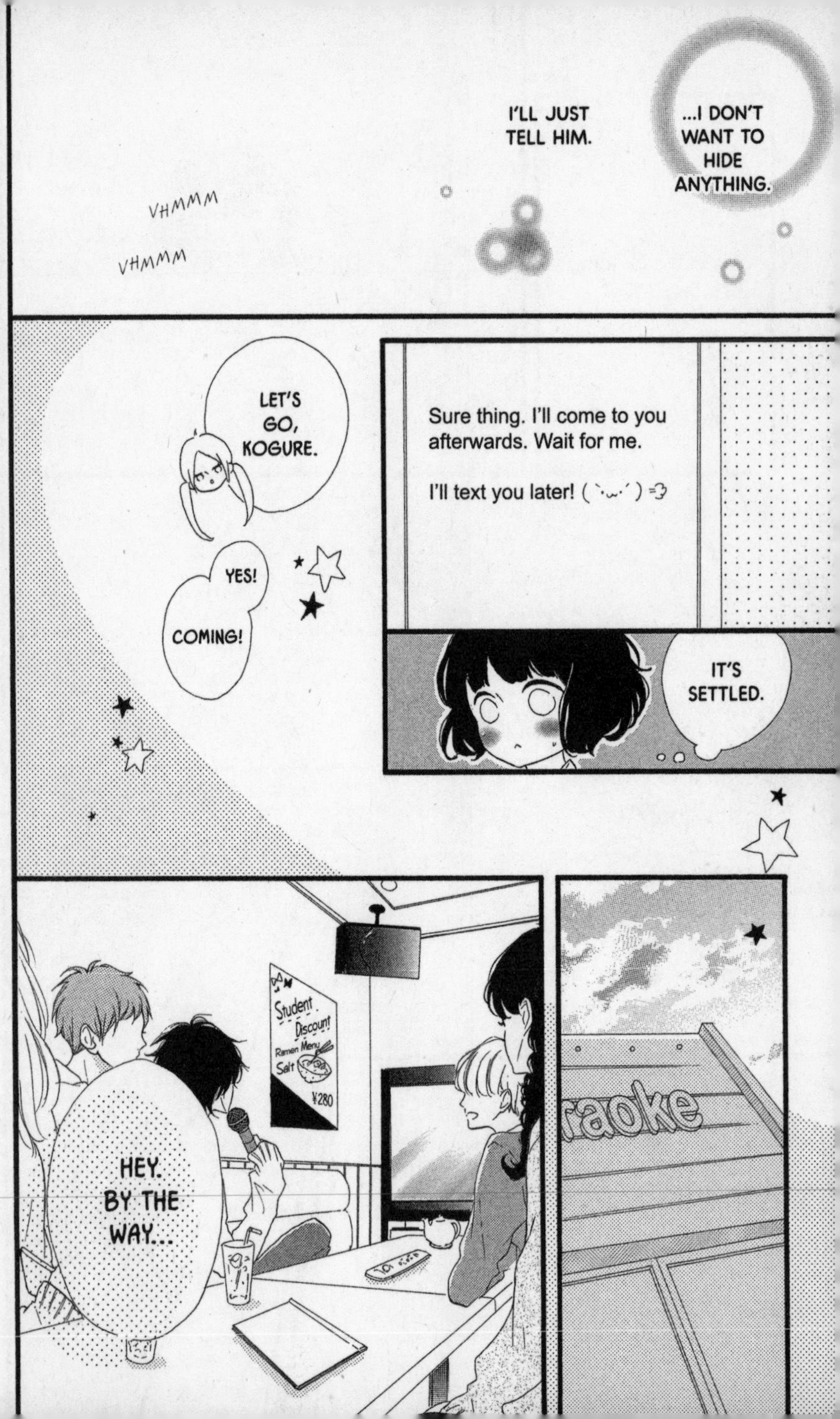
...I DON'T WANT TO HIDE ANYTHING.
I'LL JUST TELL HIM.
VHMMM
VHMMM
Sure thing. I'll come to you afterwards. Wait for me.
I'll text you later! (`･ω･´) =3
IT'S SETTLED.
LET'S GO, KOGURE.
YES! COMING!
raoke
Student Discount
Ramen Menu
Salt
¥280
HEY. BY THE WAY...

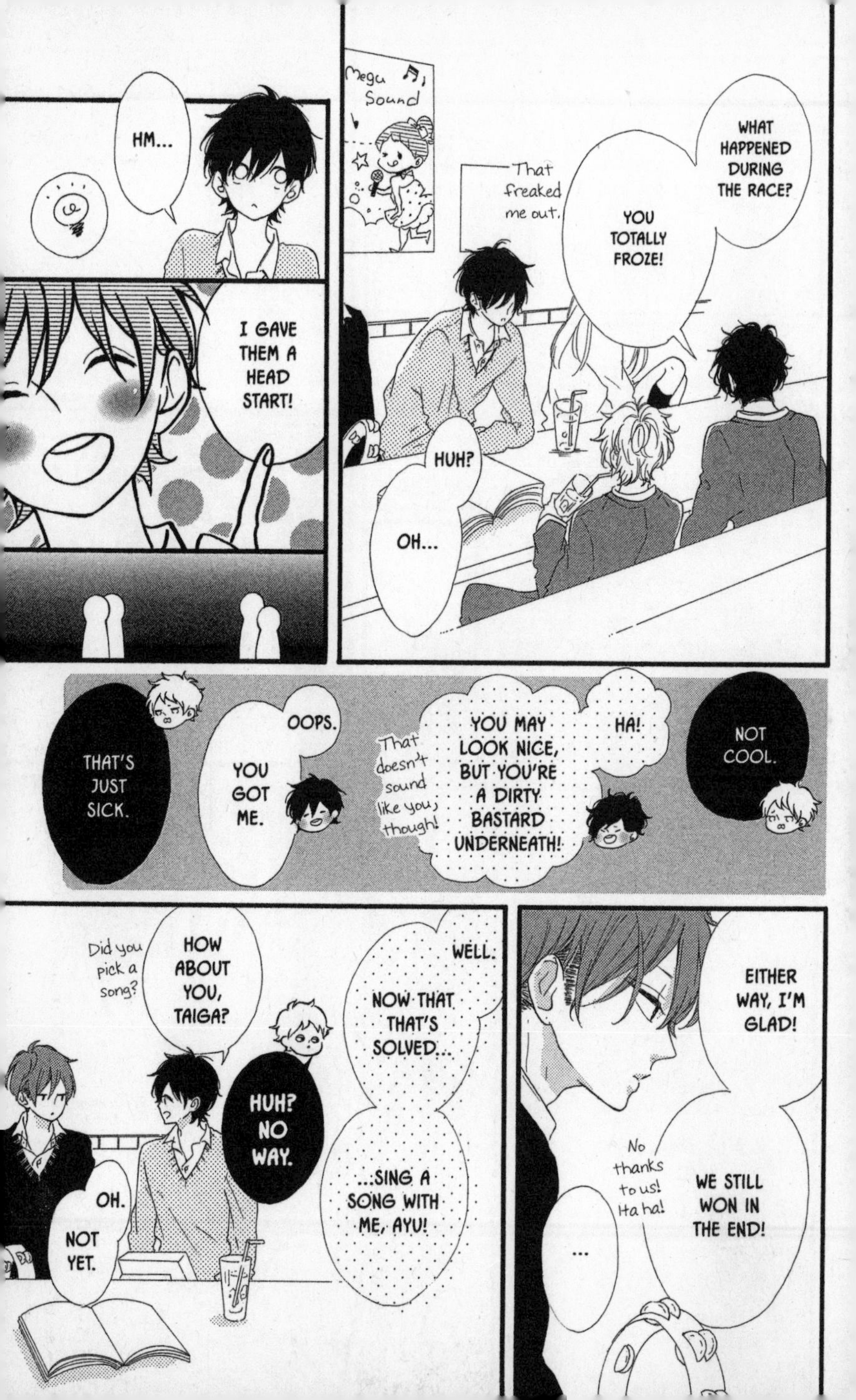
Megu Sound
WHAT HAPPENED DURING THE RACE?
YOU TOTALLY FROZE!
That freaked me out.
HUH?
OH...
HM...
I GAVE THEM A HEAD START!
NOT COOL.
HA!
YOU MAY LOOK NICE, BUT YOU'RE A DIRTY BASTARD UNDERNEATH!
That doesn't sound like you, though!
OOPS.
YOU GOT ME.
THAT'S JUST SICK.
EITHER WAY, I'M GLAD!
WE STILL WON IN THE END!
No thanks to us! Ha ha!
...
WELL.
NOW THAT THAT'S SOLVED...
...SING A SONG WITH ME, AYU!
HUH? NO WAY.
HOW ABOUT YOU, TAIGA?
Did you pick a song?
OH.
NOT YET.

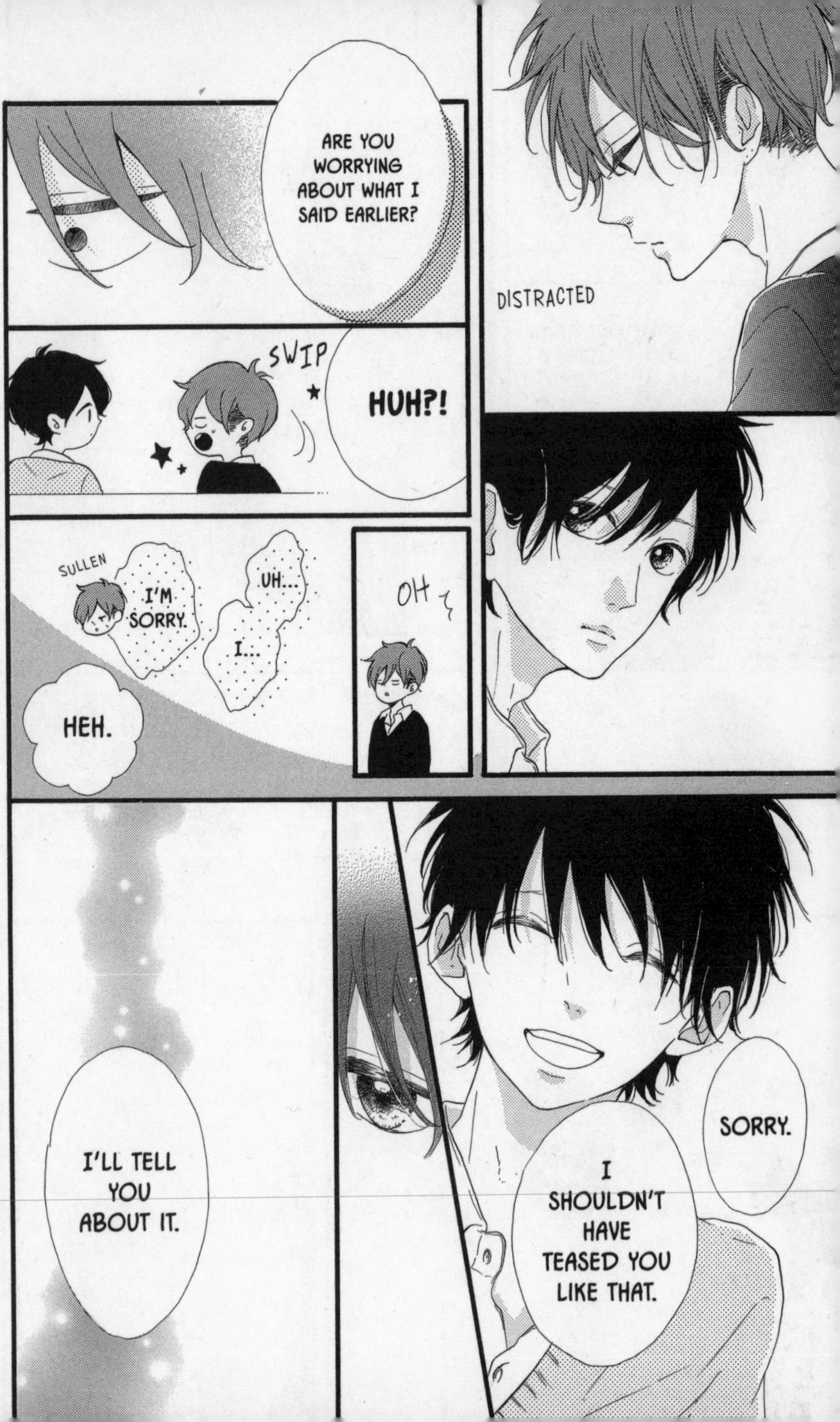
DISTRACTED
ARE YOU WORRYING ABOUT WHAT I SAID EARLIER?
SWIP
HUH?!
OH
UH...
I...
I'M SORRY.
SULLEN
HEH.
SORRY.
I SHOULDN'T HAVE TEASED YOU LIKE THAT.
I'LL TELL YOU ABOUT IT.

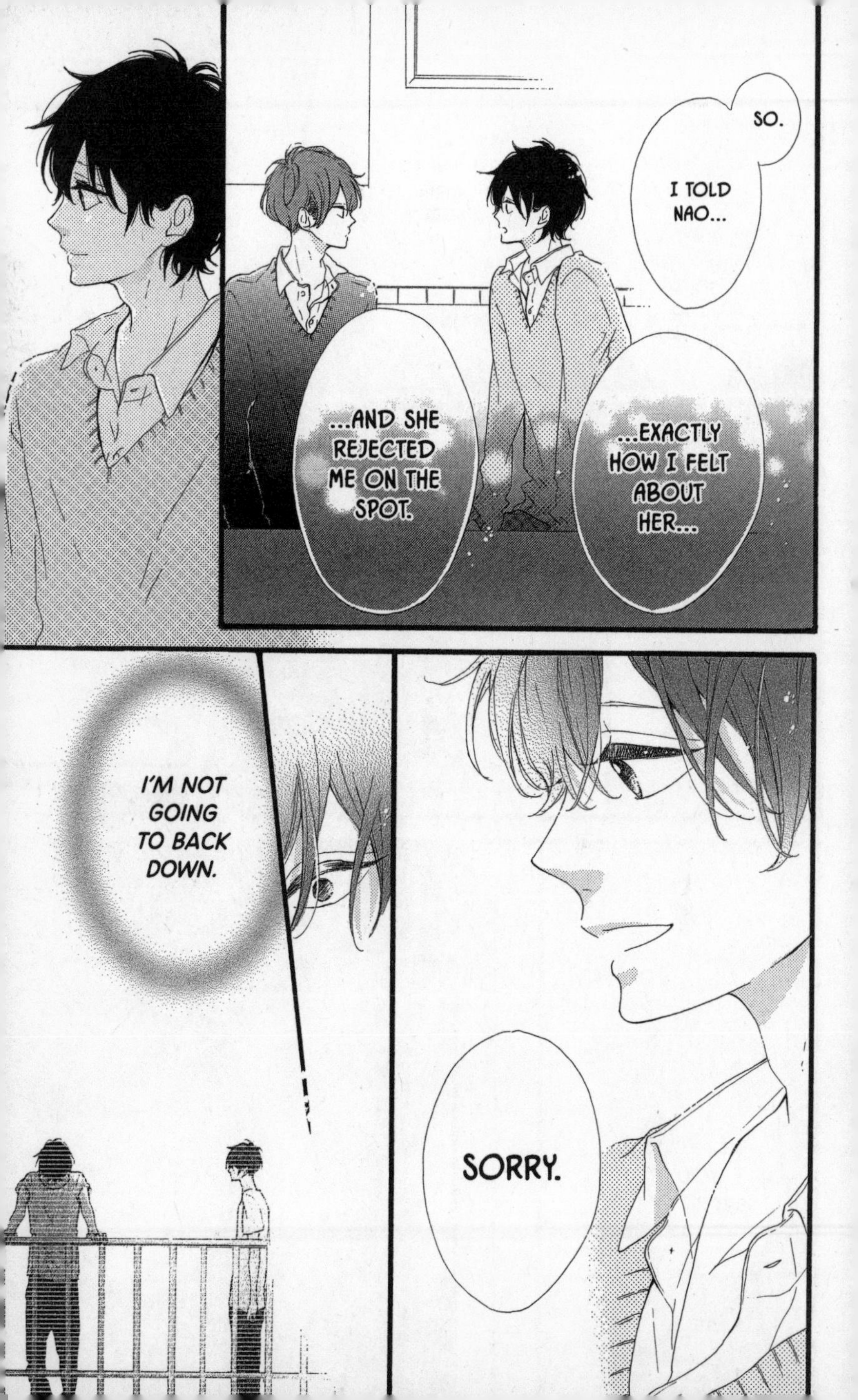
SO.
I TOLD NAO...
...EXACTLY HOW I FELT ABOUT HER...
...AND SHE REJECTED ME ON THE SPOT.
SORRY.
I'M NOT GOING TO BACK DOWN.

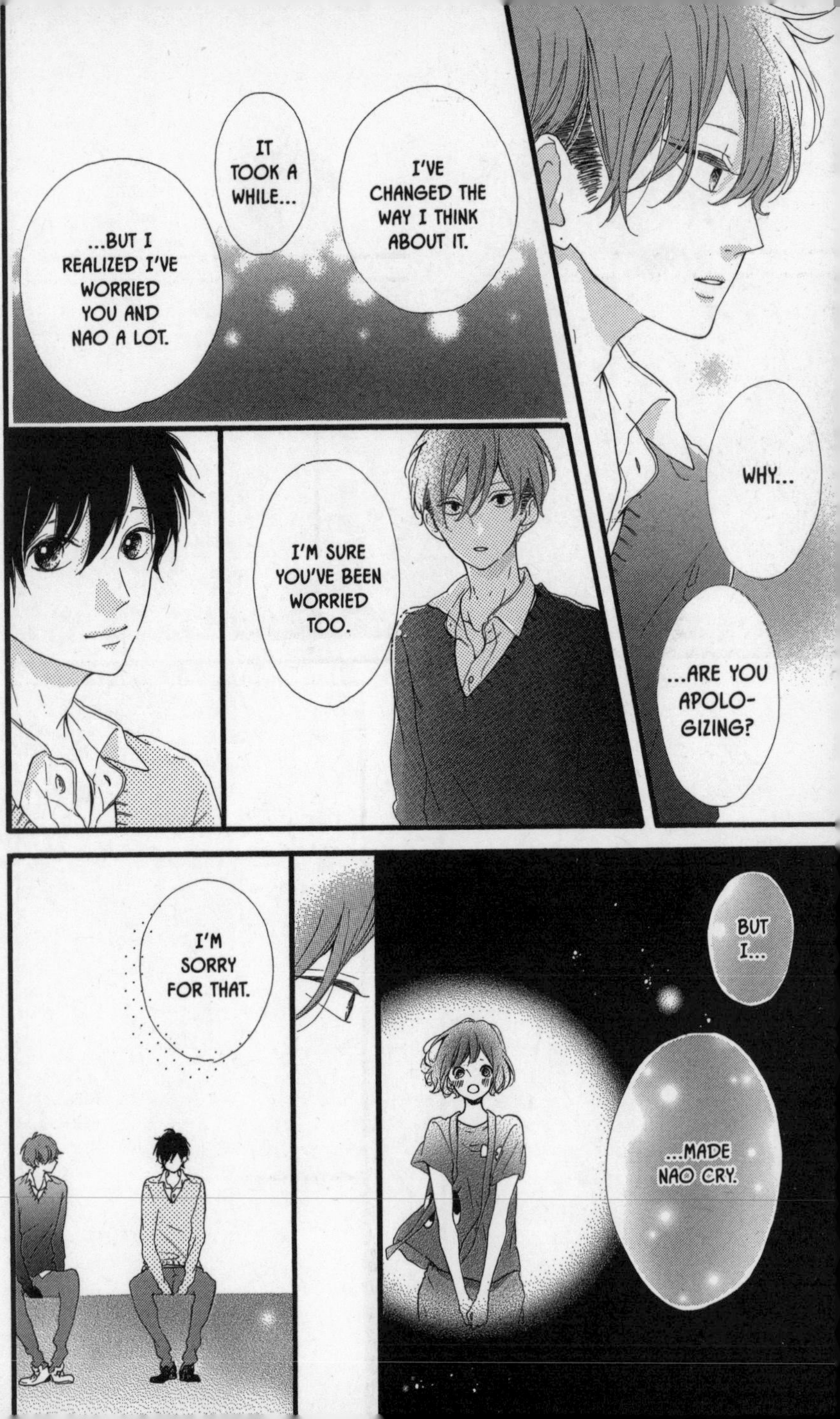
WHY...
...ARE YOU APOLO-GIZING?
I'VE CHANGED THE WAY I THINK ABOUT IT.
IT TOOK A WHILE...
...BUT I REALIZED I'VE WORRIED YOU AND NAO A LOT.
I'M SURE YOU'VE BEEN WORRIED TOO.
BUT I...
...MADE NAO CRY.
I'M SORRY FOR THAT.

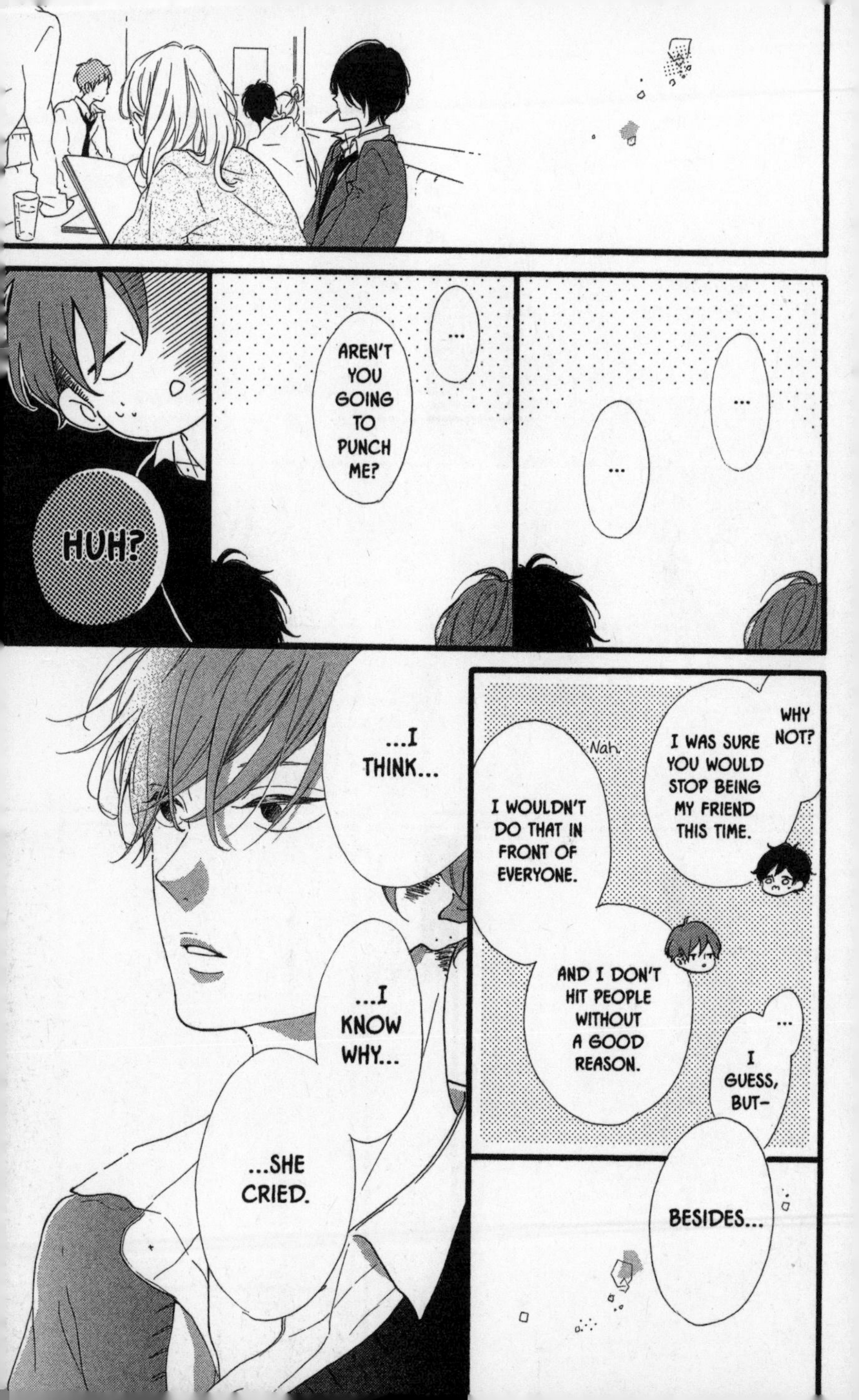
...
...
...
AREN'T YOU GOING TO PUNCH ME?
HUH?
WHY NOT?
I WAS SURE YOU WOULD STOP BEING MY FRIEND THIS TIME.
Nah.
I WOULDN'T DO THAT IN FRONT OF EVERYONE.
... I GUESS, BUT—
AND I DON'T HIT PEOPLE WITHOUT A GOOD REASON.
BESIDES...
...I THINK...
...I KNOW WHY...
...SHE CRIED.

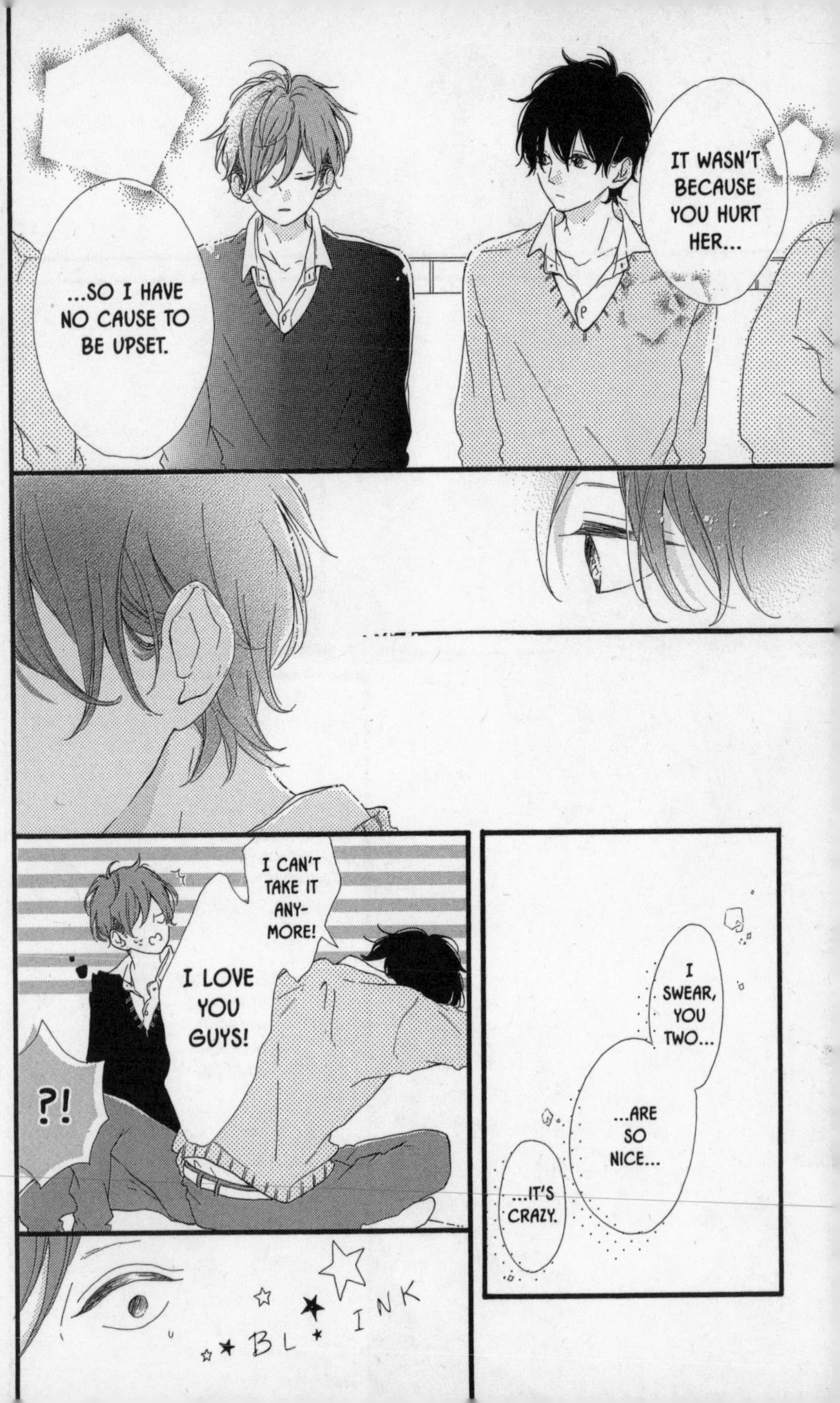
IT WASN'T BECAUSE YOU HURT HER...
...SO I HAVE NO CAUSE TO BE UPSET.
I SWEAR, YOU TWO...
...ARE SO NICE...
...IT'S CRAZY.
I CAN'T TAKE IT ANYMORE!
I LOVE YOU GUYS!
?!
BLINK

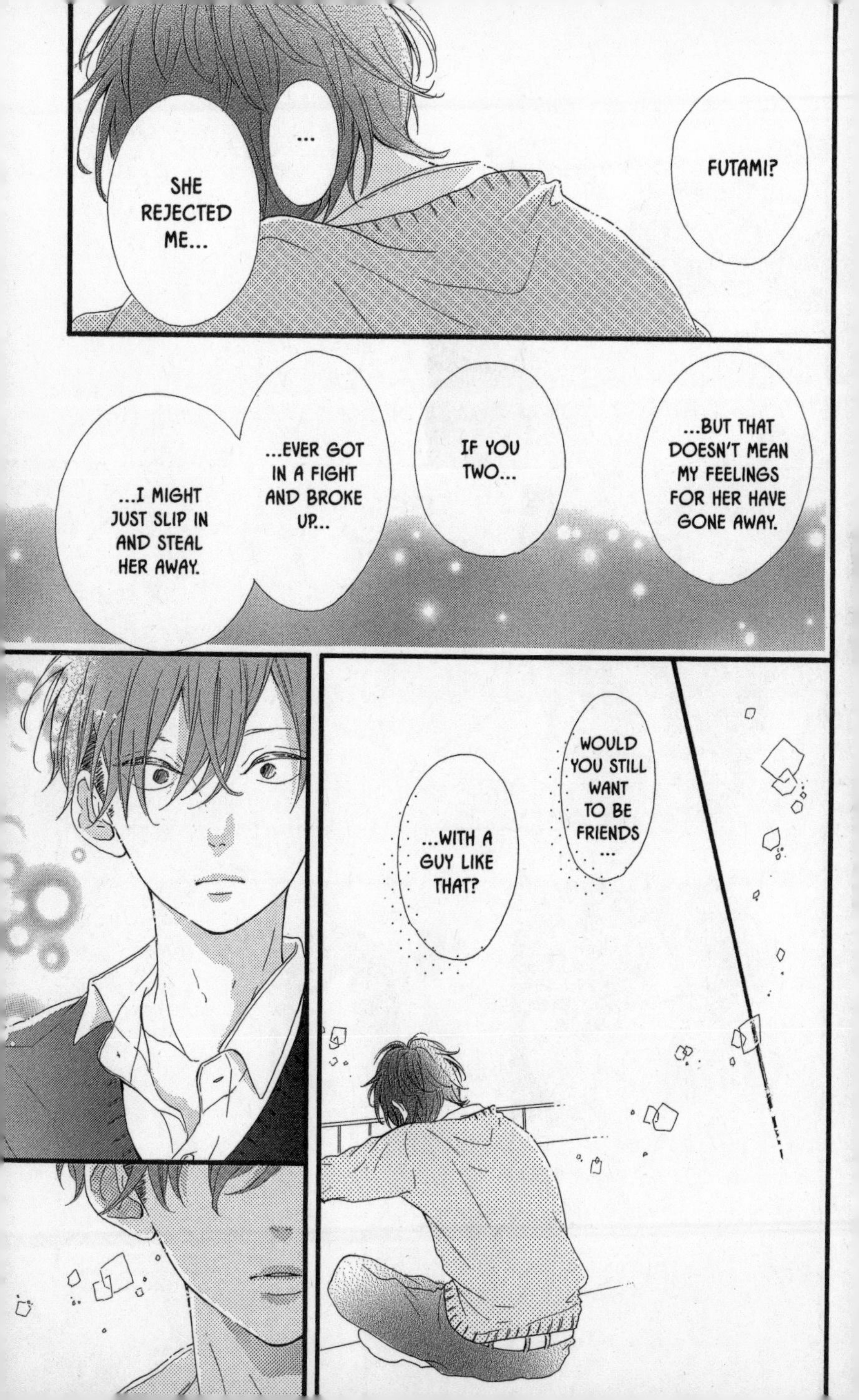
FUTAMI?
...
SHE REJECTED ME...
...BUT THAT DOESN'T MEAN MY FEELINGS FOR HER HAVE GONE AWAY.
IF YOU TWO...
...EVER GOT IN A FIGHT AND BROKE UP...
...I MIGHT JUST SLIP IN AND STEAL HER AWAY.
WOULD YOU STILL WANT TO BE FRIENDS...
...WITH A GUY LIKE THAT?

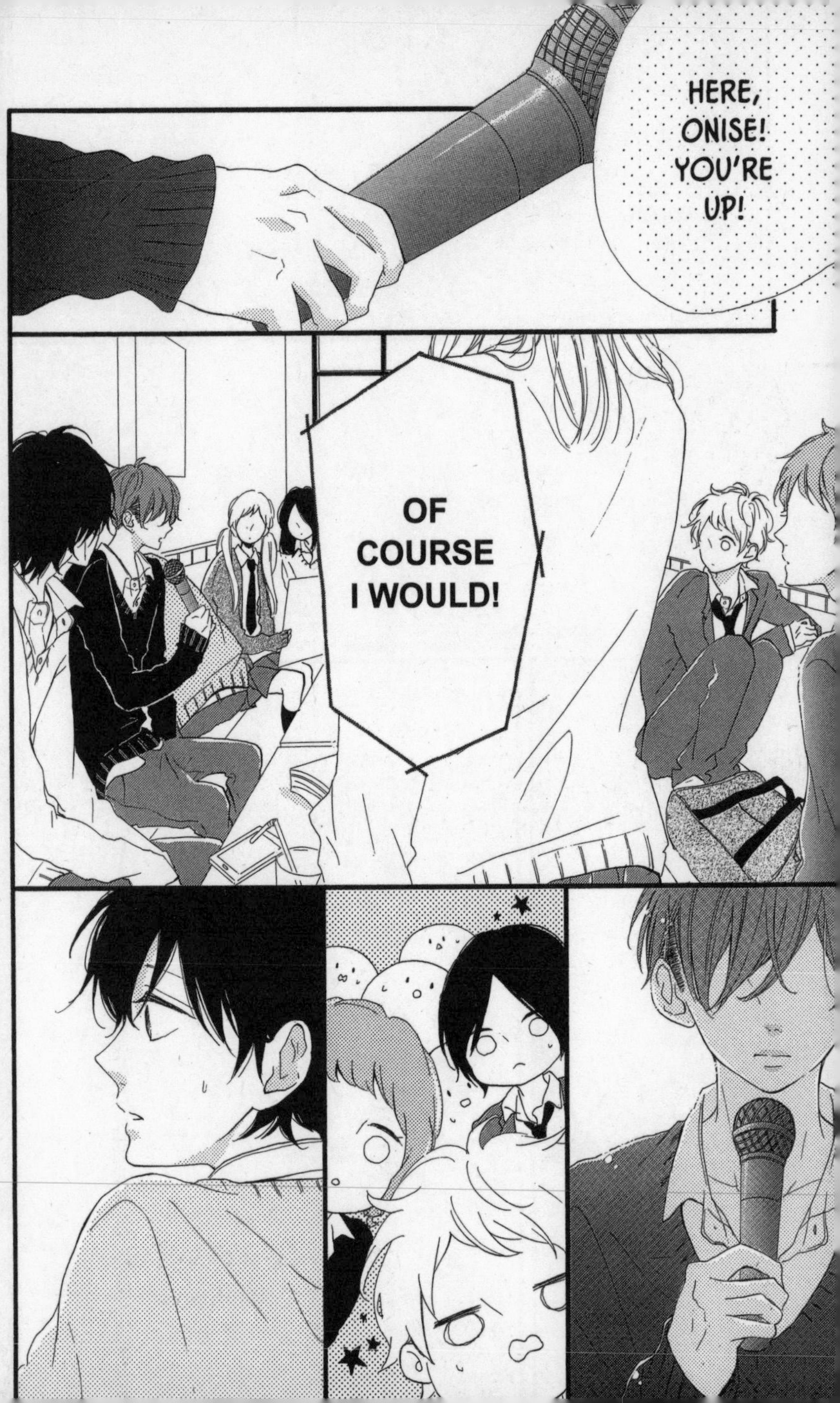
HERE, ONISE! YOU'RE UP!
OF COURSE I WOULD!

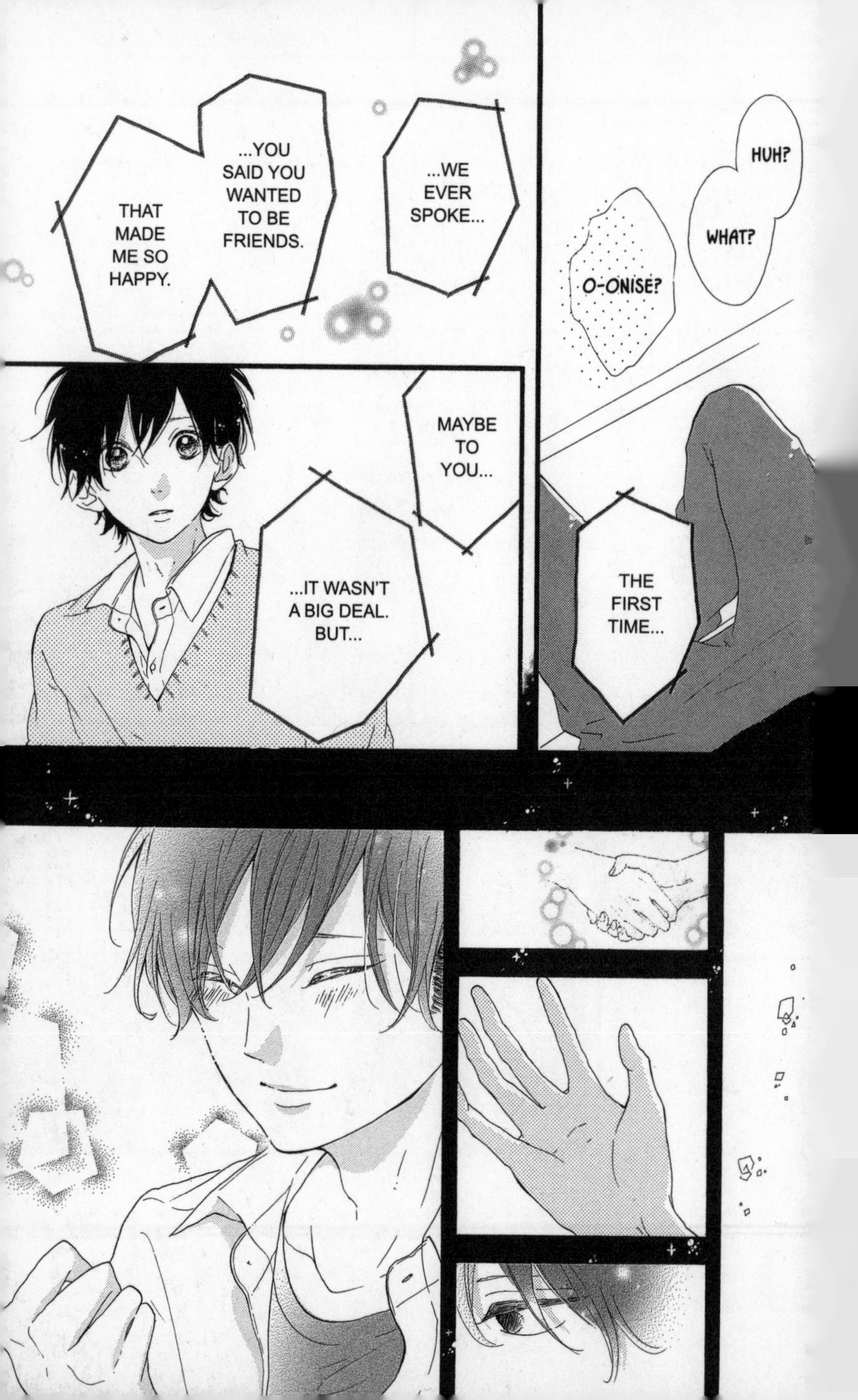
HUH?
WHAT?
O-ONISE?
THE FIRST TIME...
...WE EVER SPOKE...
...YOU SAID YOU WANTED TO BE FRIENDS.
THAT MADE ME SO HAPPY.
MAYBE TO YOU...
...IT WASN'T A BIG DEAL. BUT...

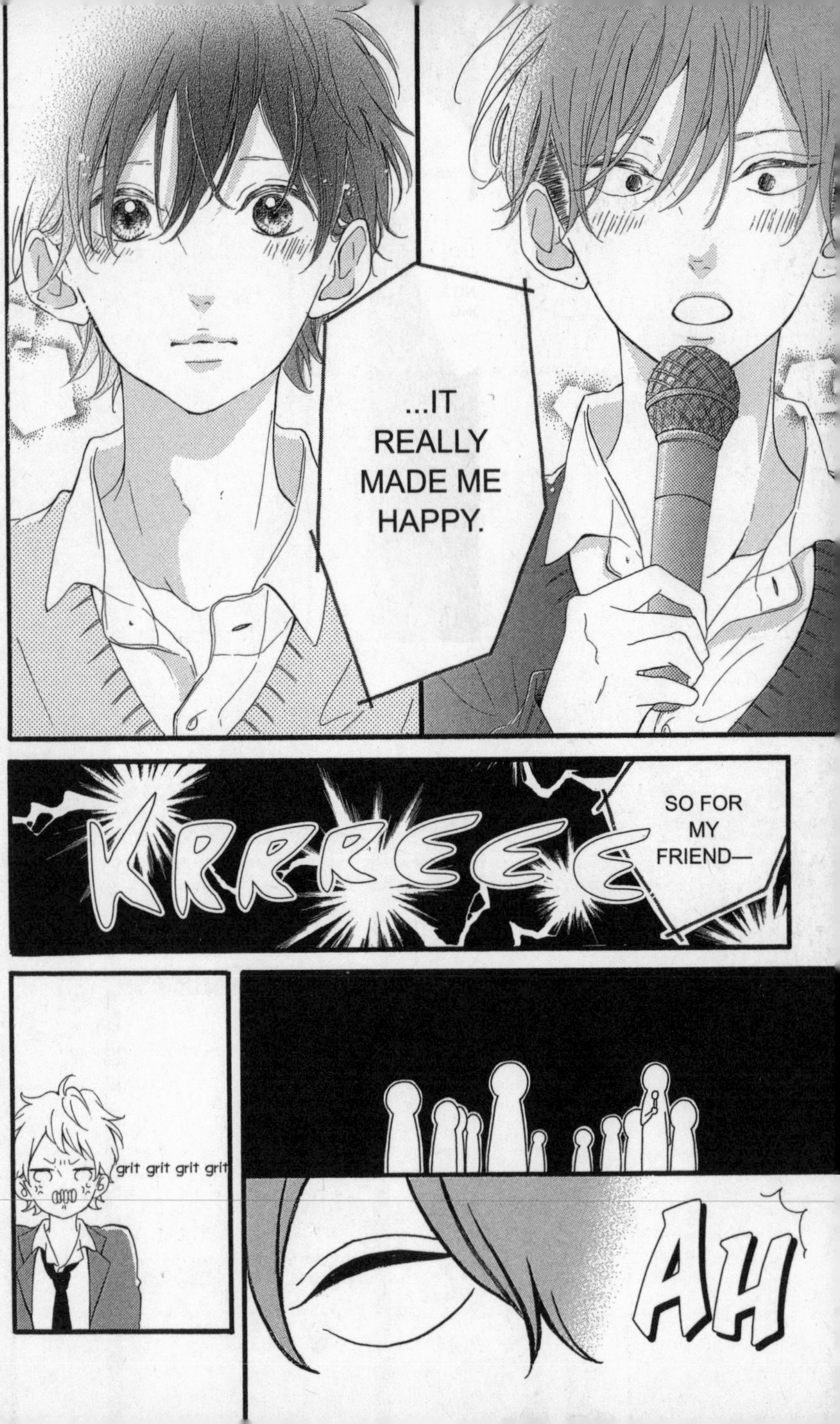
...IT REALLY MADE ME HAPPY.
SO FOR MY FRIEND—
KRRREEEE
AH
grit grit grit grit

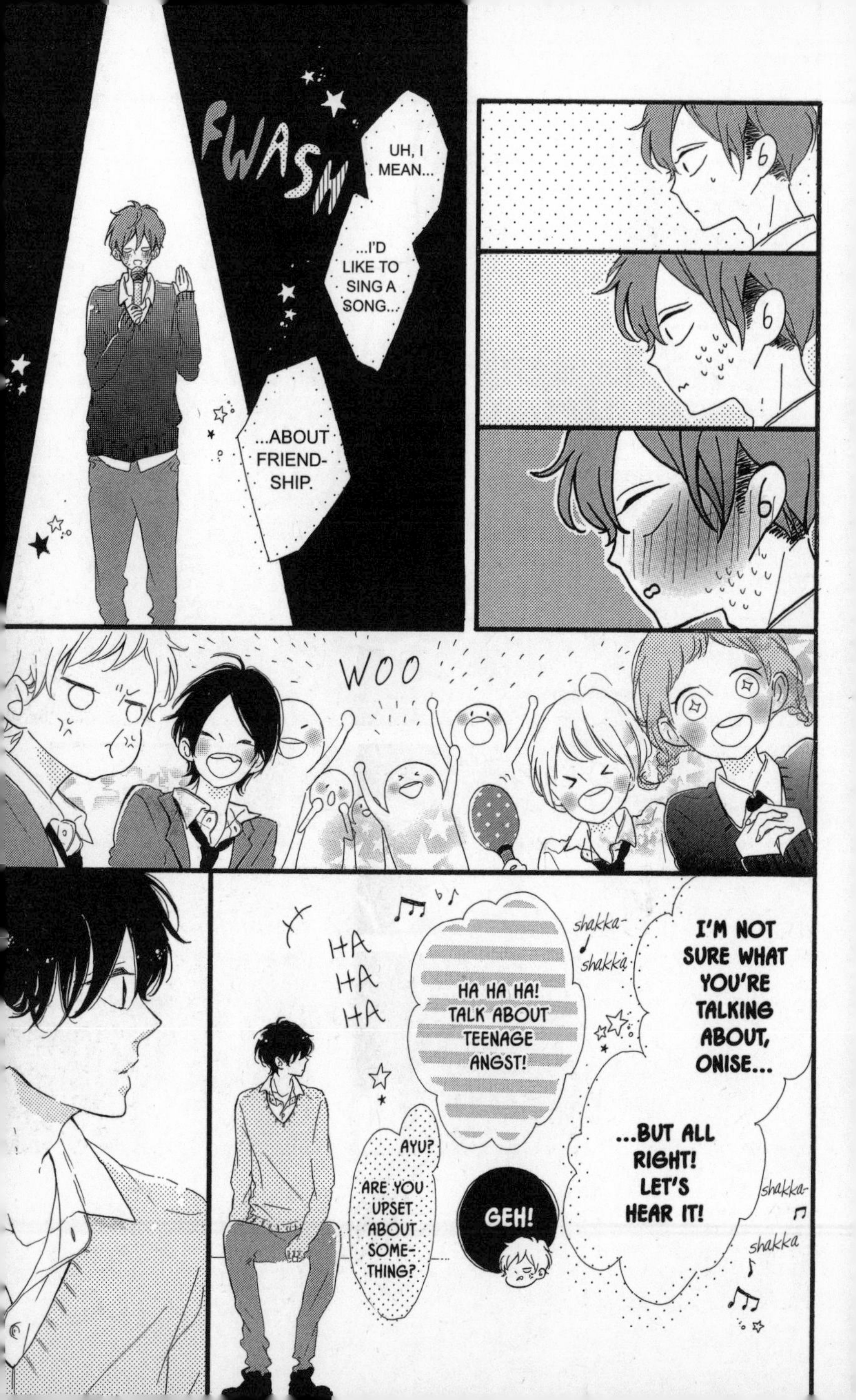
FWASH
UH, I MEAN...
...I'D LIKE TO SING A SONG...
...ABOUT FRIENDSHIP.
WOO
shakka- shakka
I'M NOT SURE WHAT YOU'RE TALKING ABOUT, ONISE...
...BUT ALL RIGHT! LET'S HEAR IT!
shakka- shakka
HA HA HA! TALK ABOUT TEENAGE ANGST!
HA HA HA
GEH!
AYU?
ARE YOU UPSET ABOUT SOMETHING?

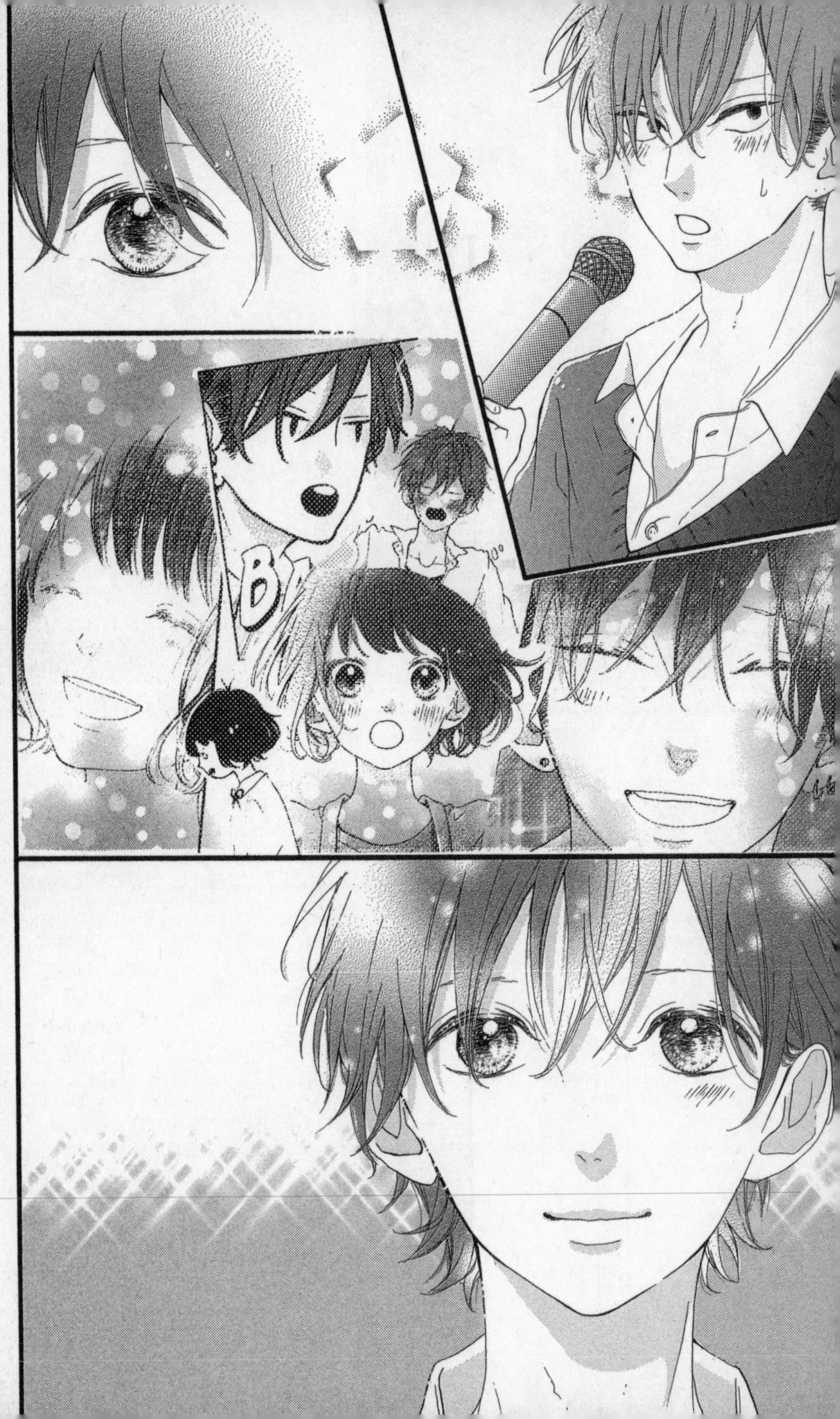
B

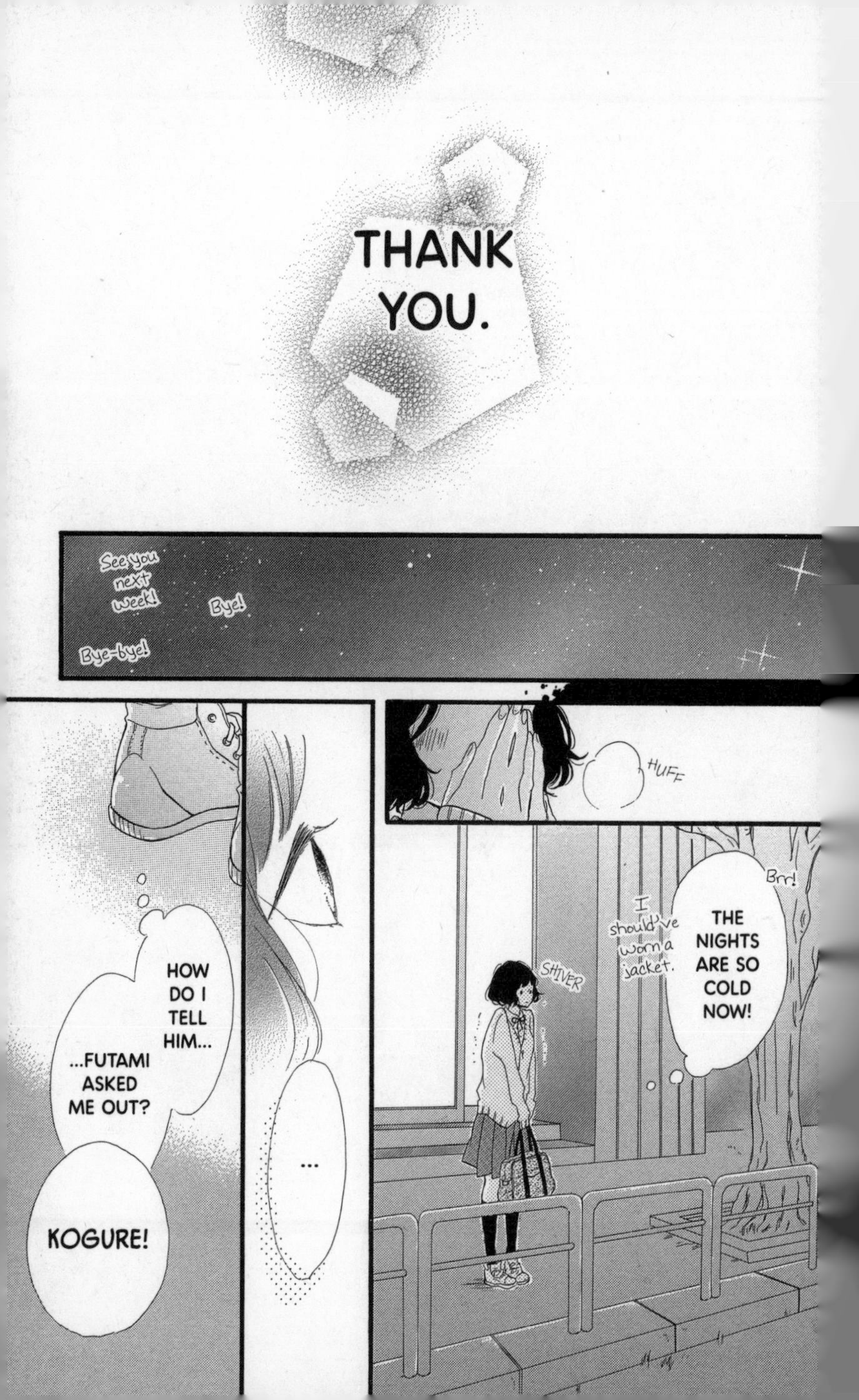
THANK YOU.
Bye!
See you next week!
Bye-bye!
HUFF
Brr!
THE NIGHTS ARE SO COLD NOW!
I should've worn a jacket.
SHIVER
...
HOW DO I TELL HIM...
...FUTAMI ASKED ME OUT?
KOGURE!

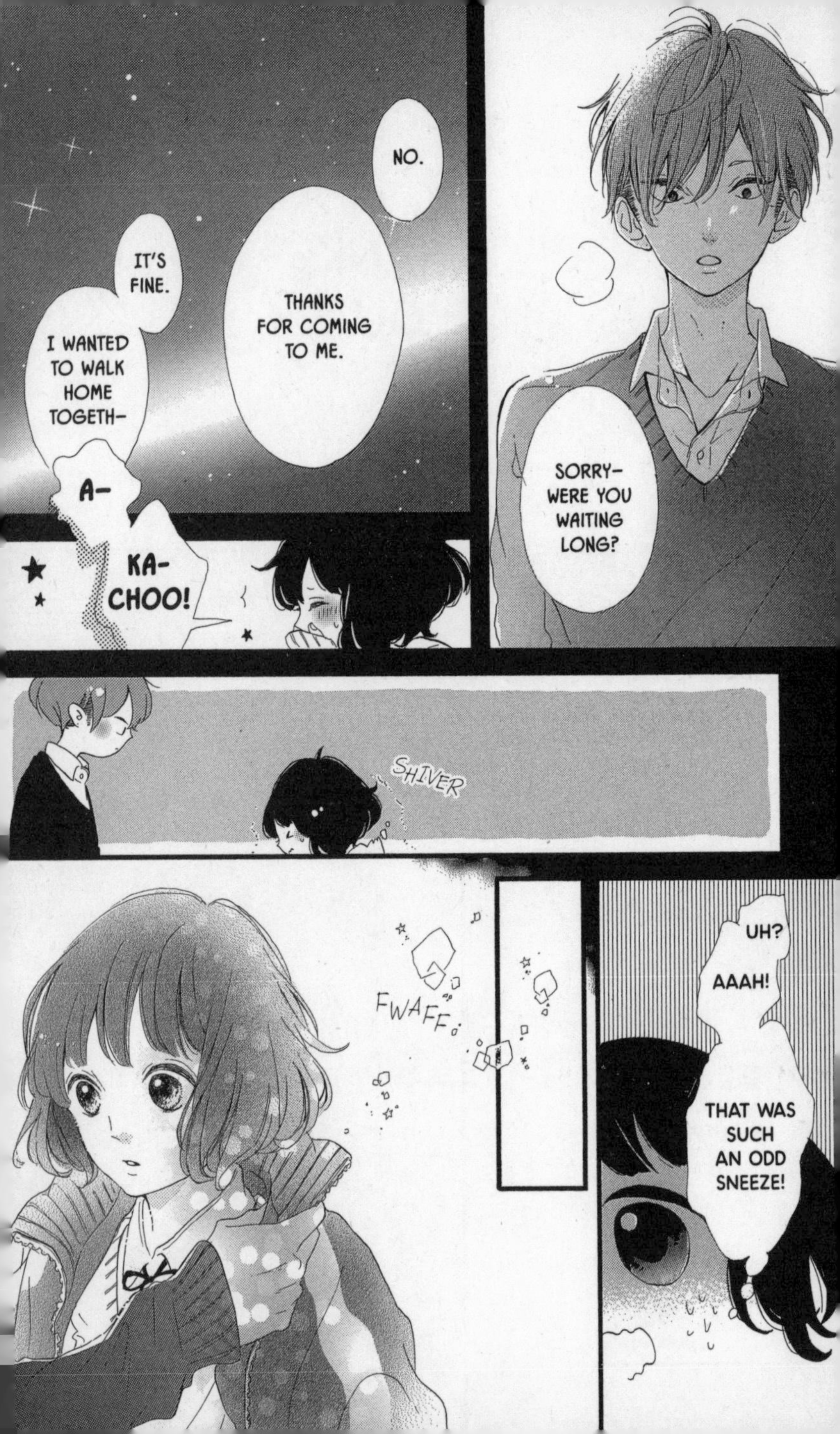
SORRY— WERE YOU WAITING LONG?
NO.
THANKS FOR COMING TO ME.
IT'S FINE.
I WANTED TO WALK HOME TOGETH—
A-
KA-CHOO!
SHIVER
UH?
AAAH!
THAT WAS SUCH AN ODD SNEEZE!
FWAFF

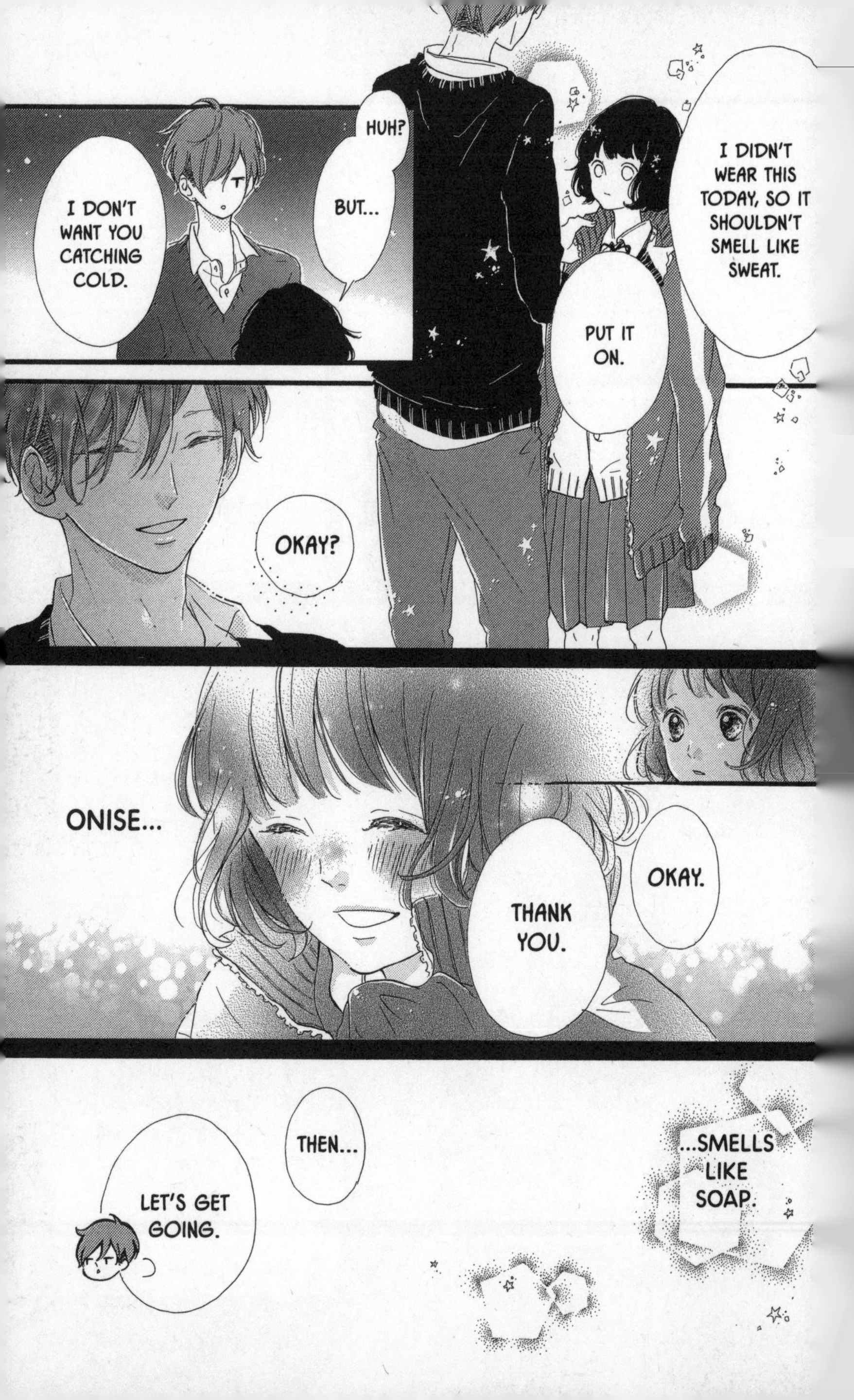

I DIDN'T WEAR THIS TODAY, SO IT SHOULDN'T SMELL LIKE SWEAT.
HUH?
PUT IT ON.
BUT...
I DON'T WANT YOU CATCHING COLD.
OKAY?
OKAY.
THANK YOU.
ONISE...
...SMELLS LIKE SOAP.
THEN...
LET'S GET GOING.

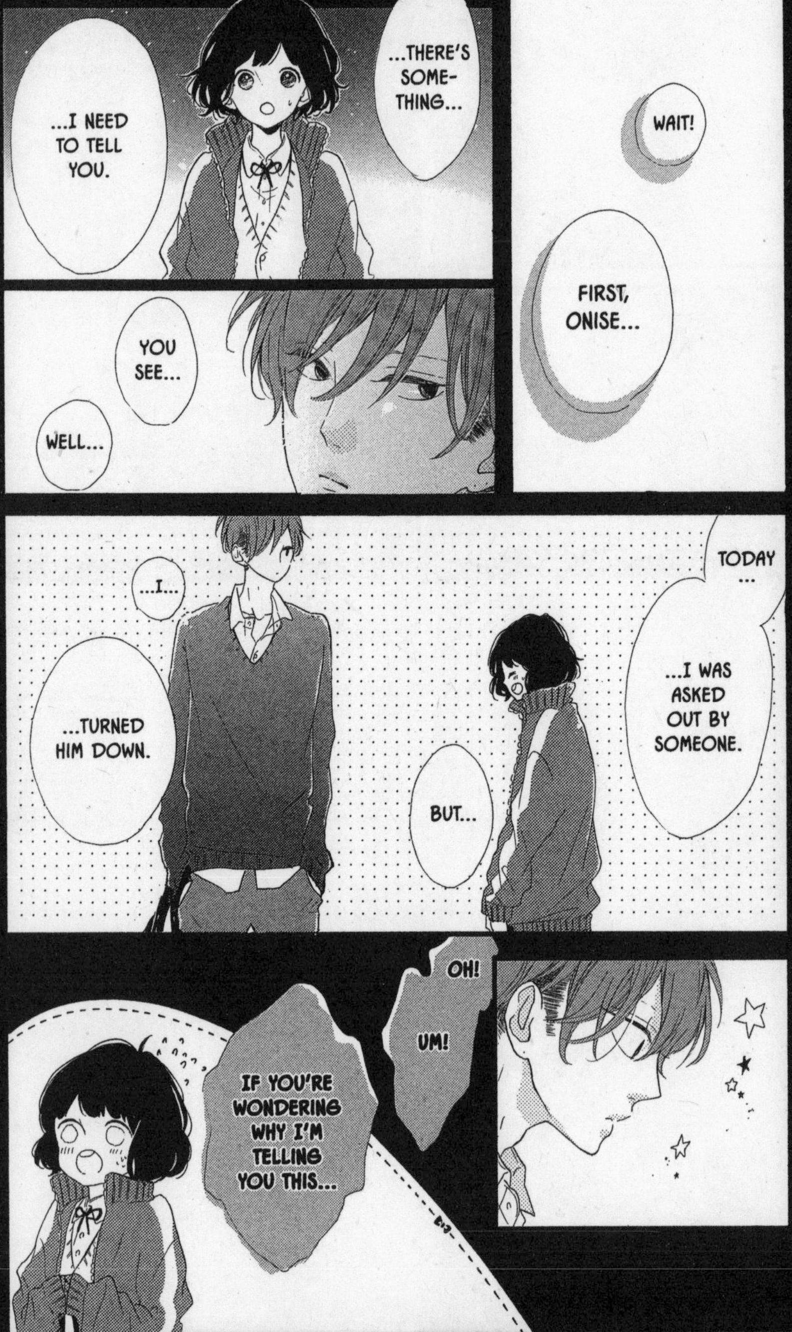
WAIT!
FIRST, ONISE...
...THERE'S SOMETHING...
...I NEED TO TELL YOU.
YOU SEE...
WELL...
TODAY...
...I WAS ASKED OUT BY SOMEONE.
BUT...
...I...
...TURNED HIM DOWN.
OH!
UM!
IF YOU'RE WONDERING WHY I'M TELLING YOU THIS...

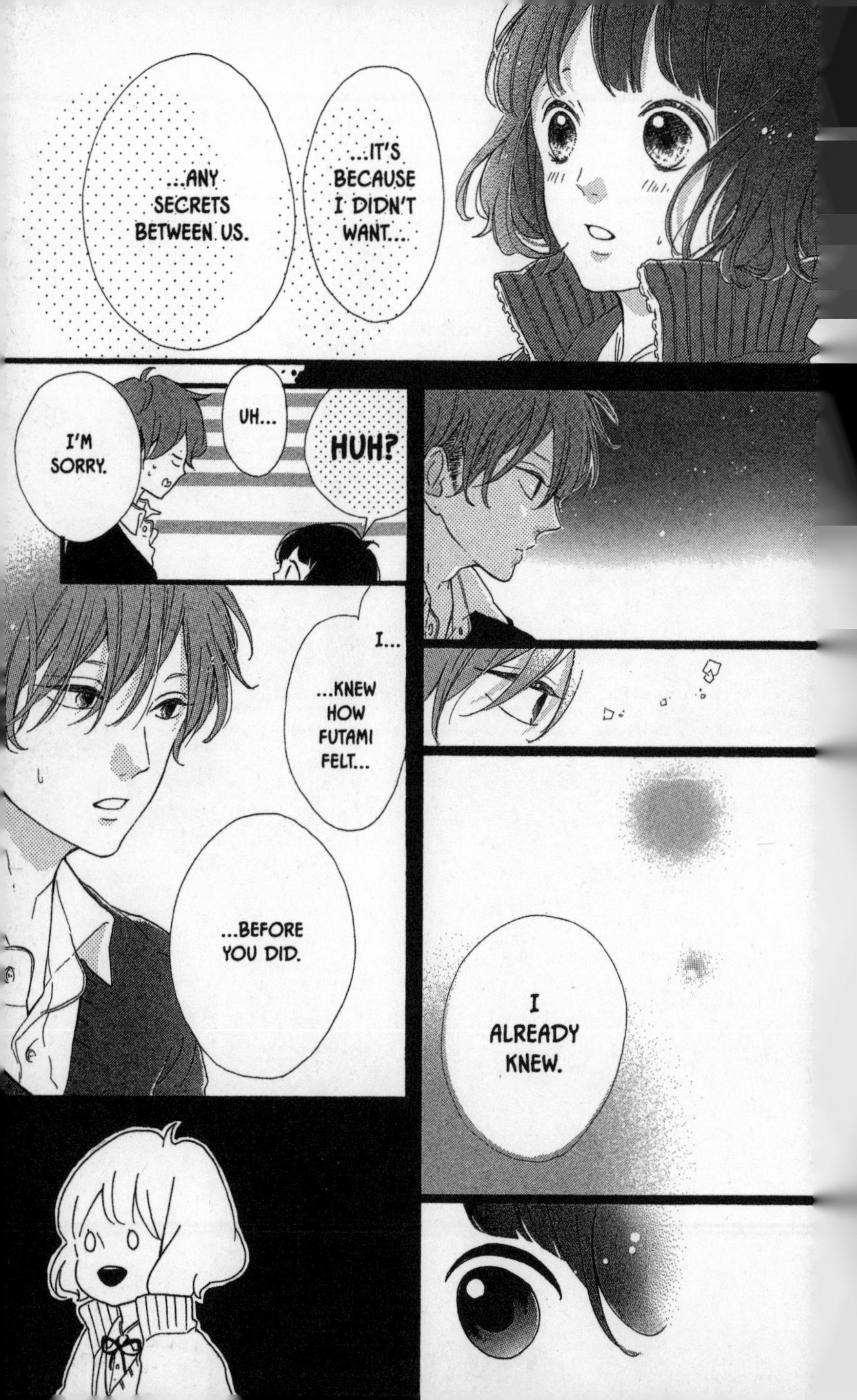
...IT'S BECAUSE I DIDN'T WANT...
...ANY SECRETS BETWEEN US.
HUH?
UH...
I'M SORRY.
I...
...KNEW HOW FUTAMI FELT...
...BEFORE YOU DID.
I ALREADY KNEW.

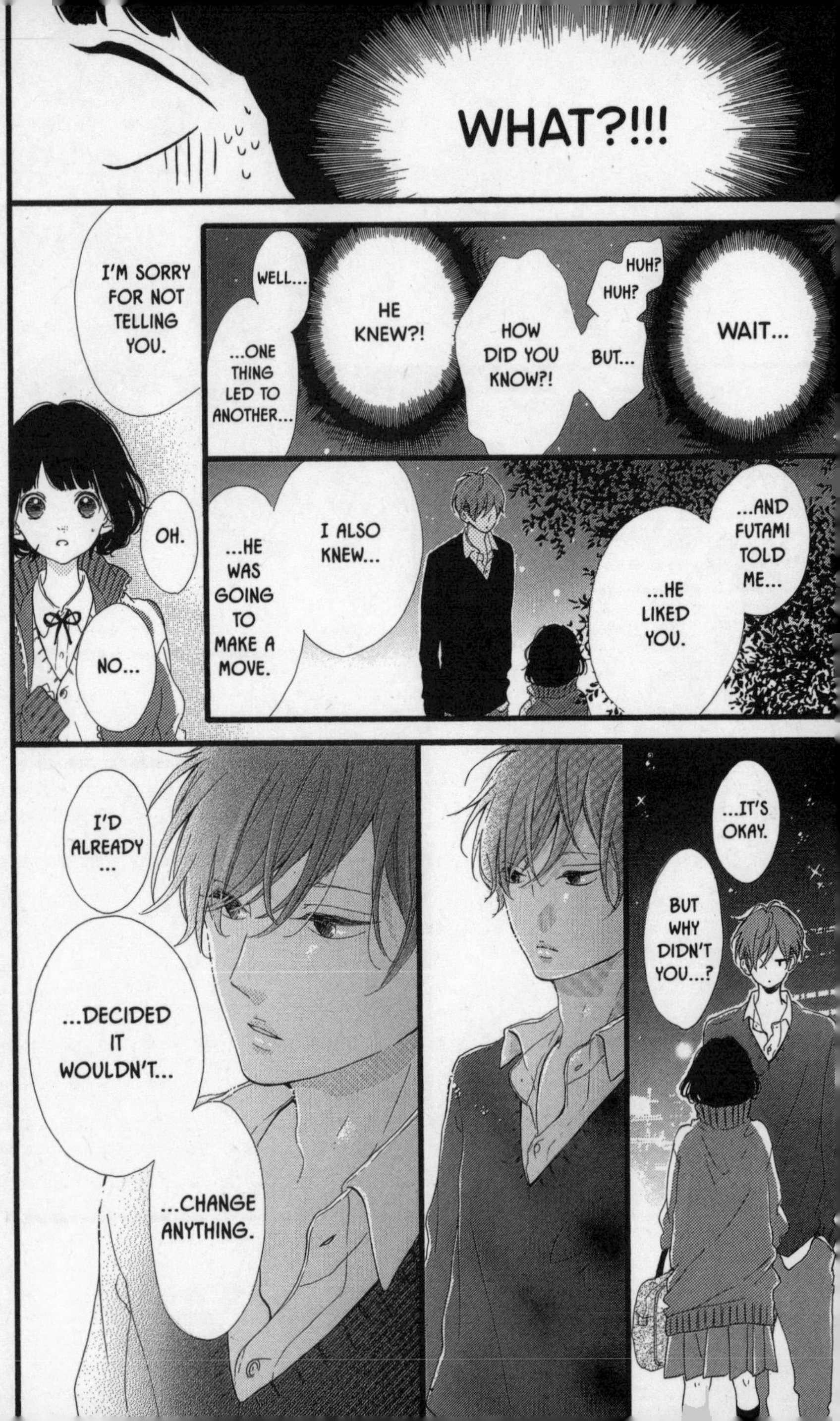
WHAT?!!!
WAIT...
HUH? HUH?
BUT...
HOW DID YOU KNOW?!
HE KNEW?!
WELL...
...ONE THING LED TO ANOTHER...
...AND FUTAMI TOLD ME...
...HE LIKED YOU.
I ALSO KNEW...
...HE WAS GOING TO MAKE A MOVE.
I'M SORRY FOR NOT TELLING YOU.
OH.
NO...
...IT'S OKAY.
BUT WHY DIDN'T YOU...?
I'D ALREADY...
...DECIDED IT WOULDN'T...
...CHANGE ANYTHING.

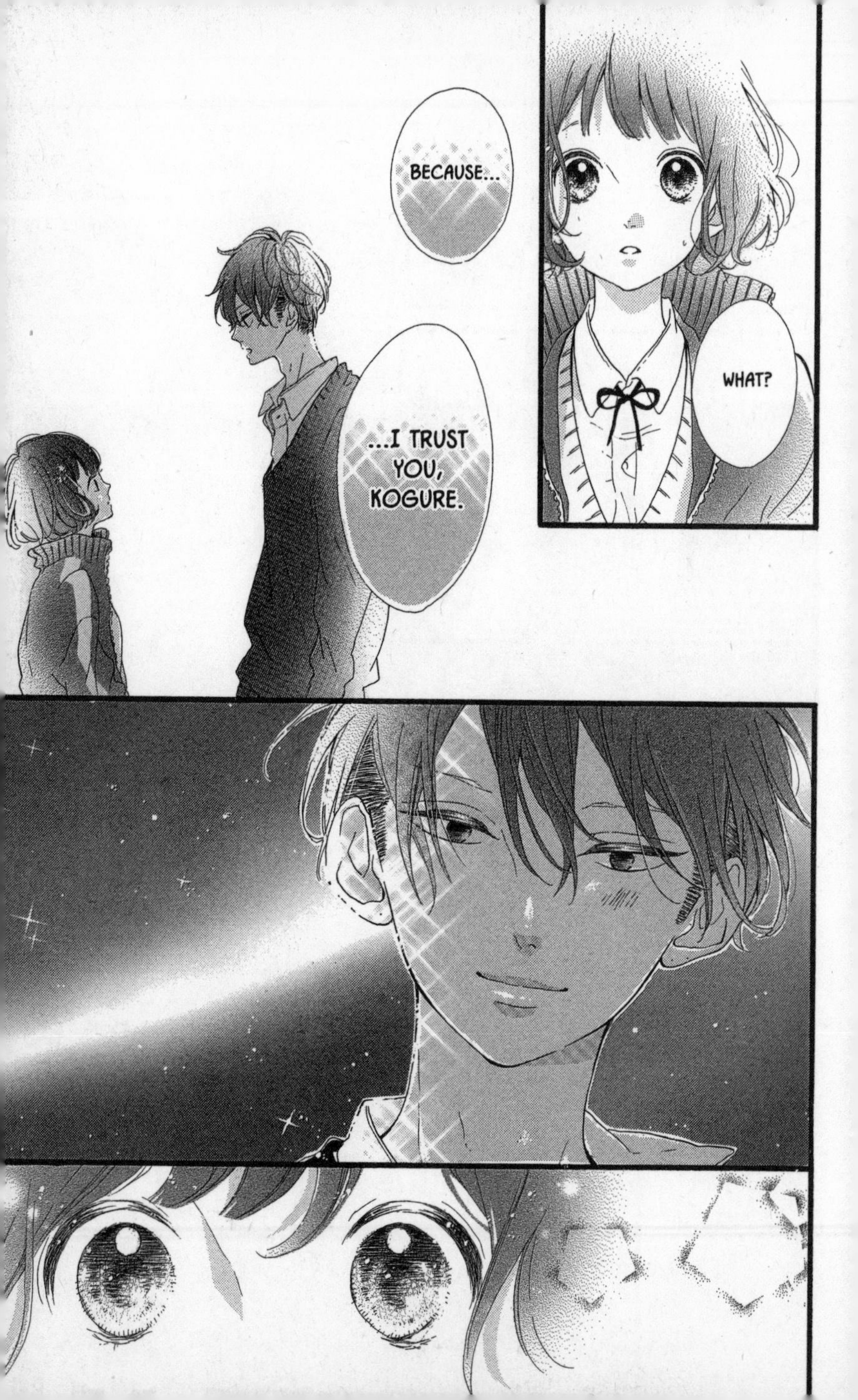
WHAT?
BECAUSE...
...I TRUST YOU, KOGURE.

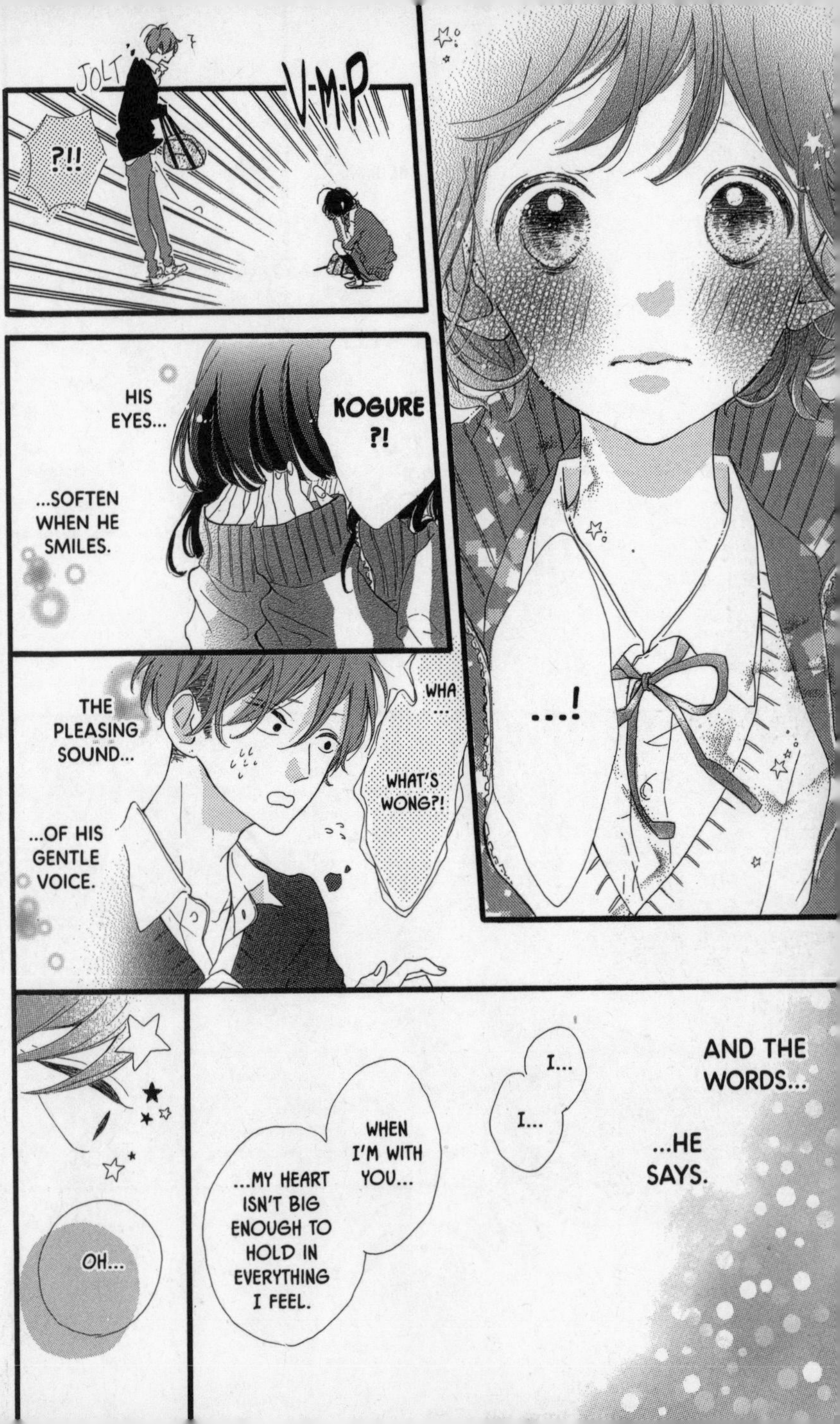
...!
V-M-P
JOLT
?!!
KOGURE ?!
HIS EYES...
...SOFTEN WHEN HE SMILES.
WHA...
WHAT'S WONG?!
THE PLEASING SOUND...
...OF HIS GENTLE VOICE.
AND THE WORDS...
...HE SAYS.
I...
I...
WHEN I'M WITH YOU...
...MY HEART ISN'T BIG ENOUGH TO HOLD IN EVERYTHING I FEEL.
OH...

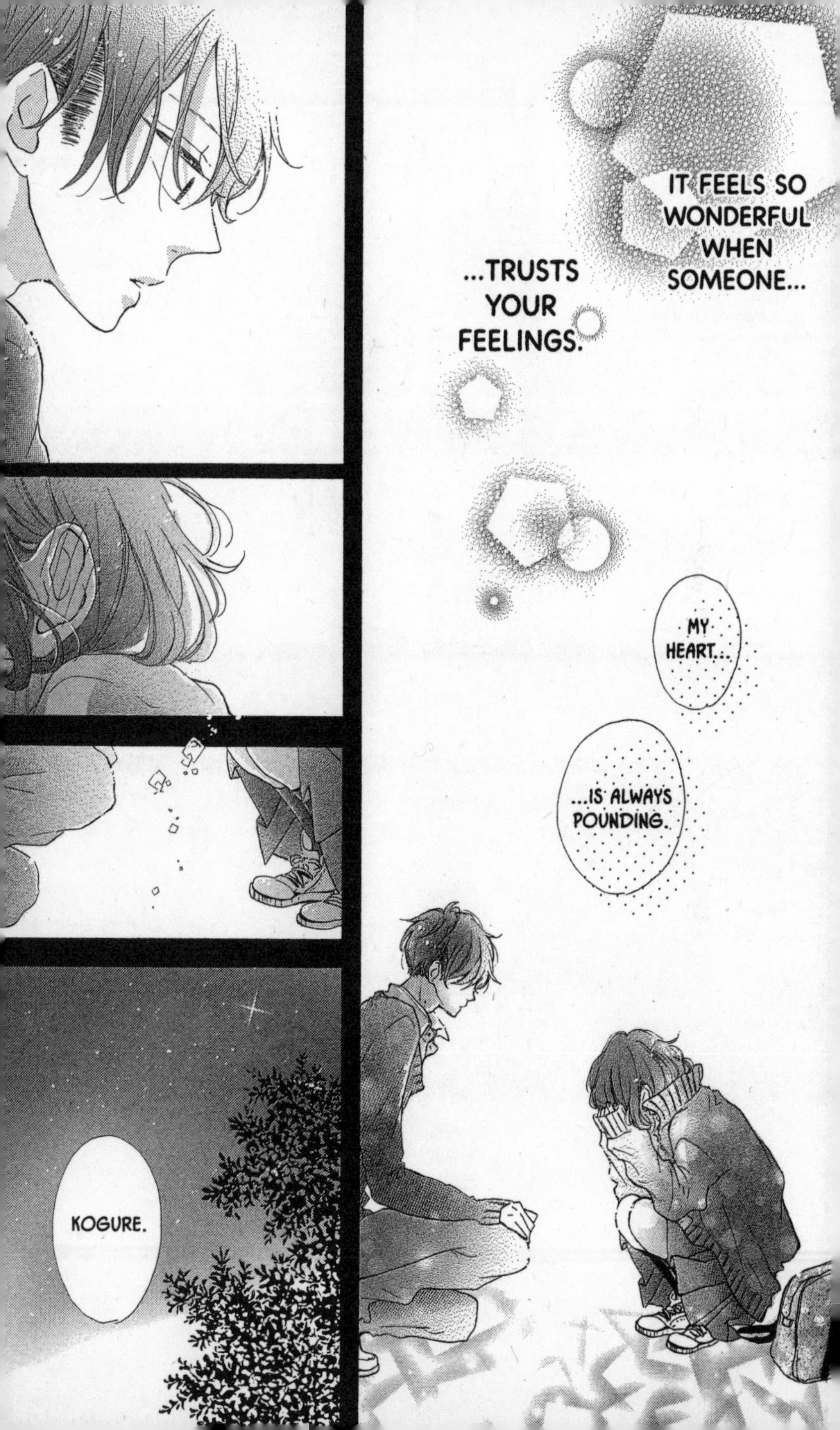
IT FEELS SO WONDERFUL WHEN SOMEONE...
...TRUSTS YOUR FEELINGS.
MY HEART...
...IS ALWAYS POUNDING.
KOGURE.

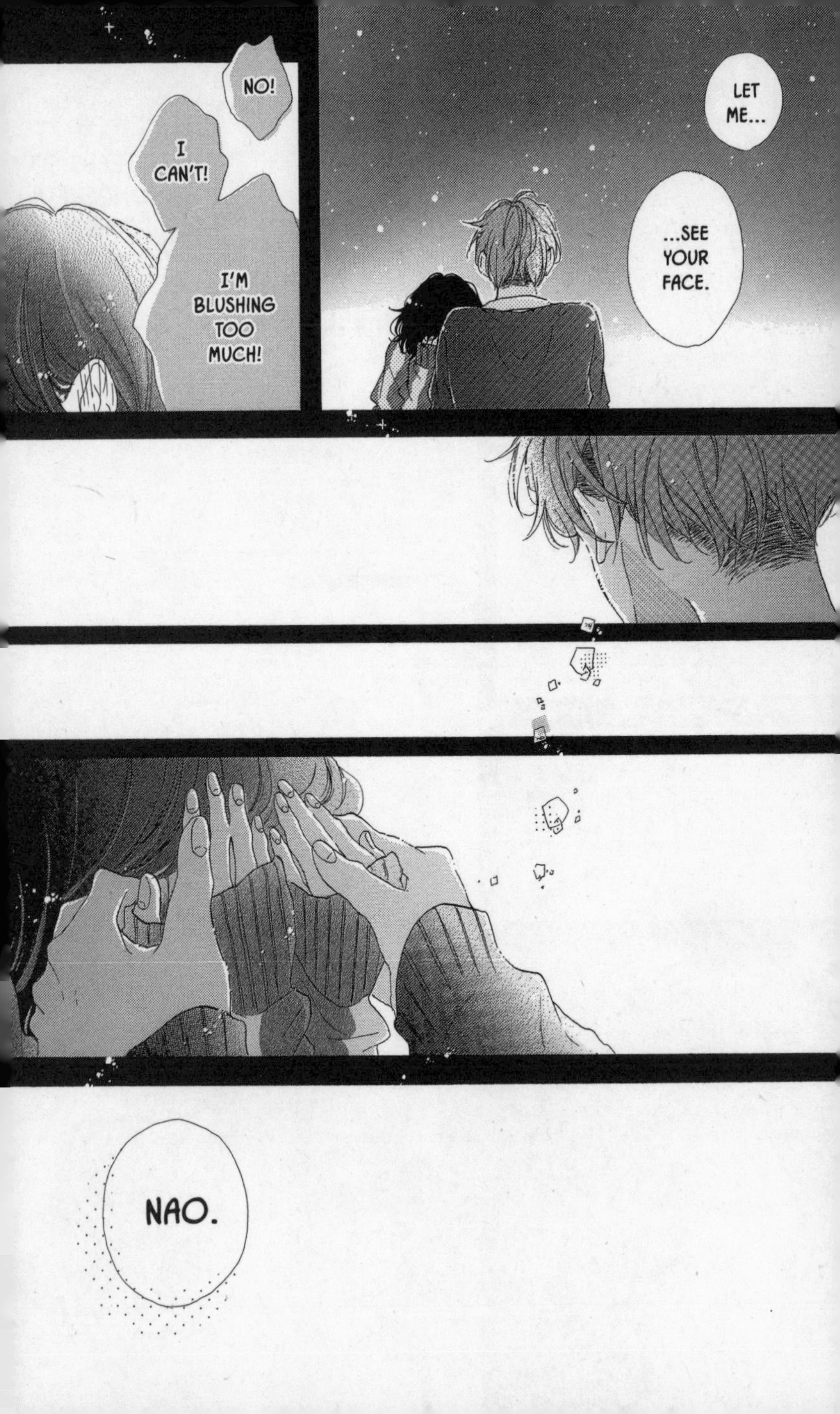
LET ME...
...SEE YOUR FACE.
NO!
I CAN'T!
I'M BLUSHING TOO MUCH!
NAO.

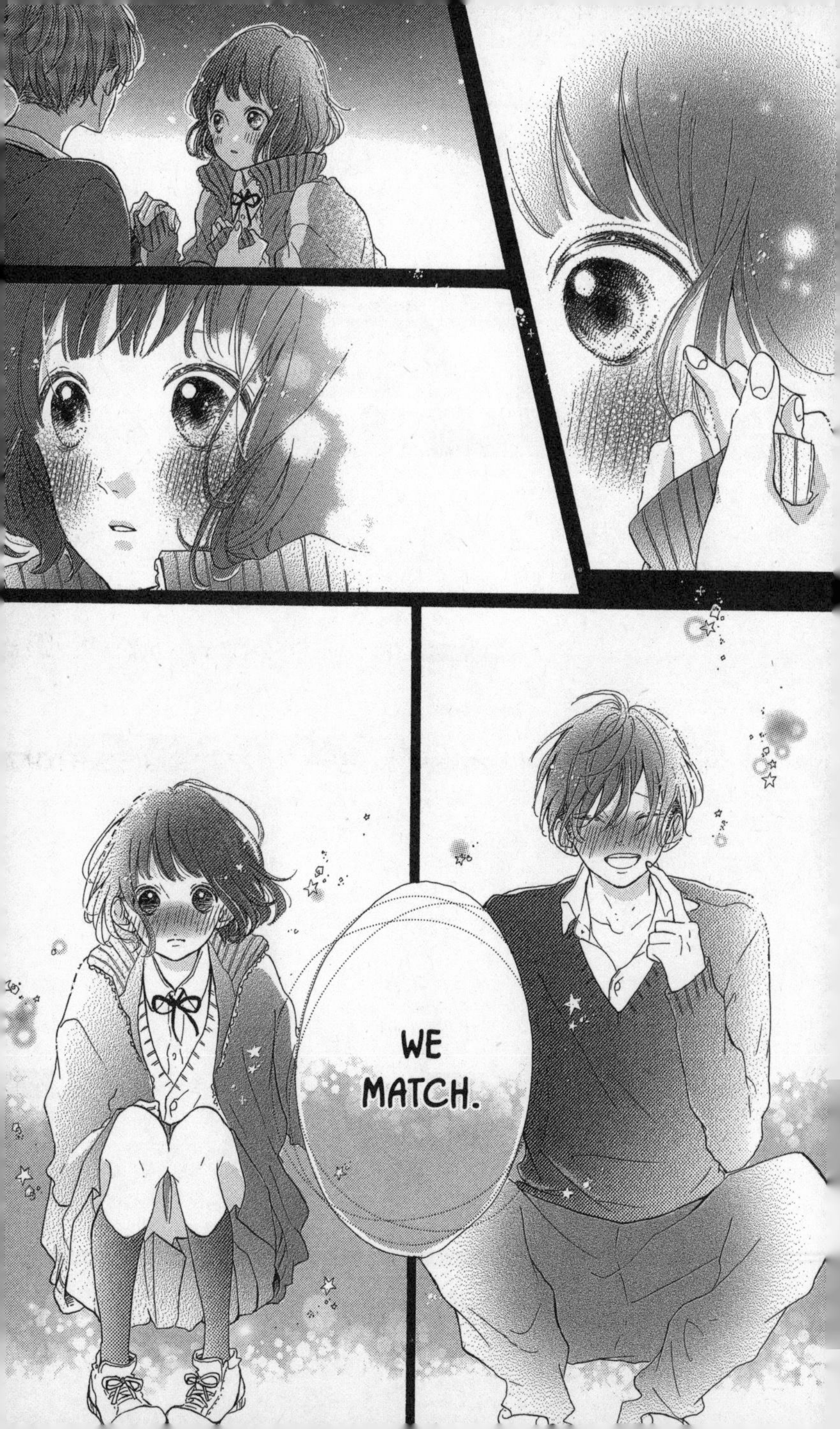
WE MATCH.

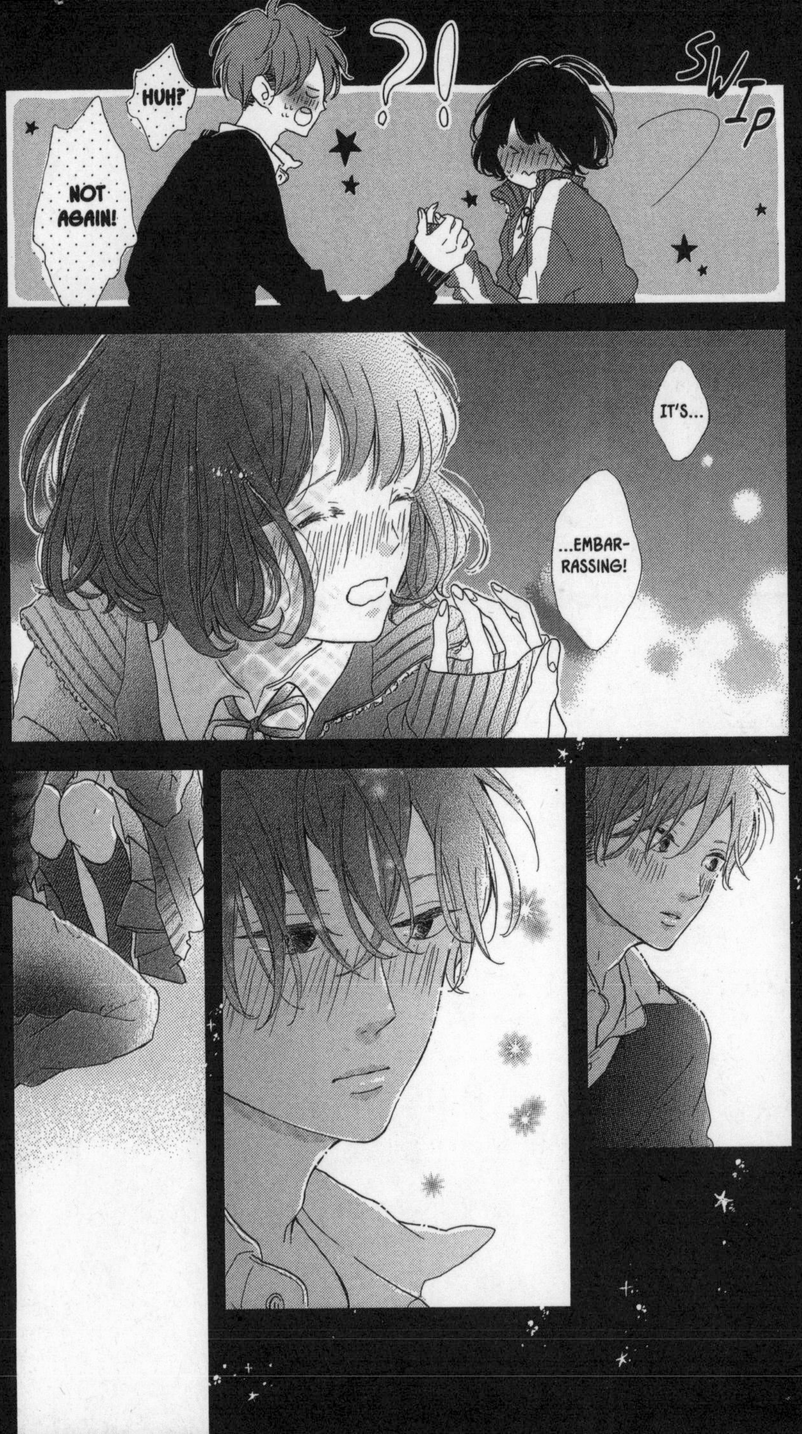
SWIP
?!
HUH?
NOT AGAIN!
IT'S...
...EMBAR-RASSING!

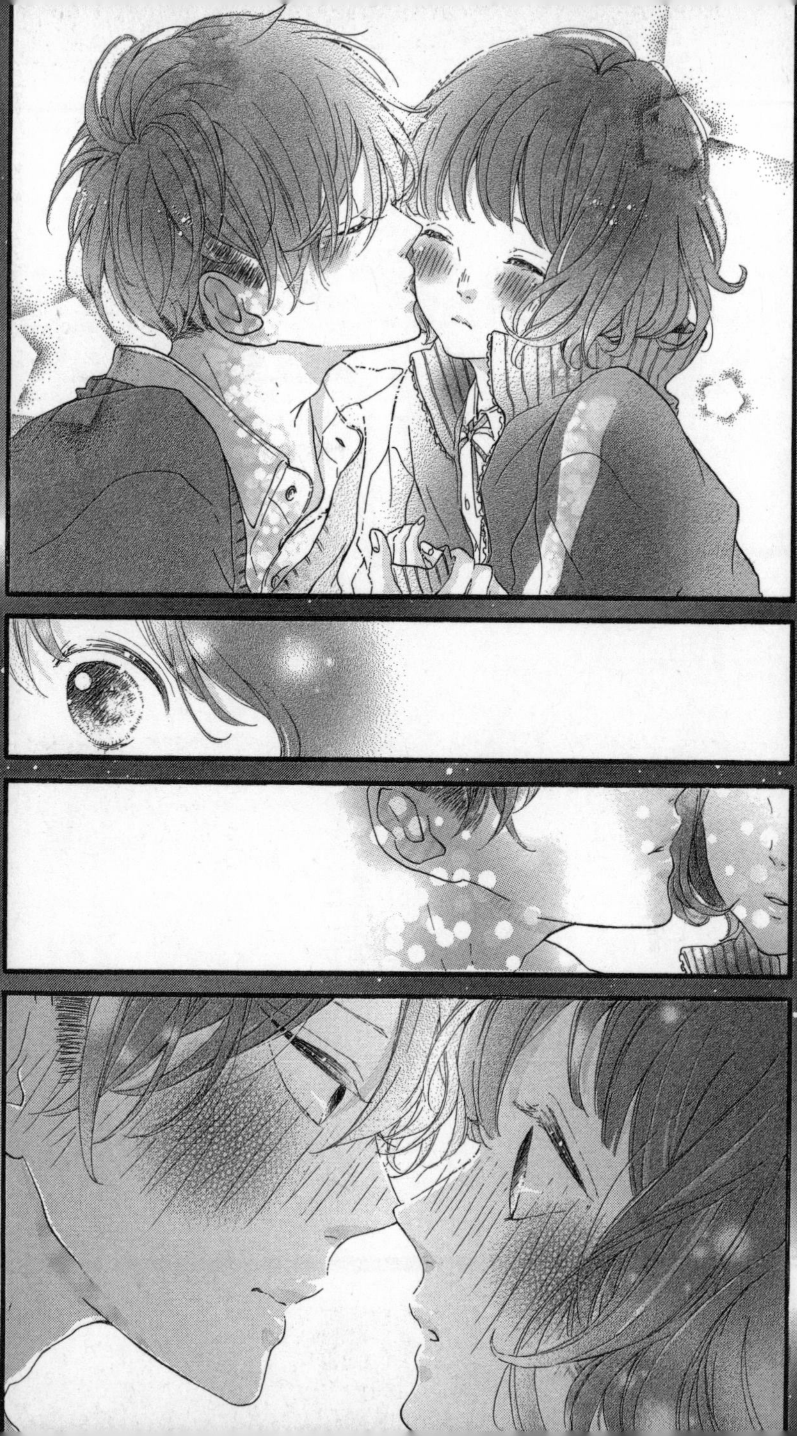

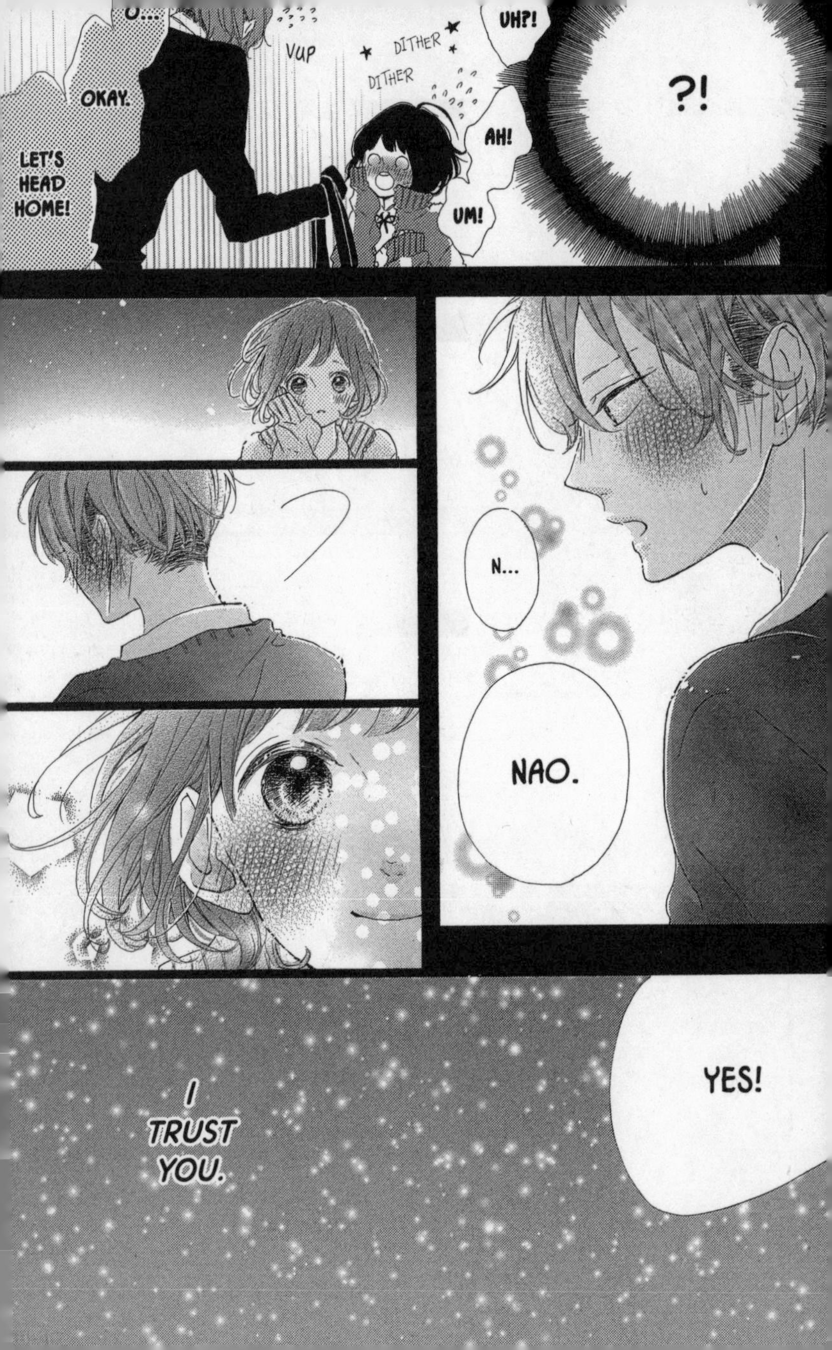
?!
UH?!
DITHER
DITHER
AH!
UM!
VUP
OKAY.
LET'S HEAD HOME!
N...
NAO.
YES!
I TRUST YOU.

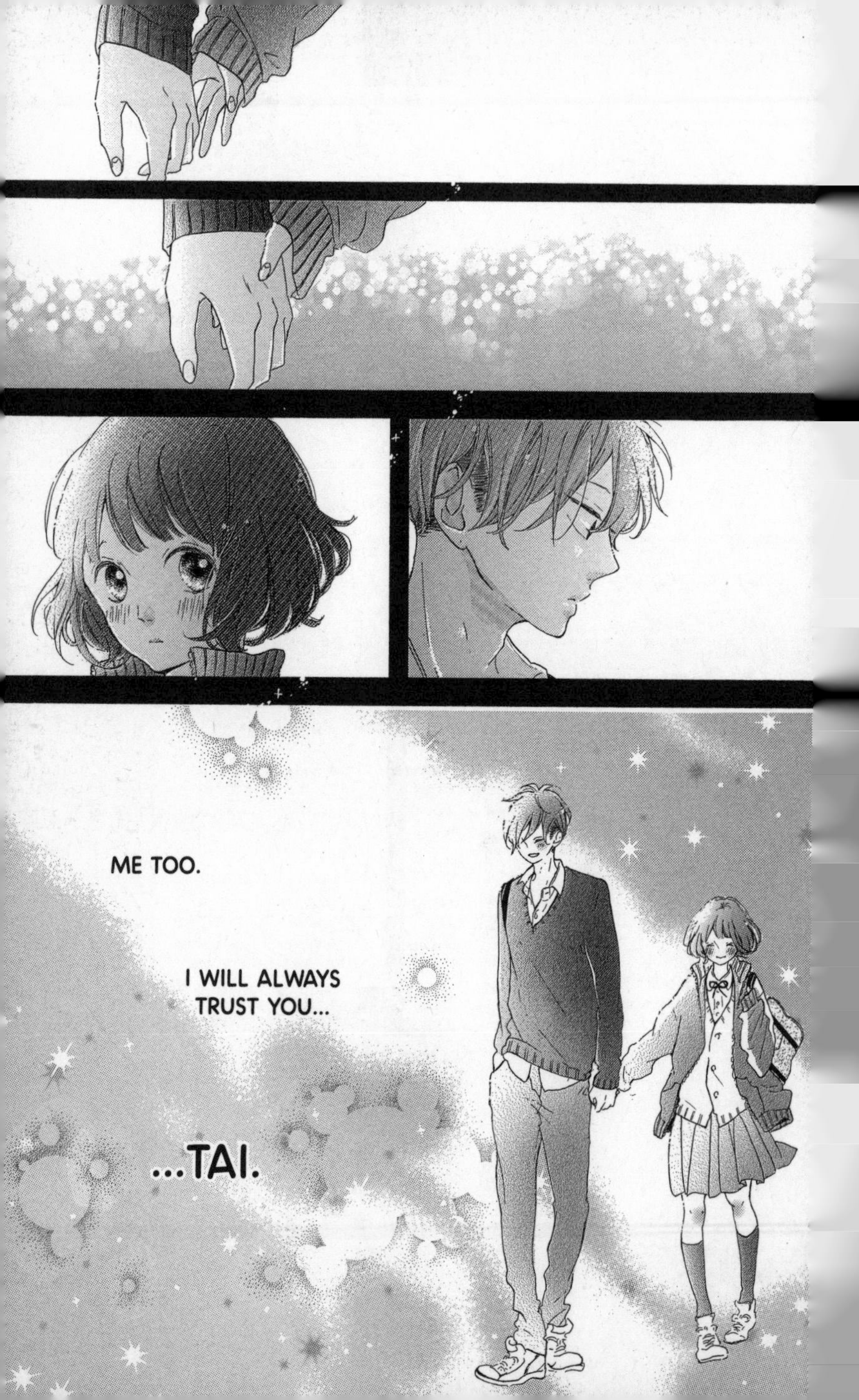
ME TOO.
I WILL ALWAYS TRUST YOU...
...TAI.

Honey So Sweet
Character Profile ♡ 2

Taiga Onise (Age 15)

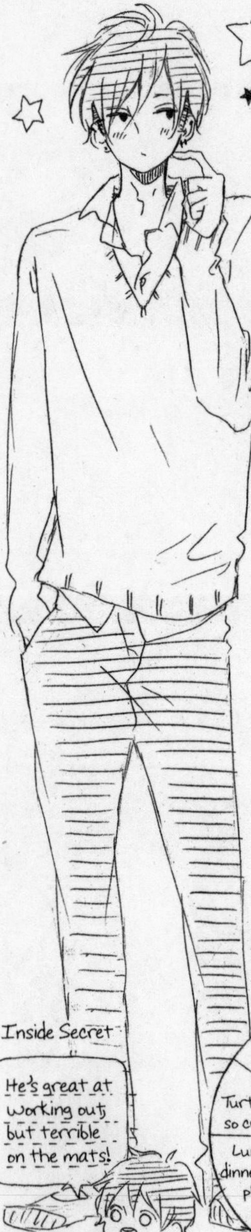

- Birthday/Blood Type: March 3/A
- Height/Weight: 5'8"/134 lbs
- Hobbies/Skills: Exercising, playing with Turty/Cooking
- Favorite/Least Favorite Food: Shortcake/Chinese onions
- Favorite Band: All Western music
- Type of Girl: The girl he's fallen in love with
- Personal Mantra: One good deed a day, daily diligence
- Favorite Thing to Do Before Bed: Good-night text to Nao, thinking over the day
- Childhood Dream: Be the Red Ranger
- Favorite Place: At school with Nao
- Current Obsession: Browsing cooking sites and creating new dishes
- Captivated By: Smiles?
- Stress Reliever: Doesn't get stressed
- Hair Colors Tried: Blond, red, brown, ash
- Mind Graph

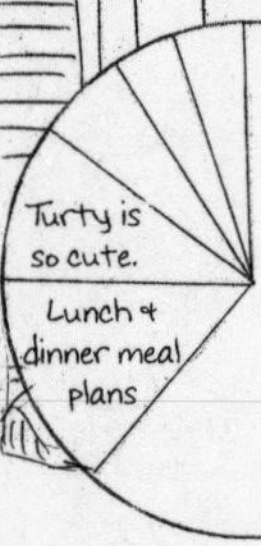

Part-time job
Being more like the Red Ranger
Making things easier on his mom
Turty is so cute.
Lunch & dinner meal plans
Nao

- Childhood Photo

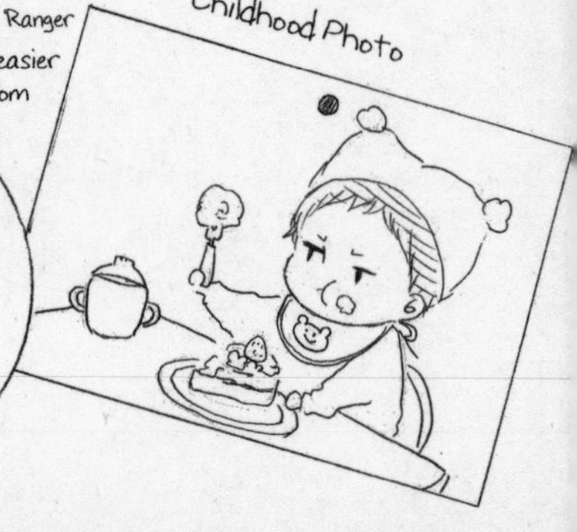

Inside Secret

He's great at working out, but terrible on the mats!

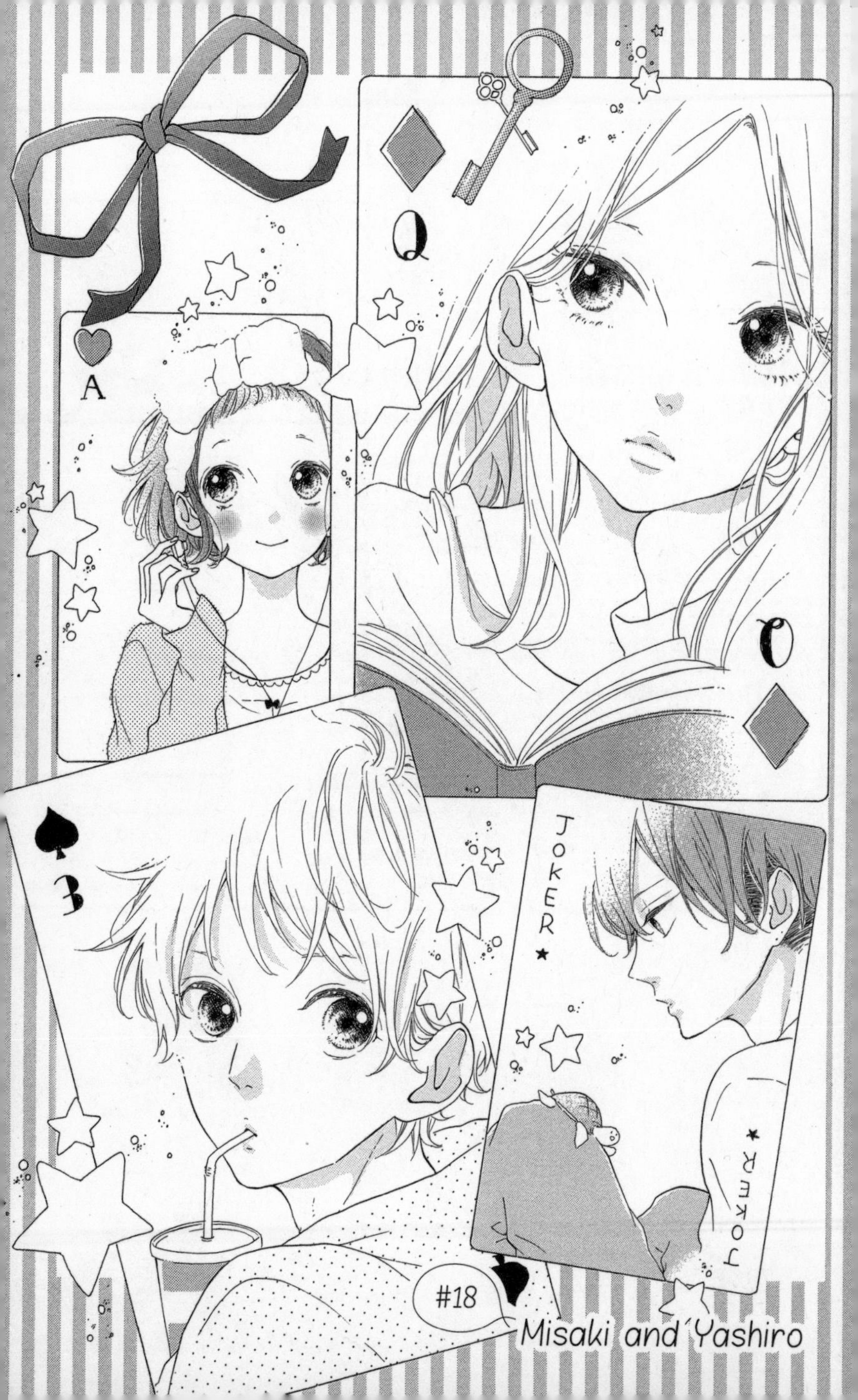
A
Q
3
JOKER
#18
Misaki and Yashiro

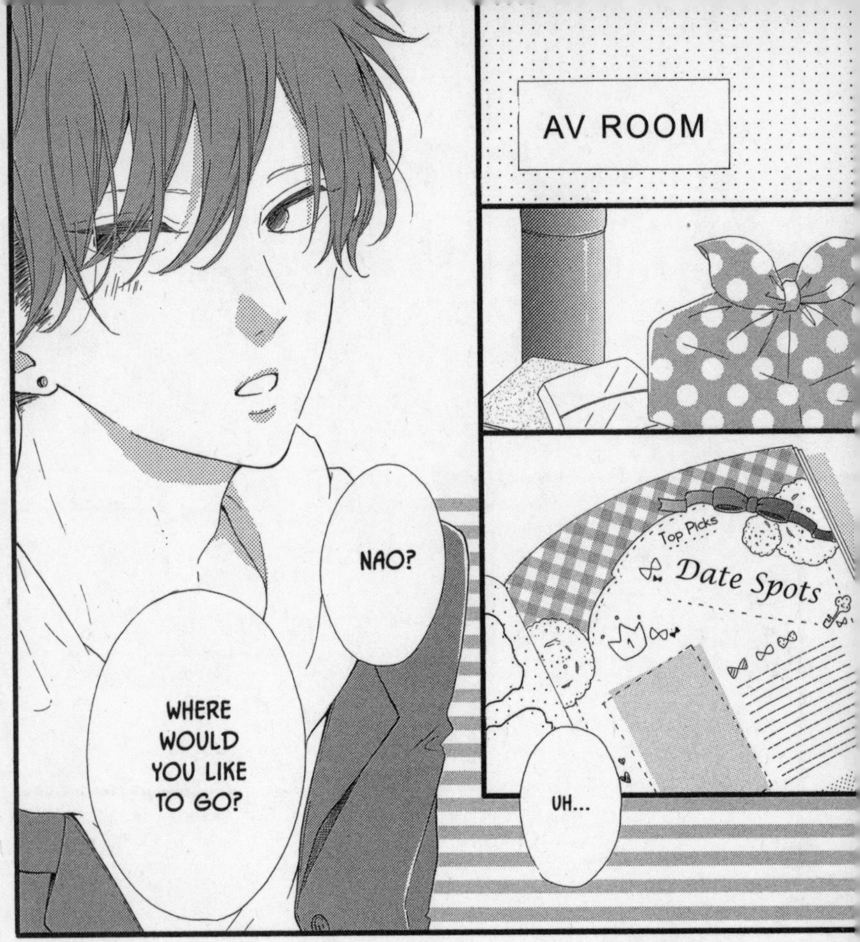
AV ROOM
Top Picks
Date Spots
UH...
NAO?
WHERE WOULD YOU LIKE TO GO?

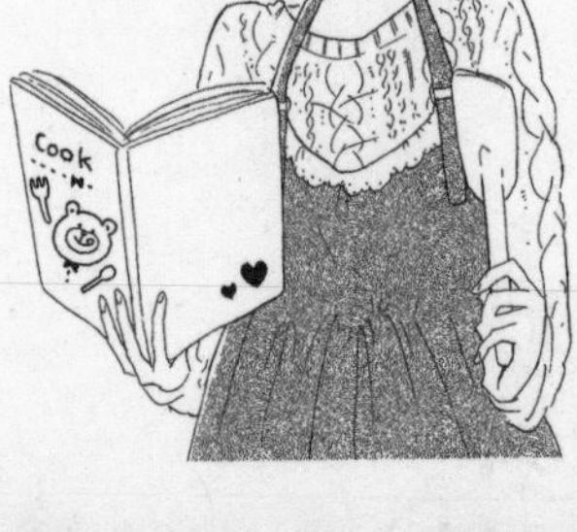
Cook

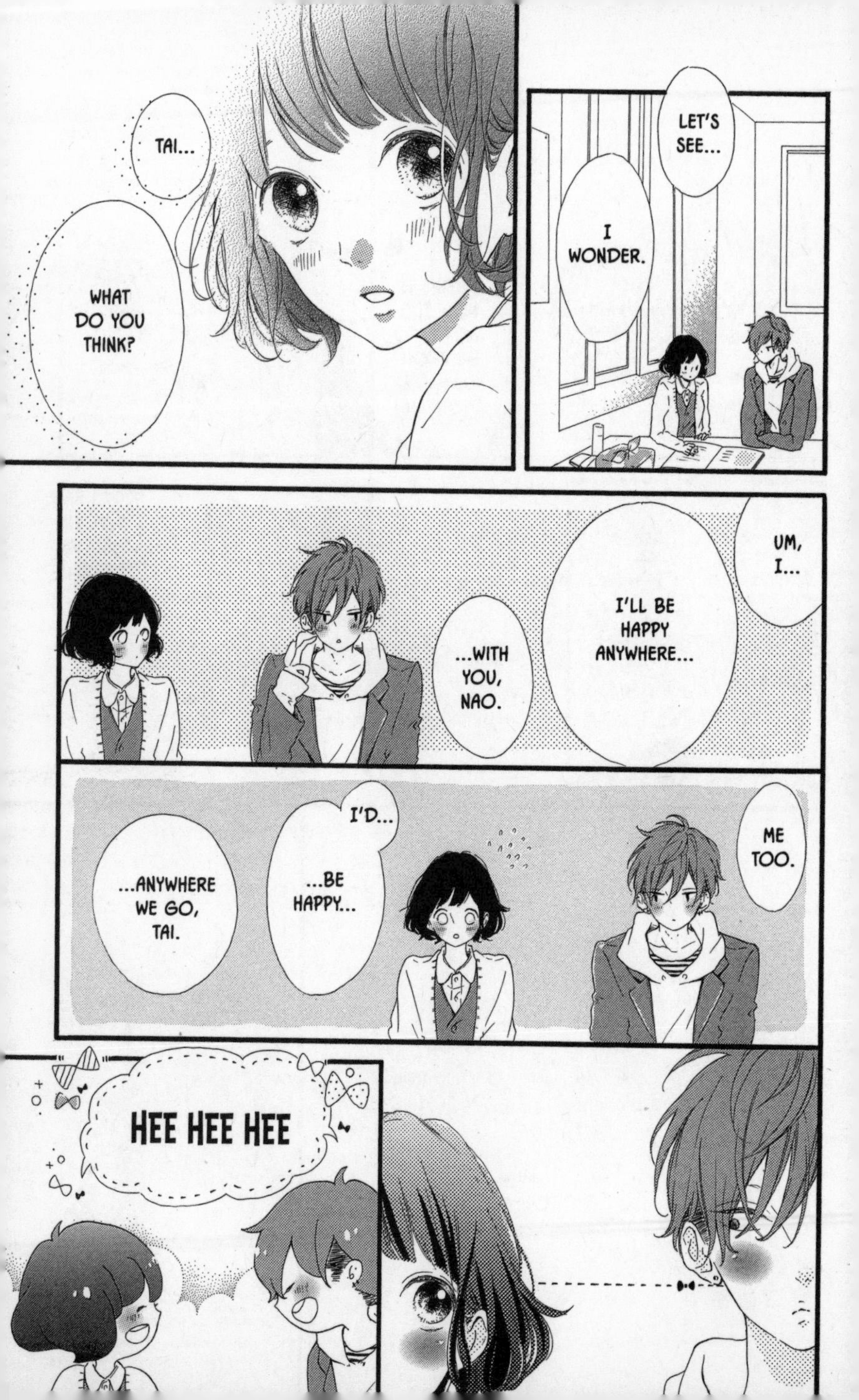
LET'S SEE...
I WONDER.
TAI...
WHAT DO YOU THINK?
UM, I...
I'LL BE HAPPY ANYWHERE...
...WITH YOU, NAO.
ME TOO.
I'D...
...BE HAPPY...
...ANYWHERE WE GO, TAI.
HEE HEE HEE

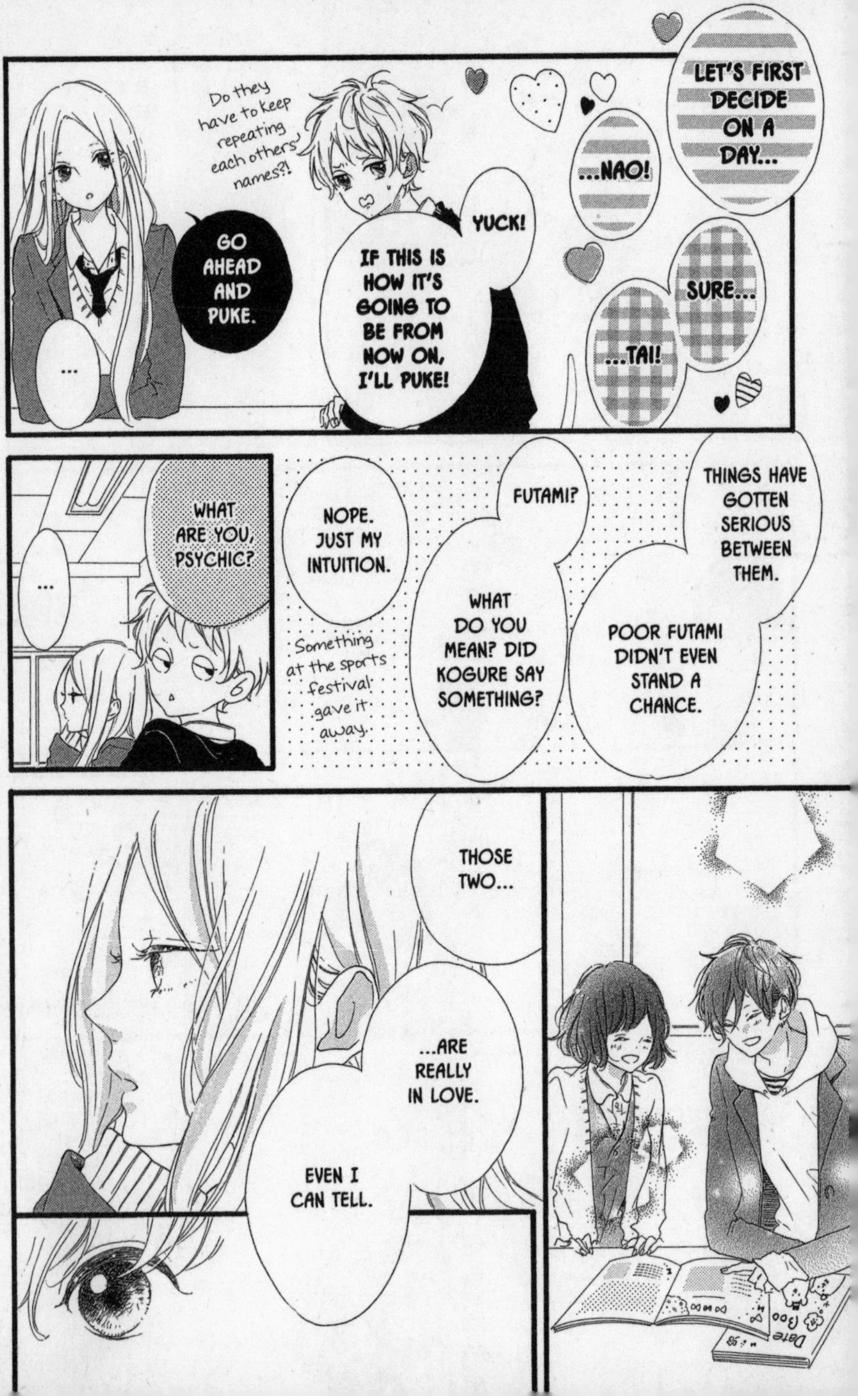
LET'S FIRST DECIDE ON A DAY...
...NAO!
SURE...
...TAI!
YUCK!
IF THIS IS HOW IT'S GOING TO BE FROM NOW ON, I'LL PUKE!
Do they have to keep repeating each others' names?!
GO AHEAD AND PUKE.
...
THINGS HAVE GOTTEN SERIOUS BETWEEN THEM.
POOR FUTAMI DIDN'T EVEN STAND A CHANCE.
FUTAMI?
WHAT DO YOU MEAN? DID KOGURE SAY SOMETHING?
NOPE. JUST MY INTUITION.
Something at the sports festival gave it away.
WHAT ARE YOU, PSYCHIC?
...
THOSE TWO...
...ARE REALLY IN LOVE.
EVEN I CAN TELL.

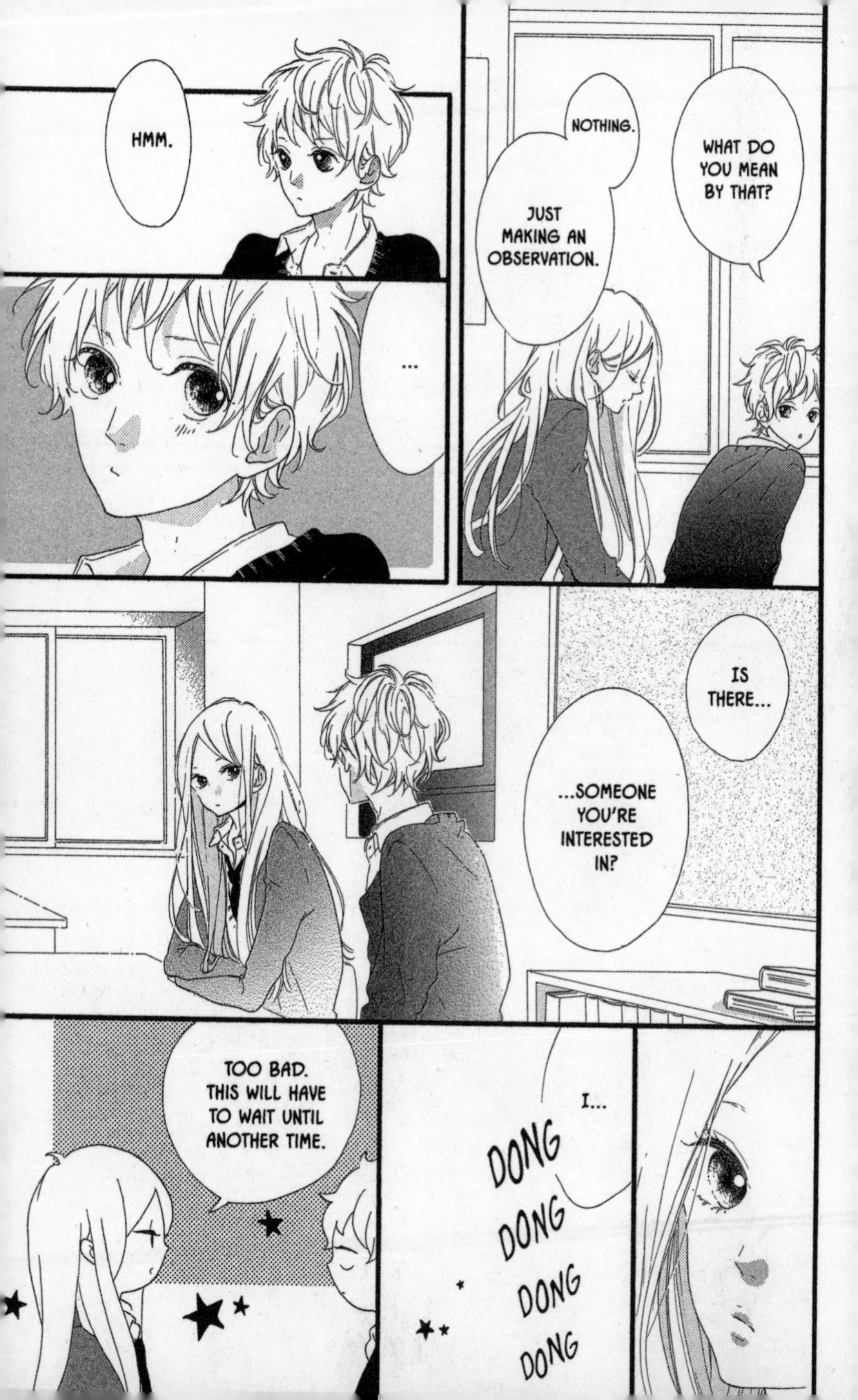
WHAT DO YOU MEAN BY THAT?
NOTHING.
JUST MAKING AN OBSERVATION.
HMM.
...
IS THERE...
...SOMEONE YOU'RE INTERESTED IN?
I...
DONG DONG DONG DONG
TOO BAD. THIS WILL HAVE TO WAIT UNTIL ANOTHER TIME.

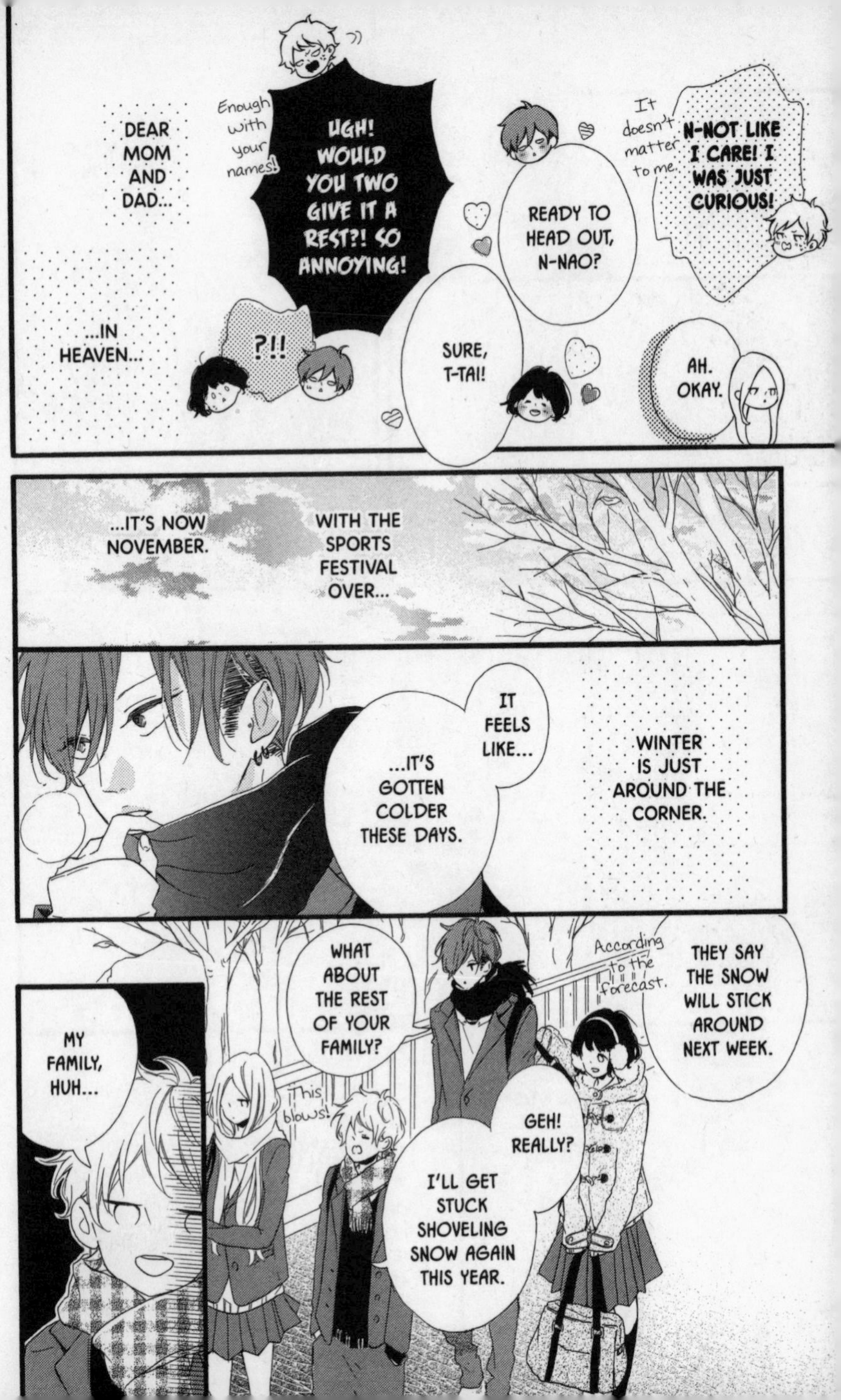
It doesn't matter to me.
N-NOT LIKE I CARE! I WAS JUST CURIOUS!
AH. OKAY.
READY TO HEAD OUT, N-NAO?
SURE, T-TAI!
UGH! WOULD YOU TWO GIVE IT A REST?! SO ANNOYING!
Enough with your names!
?!!
DEAR MOM AND DAD...
...IN HEAVEN...
WITH THE SPORTS FESTIVAL OVER...
...IT'S NOW NOVEMBER.
WINTER IS JUST AROUND THE CORNER.
IT FEELS LIKE...
...IT'S GOTTEN COLDER THESE DAYS.
THEY SAY THE SNOW WILL STICK AROUND NEXT WEEK.
According to the forecast.
GEH! REALLY?
I'LL GET STUCK SHOVELING SNOW AGAIN THIS YEAR.
This blows!
WHAT ABOUT THE REST OF YOUR FAMILY?
MY FAMILY, HUH...

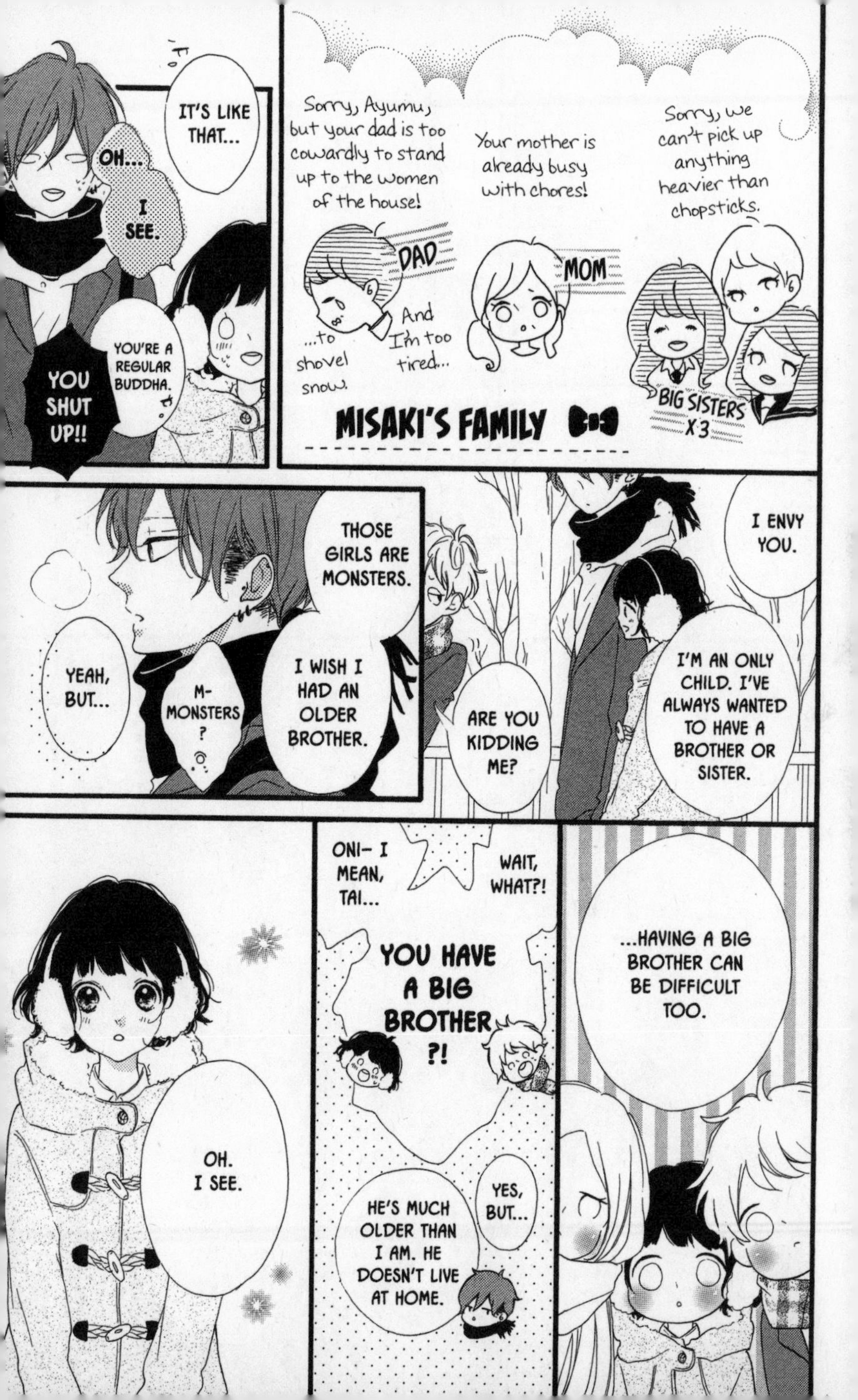
Sorry, we can't pick up anything heavier than chopsticks.
Your mother is already busy with chores!
Sorry, Ayumu, but your dad is too cowardly to stand up to the women of the house!
DAD
MOM
BIG SISTERS X 3
And I'm too tired...
...to shovel snow.
MISAKI'S FAMILY
IT'S LIKE THAT...
OH... I SEE.
YOU'RE A REGULAR BUDDHA.
YOU SHUT UP!!
I ENVY YOU.
I'M AN ONLY CHILD. I'VE ALWAYS WANTED TO HAVE A BROTHER OR SISTER.
ARE YOU KIDDING ME?
THOSE GIRLS ARE MONSTERS.
I WISH I HAD AN OLDER BROTHER.
M-MONSTERS?
YEAH, BUT...
...HAVING A BIG BROTHER CAN BE DIFFICULT TOO.
WAIT, WHAT?!
ONI- I MEAN, TAI...
YOU HAVE A BIG BROTHER?!
YES, BUT...
HE'S MUCH OLDER THAN I AM. HE DOESN'T LIVE AT HOME.
OH. I SEE.

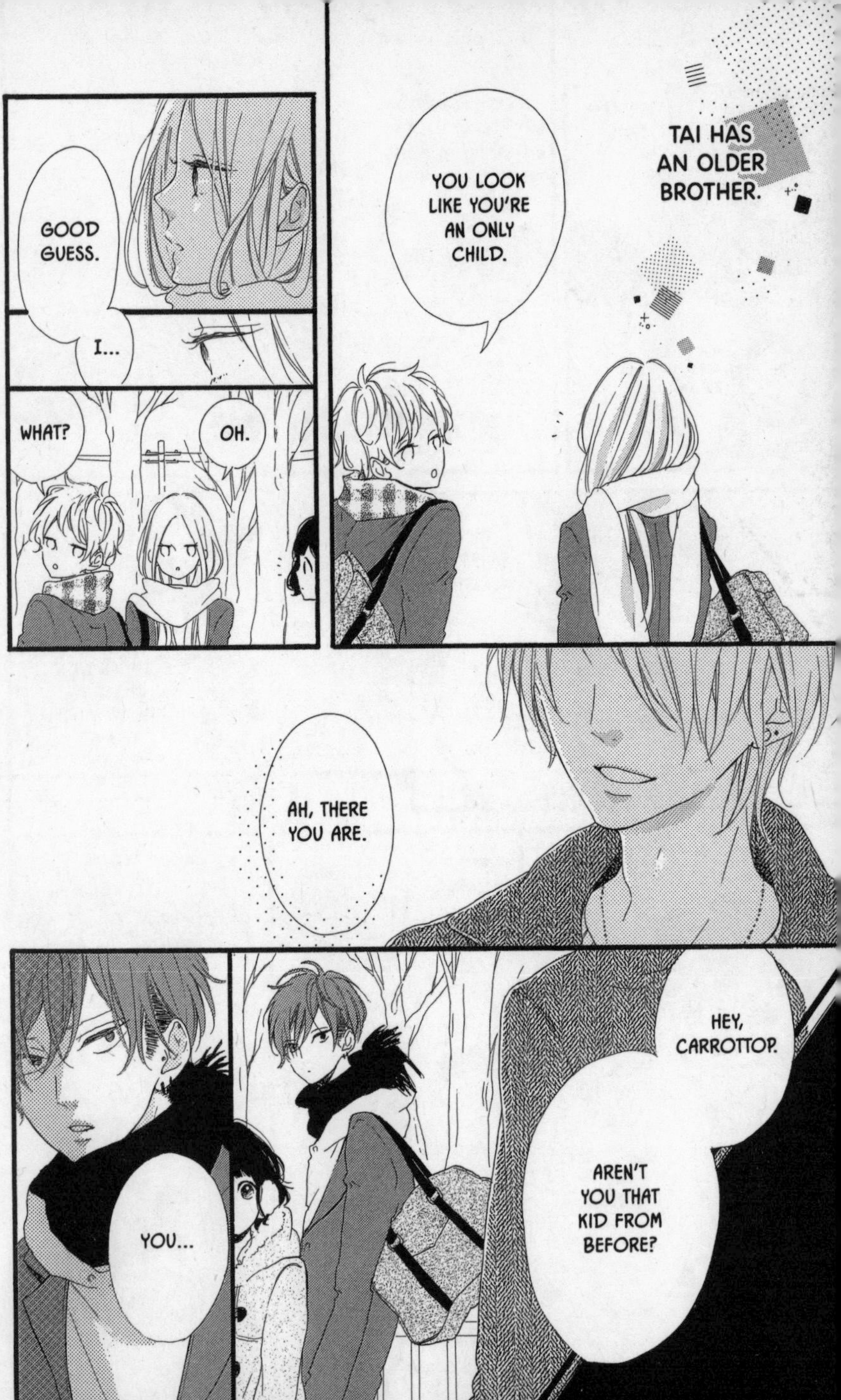
TAI HAS AN OLDER BROTHER.
YOU LOOK LIKE YOU'RE AN ONLY CHILD.
GOOD GUESS.
I...
OH.
WHAT?
AH, THERE YOU ARE.
HEY, CARROTTOP.
AREN'T YOU THAT KID FROM BEFORE?
YOU...

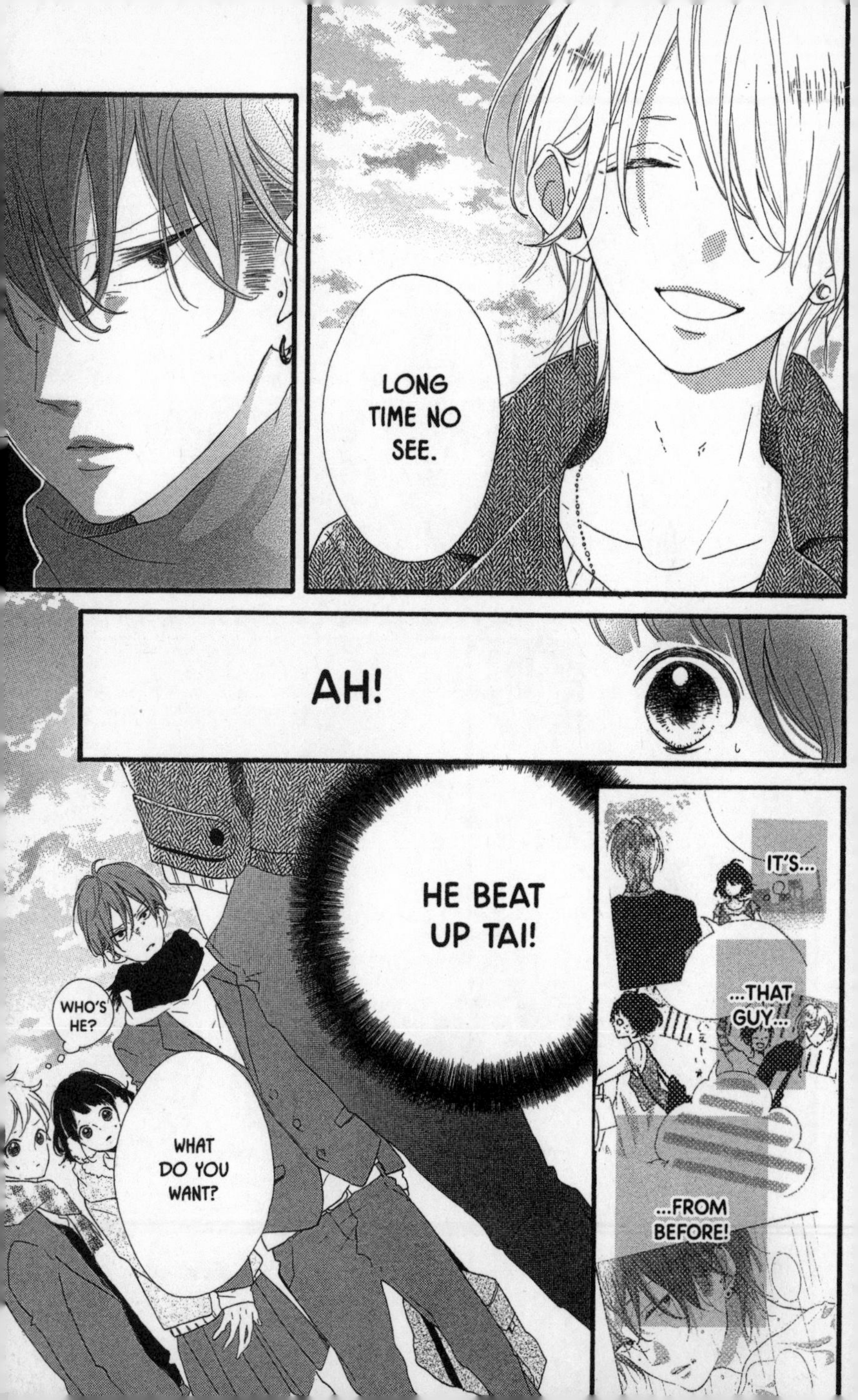

LONG TIME NO SEE.
AH!
IT'S...
...THAT GUY...
...FROM BEFORE!
HE BEAT UP TAI!
WHO'S HE?
WHAT DO YOU WANT?

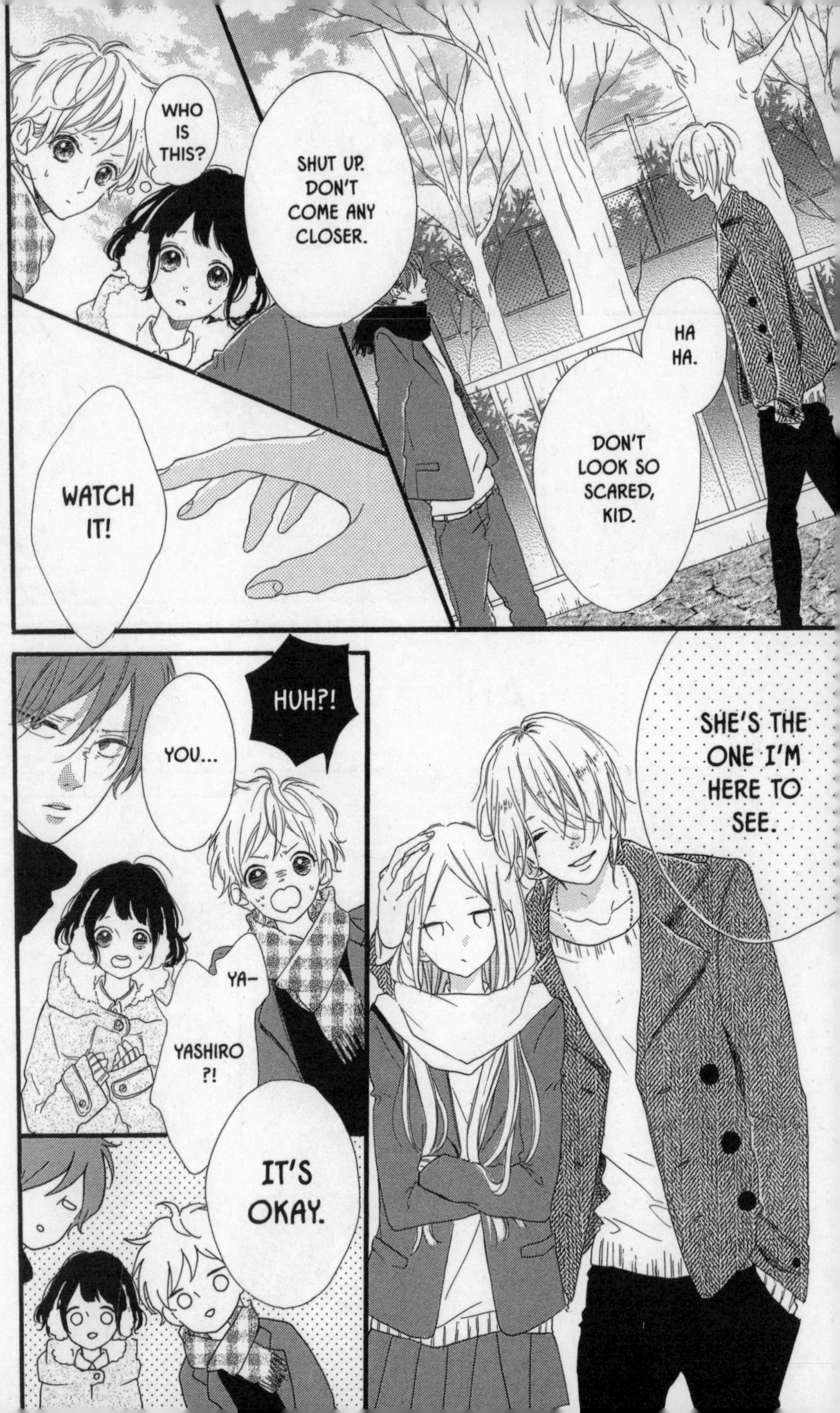

SHUT UP. DON'T COME ANY CLOSER.
WHO IS THIS?
HA HA.
DON'T LOOK SO SCARED, KID.
WATCH IT!
SHE'S THE ONE I'M HERE TO SEE.
HUH?!
YOU...
YA-
YASHIRO ?!
IT'S OKAY.

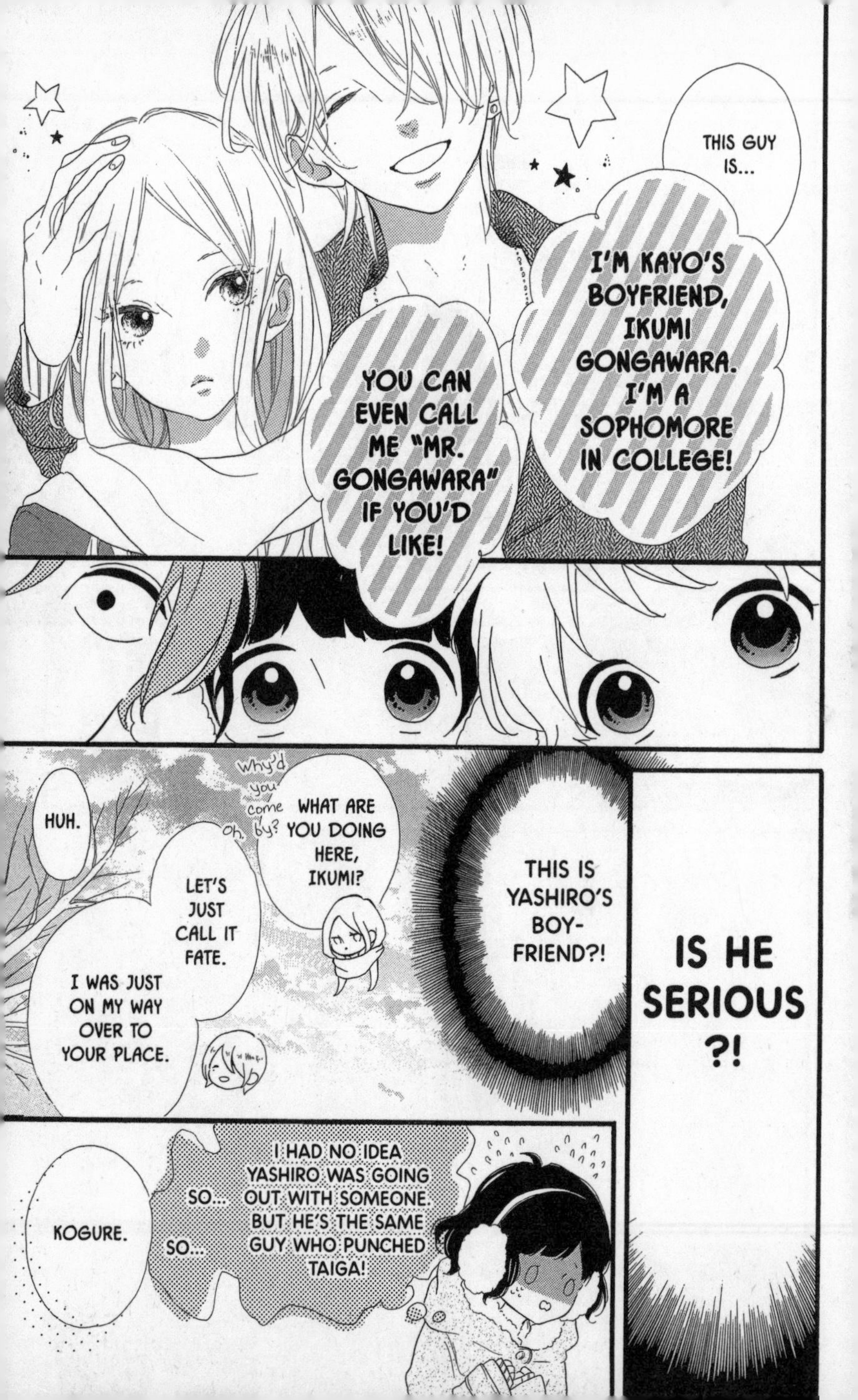
THIS GUY IS...
I'M KAYO'S BOYFRIEND, IKUMI GONGAWARA. I'M A SOPHOMORE IN COLLEGE!
YOU CAN EVEN CALL ME "MR. GONGAWARA" IF YOU'D LIKE!
IS HE SERIOUS ?!
THIS IS YASHIRO'S BOY-FRIEND?!
WHAT ARE YOU DOING HERE, IKUMI?
Why'd you come by?
Oh.
HUH.
LET'S JUST CALL IT FATE.
I WAS JUST ON MY WAY OVER TO YOUR PLACE.
I HAD NO IDEA YASHIRO WAS GOING OUT WITH SOMEONE. BUT HE'S THE SAME GUY WHO PUNCHED TAIGA!
SO...
SO...
KOGURE.

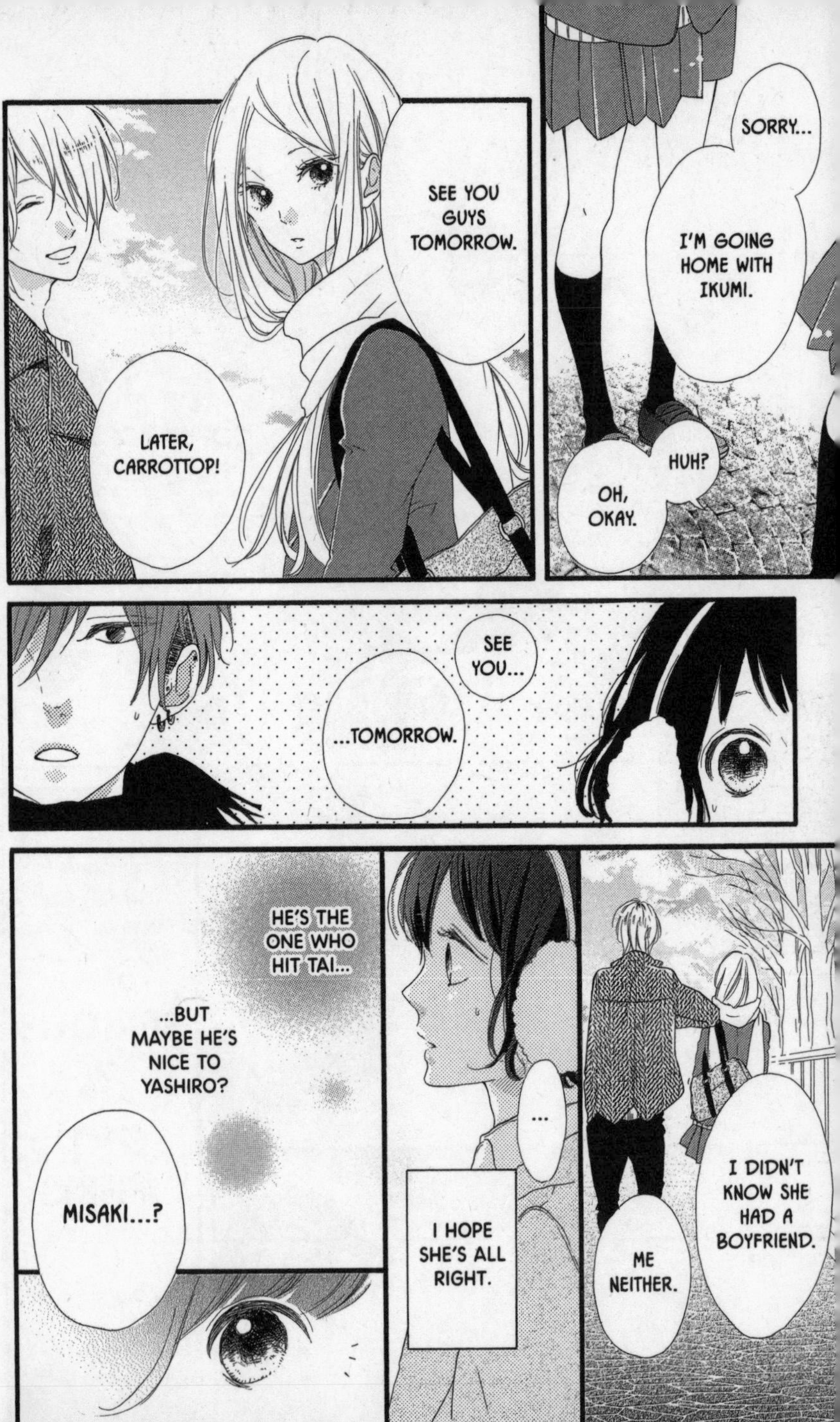
SORRY...
I'M GOING HOME WITH IKUMI.
HUH?
OH, OKAY.
SEE YOU GUYS TOMORROW.
LATER, CARROTTOP!
SEE YOU...
...TOMORROW.
I DIDN'T KNOW SHE HAD A BOYFRIEND.
ME NEITHER.
...
I HOPE SHE'S ALL RIGHT.
HE'S THE ONE WHO HIT TAI...
...BUT MAYBE HE'S NICE TO YASHIRO?
MISAKI...?

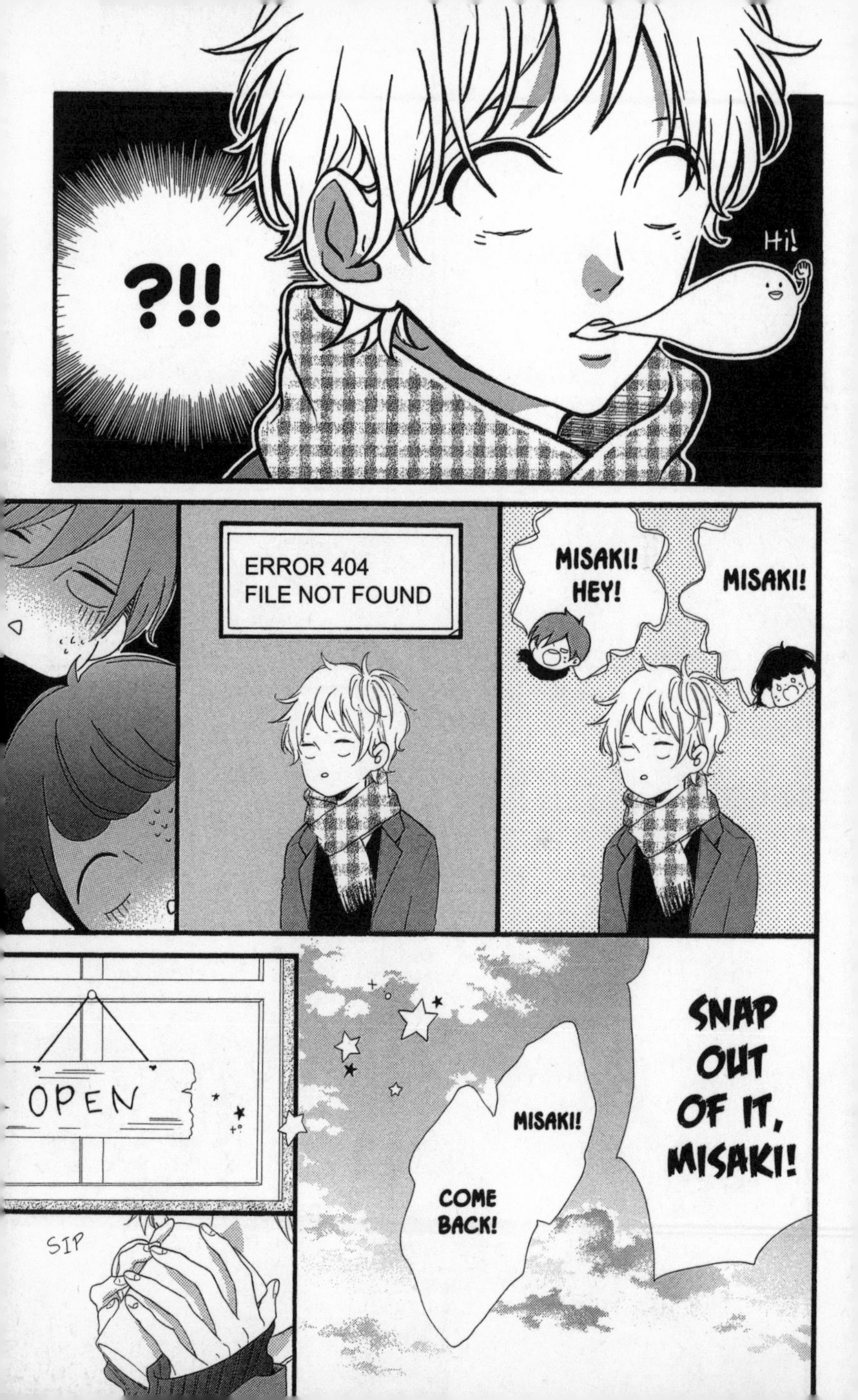

Hi!
?!!
MISAKI!
MISAKI! HEY!
ERROR 404 FILE NOT FOUND
SNAP OUT OF IT, MISAKI!
MISAKI!
COME BACK!
OPEN
SIP

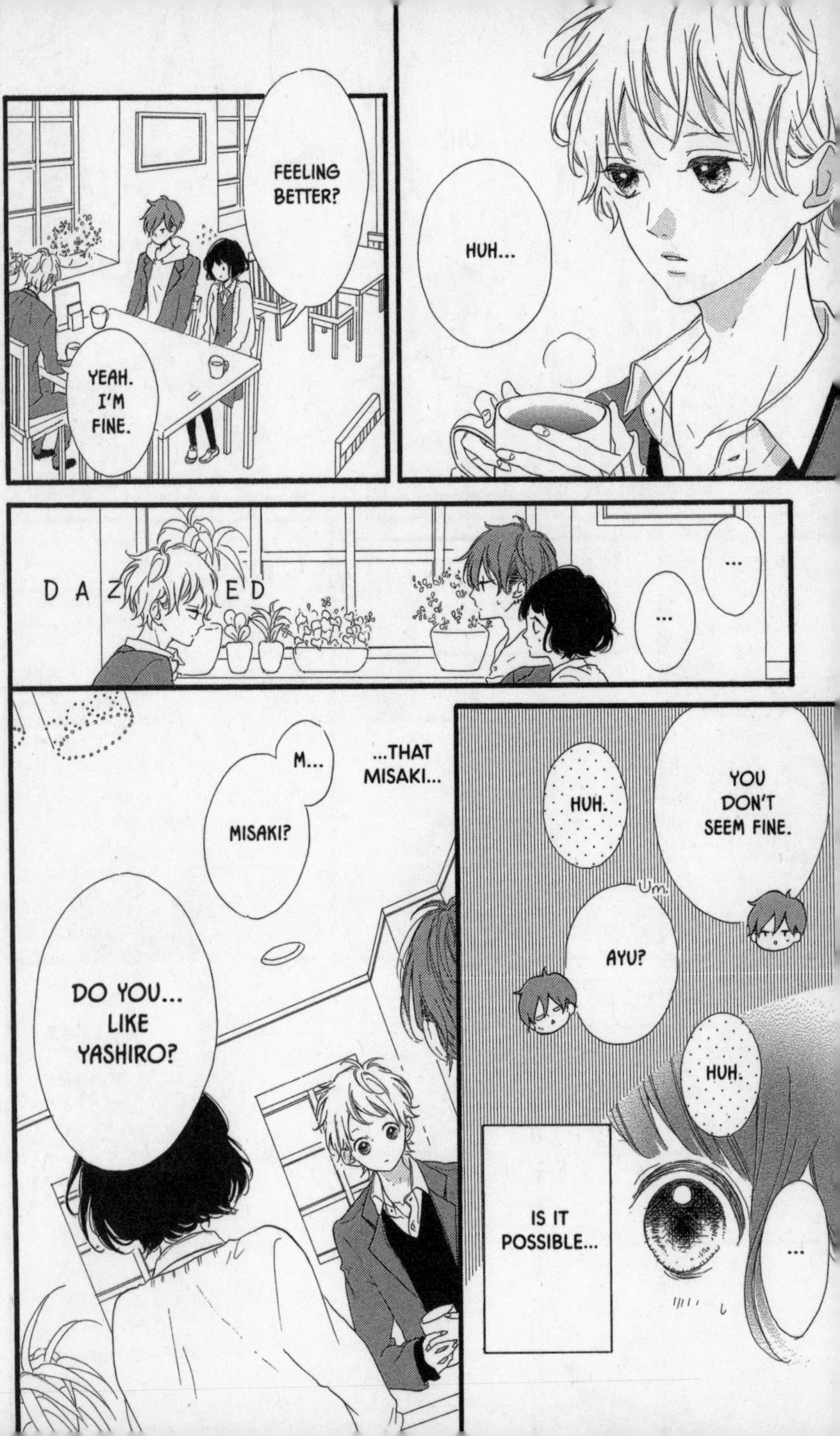
HUH...
FEELING BETTER?
YEAH. I'M FINE.
...
...
DAZED
YOU DON'T SEEM FINE.
HUH.
Um.
AYU?
HUH.
...
IS IT POSSIBLE...
...THAT MISAKI...
M...
MISAKI?
DO YOU... LIKE YASHIRO?

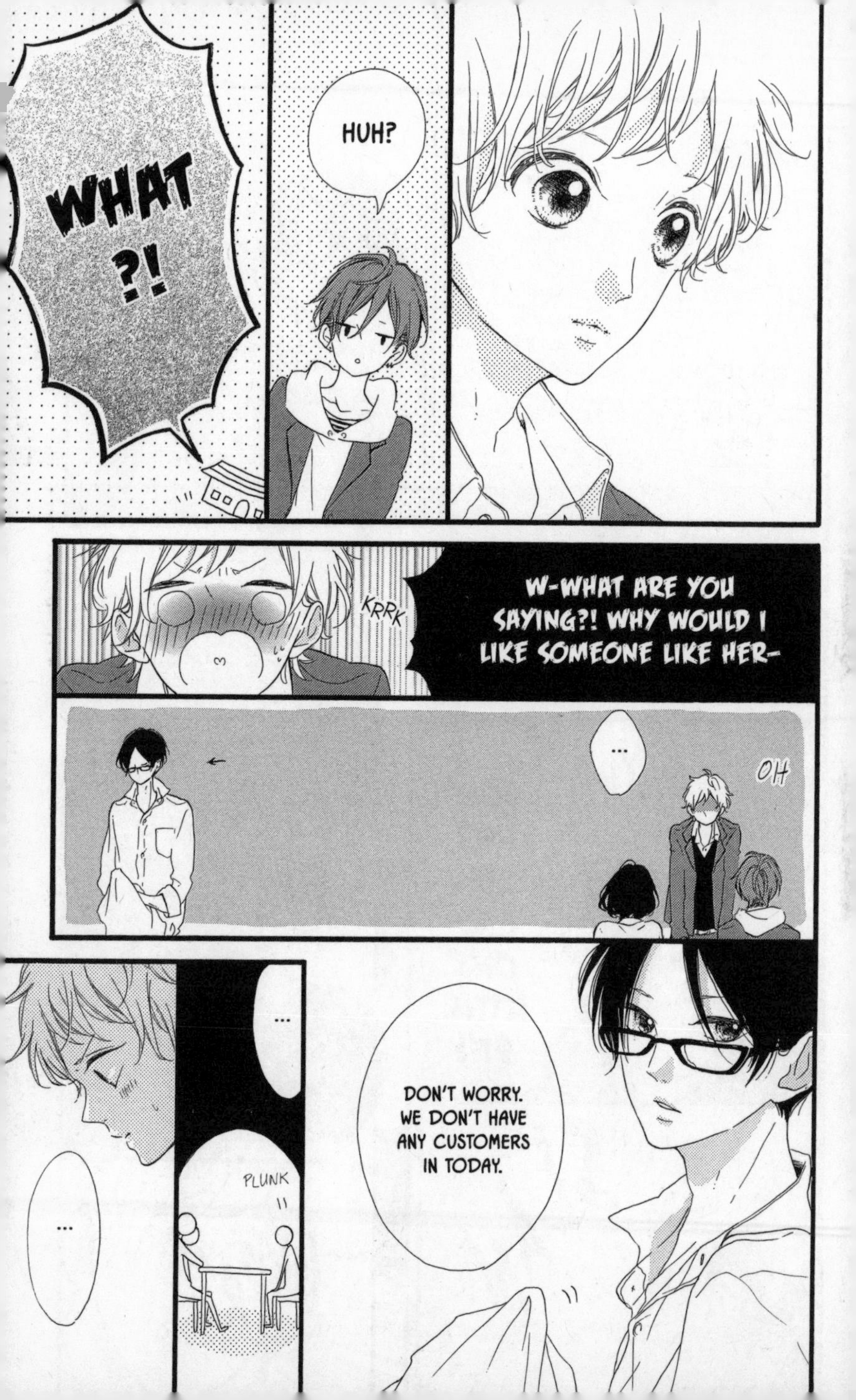
HUH?
WHAT ?!
W-WHAT ARE YOU SAYING?! WHY WOULD I LIKE SOMEONE LIKE HER-
KRRK
OH
...
DON'T WORRY. WE DON'T HAVE ANY CUSTOMERS IN TODAY.
...
PLUNK
...

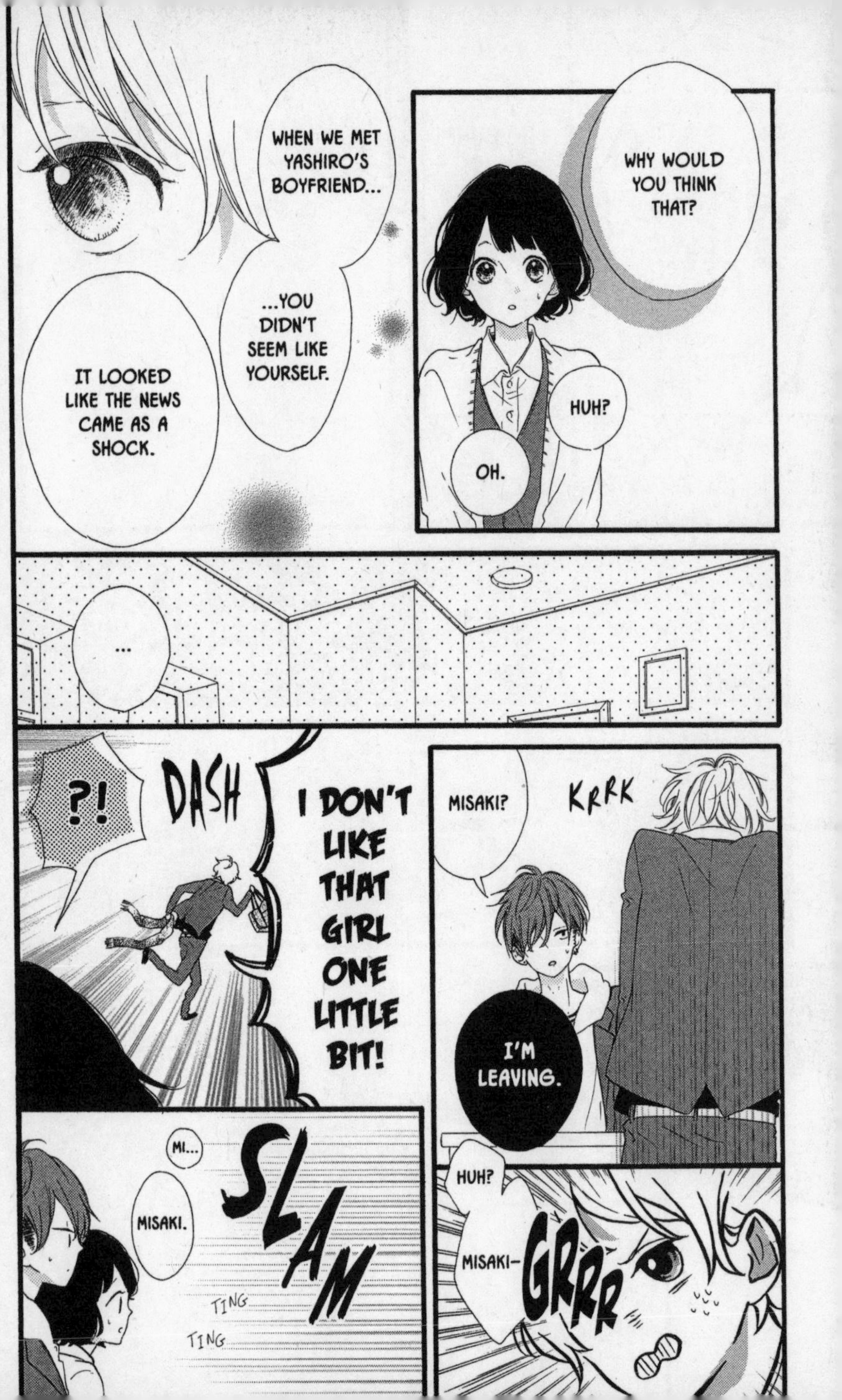
WHY WOULD YOU THINK THAT?
HUH?
OH.
WHEN WE MET YASHIRO'S BOYFRIEND...
...YOU DIDN'T SEEM LIKE YOURSELF.
IT LOOKED LIKE THE NEWS CAME AS A SHOCK.
...
KRRK
MISAKI?
I'M LEAVING.
I DON'T LIKE THAT GIRL ONE LITTLE BIT!
DASH
?!
HUH?
MISAKI-
GRRR
SLAM
MI...
MISAKI.
TING
TING

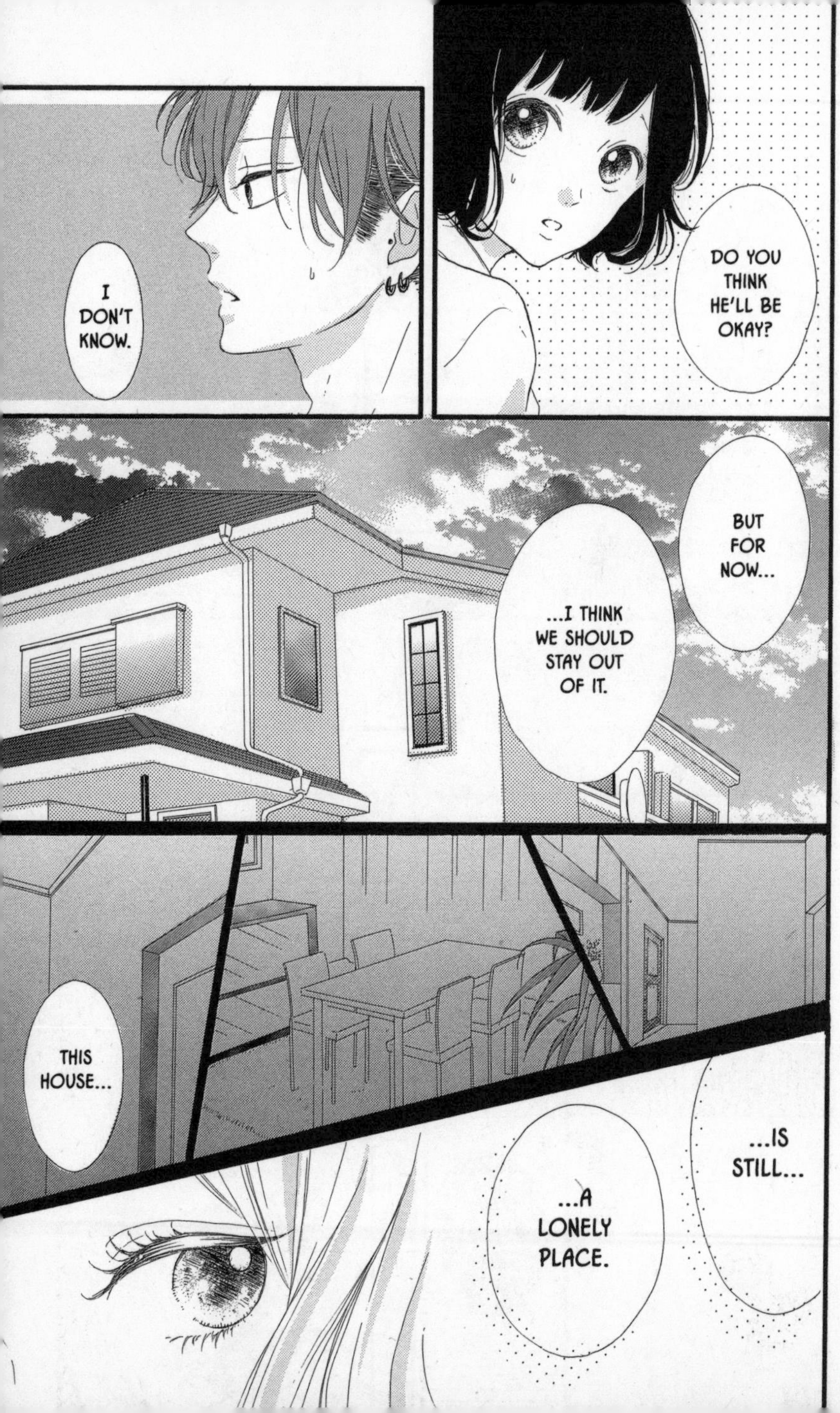
DO YOU THINK HE'LL BE OKAY?
I DON'T KNOW.
BUT FOR NOW...
...I THINK WE SHOULD STAY OUT OF IT.
THIS HOUSE...
...IS STILL...
...A LONELY PLACE.

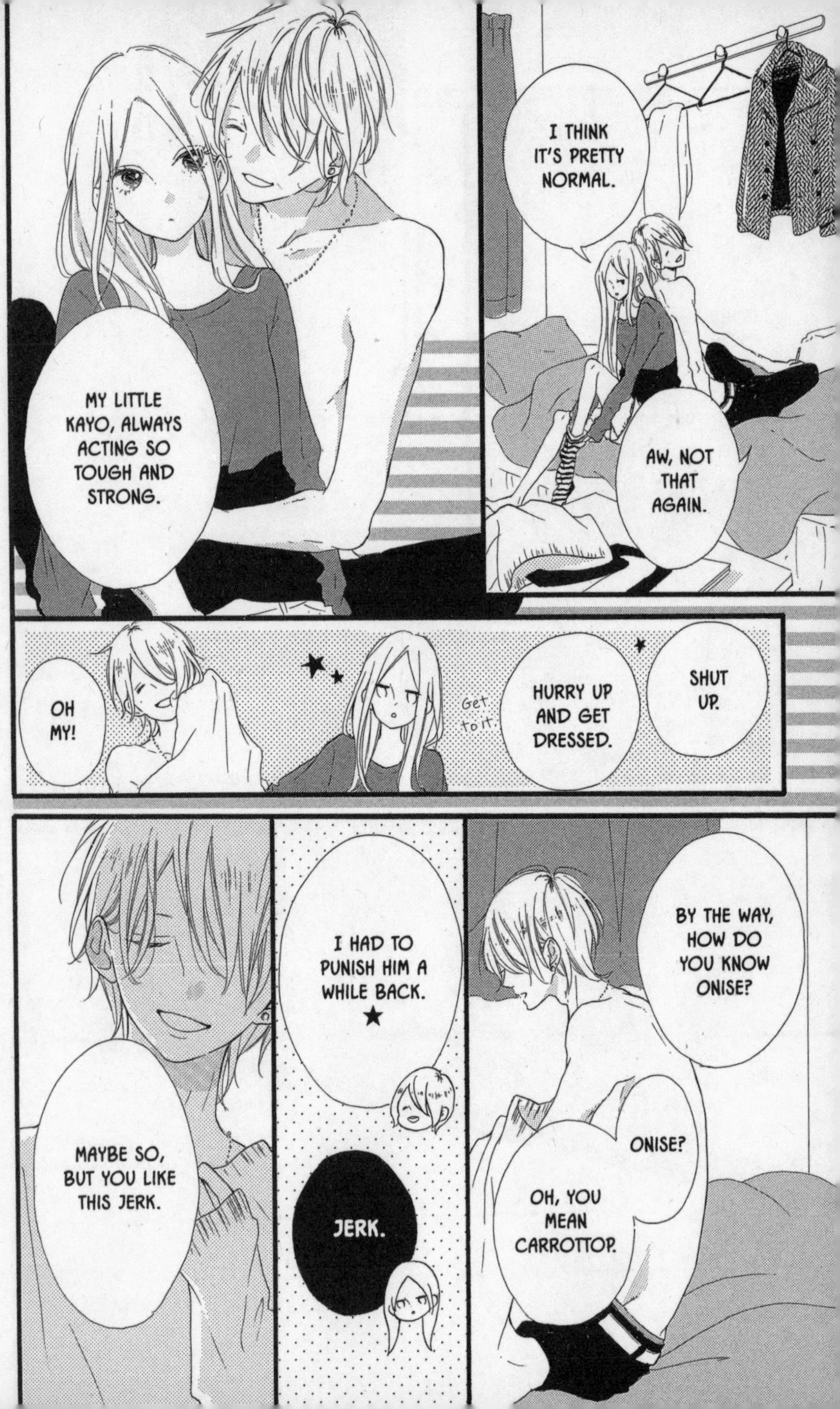

I THINK IT'S PRETTY NORMAL.
AW, NOT THAT AGAIN.
MY LITTLE KAYO, ALWAYS ACTING SO TOUGH AND STRONG.
SHUT UP.
HURRY UP AND GET DRESSED.
Get to it.
OH MY!
BY THE WAY, HOW DO YOU KNOW ONISE?
ONISE?
OH, YOU MEAN CARROTTOP.
I HAD TO PUNISH HIM A WHILE BACK. ★
JERK.
MAYBE SO, BUT YOU LIKE THIS JERK.

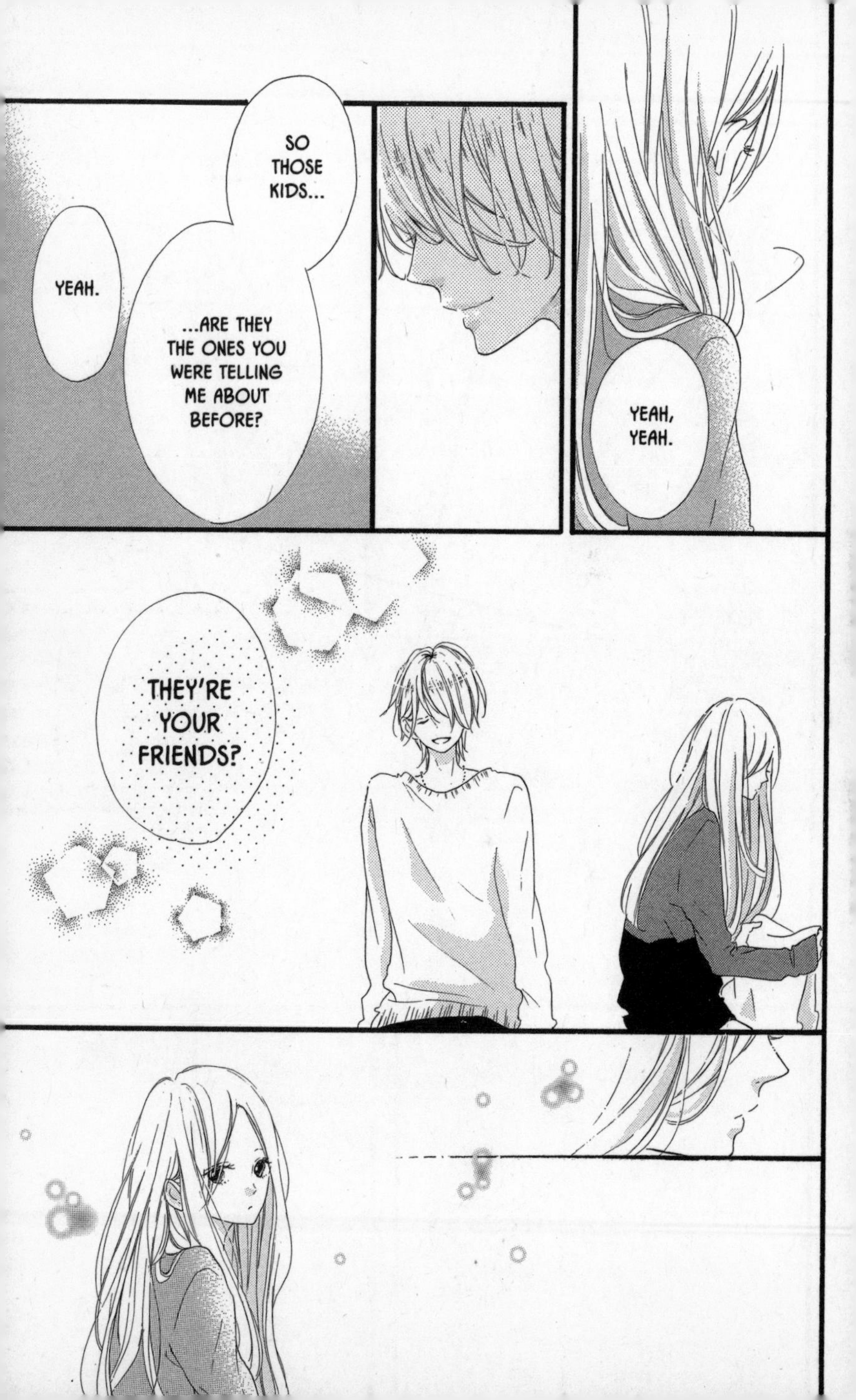
YEAH, YEAH.
SO THOSE KIDS...
...ARE THEY THE ONES YOU WERE TELLING ME ABOUT BEFORE?
YEAH.
THEY'RE YOUR FRIENDS?

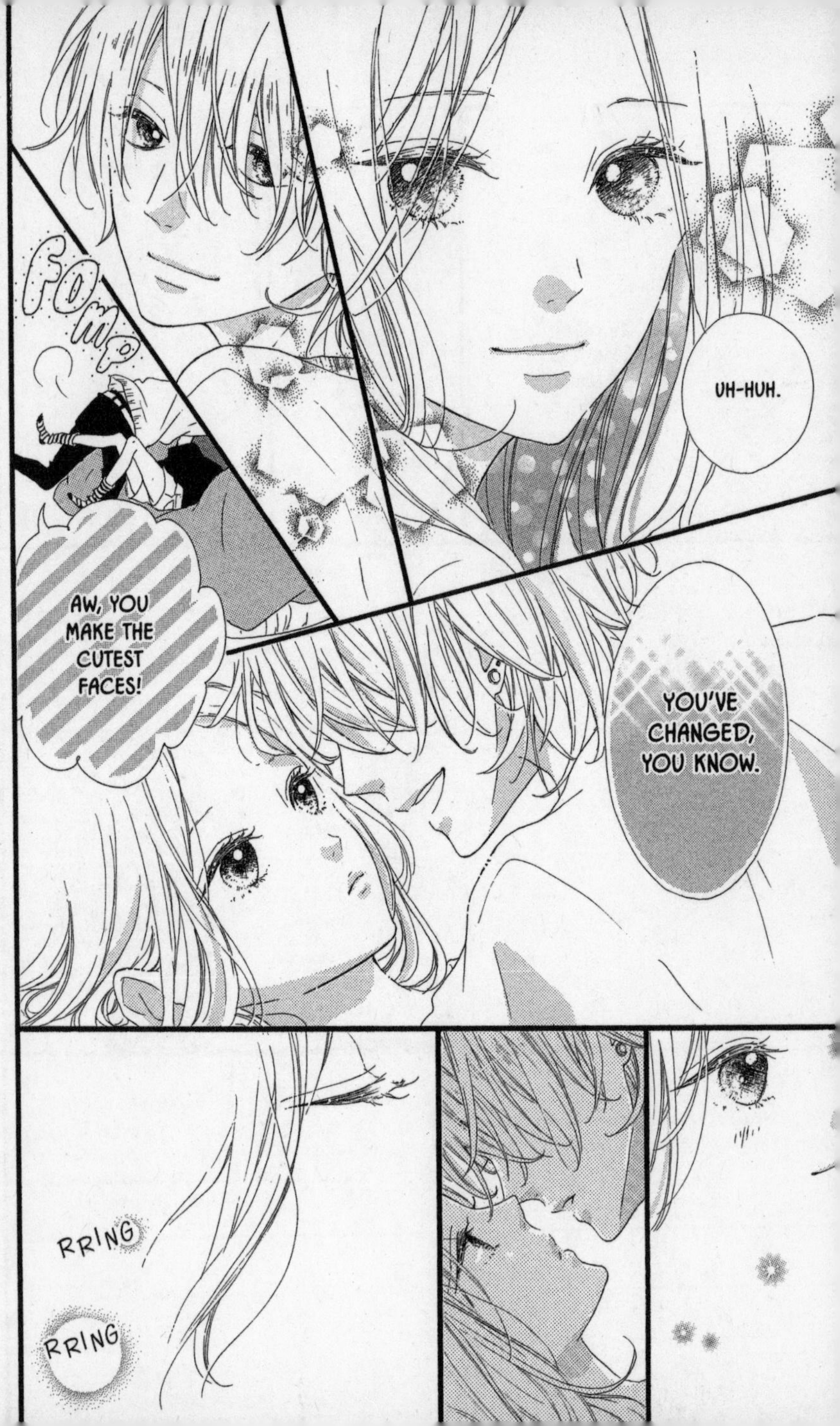
UH-HUH.
FOMP
YOU'VE CHANGED, YOU KNOW.
AW, YOU MAKE THE CUTEST FACES!
RRING
RRING

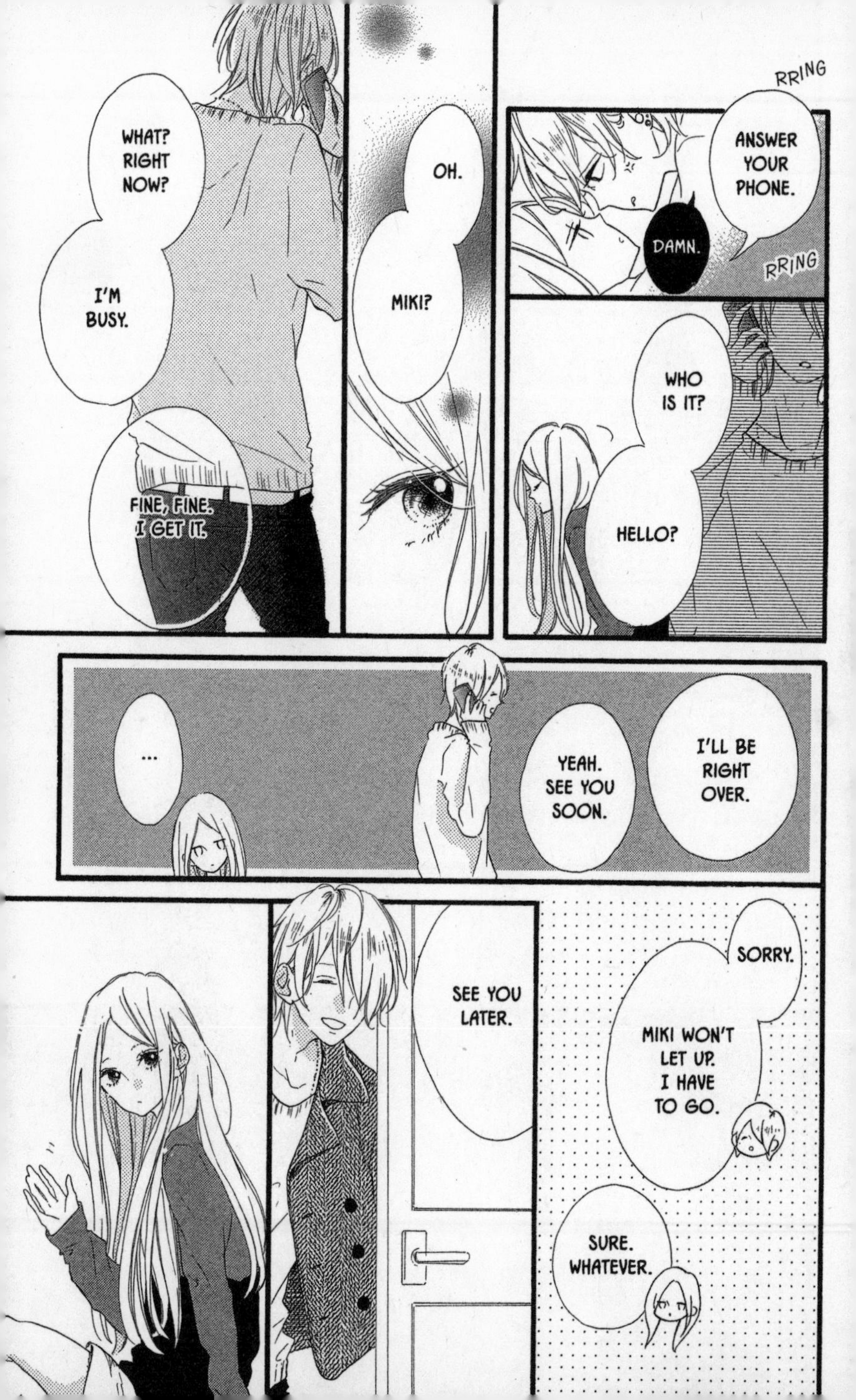
RRING
ANSWER YOUR PHONE.
DAMN.
RRING
WHO IS IT?
HELLO?
OH.
MIKI?
WHAT? RIGHT NOW?
I'M BUSY.
FINE, FINE. I GET IT.
I'LL BE RIGHT OVER.
YEAH. SEE YOU SOON.
...
SORRY.
MIKI WON'T LET UP. I HAVE TO GO.
SURE. WHATEVER.
SEE YOU LATER.

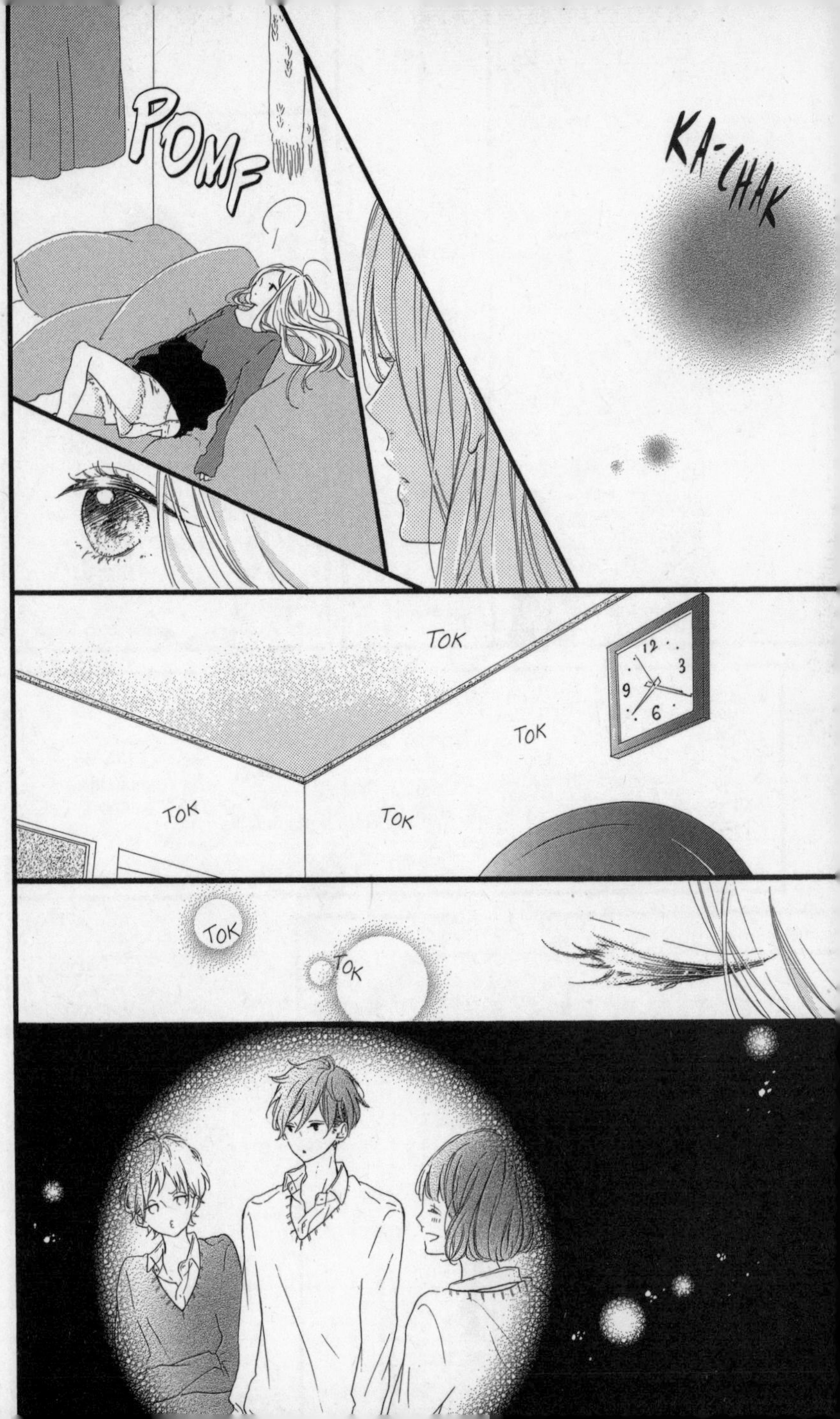
KA-CHAK
POMF
TOK
TOK
TOK
TOK
TOK
TOK

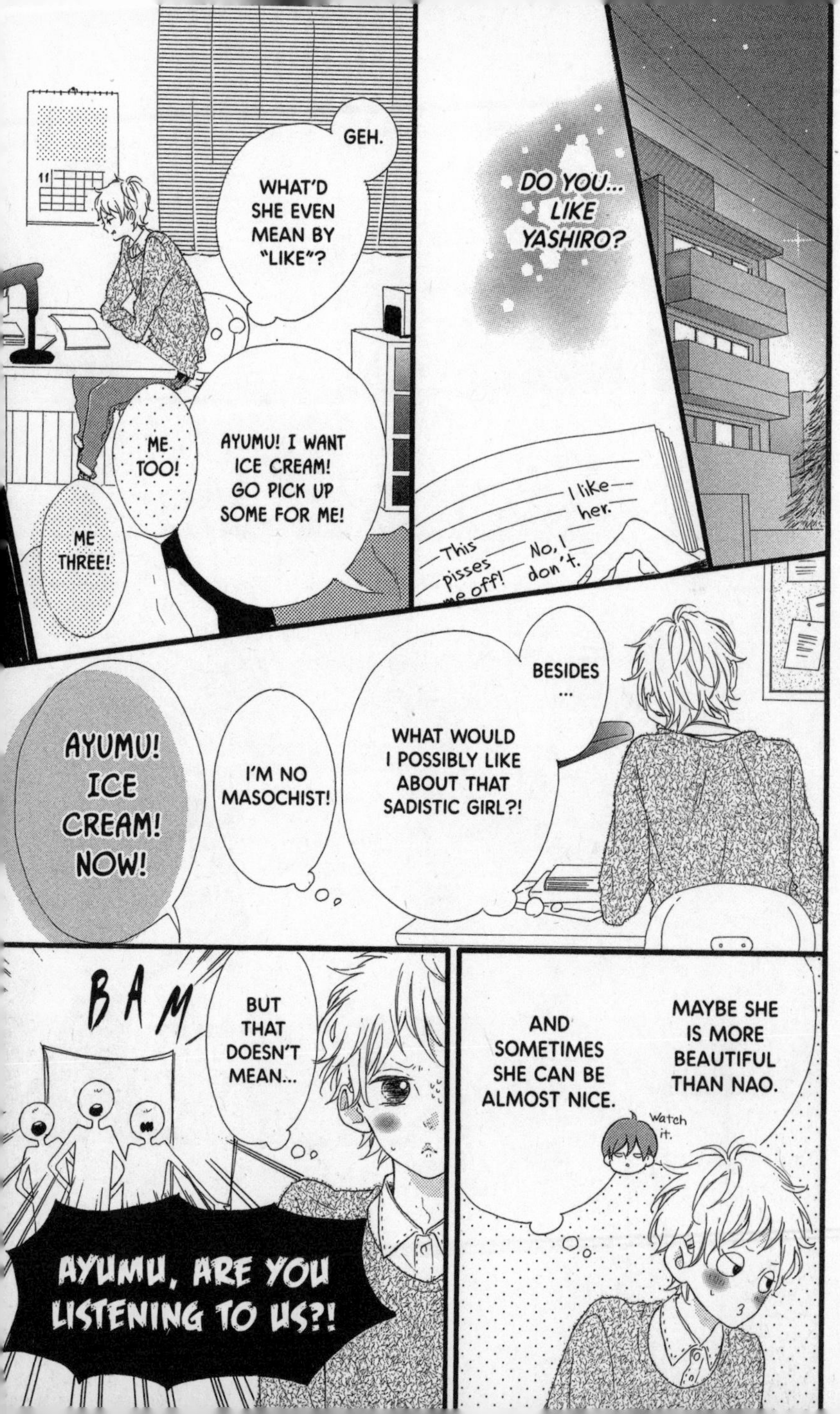
DO YOU... LIKE YASHIRO?
I like her.
No, I don't.
This pisses me off!
GEH.
WHAT'D SHE EVEN MEAN BY "LIKE"?
AYUMU! I WANT ICE CREAM! GO PICK UP SOME FOR ME!
ME TOO!
ME THREE!
BESIDES...
WHAT WOULD I POSSIBLY LIKE ABOUT THAT SADISTIC GIRL?!
I'M NO MASOCHIST!
AYUMU! ICE CREAM! NOW!
MAYBE SHE IS MORE BEAUTIFUL THAN NAO.
AND SOMETIMES SHE CAN BE ALMOST NICE.
Watch it.
BUT THAT DOESN'T MEAN...
BAM
AYUMU, ARE YOU LISTENING TO US?!

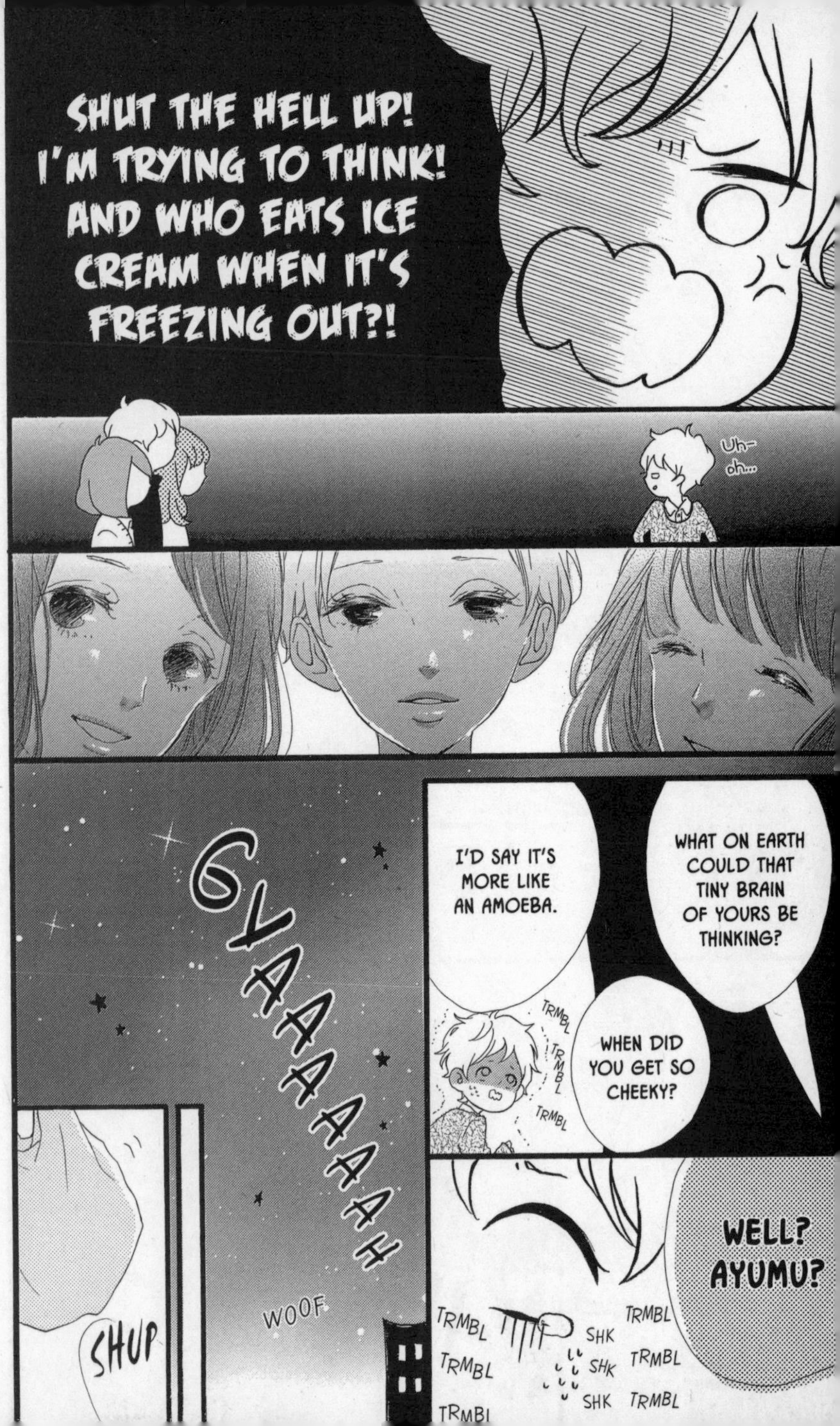
SHUT THE HELL UP! I'M TRYING TO THINK! AND WHO EATS ICE CREAM WHEN IT'S FREEZING OUT?!
Uh-oh...
WHAT ON EARTH COULD THAT TINY BRAIN OF YOURS BE THINKING?
I'D SAY IT'S MORE LIKE AN AMOEBA.
TRMBL TRMBL TRMBL
WHEN DID YOU GET SO CHEEKY?
WELL? AYUMU?
TRMBL TRMBL TRMBL
SHK SHK SHK
TRMBL TRMBL TRMBL
GYAAAAAAAH
WOOF
SHUP

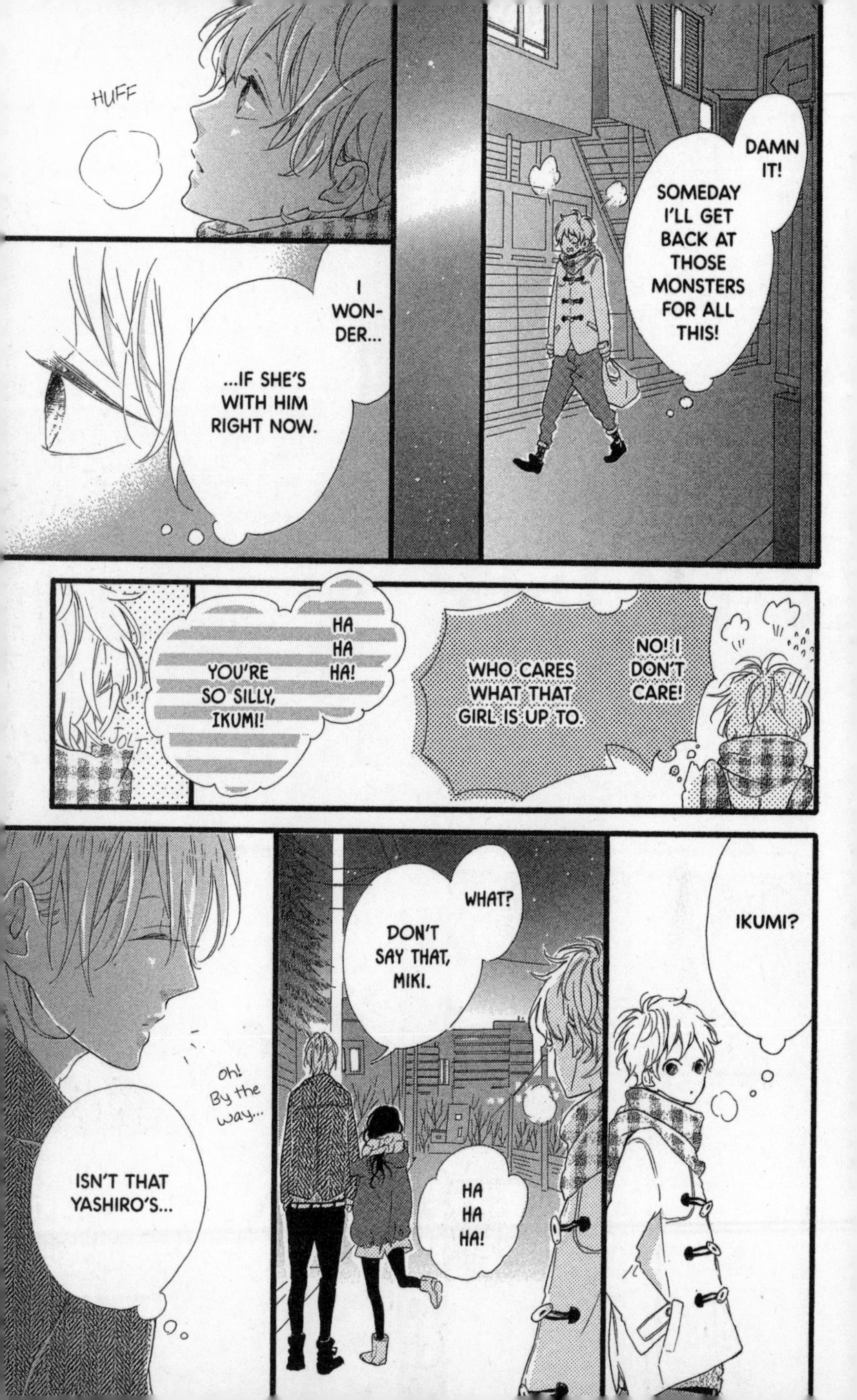
DAMN IT!
SOMEDAY I'LL GET BACK AT THOSE MONSTERS FOR ALL THIS!
HUFF
I WONDER...
...IF SHE'S WITH HIM RIGHT NOW.
NO! I DON'T CARE!
WHO CARES WHAT THAT GIRL IS UP TO.
HA HA HA!
YOU'RE SO SILLY, IKUMI!
JOLT
IKUMI?
WHAT?
DON'T SAY THAT, MIKI.
HA HA HA!
Oh! By the way...
ISN'T THAT YASHIRO'S...

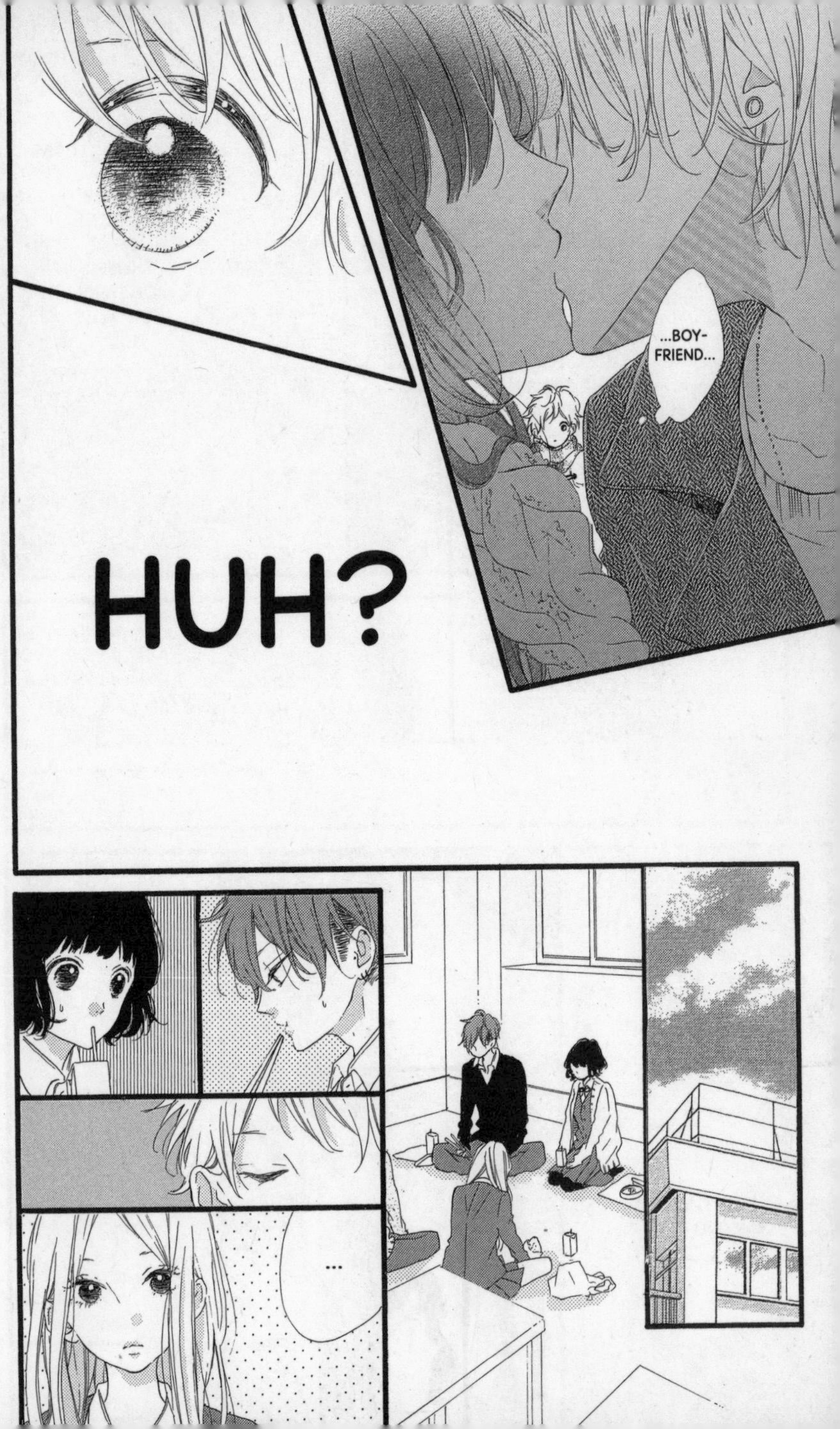
...BOY-FRIEND...
HUH?
...

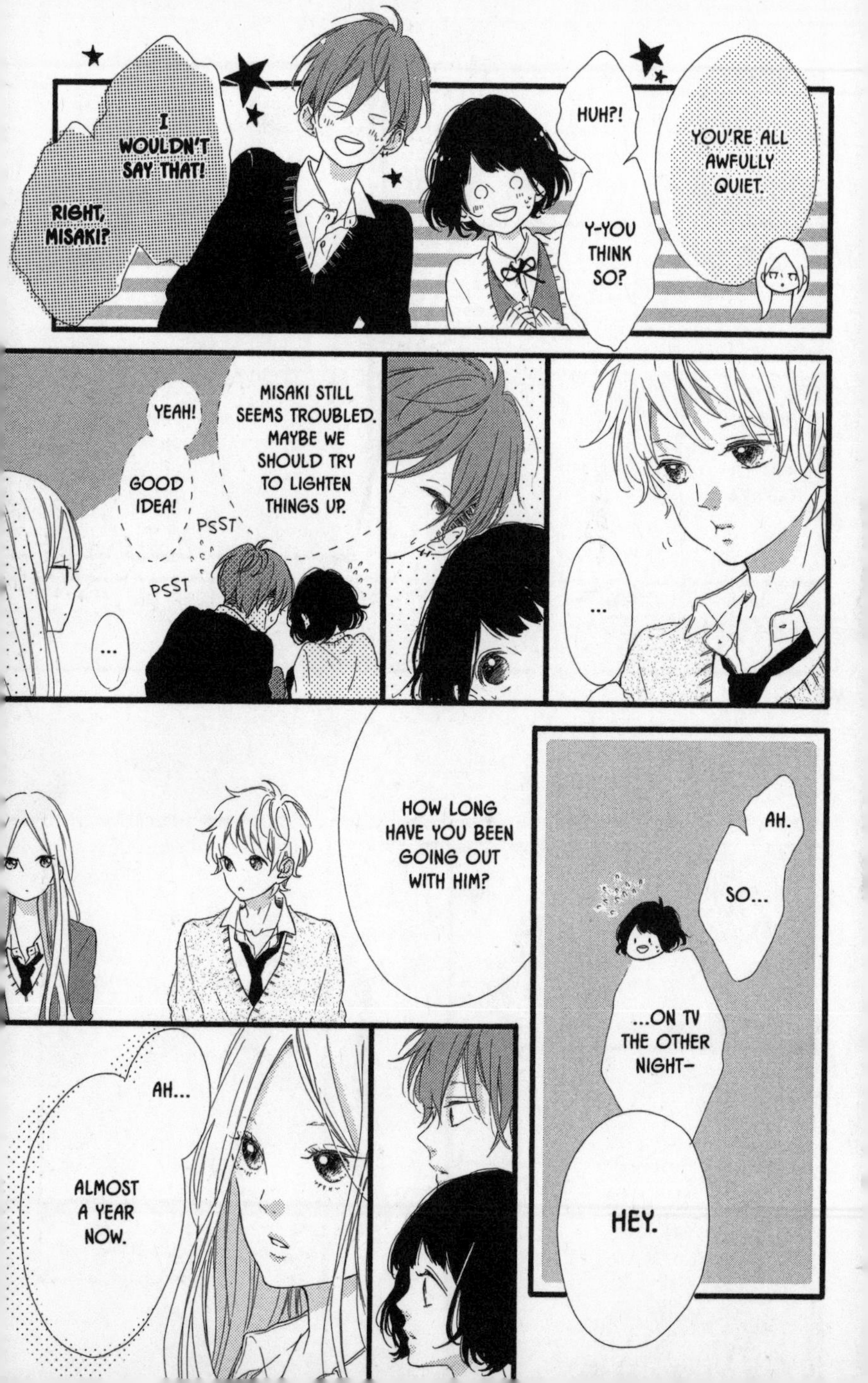
YOU'RE ALL AWFULLY QUIET.
HUH?!
Y-YOU THINK SO?
I WOULDN'T SAY THAT!
RIGHT, MISAKI?
...
MISAKI STILL SEEMS TROUBLED. MAYBE WE SHOULD TRY TO LIGHTEN THINGS UP.
YEAH!
GOOD IDEA!
PSST
PSST
...
AH.
SO...
...ON TV THE OTHER NIGHT–
HEY.
HOW LONG HAVE YOU BEEN GOING OUT WITH HIM?
AH...
ALMOST A YEAR NOW.

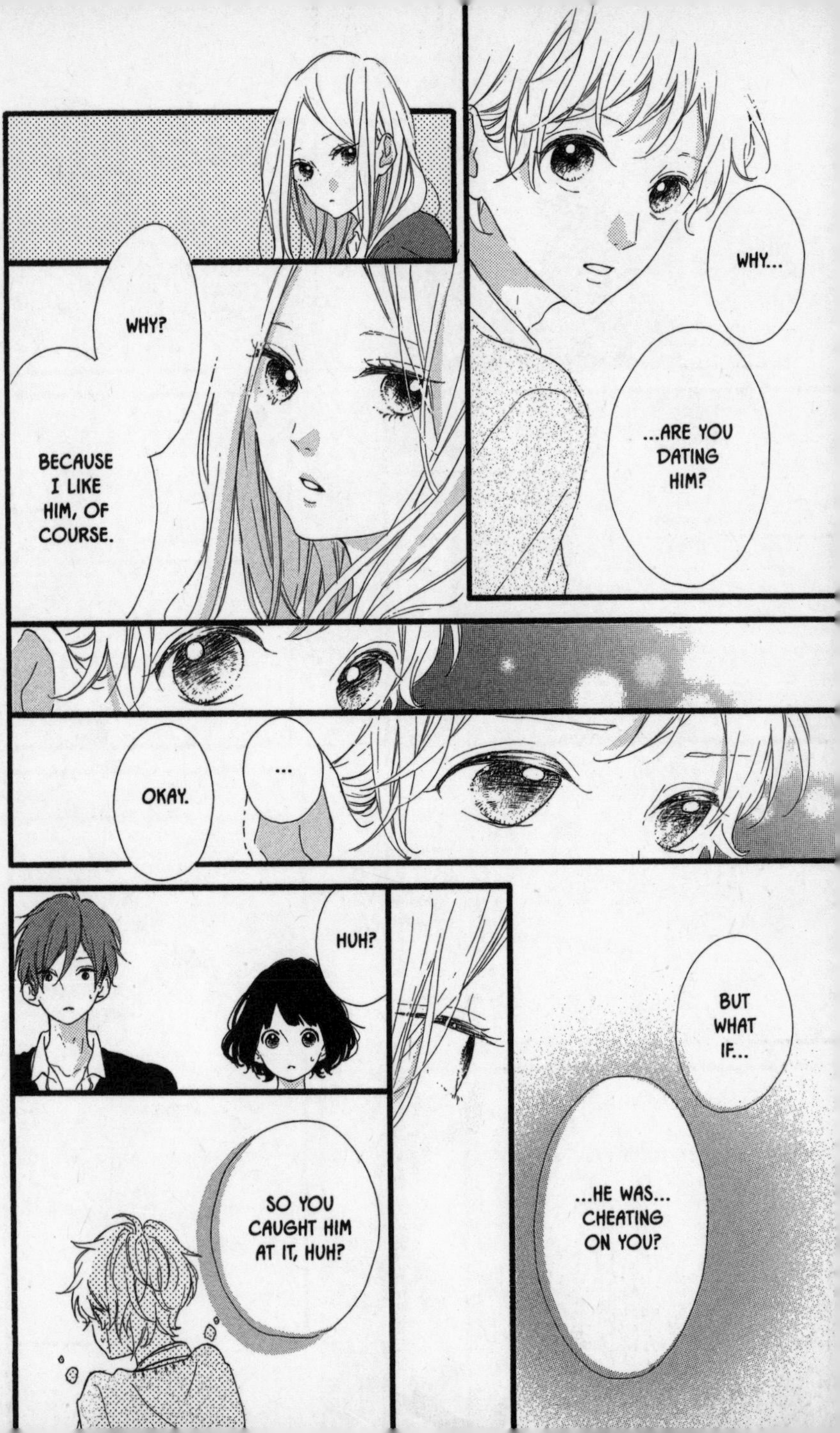
WHY...
...ARE YOU DATING HIM?
WHY?
BECAUSE I LIKE HIM, OF COURSE.
...
OKAY.
BUT WHAT IF...
...HE WAS... CHEATING ON YOU?
HUH?
SO YOU CAUGHT HIM AT IT, HUH?

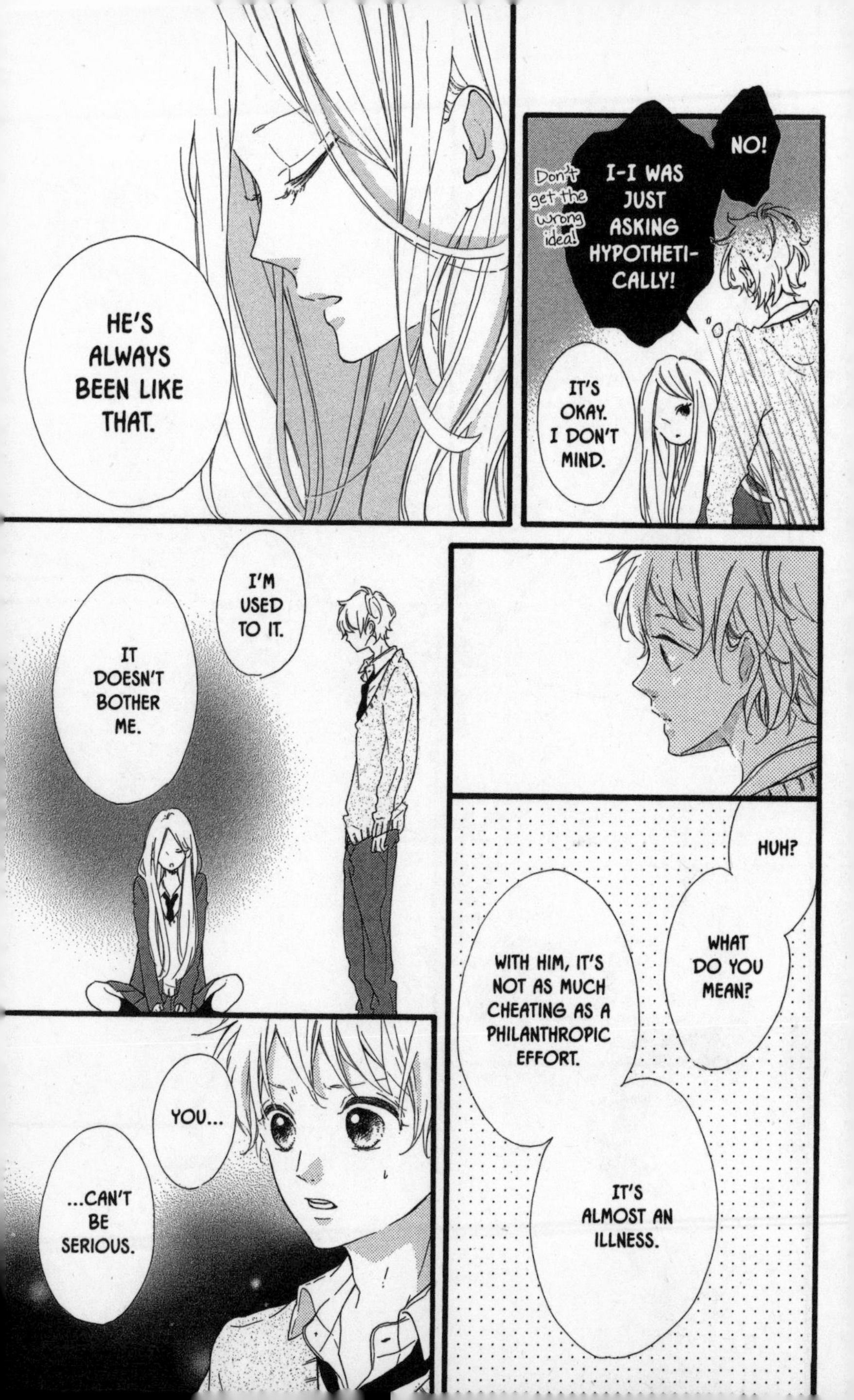
NO!
I-I WAS JUST ASKING HYPOTHETICALLY!
Don't get the wrong idea!
IT'S OKAY. I DON'T MIND.
HE'S ALWAYS BEEN LIKE THAT.
HUH?
WHAT DO YOU MEAN?
WITH HIM, IT'S NOT AS MUCH CHEATING AS A PHILANTHROPIC EFFORT.
IT'S ALMOST AN ILLNESS.
I'M USED TO IT.
IT DOESN'T BOTHER ME.
YOU...
...CAN'T BE SERIOUS.

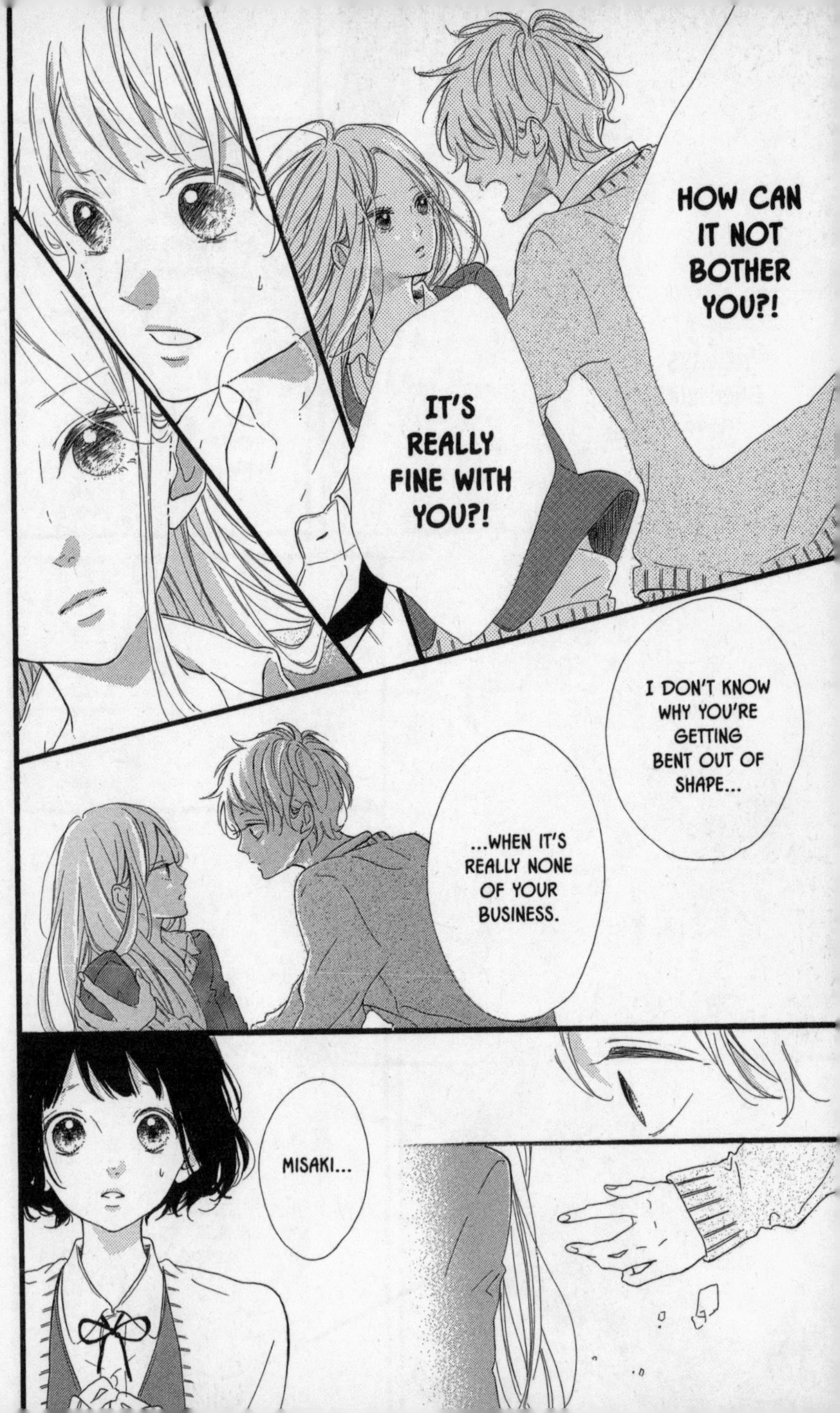
HOW CAN IT NOT BOTHER YOU?!
IT'S REALLY FINE WITH YOU?!
I DON'T KNOW WHY YOU'RE GETTING BENT OUT OF SHAPE...
...WHEN IT'S REALLY NONE OF YOUR BUSINESS.
MISAKI...

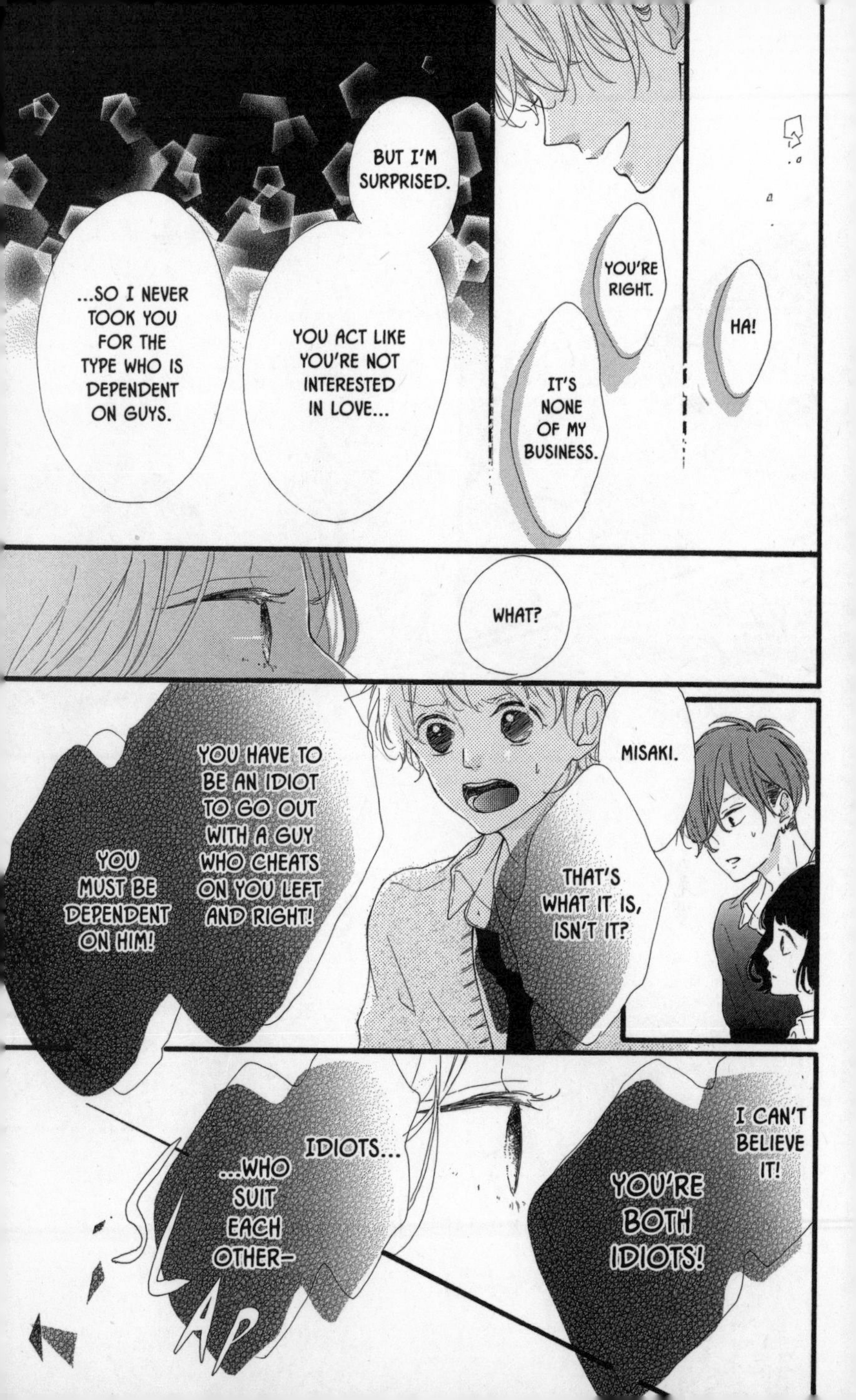
HA!
YOU'RE RIGHT.
IT'S NONE OF MY BUSINESS.
BUT I'M SURPRISED.
YOU ACT LIKE YOU'RE NOT INTERESTED IN LOVE...
...SO I NEVER TOOK YOU FOR THE TYPE WHO IS DEPENDENT ON GUYS.
WHAT?
MISAKI.
THAT'S WHAT IT IS, ISN'T IT?
YOU HAVE TO BE AN IDIOT TO GO OUT WITH A GUY WHO CHEATS ON YOU LEFT AND RIGHT!
YOU MUST BE DEPENDENT ON HIM!
I CAN'T BELIEVE IT!
YOU'RE BOTH IDIOTS!
IDIOTS...
...WHO SUIT EACH OTHER–
SLAP

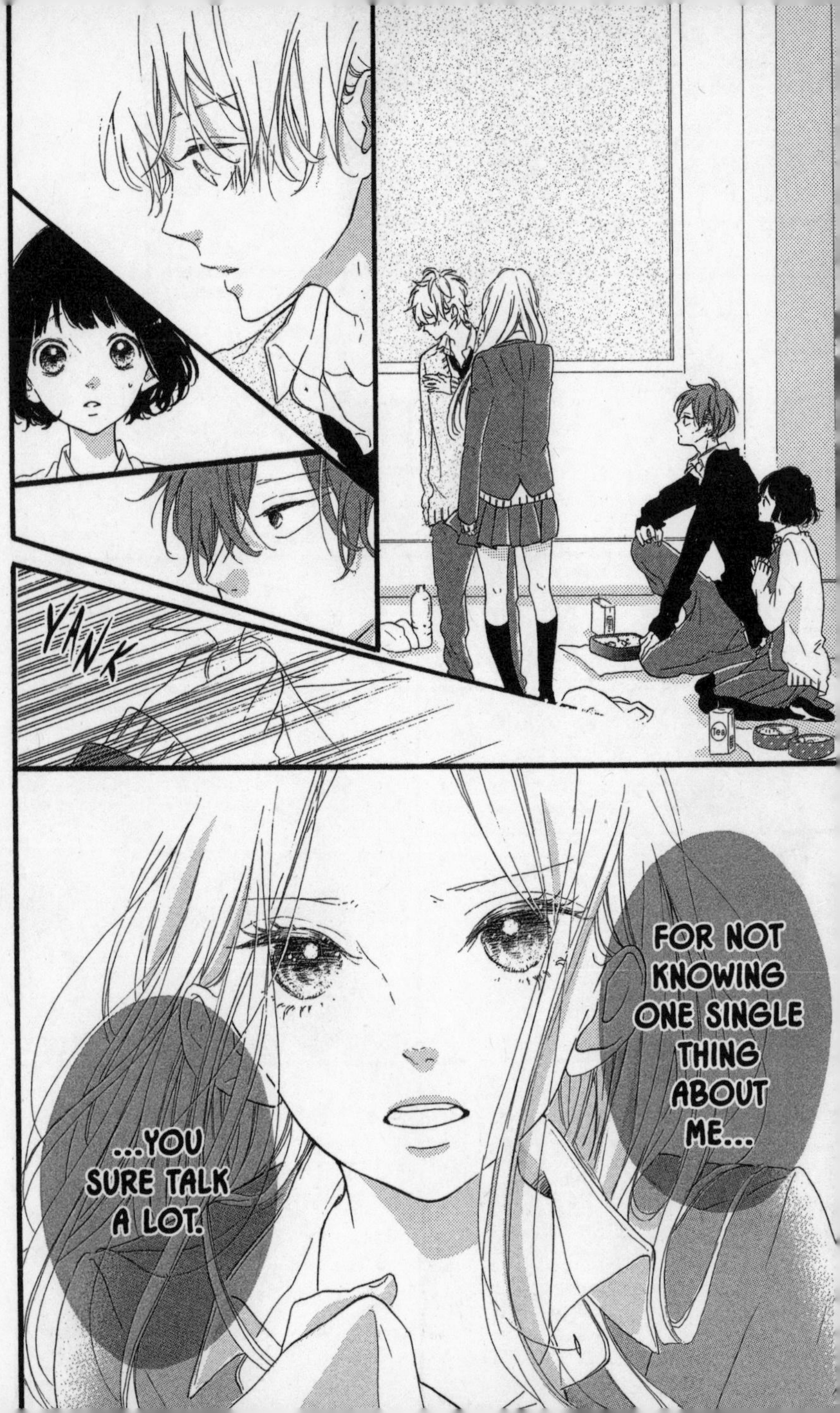
YANK
FOR NOT KNOWING ONE SINGLE THING ABOUT ME...
...YOU SURE TALK A LOT.

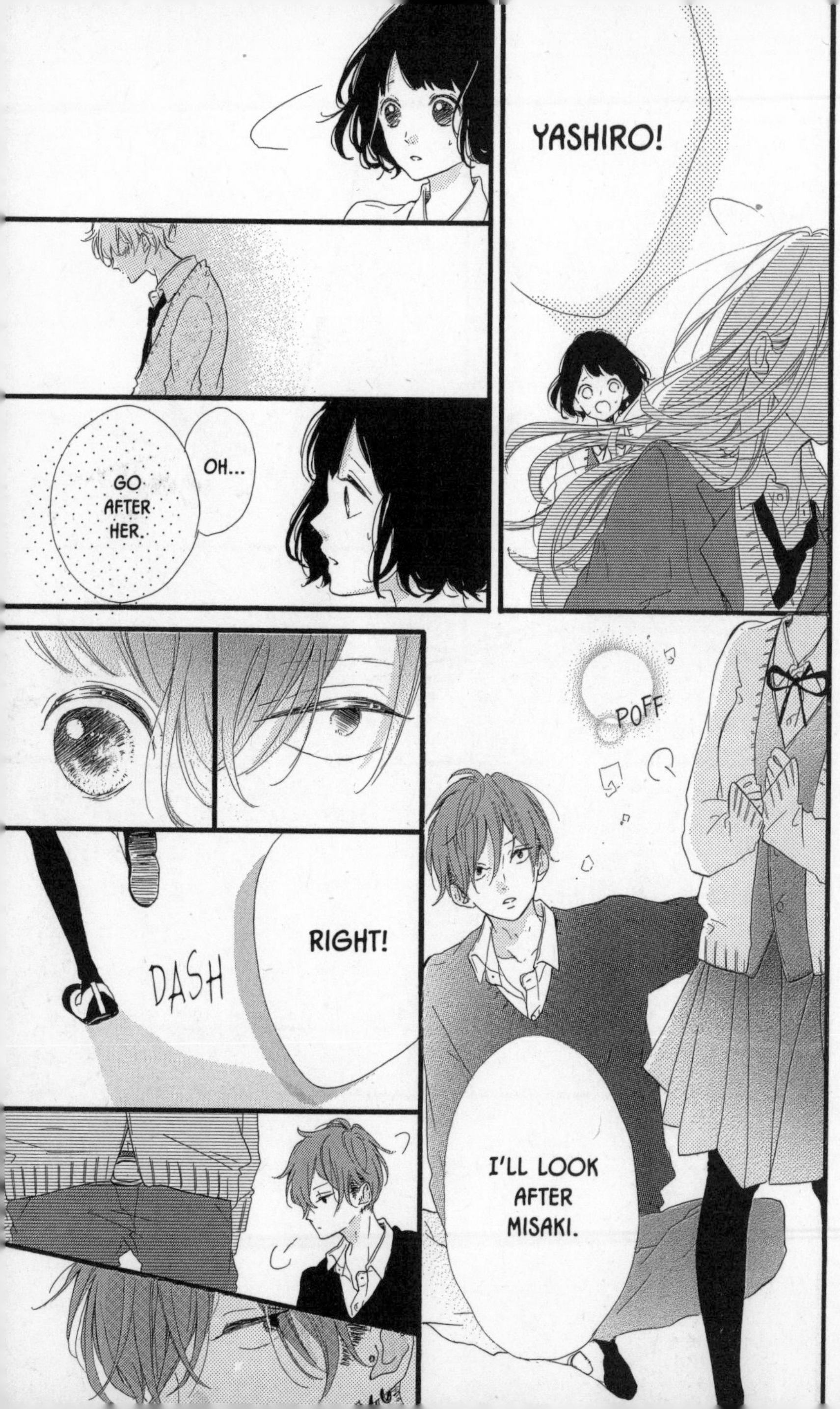
YASHIRO!
OH...
GO AFTER HER.
POFF
I'LL LOOK AFTER MISAKI.
RIGHT!
DASH

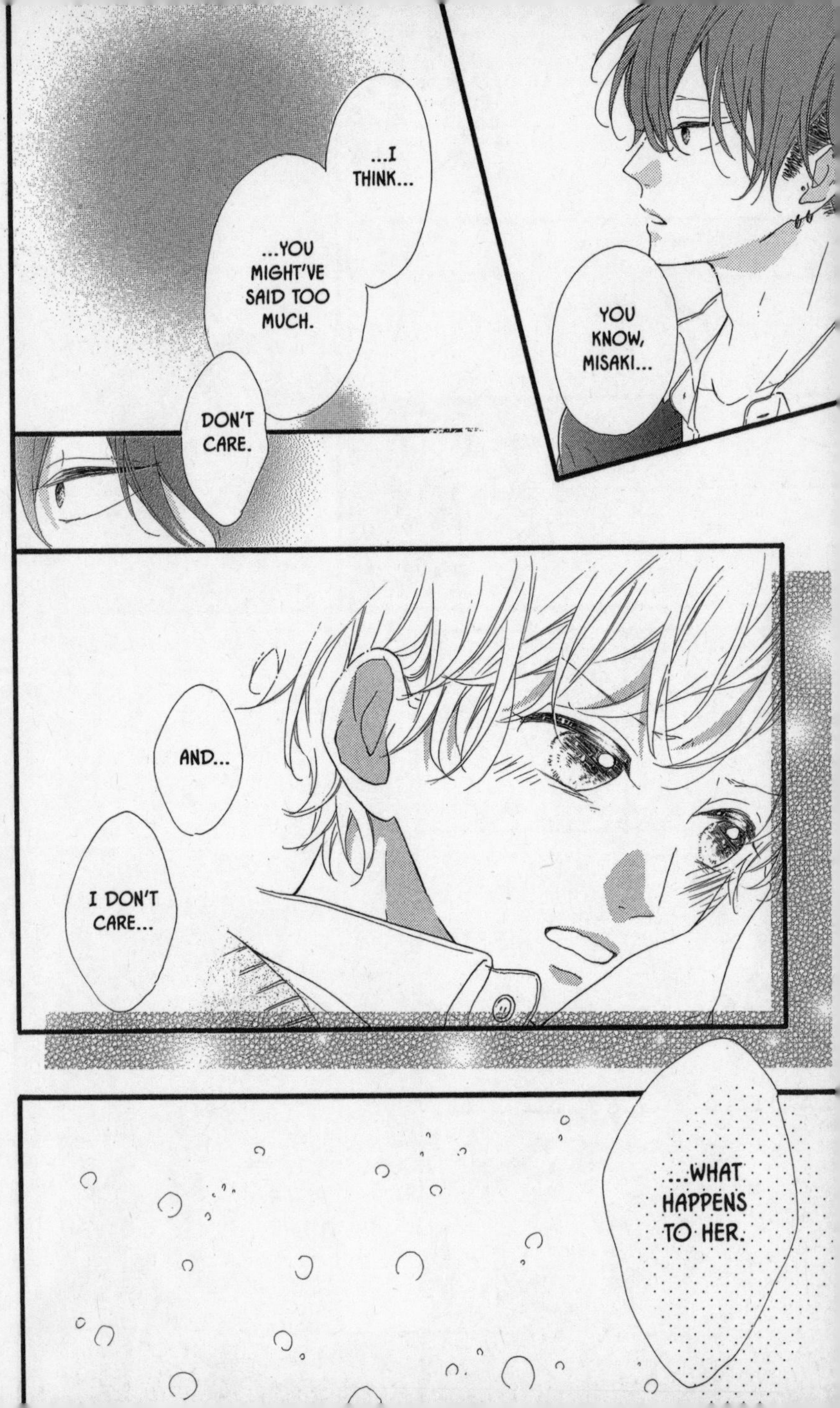
YOU KNOW, MISAKI...
...I THINK...
...YOU MIGHT'VE SAID TOO MUCH.
DON'T CARE.
AND...
I DON'T CARE...
...WHAT HAPPENS TO HER.

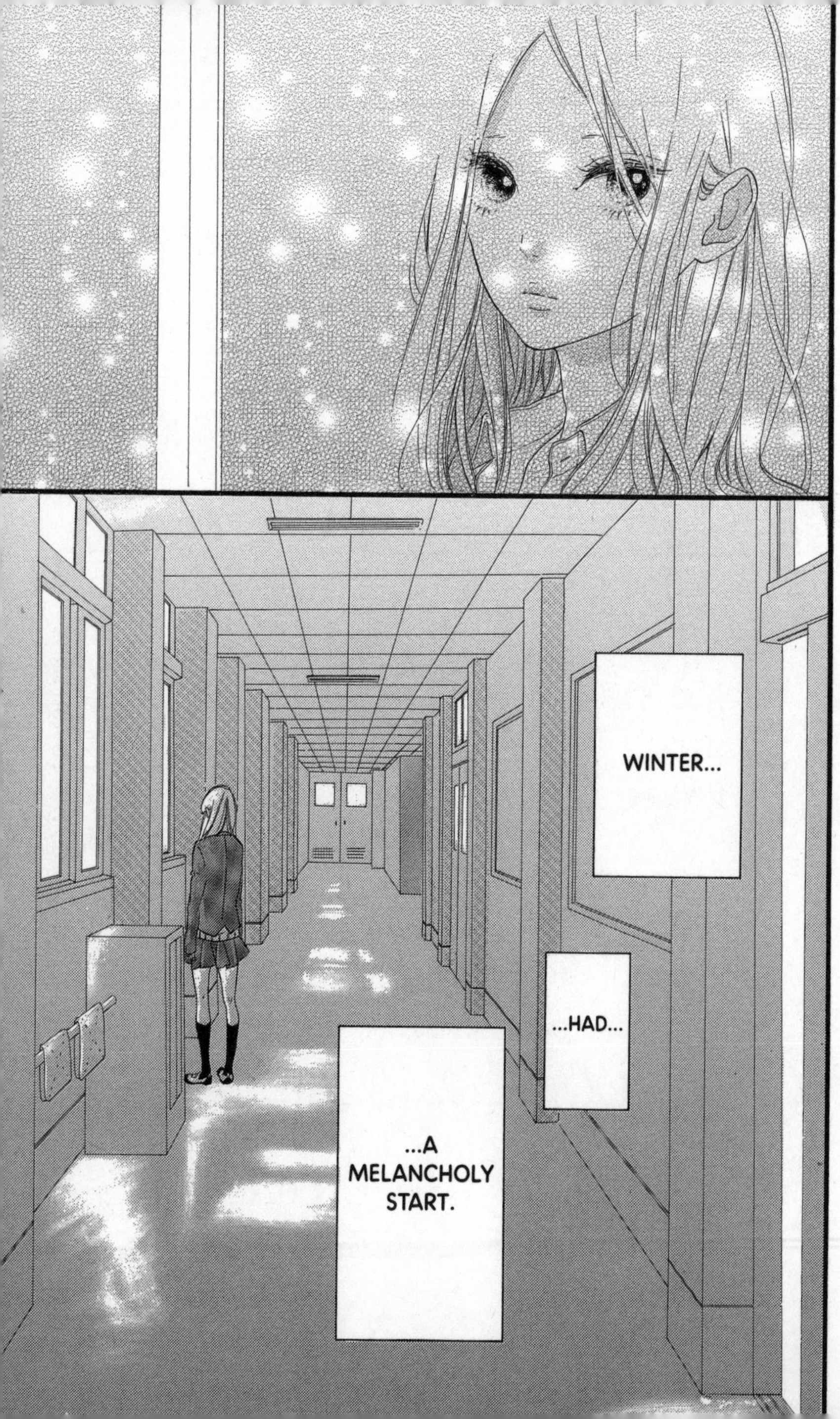
WINTER...
...HAD...
...A MELANCHOLY START.

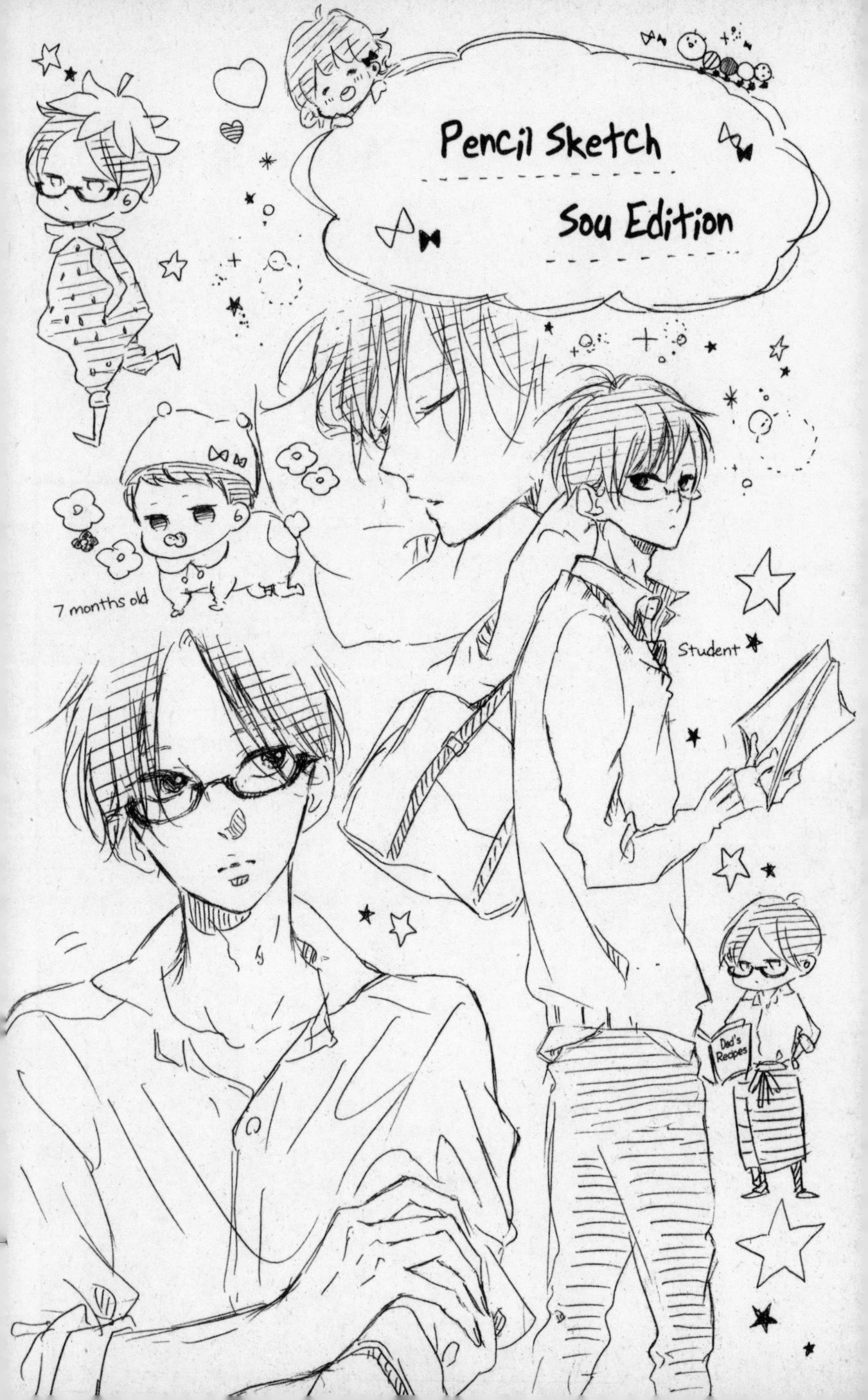
Pencil Sketch
Sou Edition
7 months old
Student
Dad's Recipes

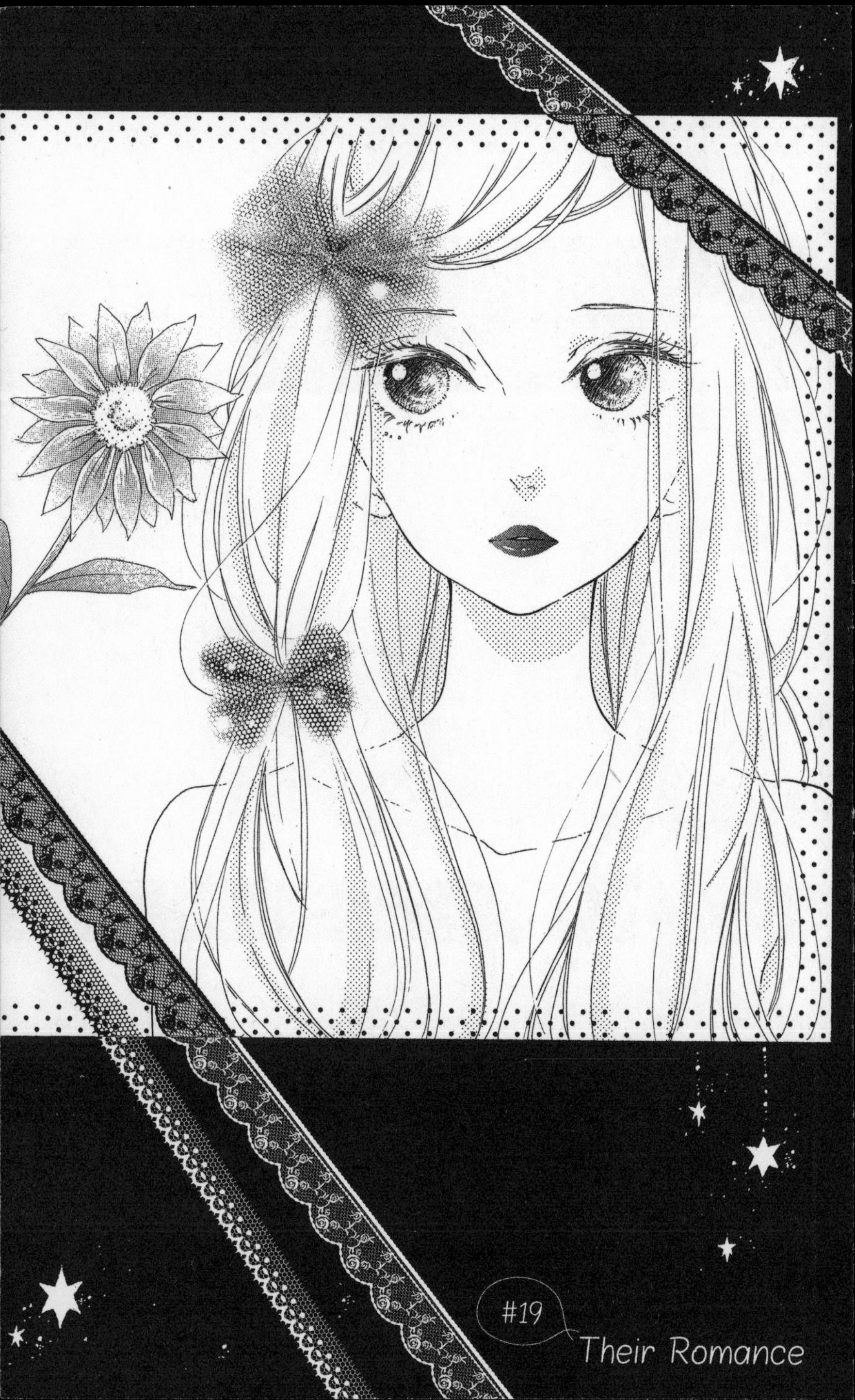
#19
Their Romance

I NEVER TOOK YOU FOR THE TYPE WHO IS DEPENDENT ON GUYS.

HE MIGHT HAVE...

...HIT THE NAIL ON THE HEAD WITH THAT ONE.

AL- THOUGH...

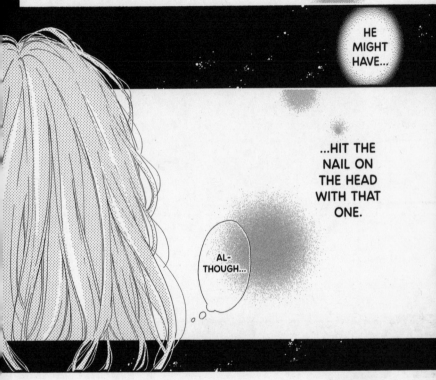

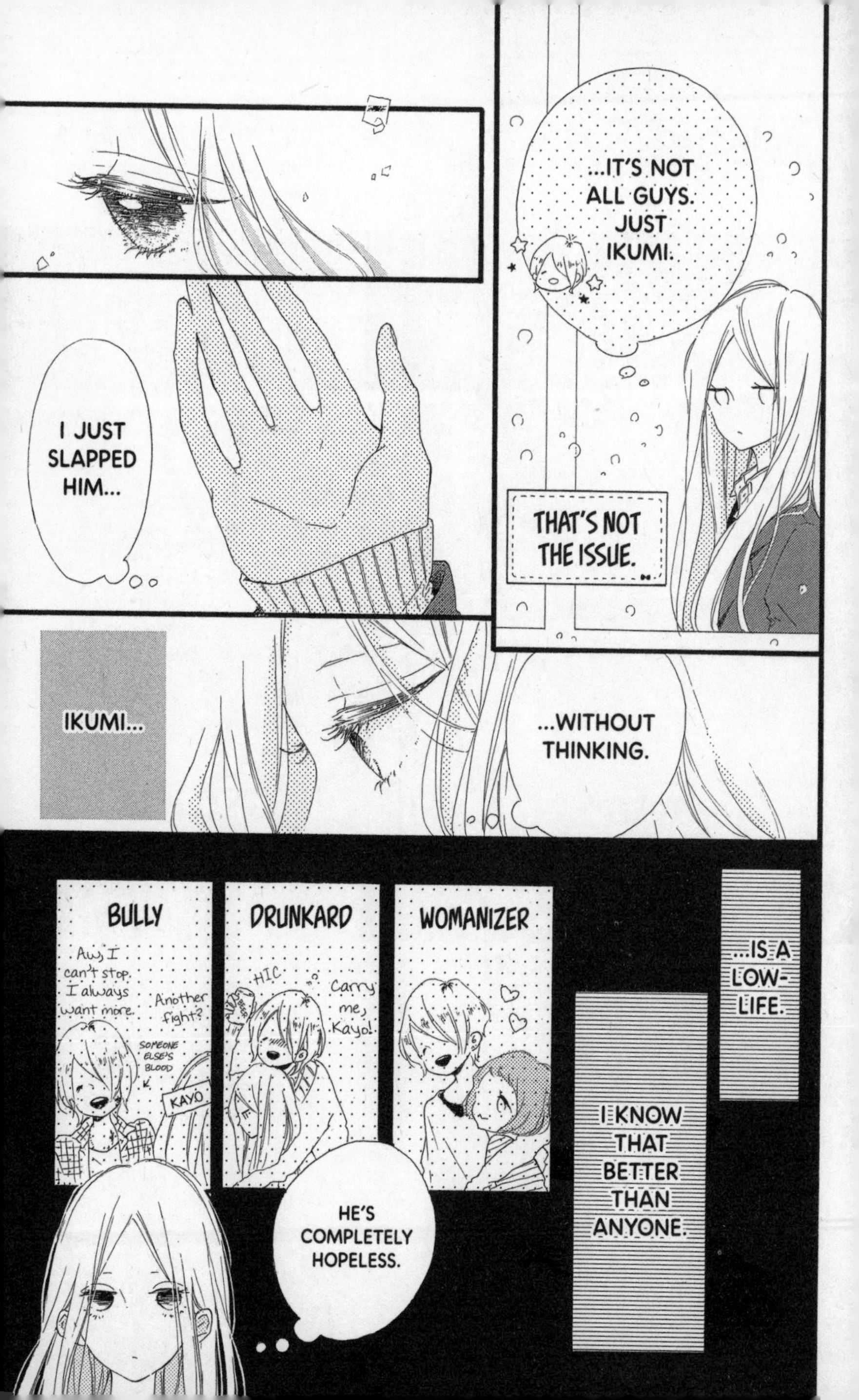
...IT'S NOT ALL GUYS. JUST IKUMI.
THAT'S NOT THE ISSUE.
I JUST SLAPPED HIM...
...WITHOUT THINKING.
IKUMI...
...IS A LOW-LIFE.
I KNOW THAT BETTER THAN ANYONE.
WOMANIZER
DRUNKARD
HIC
Carry me, Kayo!
BULLY
Aw, I can't stop. I always want more.
Another fight?
SOMEONE ELSE'S BLOOD
KAYO
HE'S COMPLETELY HOPELESS.

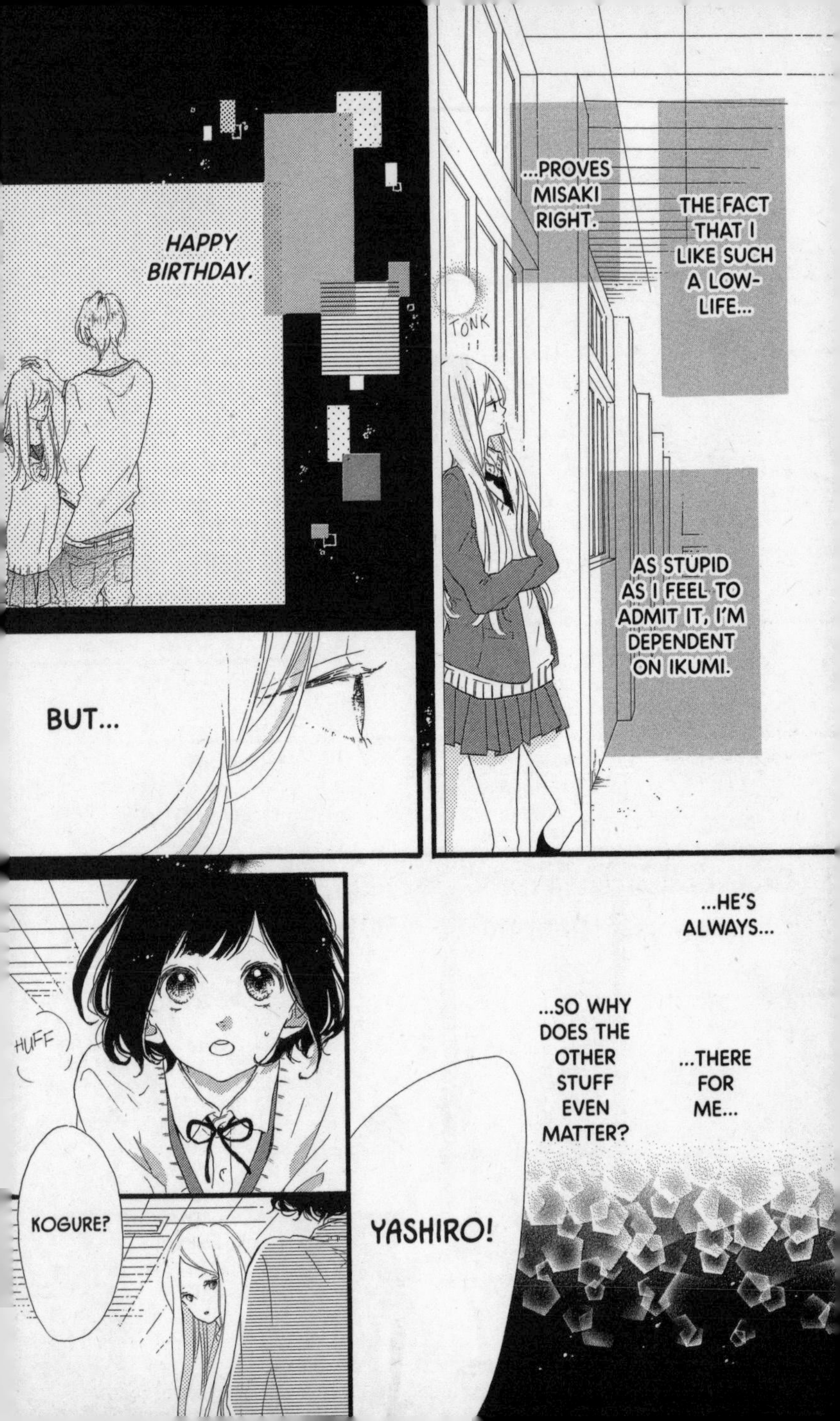
THE FACT THAT I LIKE SUCH A LOW-LIFE...
...PROVES MISAKI RIGHT.
TONK
AS STUPID AS I FEEL TO ADMIT IT, I'M DEPENDENT ON IKUMI.
HAPPY BIRTHDAY.
BUT...
...HE'S ALWAYS...
...THERE FOR ME...
...SO WHY DOES THE OTHER STUFF EVEN MATTER?
YASHIRO!
HUFF
KOGURE?

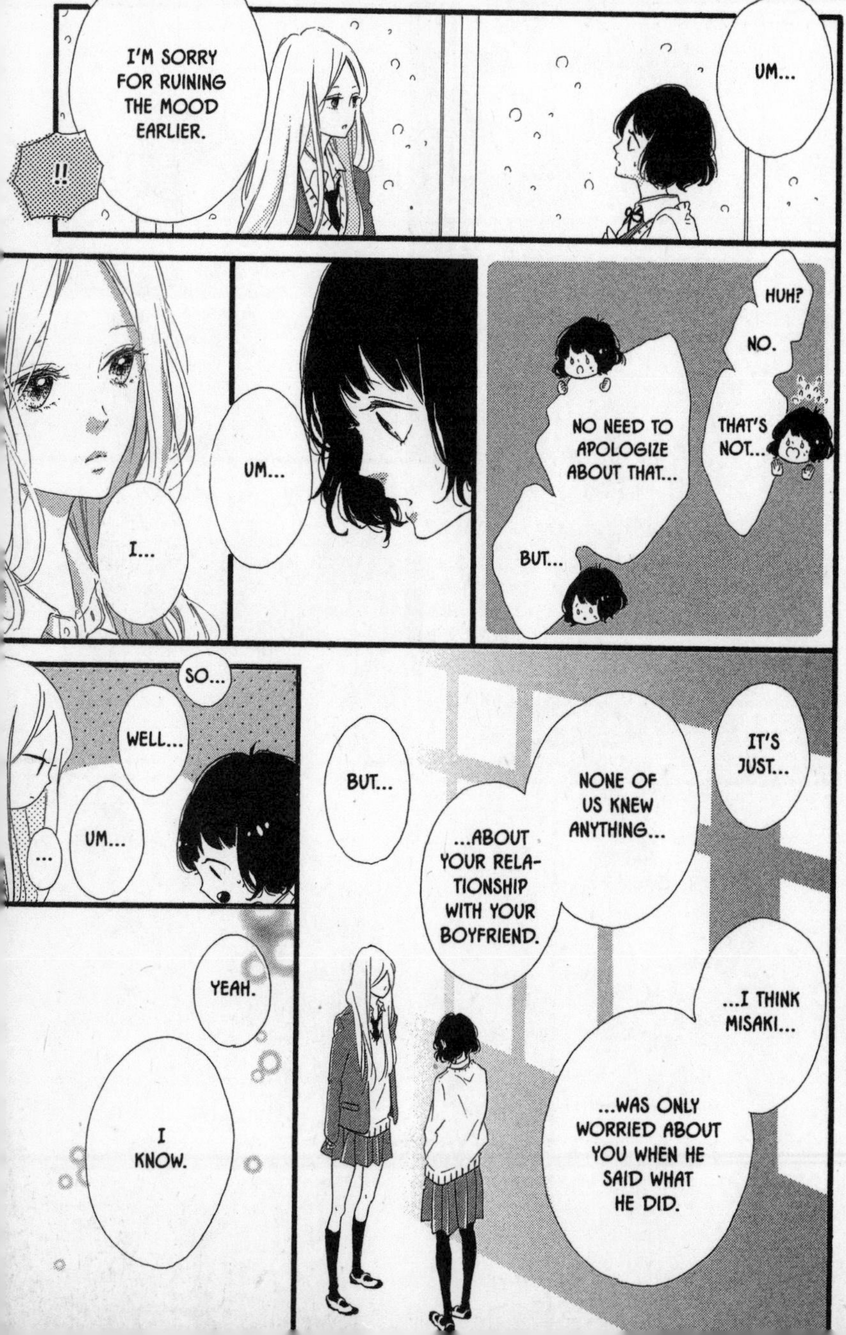
UM...
I'M SORRY FOR RUINING THE MOOD EARLIER.
!!
HUH?
NO.
THAT'S NOT...
NO NEED TO APOLOGIZE ABOUT THAT...
BUT...
UM...
I...
IT'S JUST...
NONE OF US KNEW ANYTHING...
...ABOUT YOUR RELA-TIONSHIP WITH YOUR BOYFRIEND.
BUT...
...I THINK MISAKI...
...WAS ONLY WORRIED ABOUT YOU WHEN HE SAID WHAT HE DID.
SO...
WELL...
UM...
...
YEAH.
I KNOW.

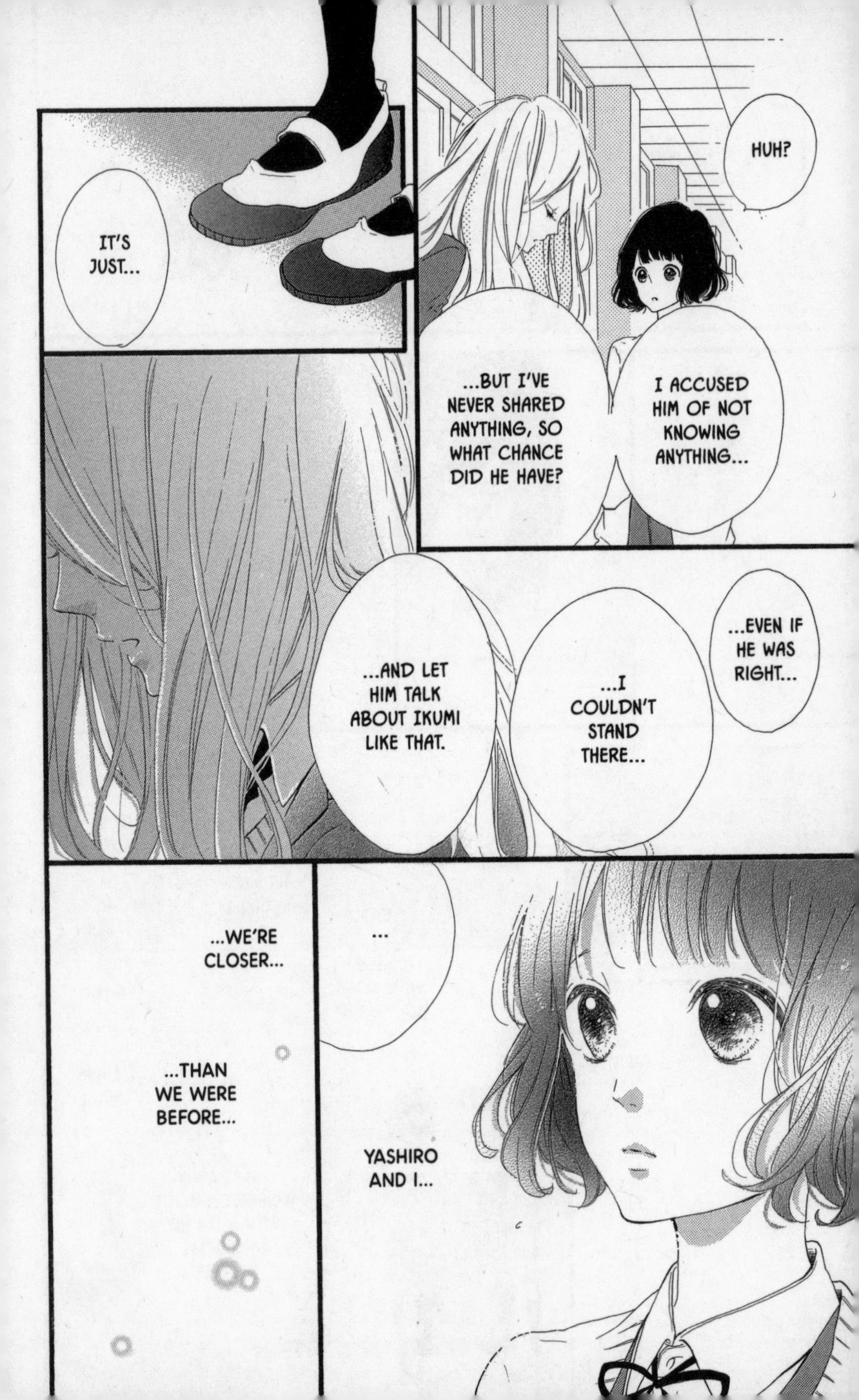
HUH?
I ACCUSED HIM OF NOT KNOWING ANYTHING...
...BUT I'VE NEVER SHARED ANYTHING, SO WHAT CHANCE DID HE HAVE?
IT'S JUST...
...EVEN IF HE WAS RIGHT...
...I COULDN'T STAND THERE...
...AND LET HIM TALK ABOUT IKUMI LIKE THAT.
...
YASHIRO AND I...
...WE'RE CLOSER...
...THAN WE WERE BEFORE...

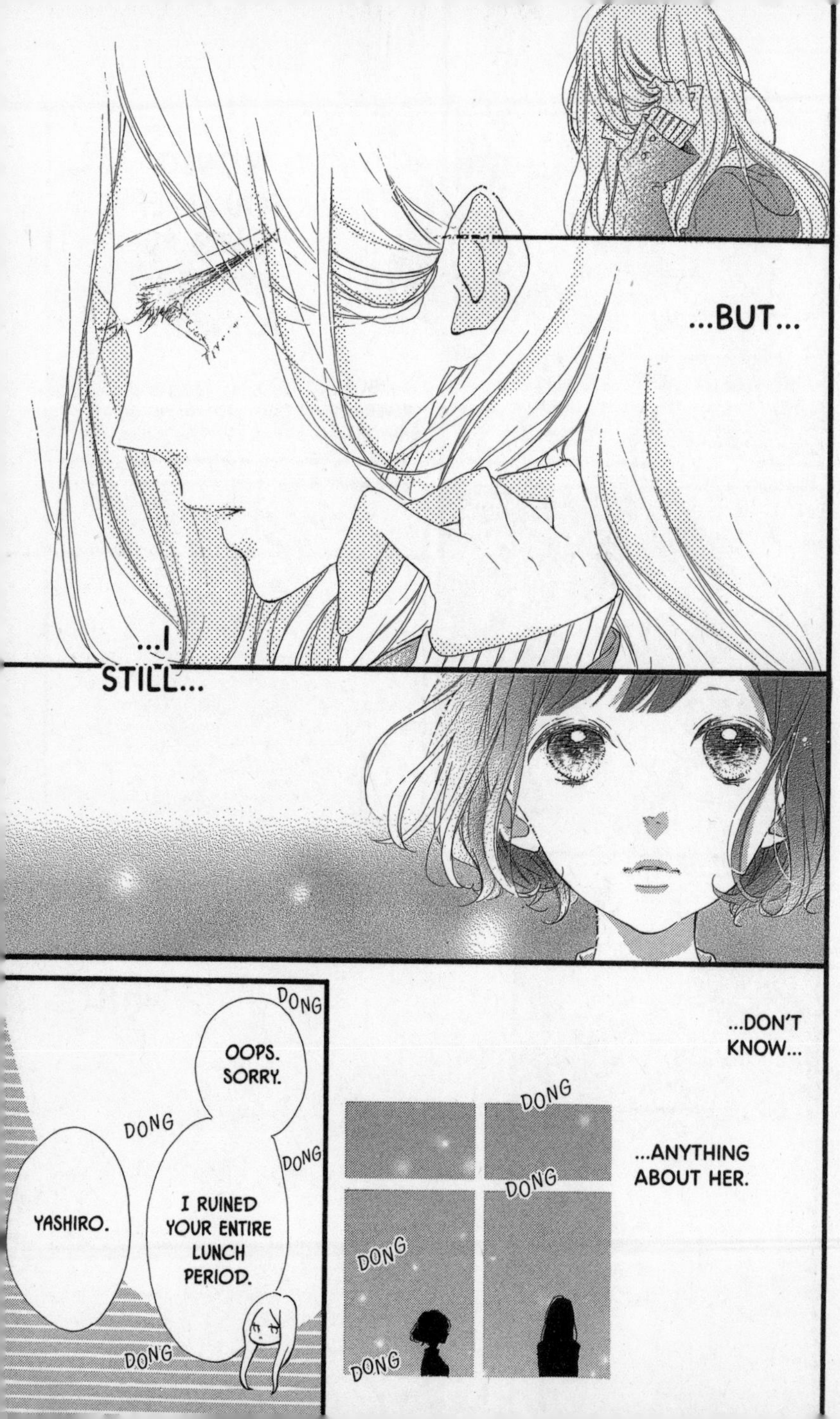
...BUT...
...I STILL...
...DON'T KNOW...
DONG
DONG
...ANYTHING ABOUT HER.
DONG
DONG
DONG
OOPS. SORRY.
DONG
DONG
I RUINED YOUR ENTIRE LUNCH PERIOD.
YASHIRO.
DONG

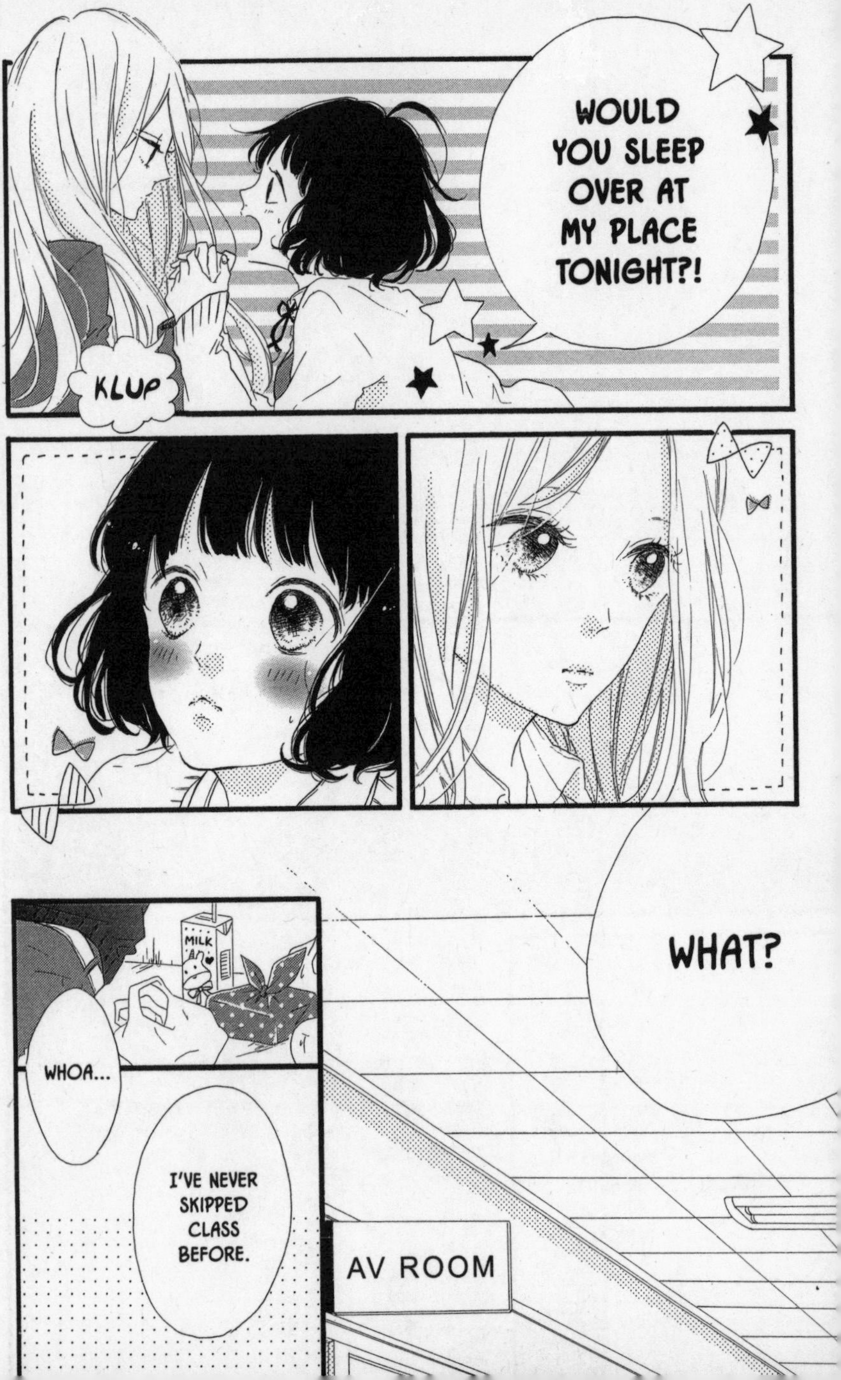

WOULD YOU SLEEP OVER AT MY PLACE TONIGHT?!
KLUP
WHAT?
AV ROOM
WHOA...
I'VE NEVER SKIPPED CLASS BEFORE.
MILK

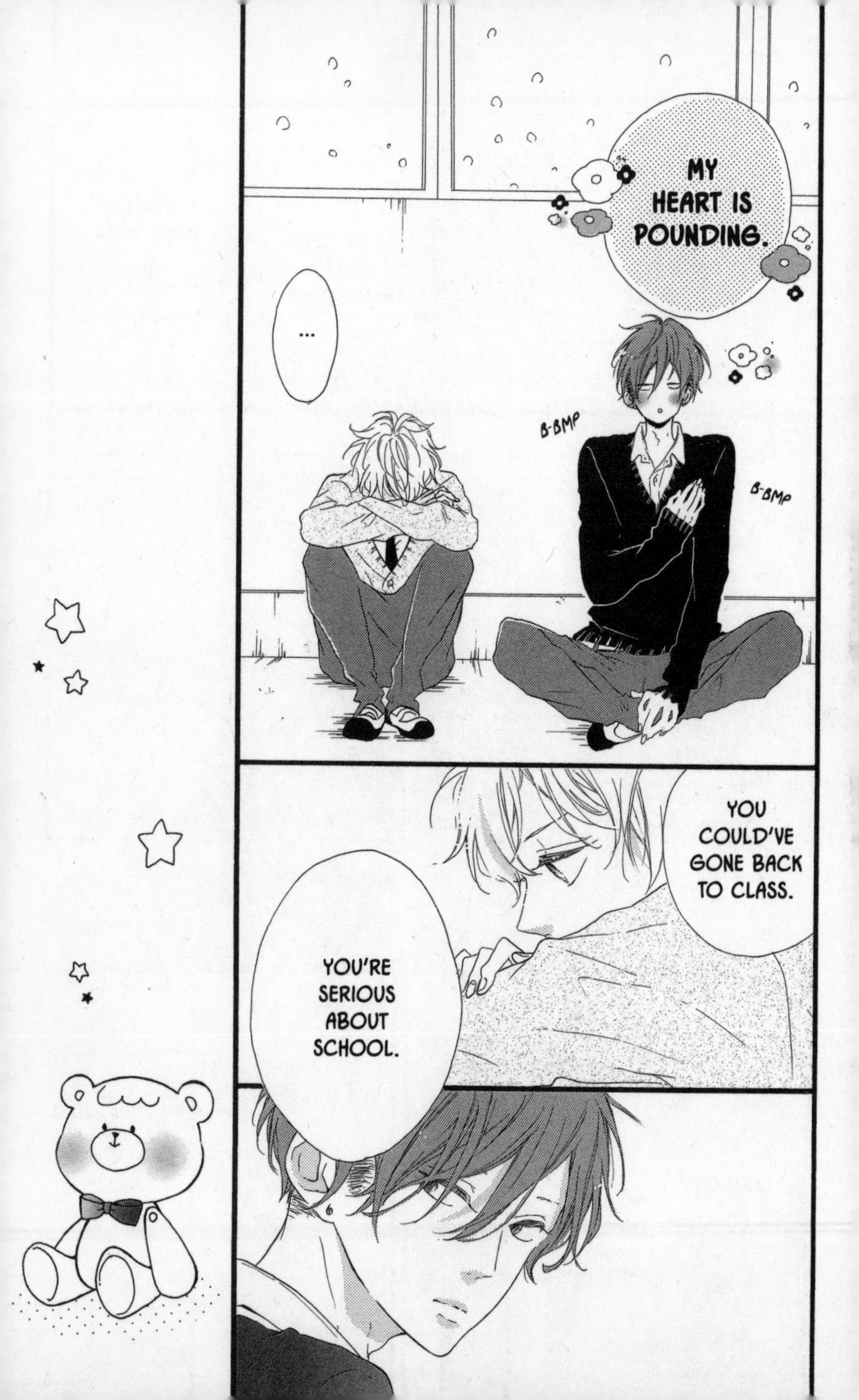
MY HEART IS POUNDING.
...
B-BMP
B-BMP
YOU COULD'VE GONE BACK TO CLASS.
YOU'RE SERIOUS ABOUT SCHOOL.

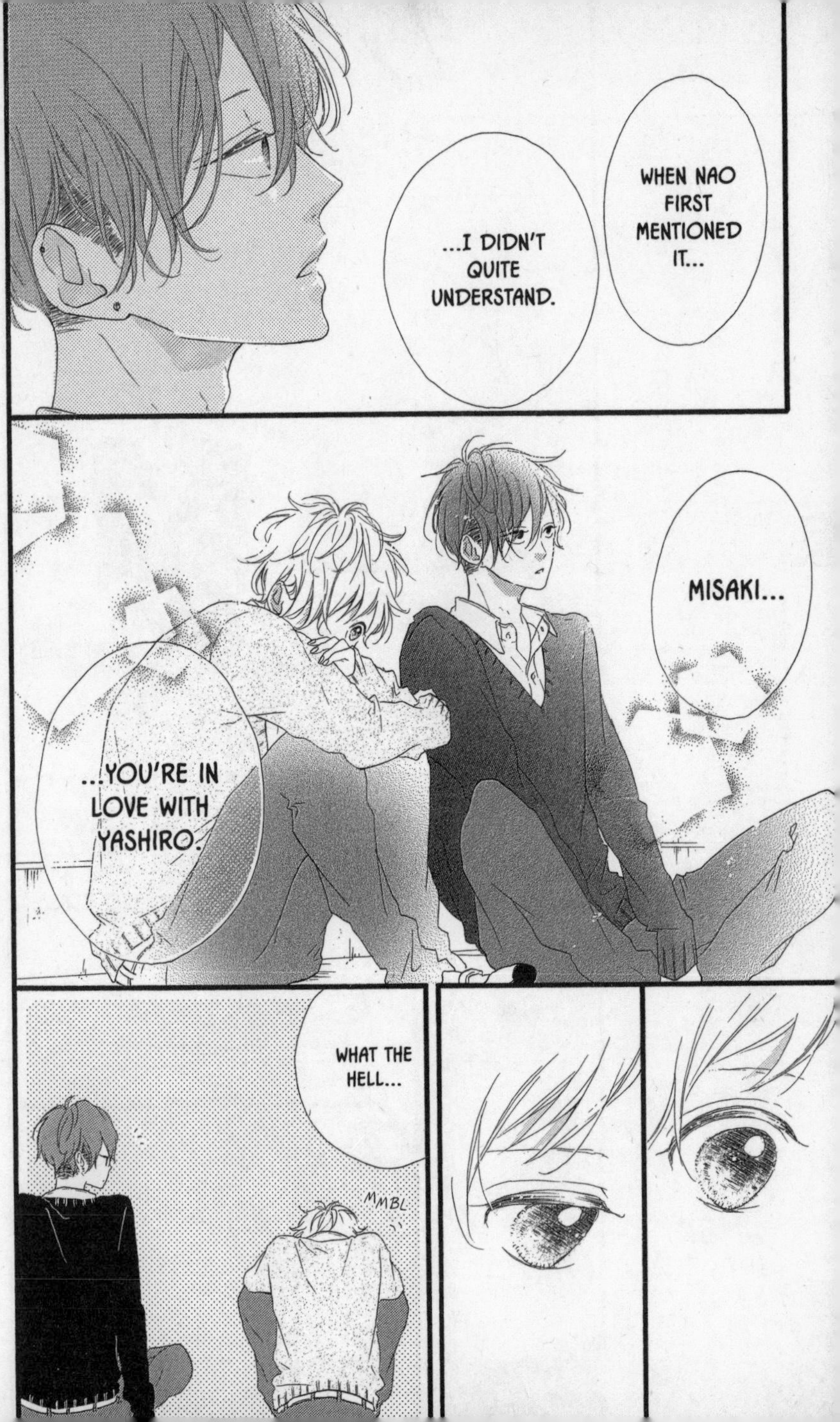
WHEN NAO FIRST MENTIONED IT...
...I DIDN'T QUITE UNDERSTAND.
MISAKI...
...YOU'RE IN LOVE WITH YASHIRO.
WHAT THE HELL...
MMBL

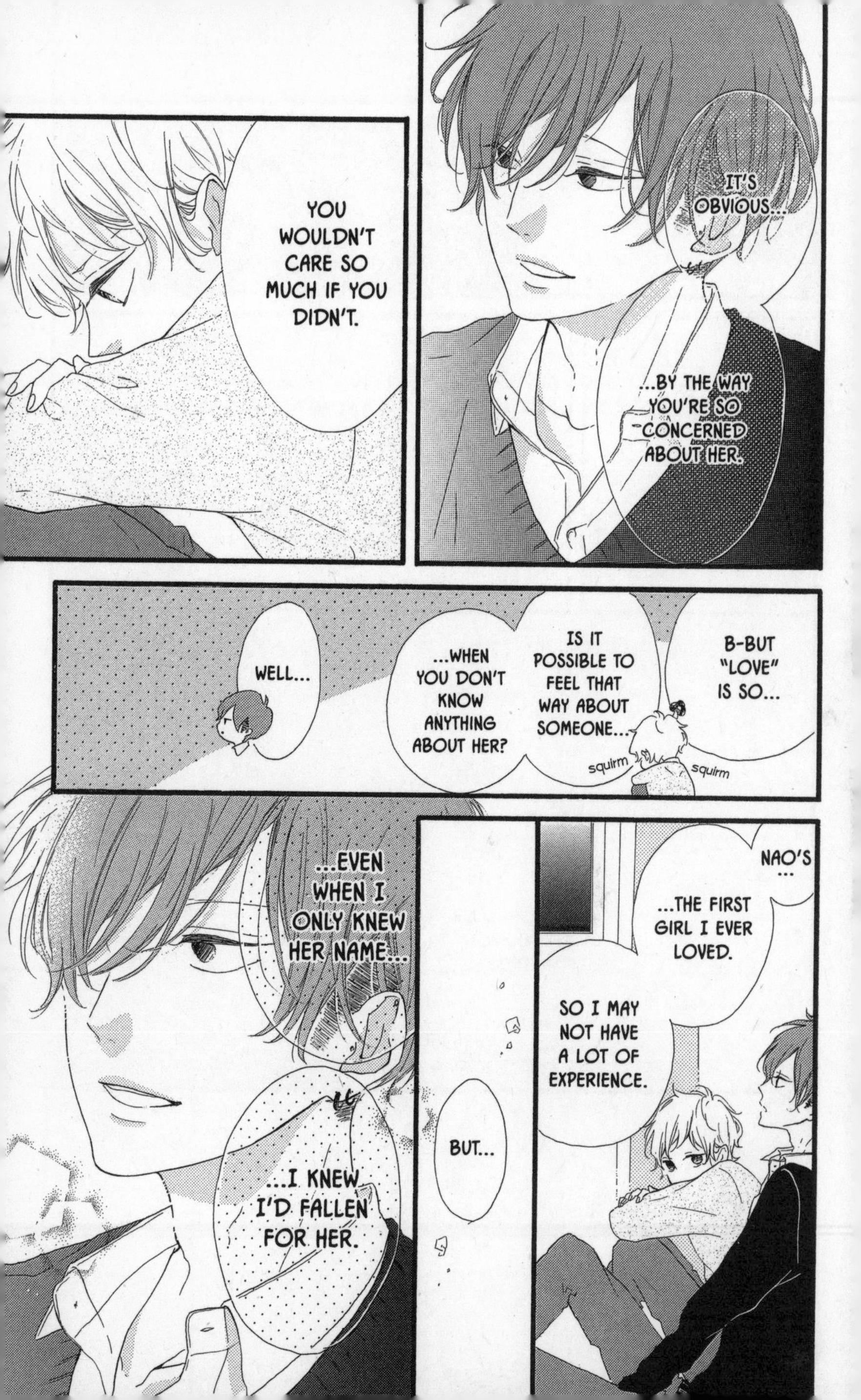
IT'S OBVIOUS...
...BY THE WAY YOU'RE SO CONCERNED ABOUT HER.
YOU WOULDN'T CARE SO MUCH IF YOU DIDN'T.
B-BUT "LOVE" IS SO...
IS IT POSSIBLE TO FEEL THAT WAY ABOUT SOMEONE...
...WHEN YOU DON'T KNOW ANYTHING ABOUT HER?
squirm
squirm
WELL...
NAO'S...
...THE FIRST GIRL I EVER LOVED.
SO I MAY NOT HAVE A LOT OF EXPERIENCE.
BUT...
...EVEN WHEN I ONLY KNEW HER NAME...
...I KNEW I'D FALLEN FOR HER.

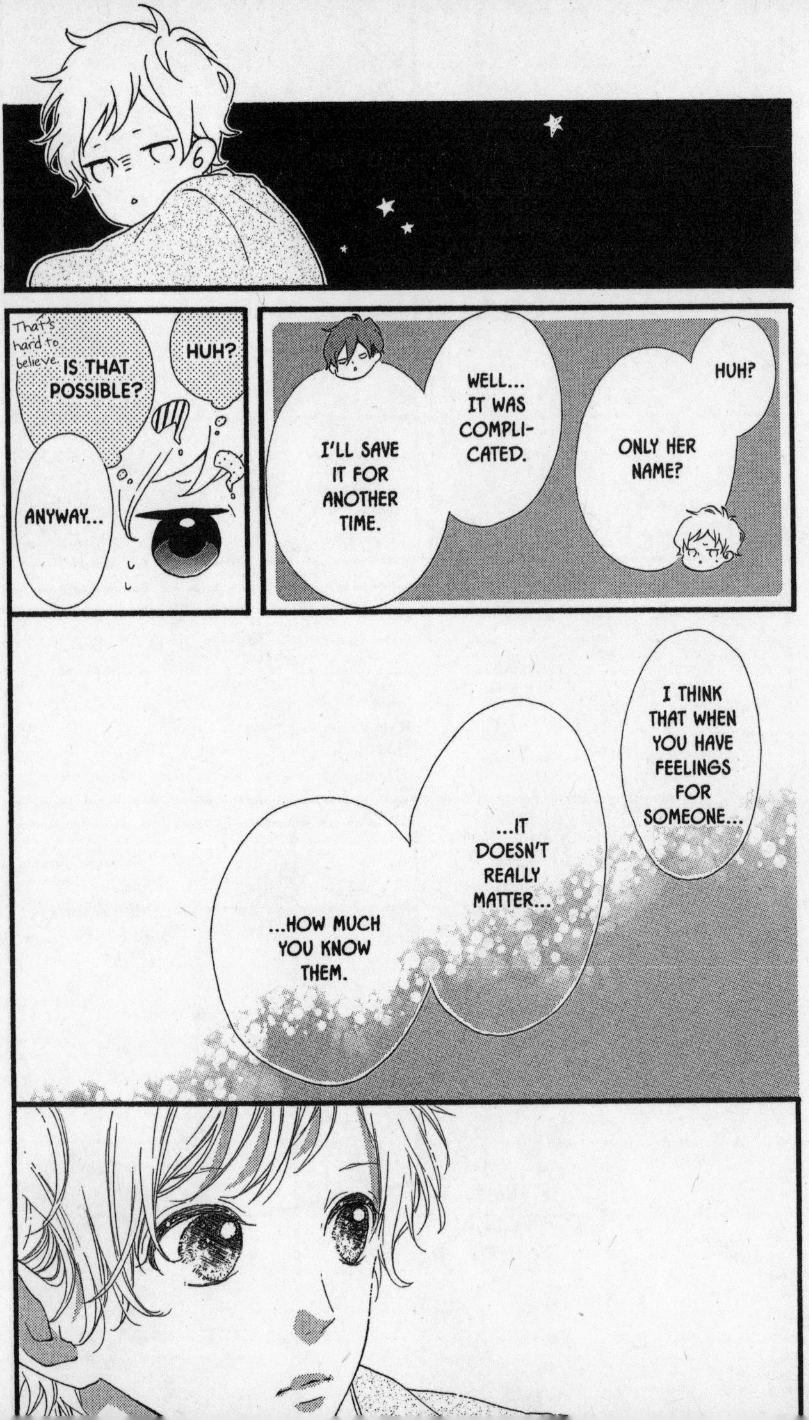
HUH?
ONLY HER NAME?
WELL... IT WAS COMPLICATED.
I'LL SAVE IT FOR ANOTHER TIME.
HUH?
That's hard to believe.
IS THAT POSSIBLE?
ANYWAY...
I THINK THAT WHEN YOU HAVE FEELINGS FOR SOMEONE...
...IT DOESN'T REALLY MATTER...
...HOW MUCH YOU KNOW THEM.

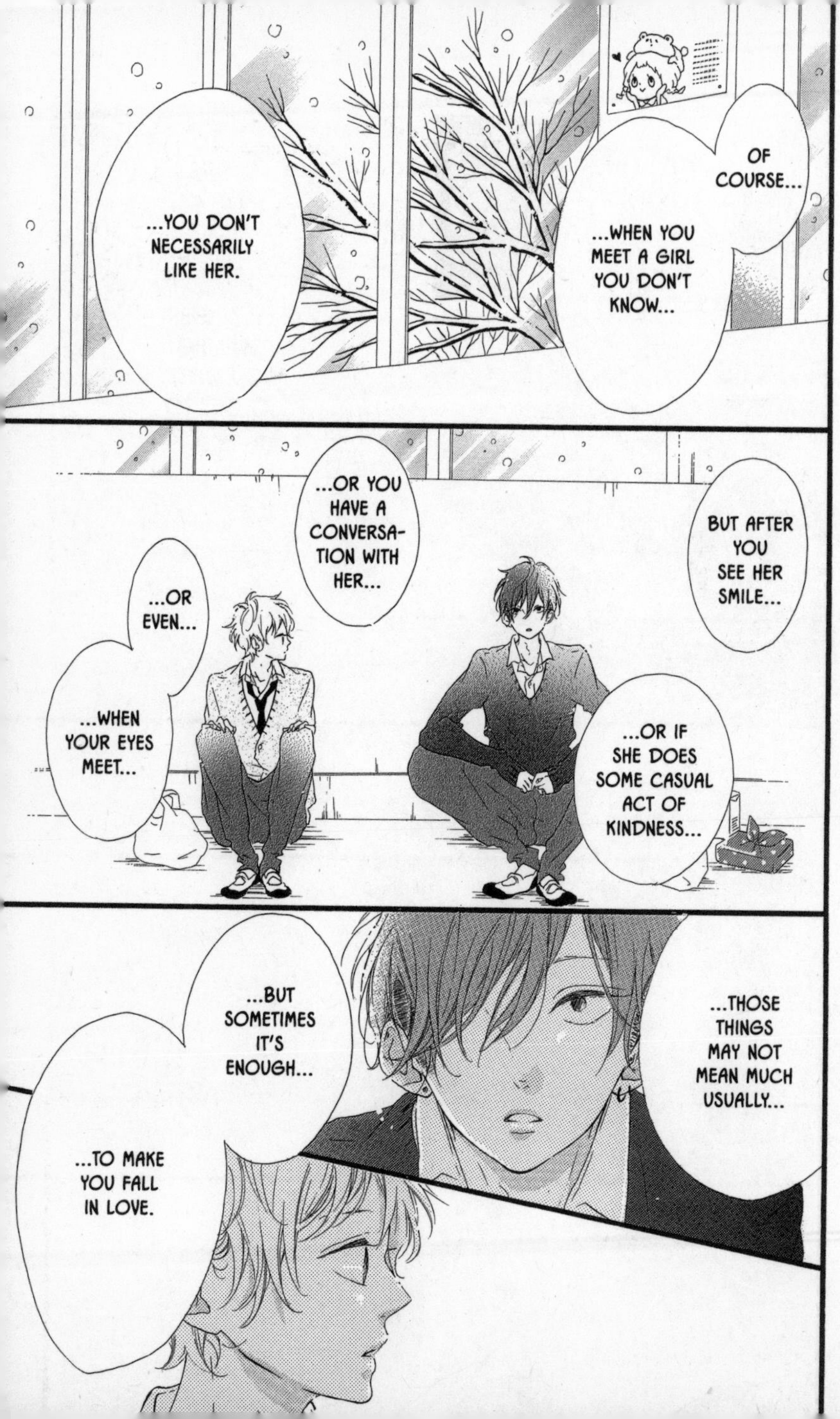
OF COURSE...
...WHEN YOU MEET A GIRL YOU DON'T KNOW...
...YOU DON'T NECESSARILY LIKE HER.
BUT AFTER YOU SEE HER SMILE...
...OR IF SHE DOES SOME CASUAL ACT OF KINDNESS...
...OR YOU HAVE A CONVERSA-TION WITH HER...
...OR EVEN...
...WHEN YOUR EYES MEET...
...THOSE THINGS MAY NOT MEAN MUCH USUALLY...
...BUT SOMETIMES IT'S ENOUGH...
...TO MAKE YOU FALL IN LOVE.

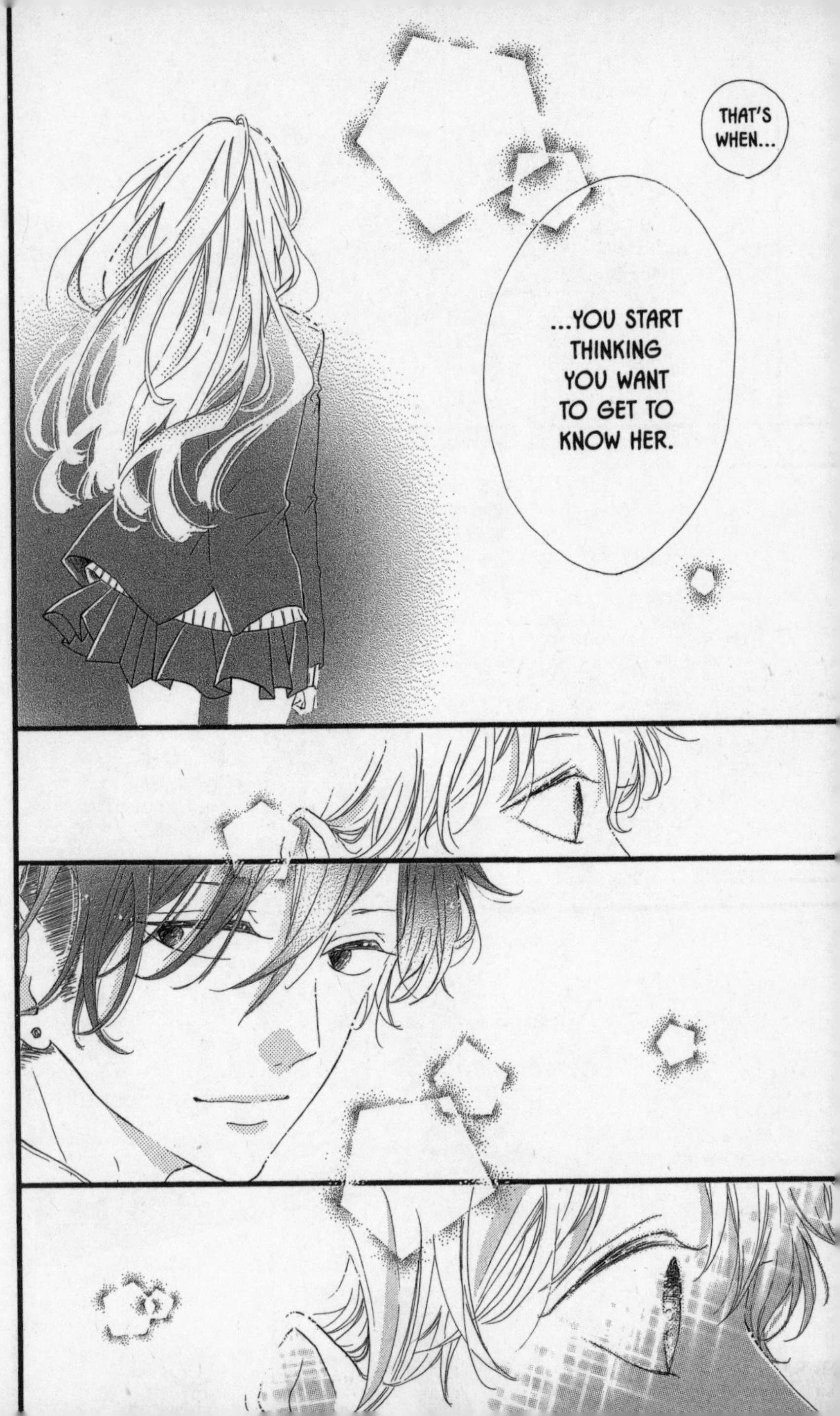
THAT'S WHEN...
...YOU START THINKING YOU WANT TO GET TO KNOW HER.

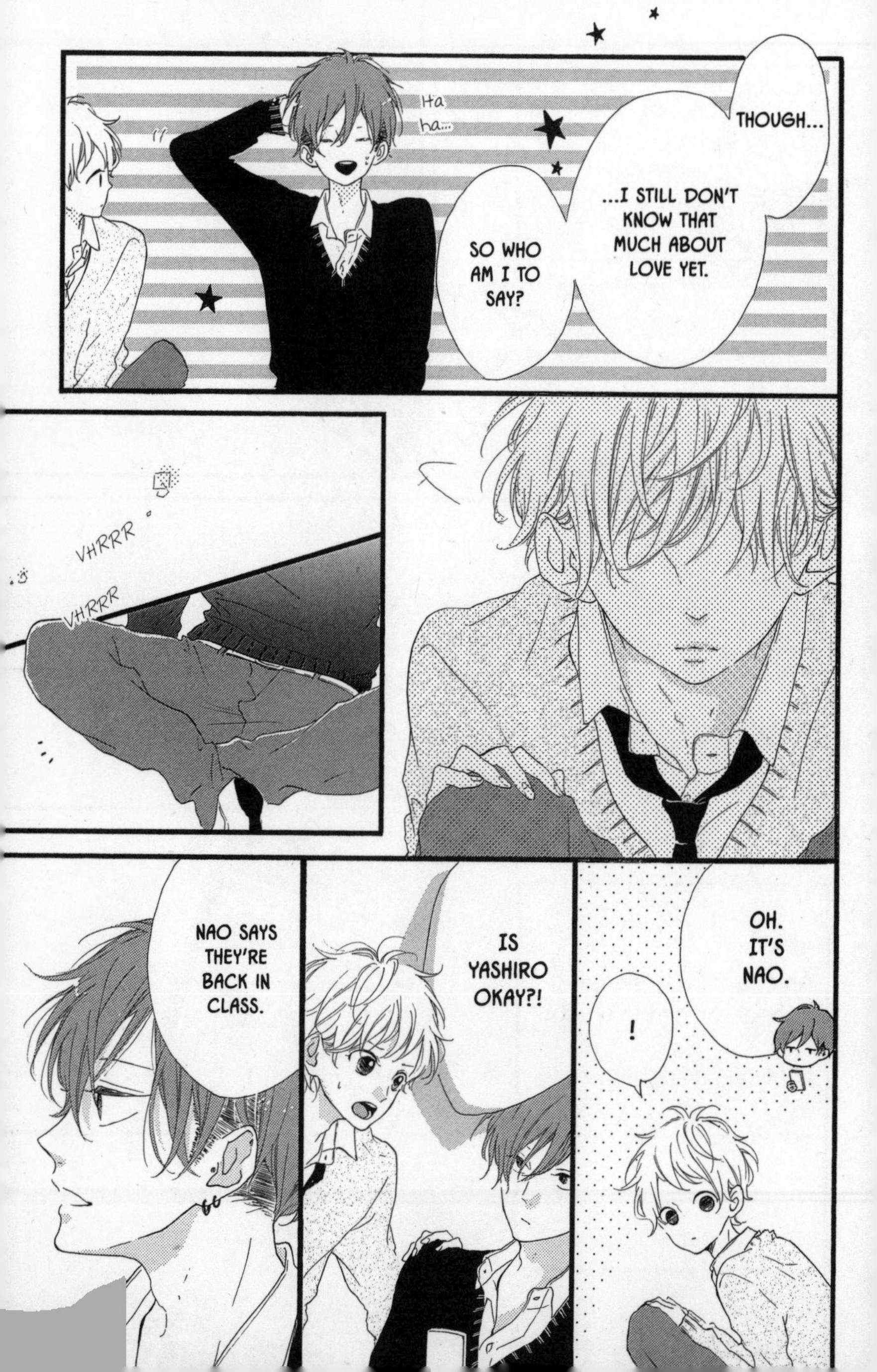
THOUGH...
...I STILL DON'T KNOW THAT MUCH ABOUT LOVE YET.
SO WHO AM I TO SAY?
Ha ha...
VHRRR
VHRRR
OH. IT'S NAO.
!
IS YASHIRO OKAY?!
NAO SAYS THEY'RE BACK IN CLASS.

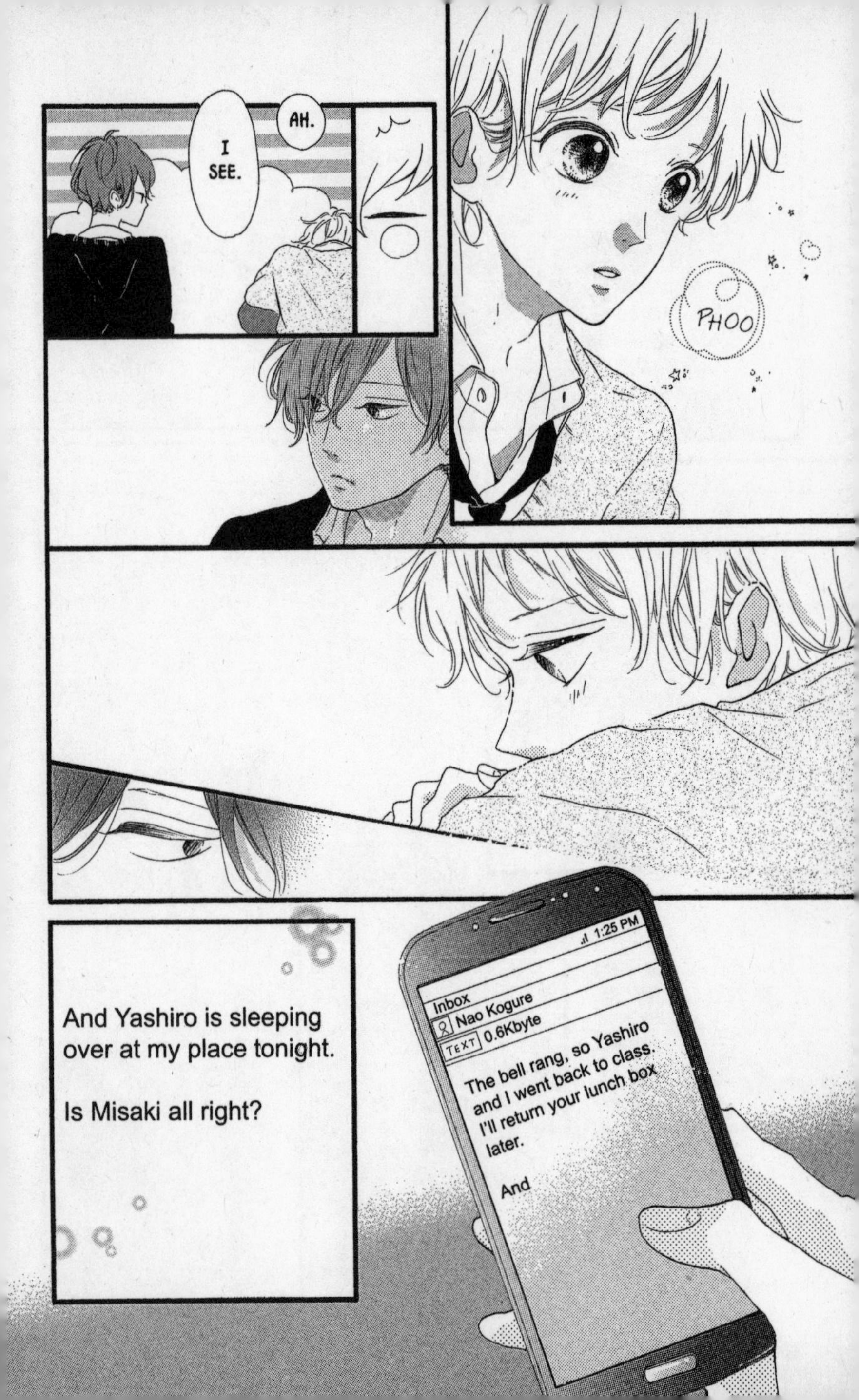
PHOO
AH.
I SEE.
1:25 PM
Inbox
Nao Kogure
TEXT 0.6Kbyte
The bell rang, so Yashiro and I went back to class. I'll return your lunch box later.

And
And Yashiro is sleeping over at my place tonight.

Is Misaki all right?

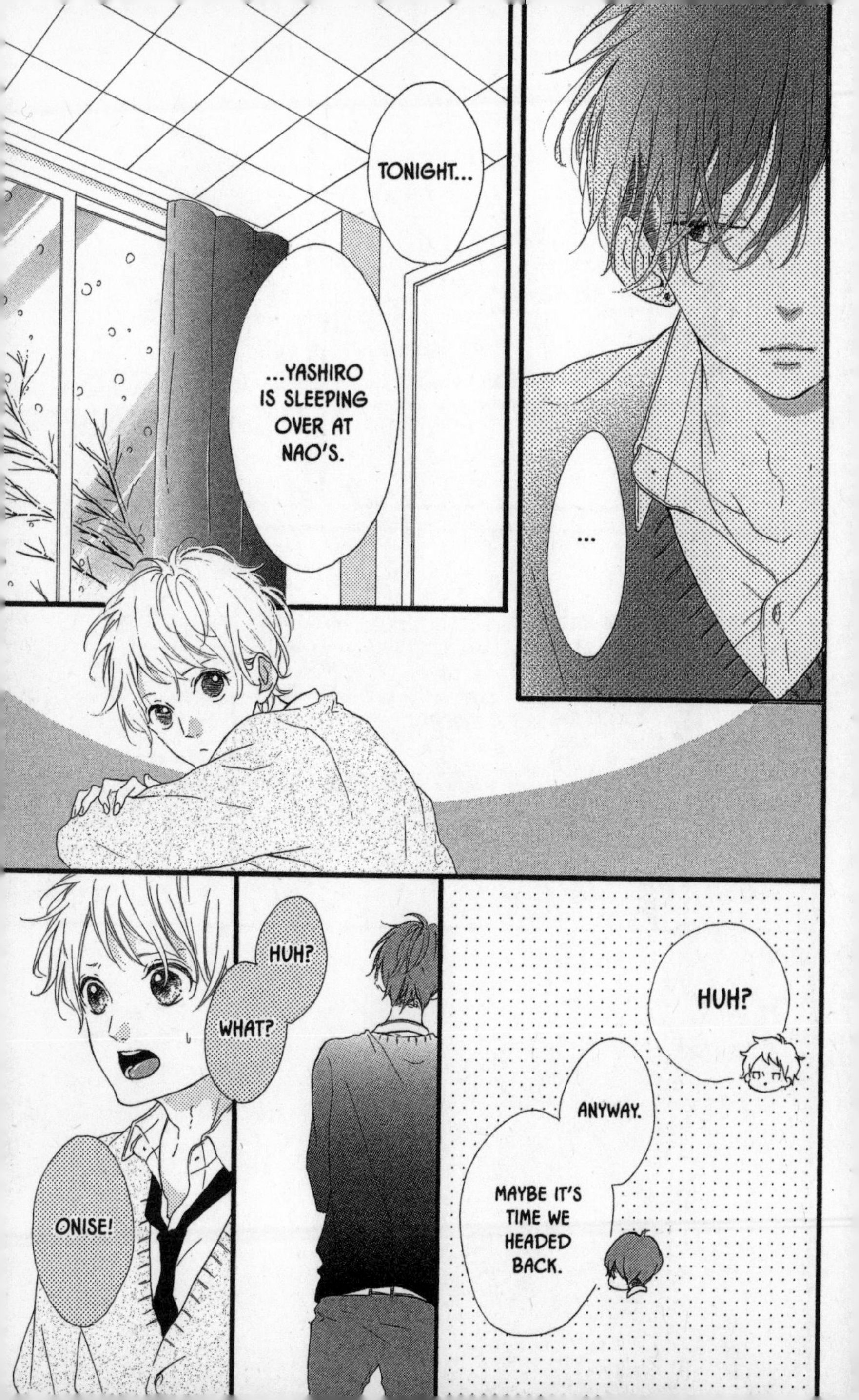
...
TONIGHT...
...YASHIRO IS SLEEPING OVER AT NAO'S.
HUH?
ANYWAY.
MAYBE IT'S TIME WE HEADED BACK.
HUH?
WHAT?
ONISE!

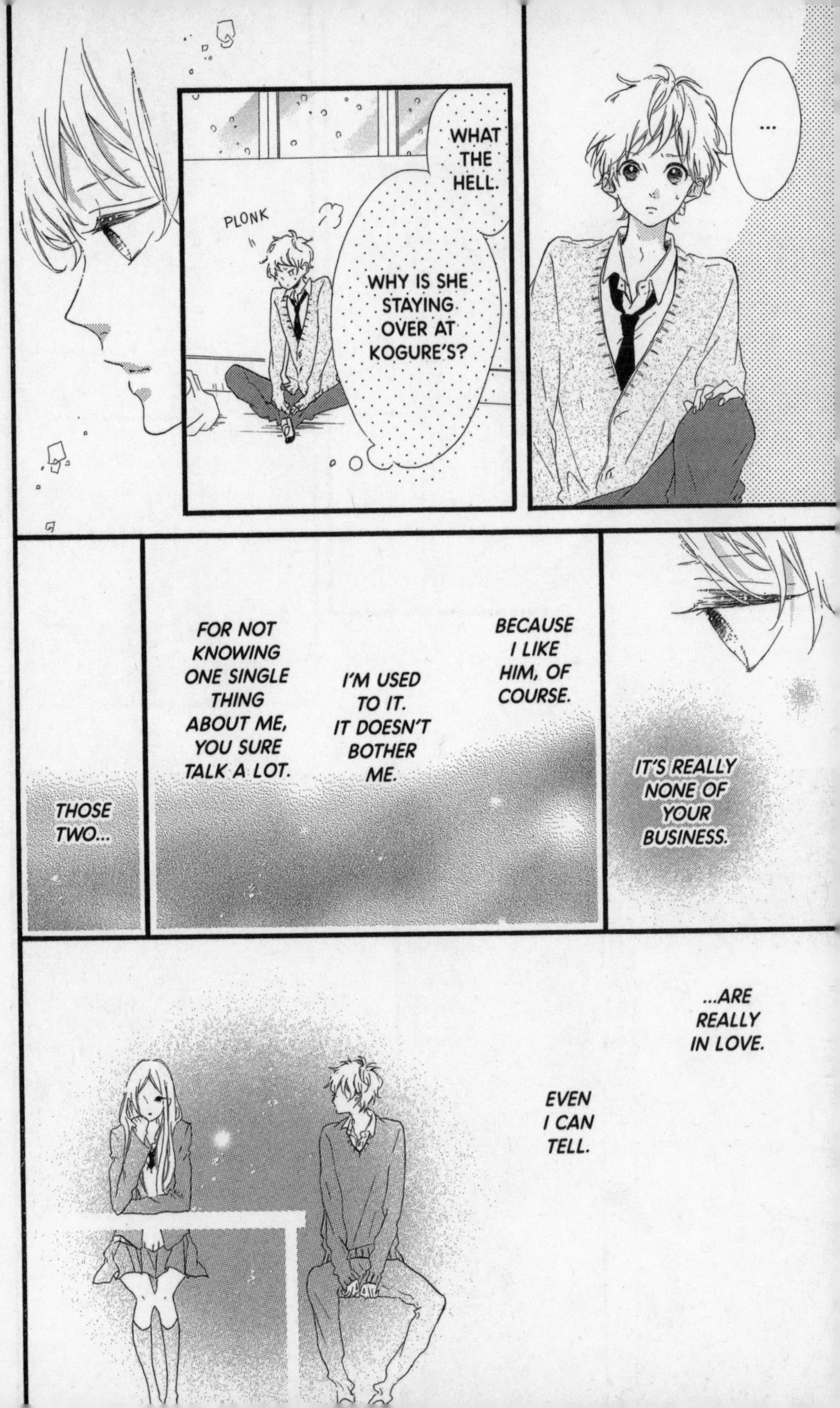
...
WHAT THE HELL.
PLONK
WHY IS SHE STAYING OVER AT KOGURE'S?
IT'S REALLY NONE OF YOUR BUSINESS.
BECAUSE I LIKE HIM, OF COURSE.
I'M USED TO IT. IT DOESN'T BOTHER ME.
FOR NOT KNOWING ONE SINGLE THING ABOUT ME, YOU SURE TALK A LOT.
THOSE TWO...
...ARE REALLY IN LOVE.
EVEN I CAN TELL.

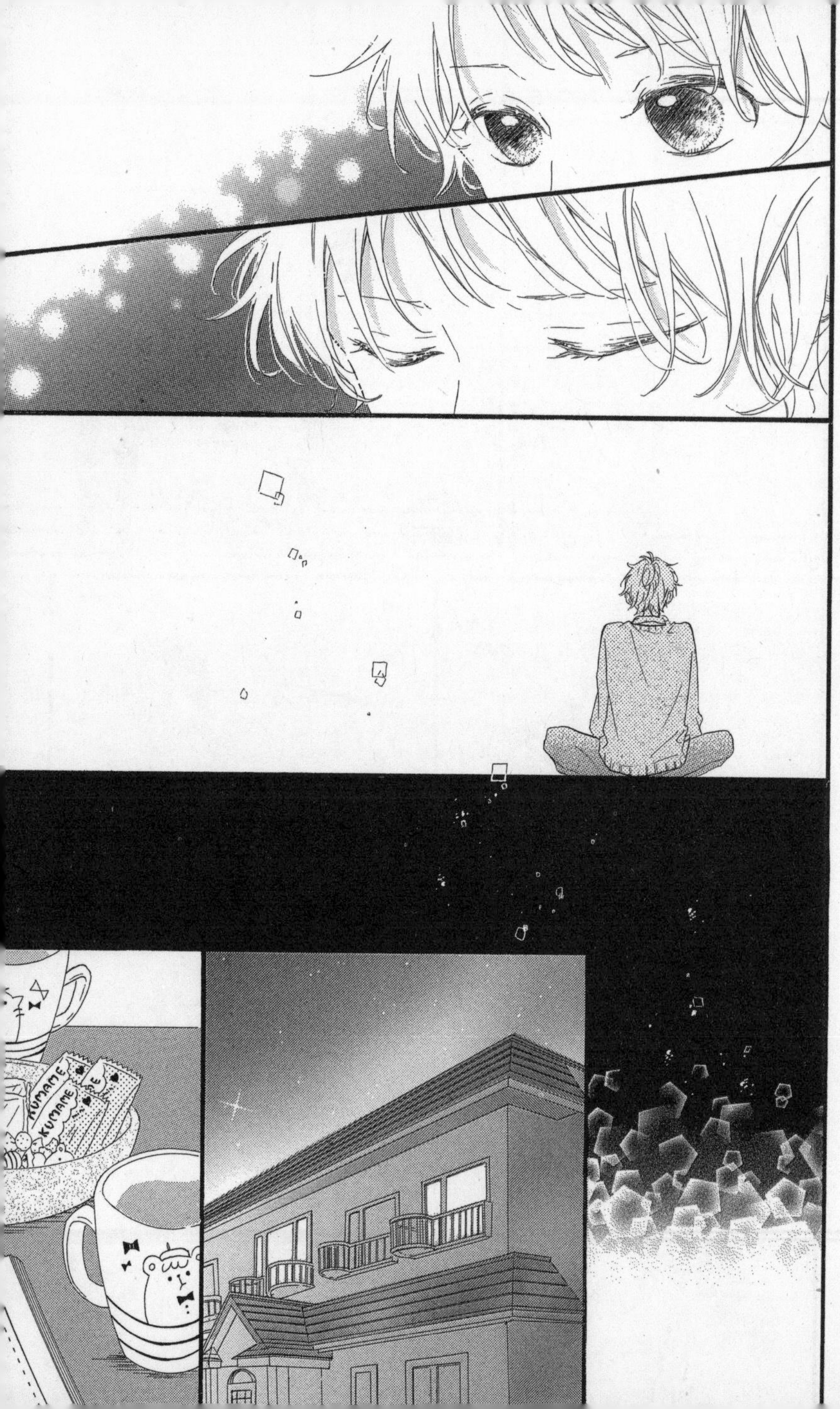
KUMAME
KUMAME

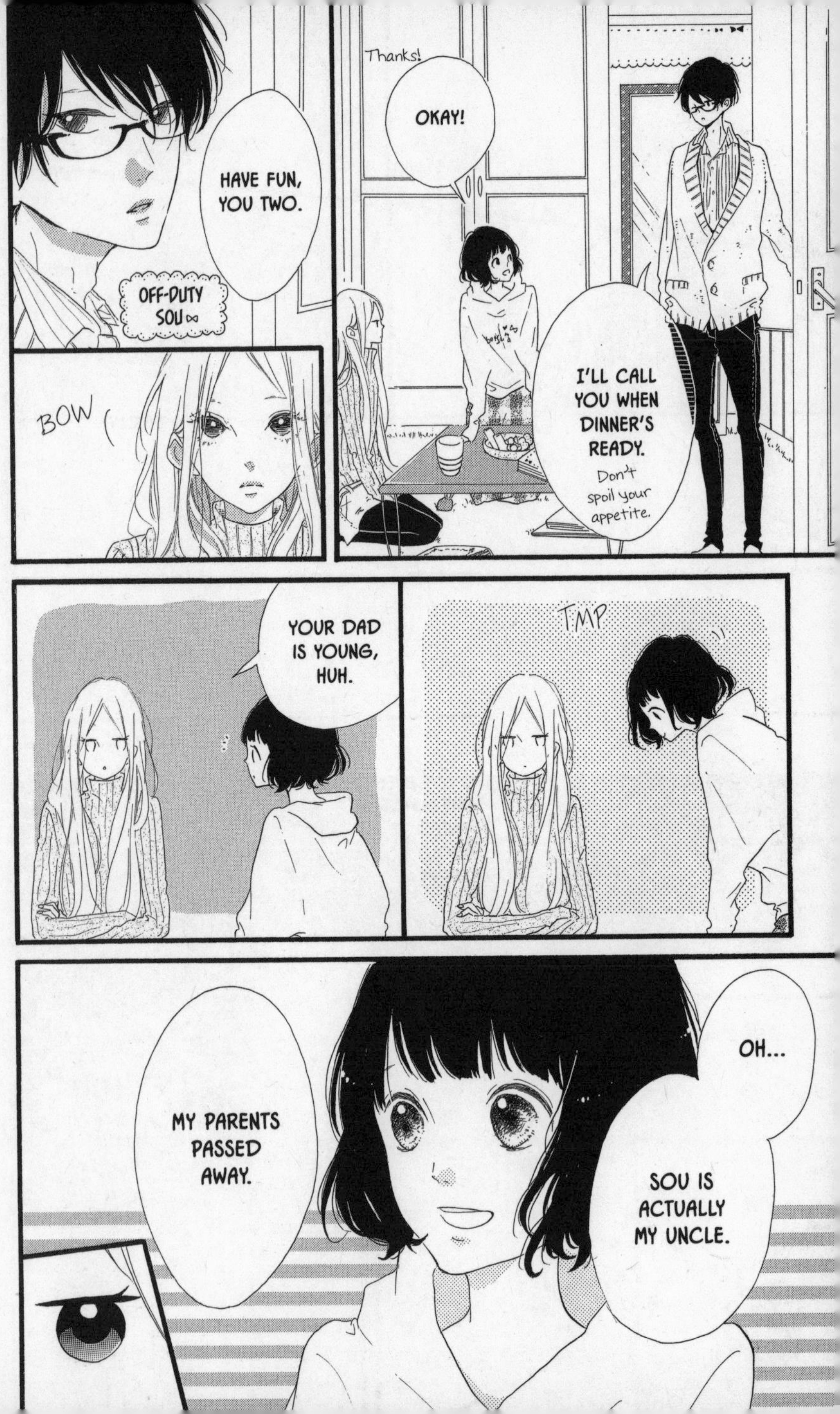
I'LL CALL YOU WHEN DINNER'S READY.
Don't spoil your appetite.
OKAY!
Thanks!
HAVE FUN, YOU TWO.
OFF-DUTY SOU∞
BOW
TMP
YOUR DAD IS YOUNG, HUH.
OH...
SOU IS ACTUALLY MY UNCLE.
MY PARENTS PASSED AWAY.

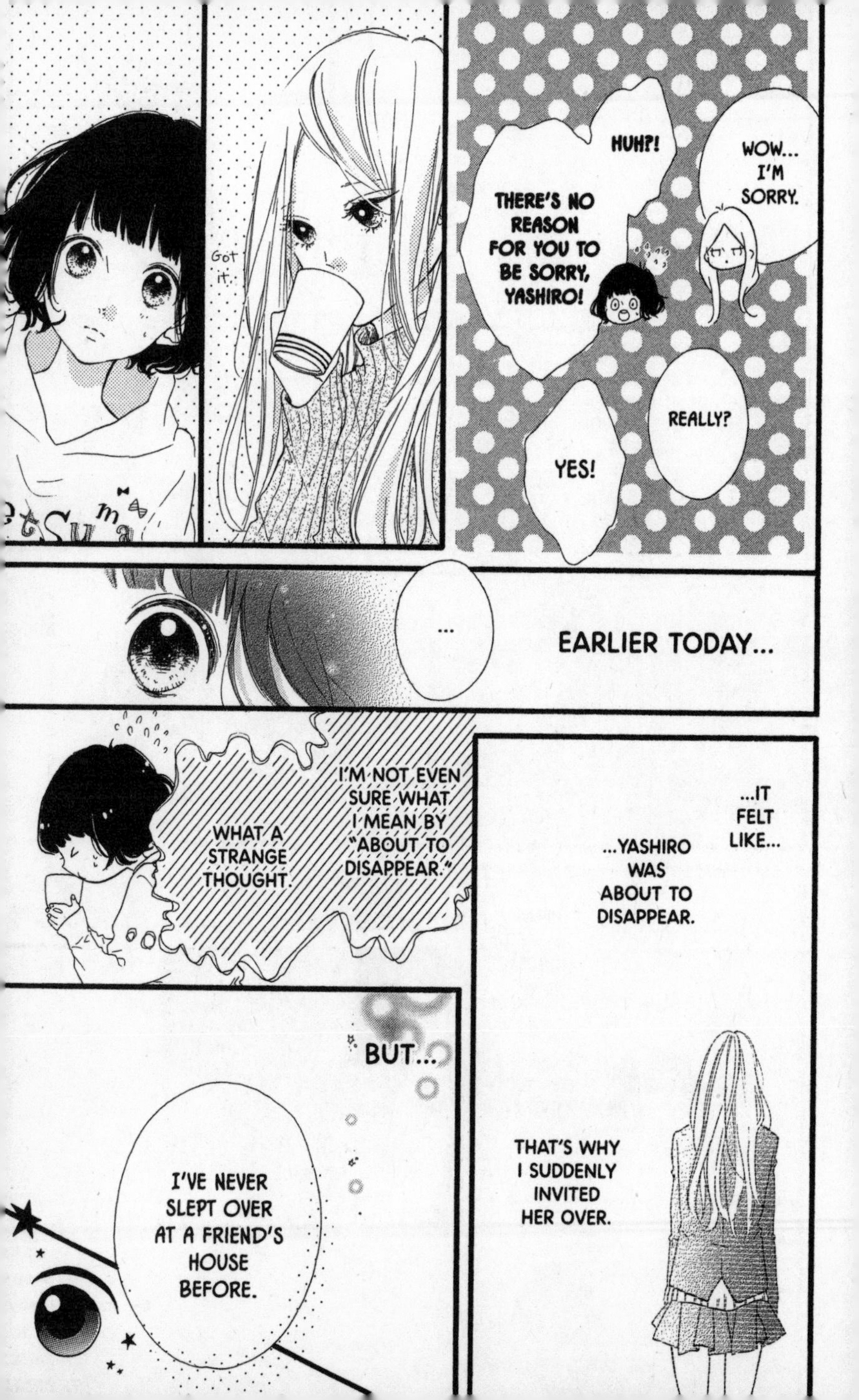
WOW... I'M SORRY.
HUH?!
THERE'S NO REASON FOR YOU TO BE SORRY, YASHIRO!
REALLY?
YES!
Got it.
EARLIER TODAY...
...
...IT FELT LIKE...
...YASHIRO WAS ABOUT TO DISAPPEAR.
THAT'S WHY I SUDDENLY INVITED HER OVER.
I'M NOT EVEN SURE WHAT I MEAN BY "ABOUT TO DISAPPEAR."
WHAT A STRANGE THOUGHT.
BUT...
I'VE NEVER SLEPT OVER AT A FRIEND'S HOUSE BEFORE.

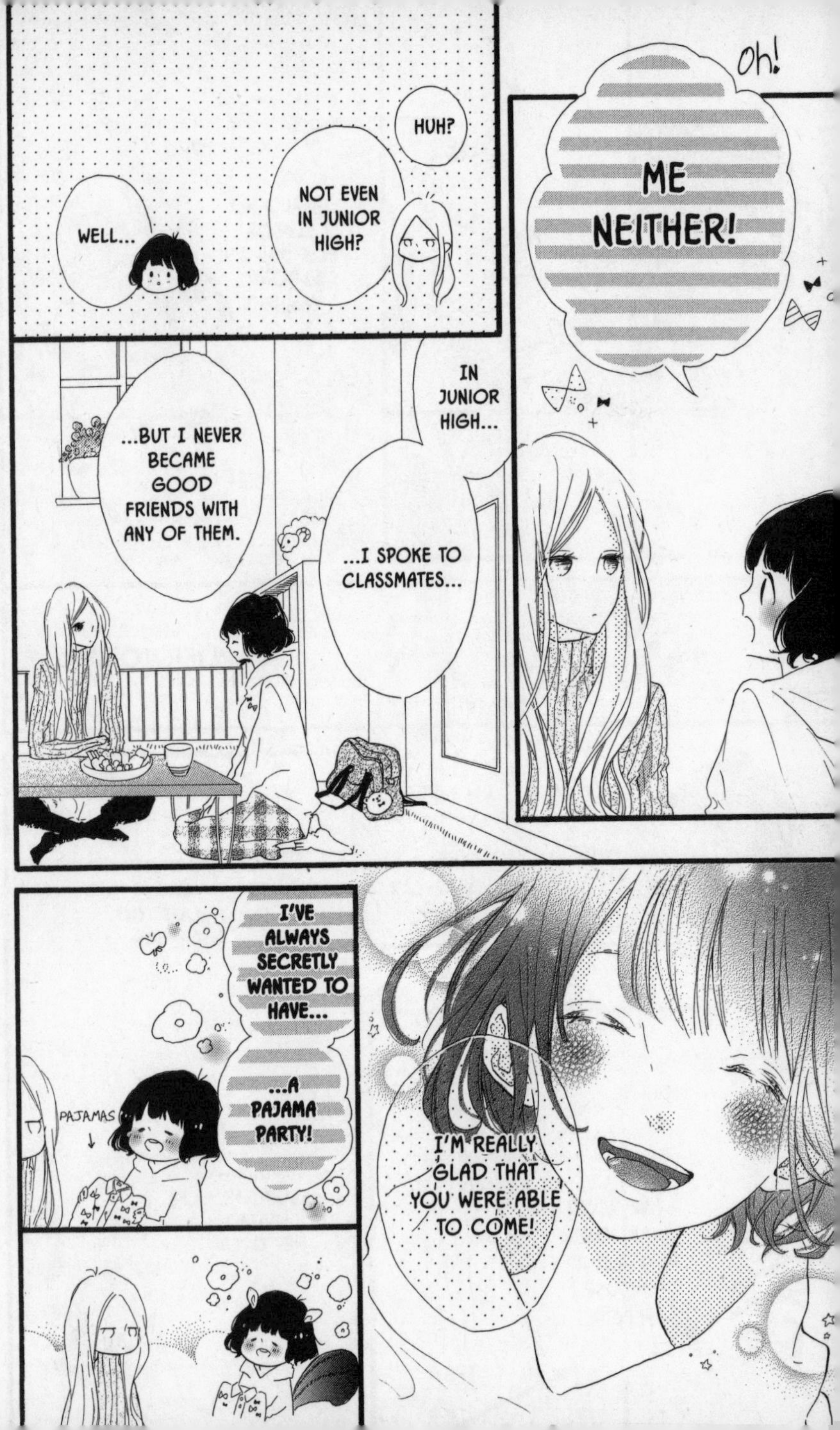
HUH?
NOT EVEN IN JUNIOR HIGH?
WELL...
IN JUNIOR HIGH...
...I SPOKE TO CLASSMATES...
...BUT I NEVER BECAME GOOD FRIENDS WITH ANY OF THEM.
Oh!
ME NEITHER!
I'M REALLY GLAD THAT YOU WERE ABLE TO COME!
I'VE ALWAYS SECRETLY WANTED TO HAVE...
...A PAJAMA PARTY!
PAJAMAS

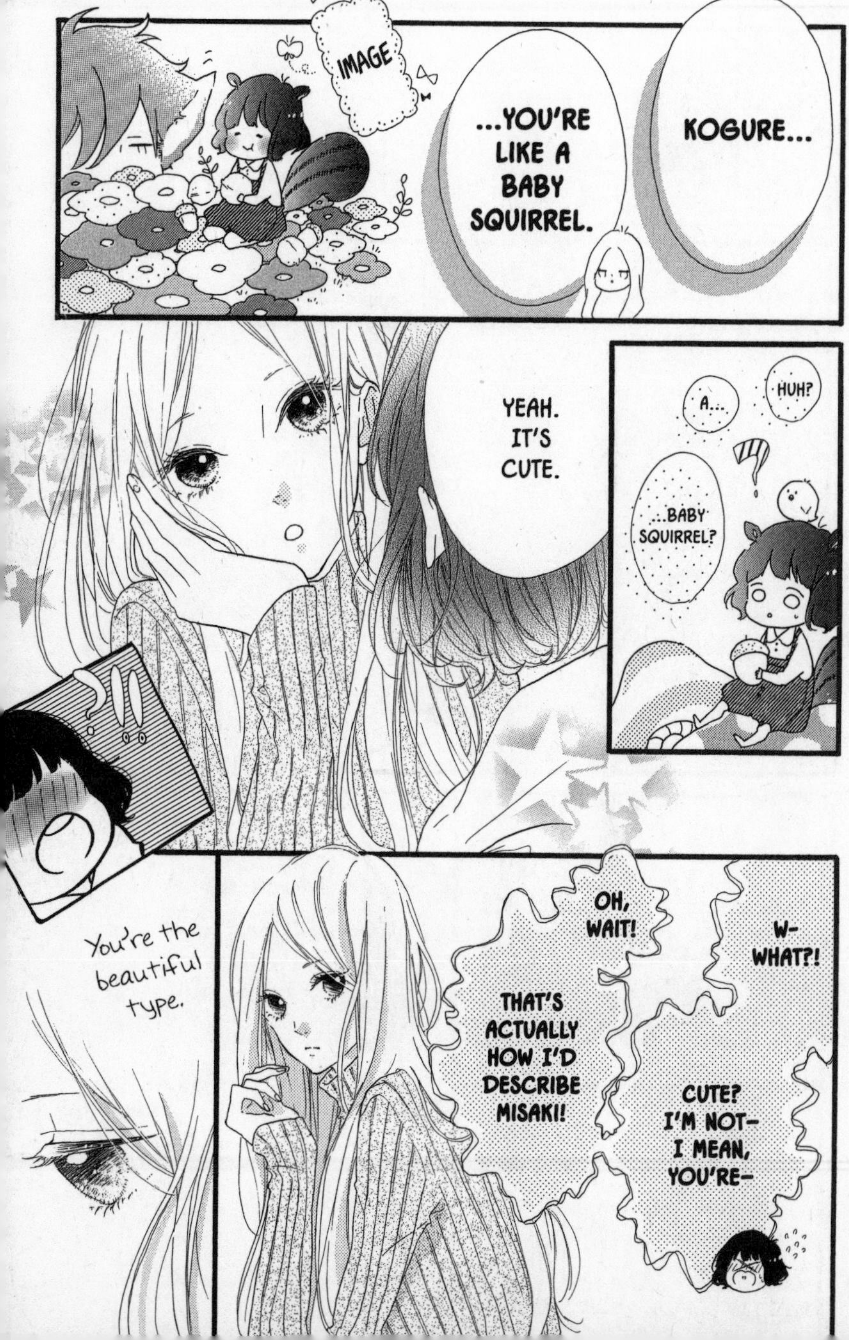
KOGURE...
...YOU'RE LIKE A BABY SQUIRREL.
IMAGE
HUH?
A...
...BABY SQUIRREL?
YEAH. IT'S CUTE.
W-WHAT?!
CUTE? I'M NOT- I MEAN, YOU'RE-
OH, WAIT!
THAT'S ACTUALLY HOW I'D DESCRIBE MISAKI!
You're the beautiful type.

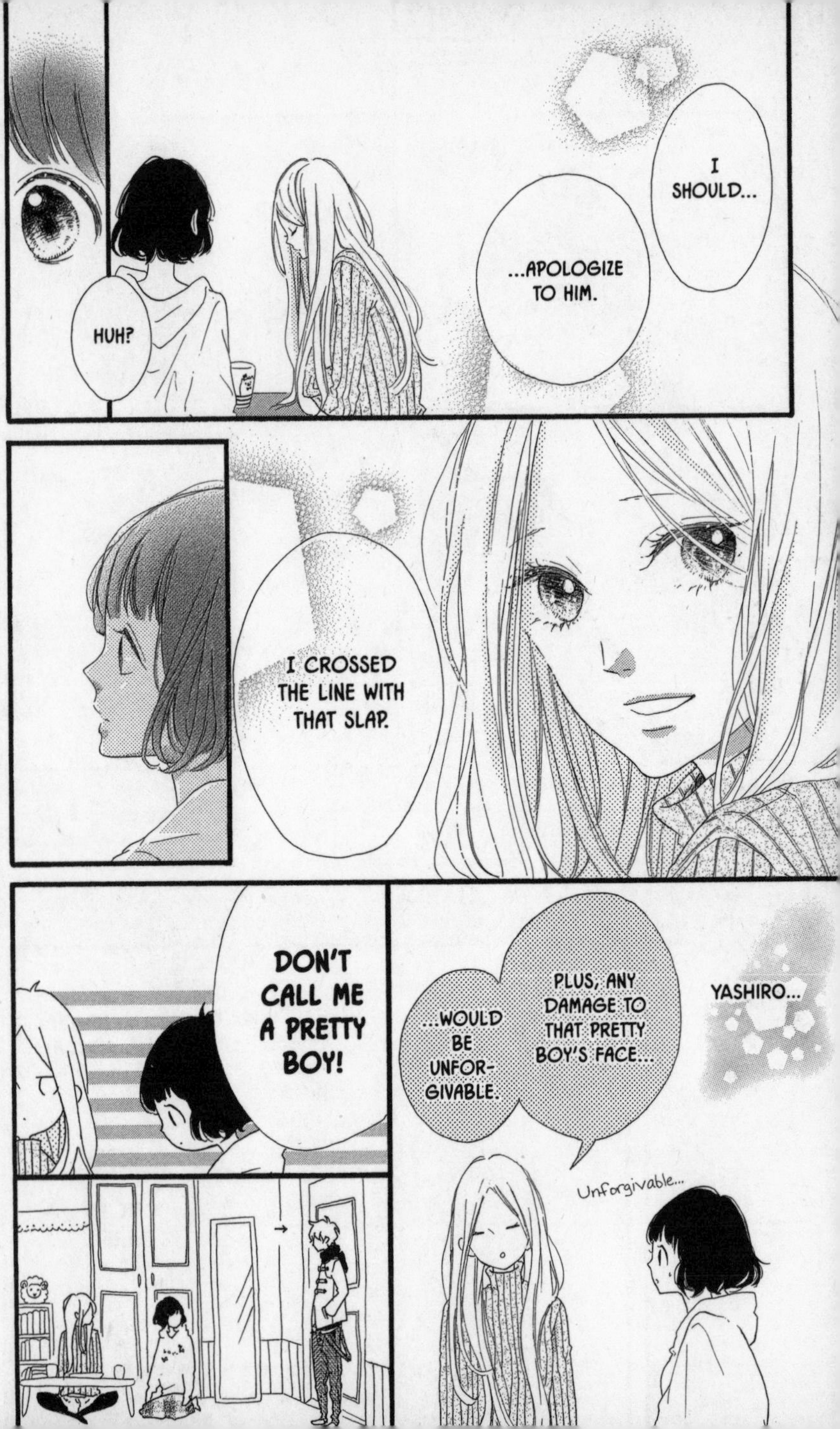
I SHOULD...
...APOLOGIZE TO HIM.
HUH?
I CROSSED THE LINE WITH THAT SLAP.
YASHIRO...
PLUS, ANY DAMAGE TO THAT PRETTY BOY'S FACE...
...WOULD BE UNFORGIVABLE.
Unforgivable...
DON'T CALL ME A PRETTY BOY!

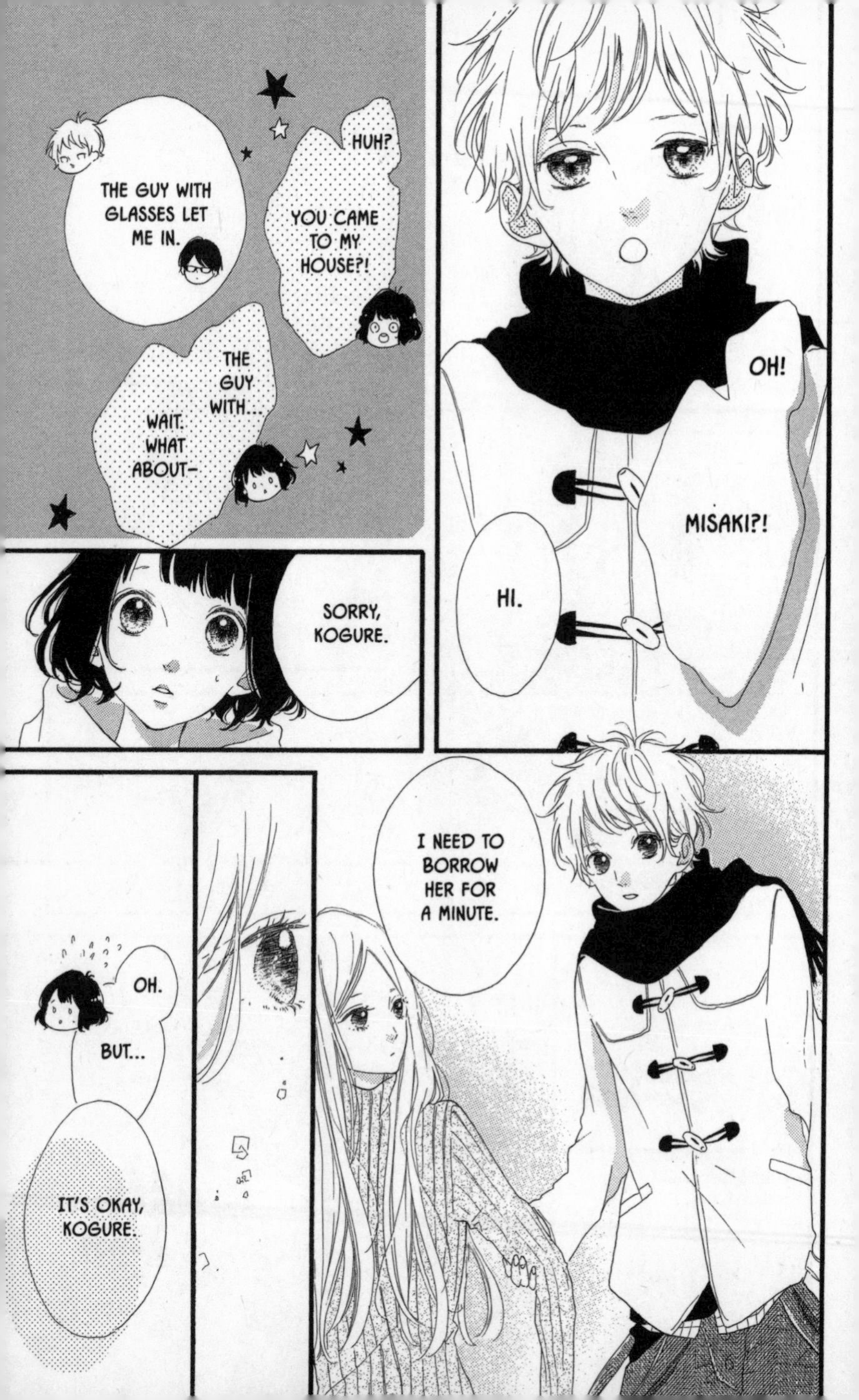
OH!
MISAKI?!
HI.
HUH?
YOU CAME TO MY HOUSE?!
THE GUY WITH GLASSES LET ME IN.
THE GUY WITH...
WAIT. WHAT ABOUT-
SORRY, KOGURE.
I NEED TO BORROW HER FOR A MINUTE.
OH.
BUT...
IT'S OKAY, KOGURE.

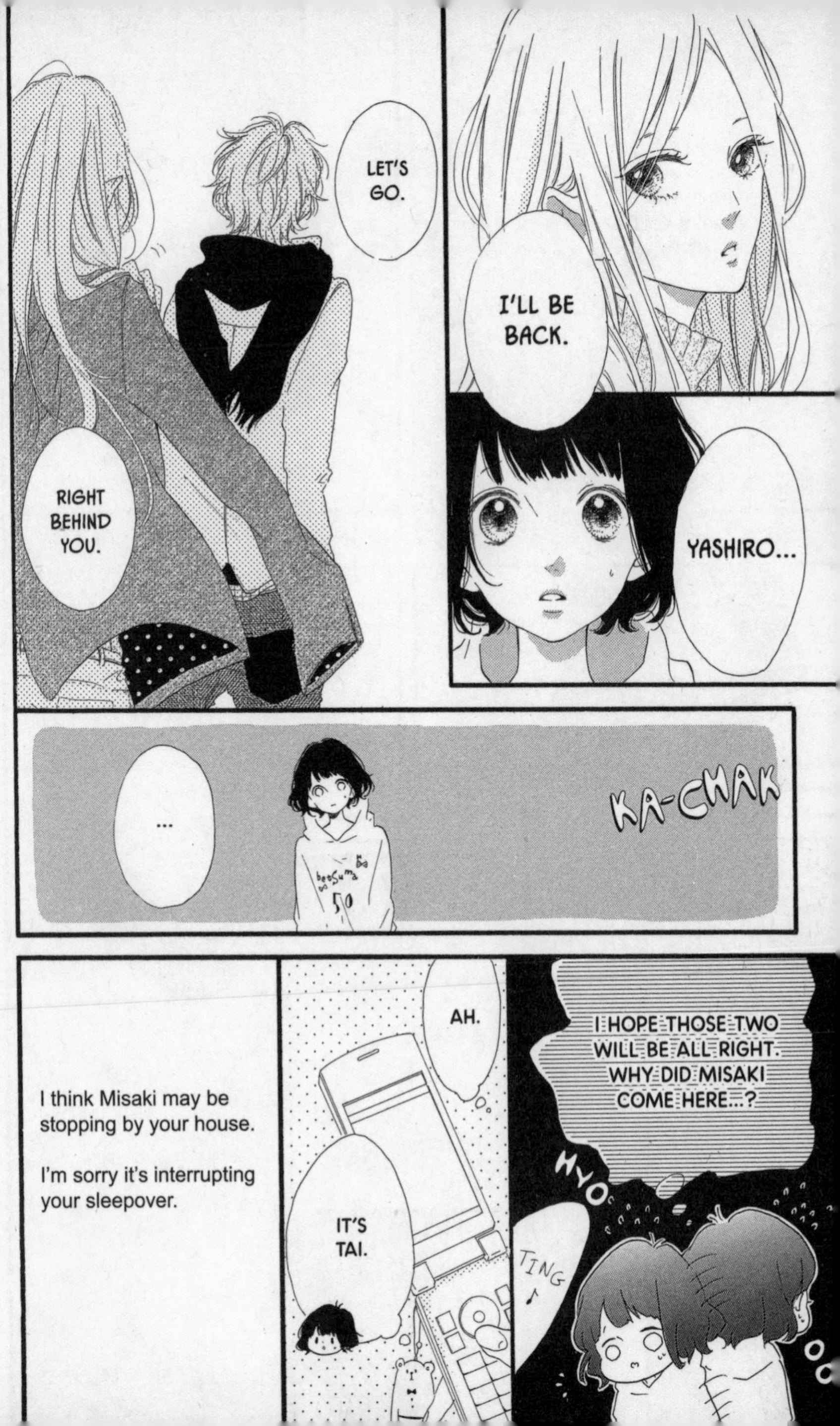

I'LL BE BACK.
YASHIRO...
LET'S GO.
RIGHT BEHIND YOU.
KA-CHAK
...
I HOPE THOSE TWO WILL BE ALL RIGHT. WHY DID MISAKI COME HERE...?
HYO
TING
AH.
IT'S TAI.
I think Misaki may be stopping by your house.
I'm sorry it's interrupting your sleepover.

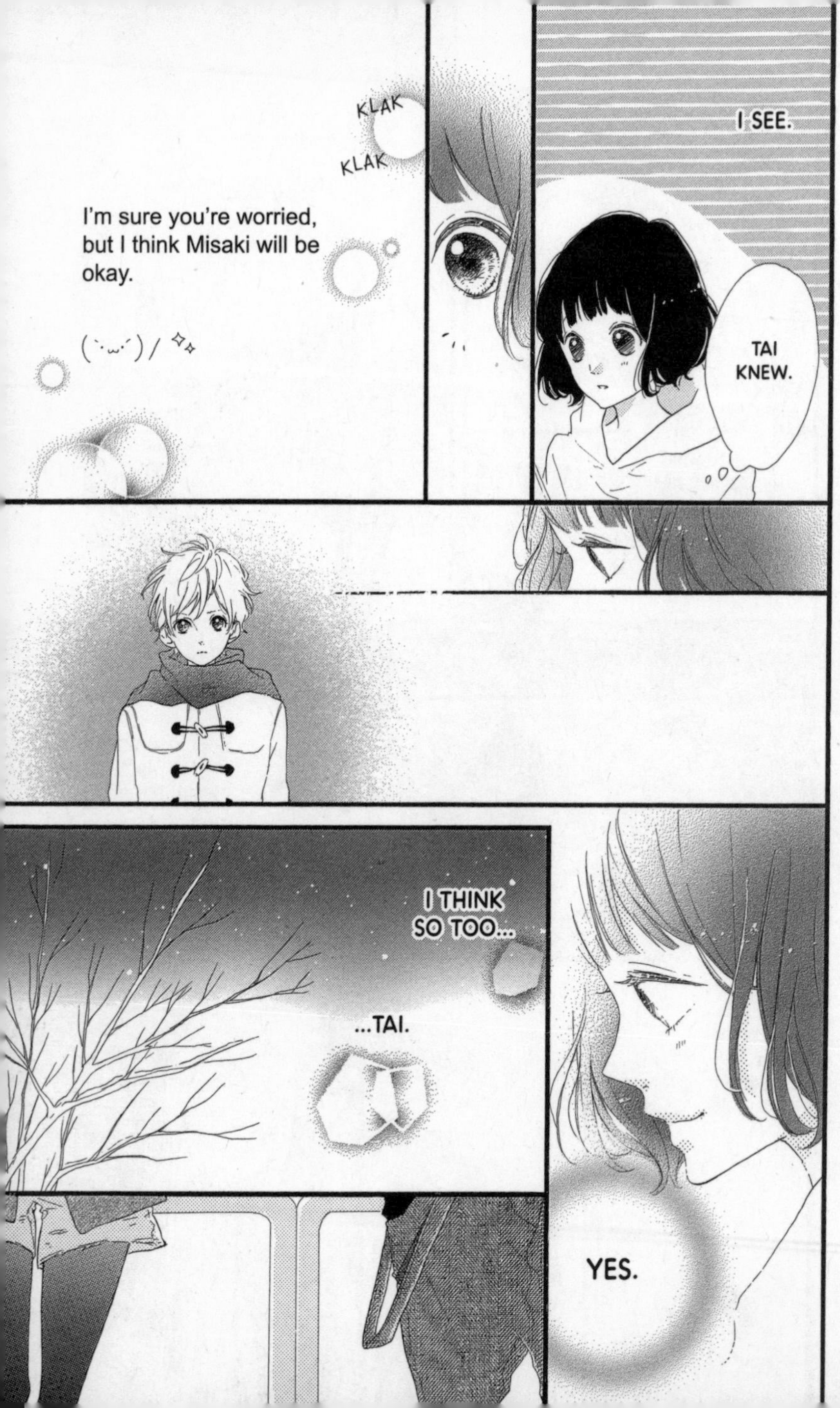
I SEE.
TAI KNEW.
KLAK
KLAK
I'm sure you're worried, but I think Misaki will be okay.
(`･ω･´)/ ✧
YES.
I THINK SO TOO...
...TAI.

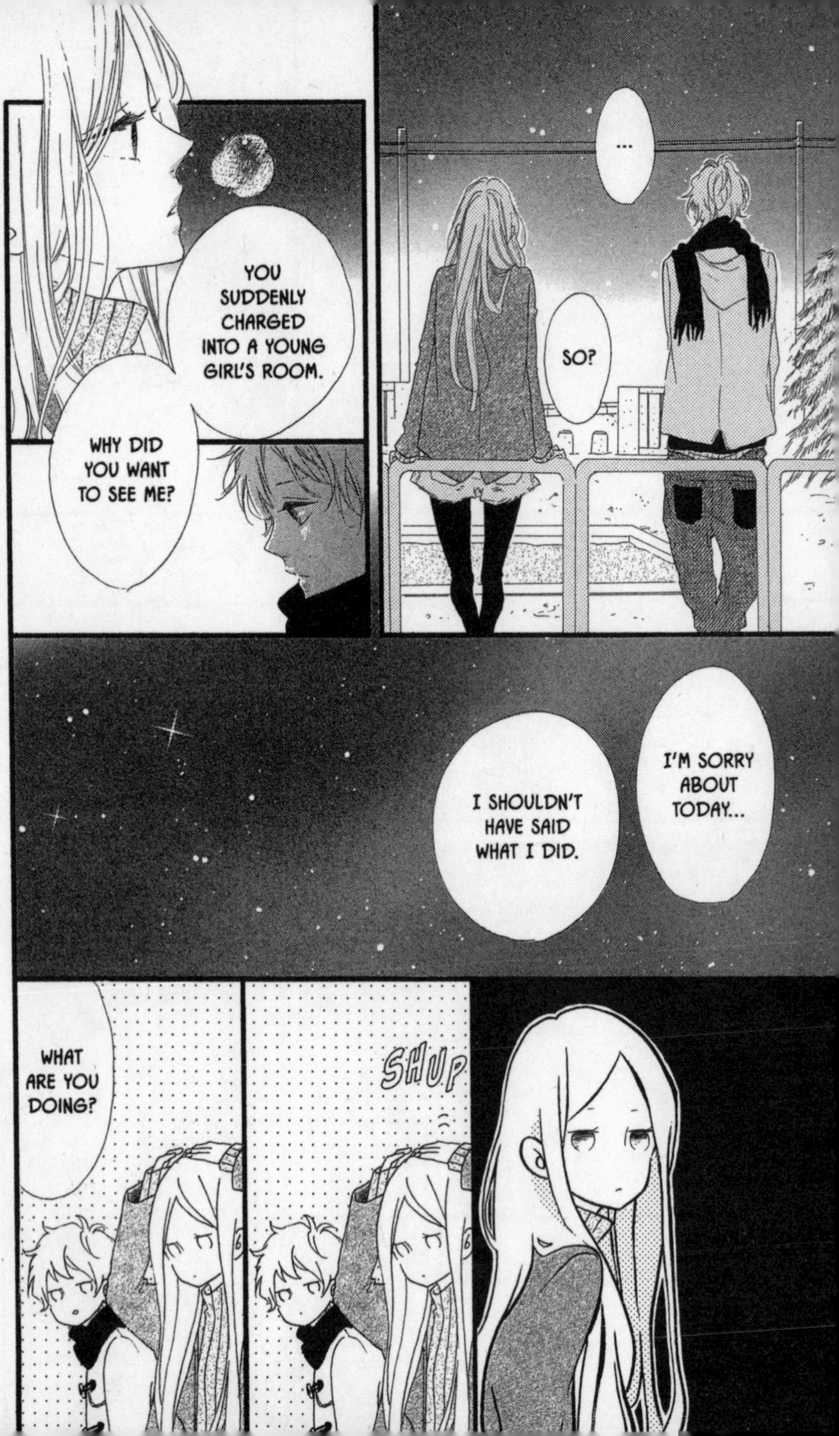
...
SO?
YOU SUDDENLY CHARGED INTO A YOUNG GIRL'S ROOM.
WHY DID YOU WANT TO SEE ME?
I'M SORRY ABOUT TODAY...
I SHOULDN'T HAVE SAID WHAT I DID.
SHUP
WHAT ARE YOU DOING?

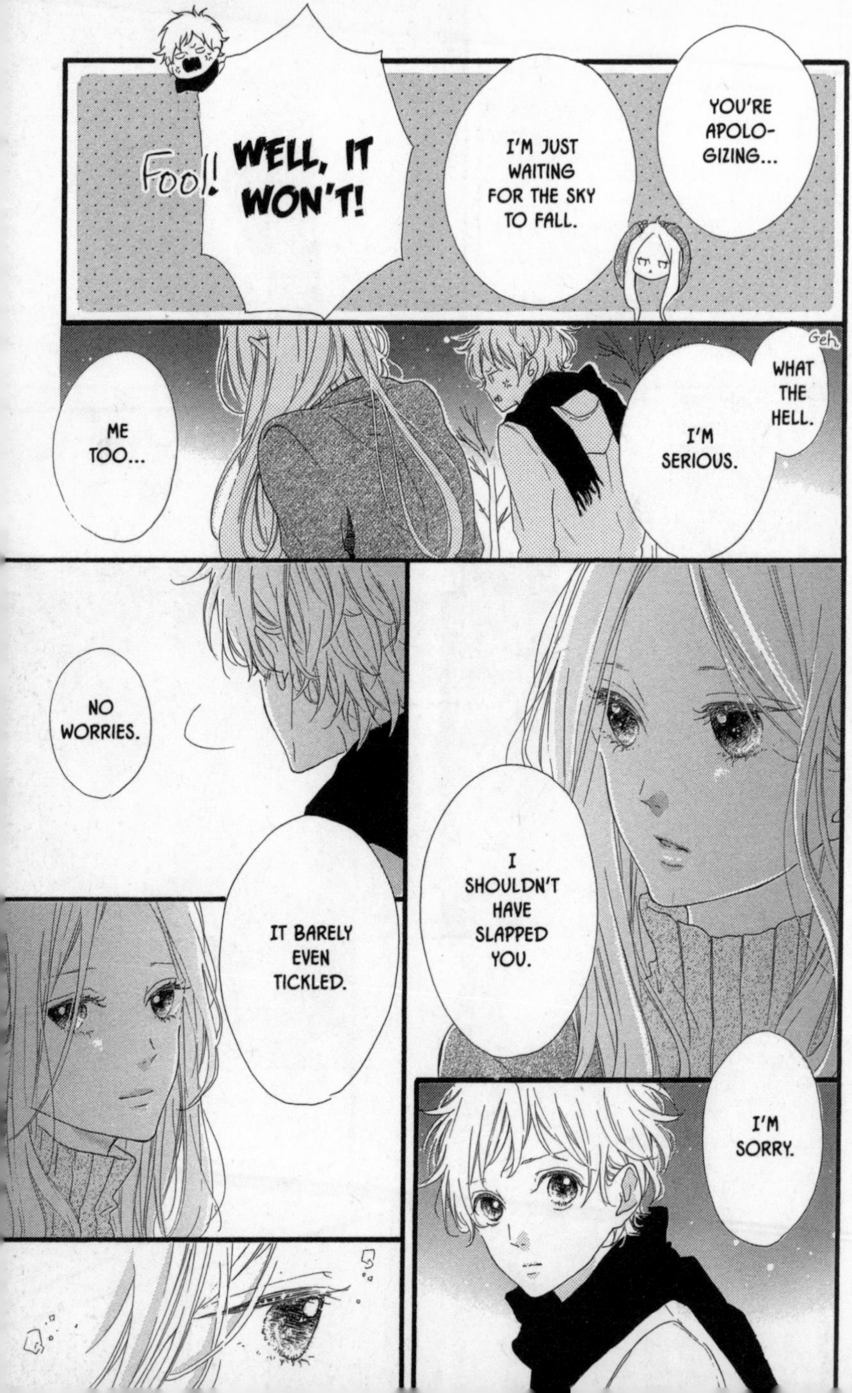
YOU'RE APOLO-GIZING...
I'M JUST WAITING FOR THE SKY TO FALL.
WELL, IT WON'T!
Fool!
Geh
WHAT THE HELL.
I'M SERIOUS.
ME TOO...
I SHOULDN'T HAVE SLAPPED YOU.
I'M SORRY.
NO WORRIES.
IT BARELY EVEN TICKLED.

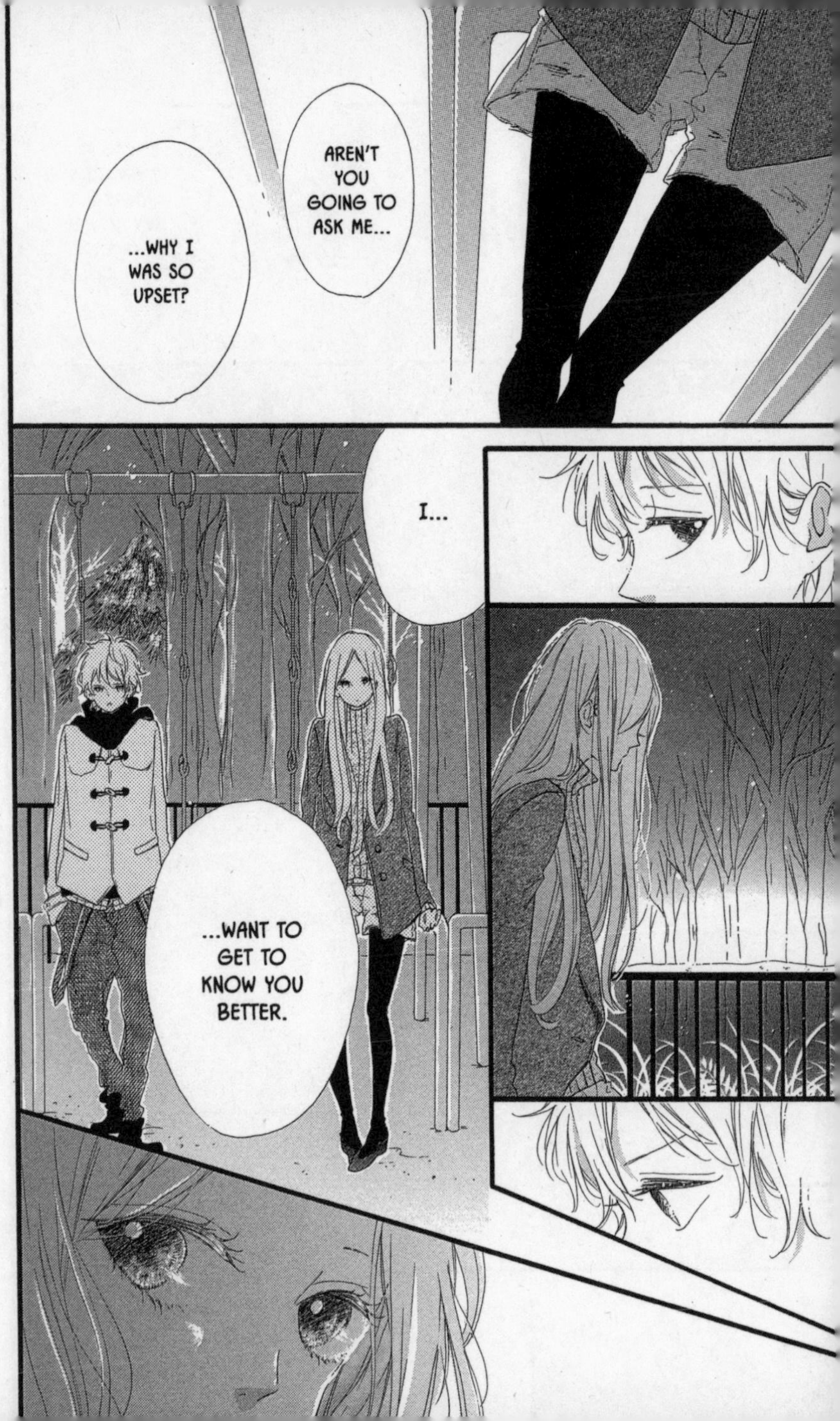
AREN'T YOU GOING TO ASK ME...
...WHY I WAS SO UPSET?
I...
...WANT TO GET TO KNOW YOU BETTER.

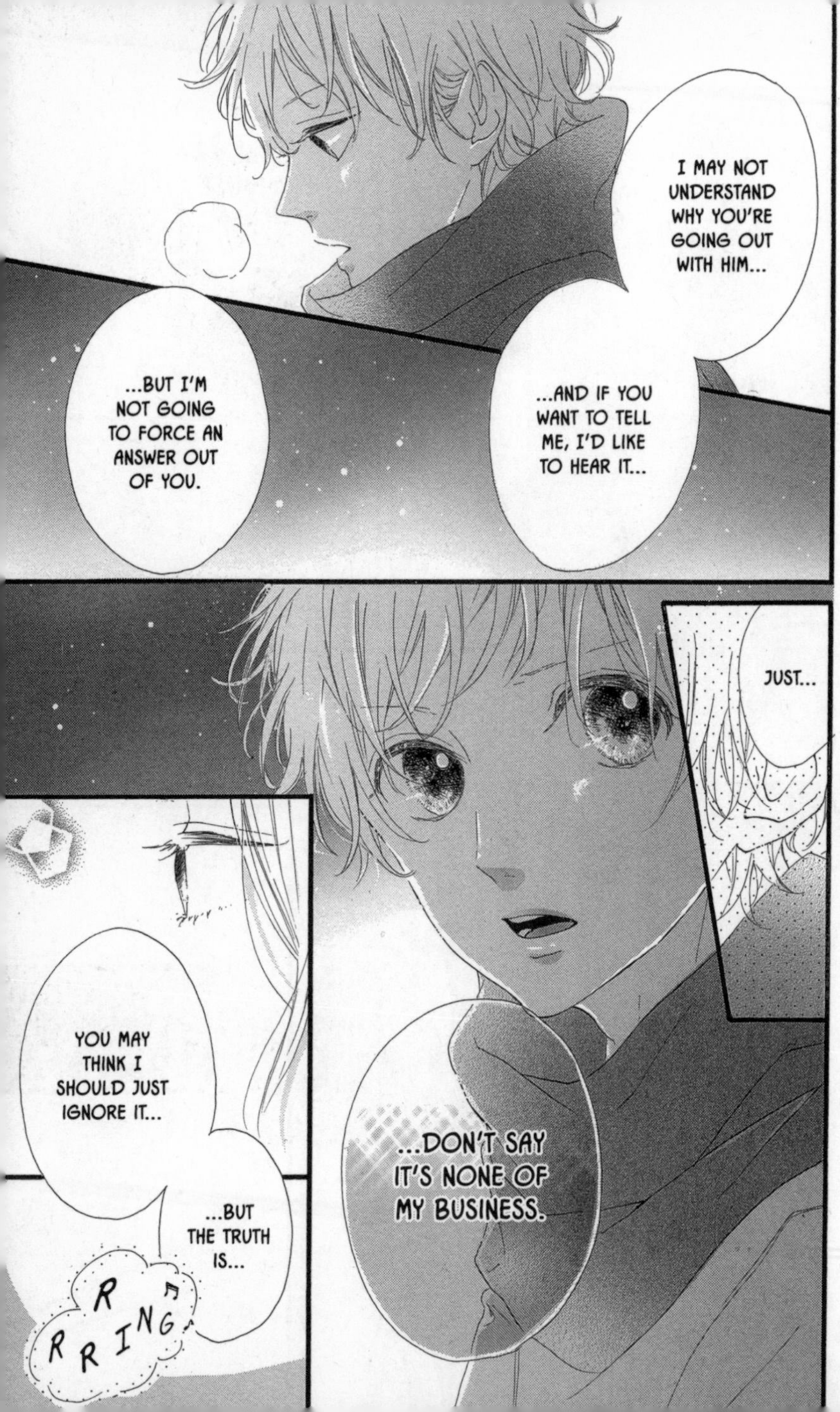
I MAY NOT UNDERSTAND WHY YOU'RE GOING OUT WITH HIM...
...AND IF YOU WANT TO TELL ME, I'D LIKE TO HEAR IT...
...BUT I'M NOT GOING TO FORCE AN ANSWER OUT OF YOU.
JUST...
...DON'T SAY IT'S NONE OF MY BUSINESS.
YOU MAY THINK I SHOULD JUST IGNORE IT...
...BUT THE TRUTH IS...
RRRING

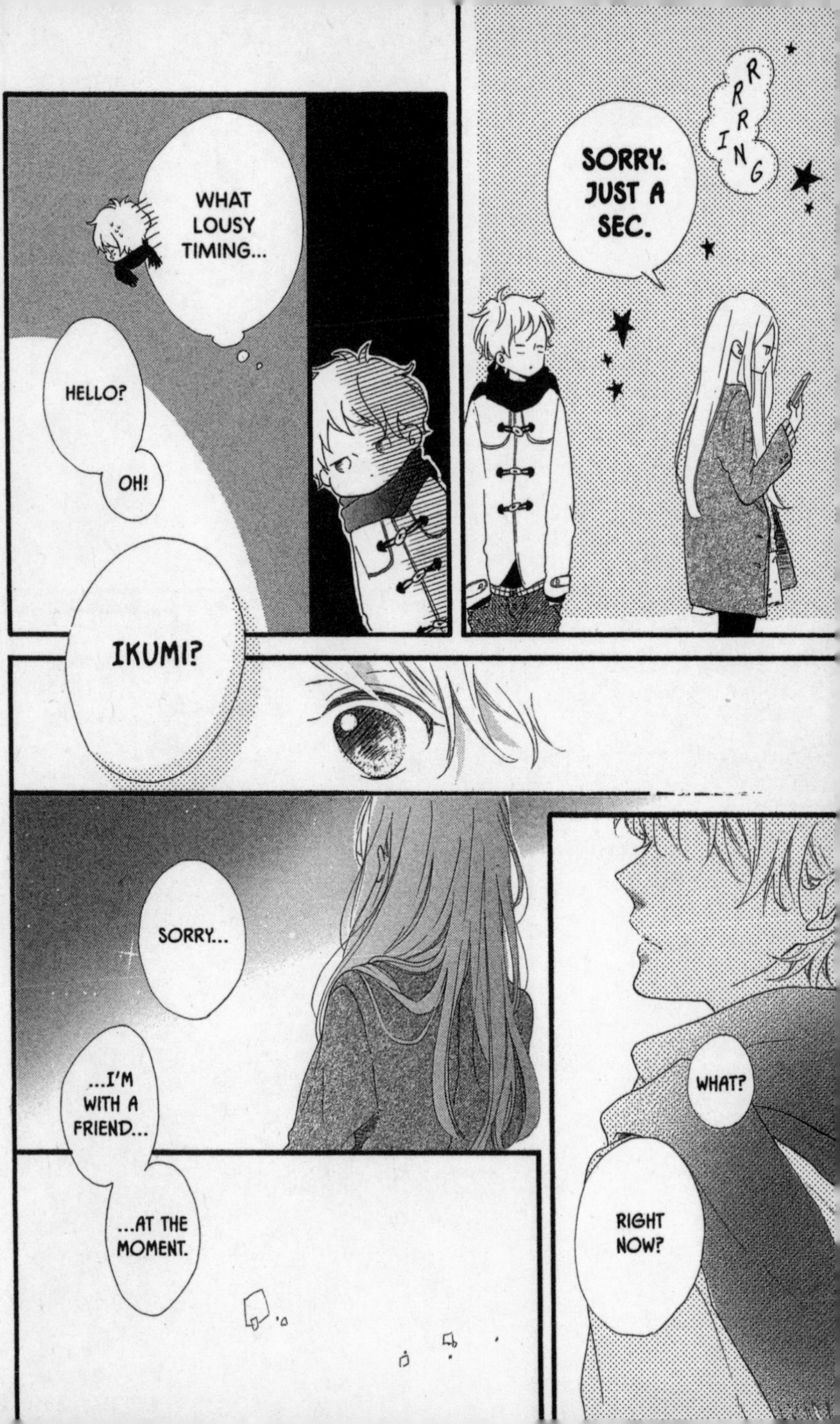
RRRING
SORRY. JUST A SEC.
WHAT LOUSY TIMING...
HELLO?
OH!
IKUMI?
WHAT?
RIGHT NOW?
SORRY...
...I'M WITH A FRIEND...
...AT THE MOMENT.

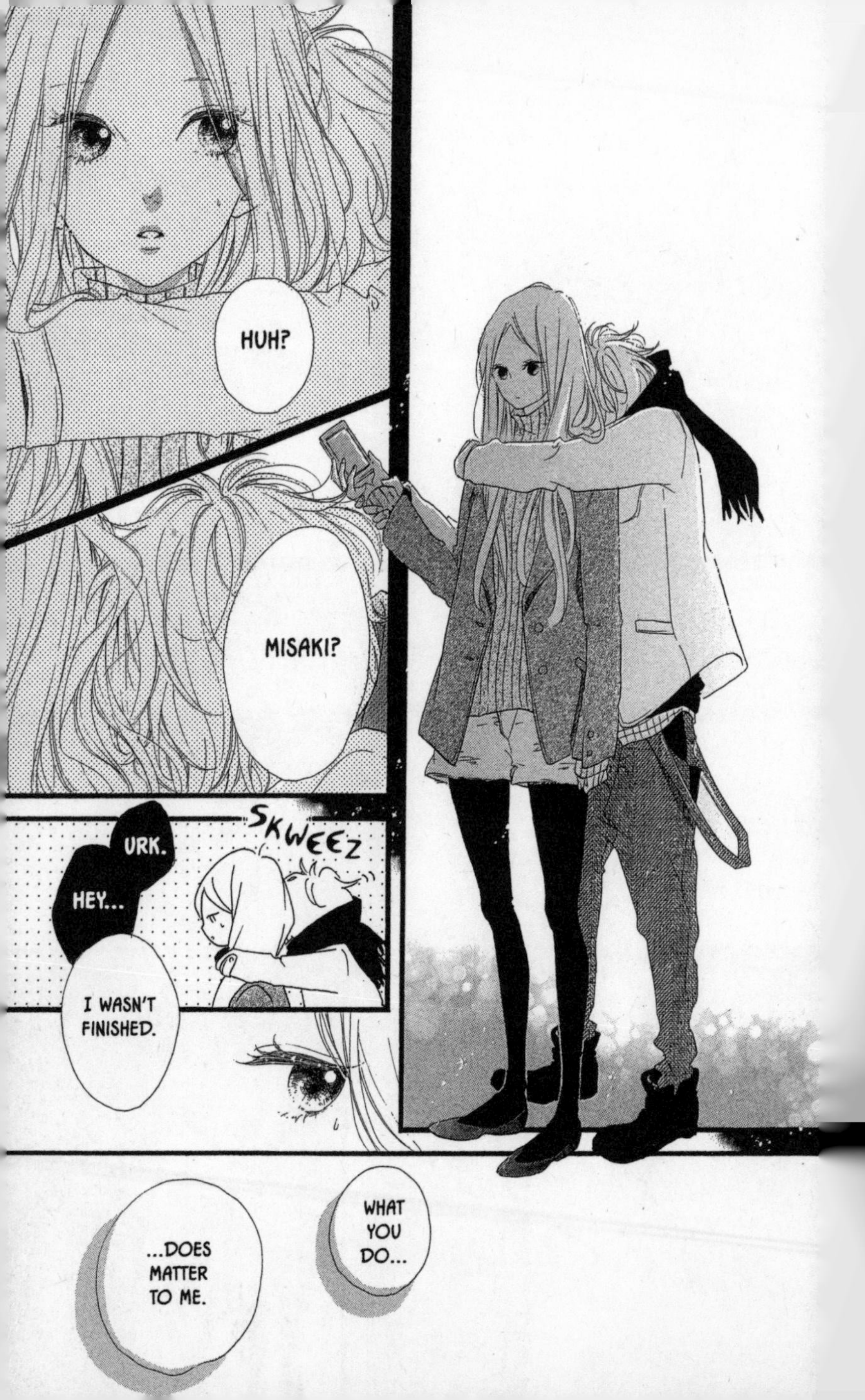
HUH?
MISAKI?
SKWEEZ
URK.
HEY...
I WASN'T FINISHED.
WHAT YOU DO...
...DOES MATTER TO ME.

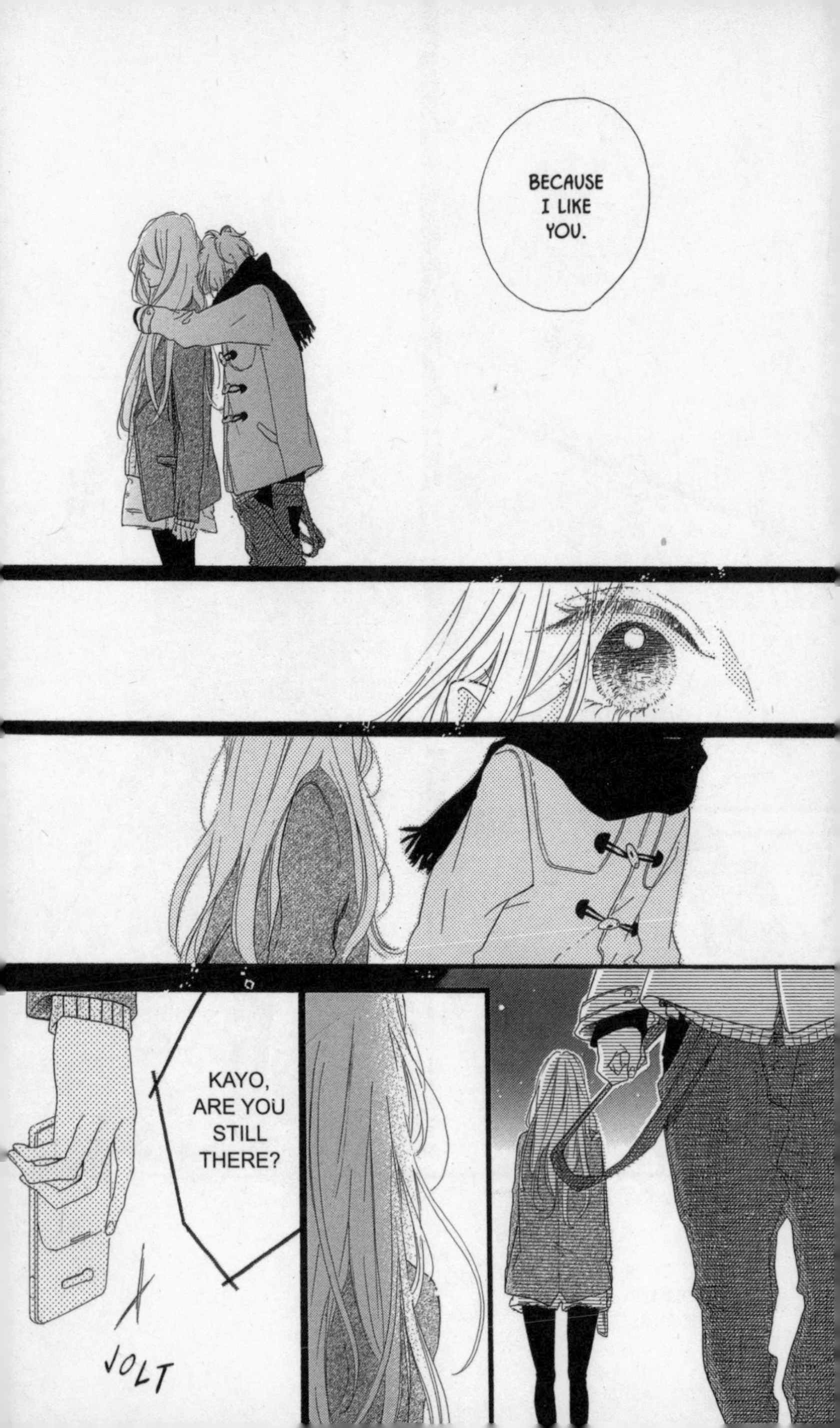
BECAUSE I LIKE YOU.
KAYO, ARE YOU STILL THERE?
JOLT

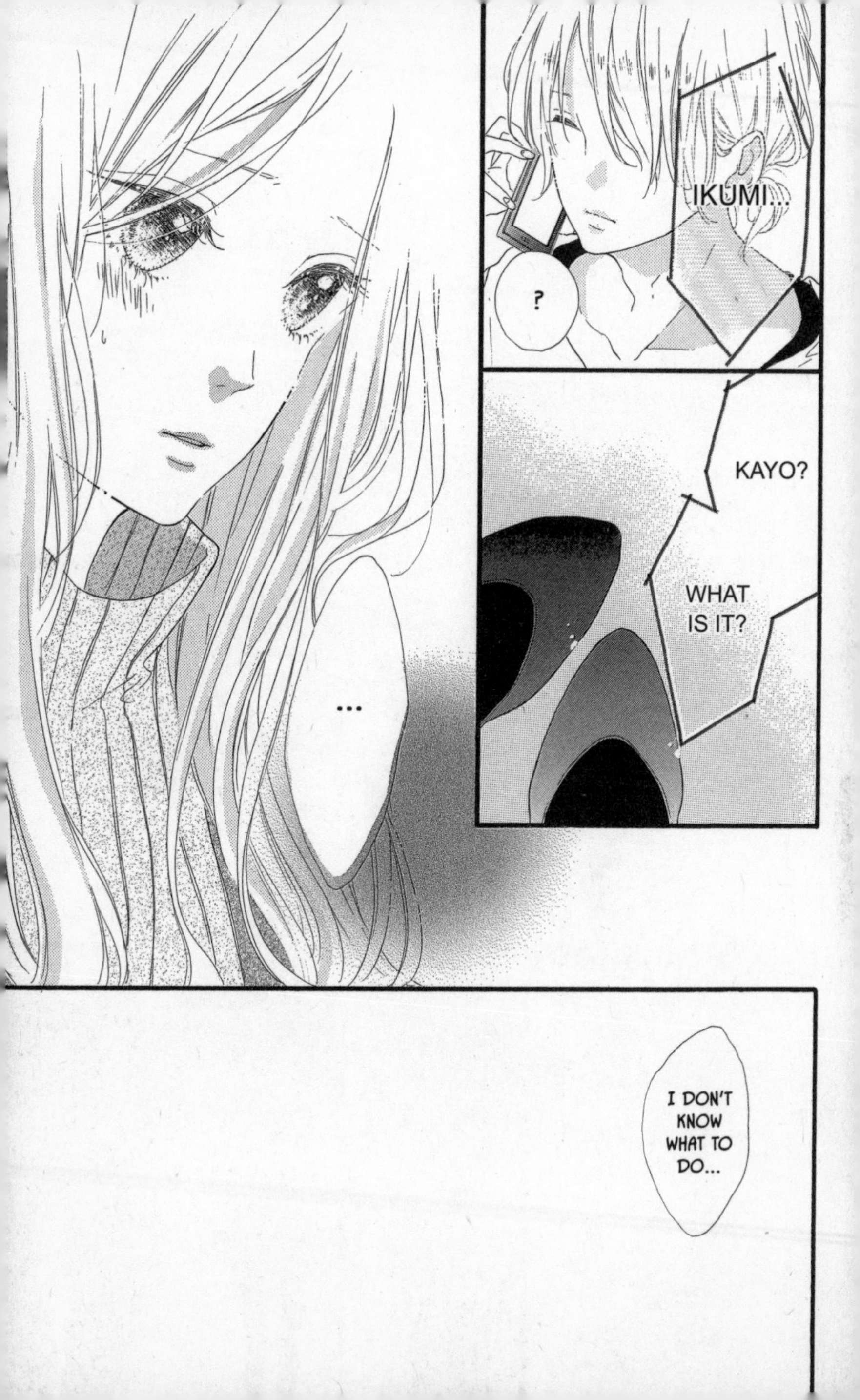
IKUMI...
?
KAYO?
WHAT IS IT?
...
I DON'T KNOW WHAT TO DO...

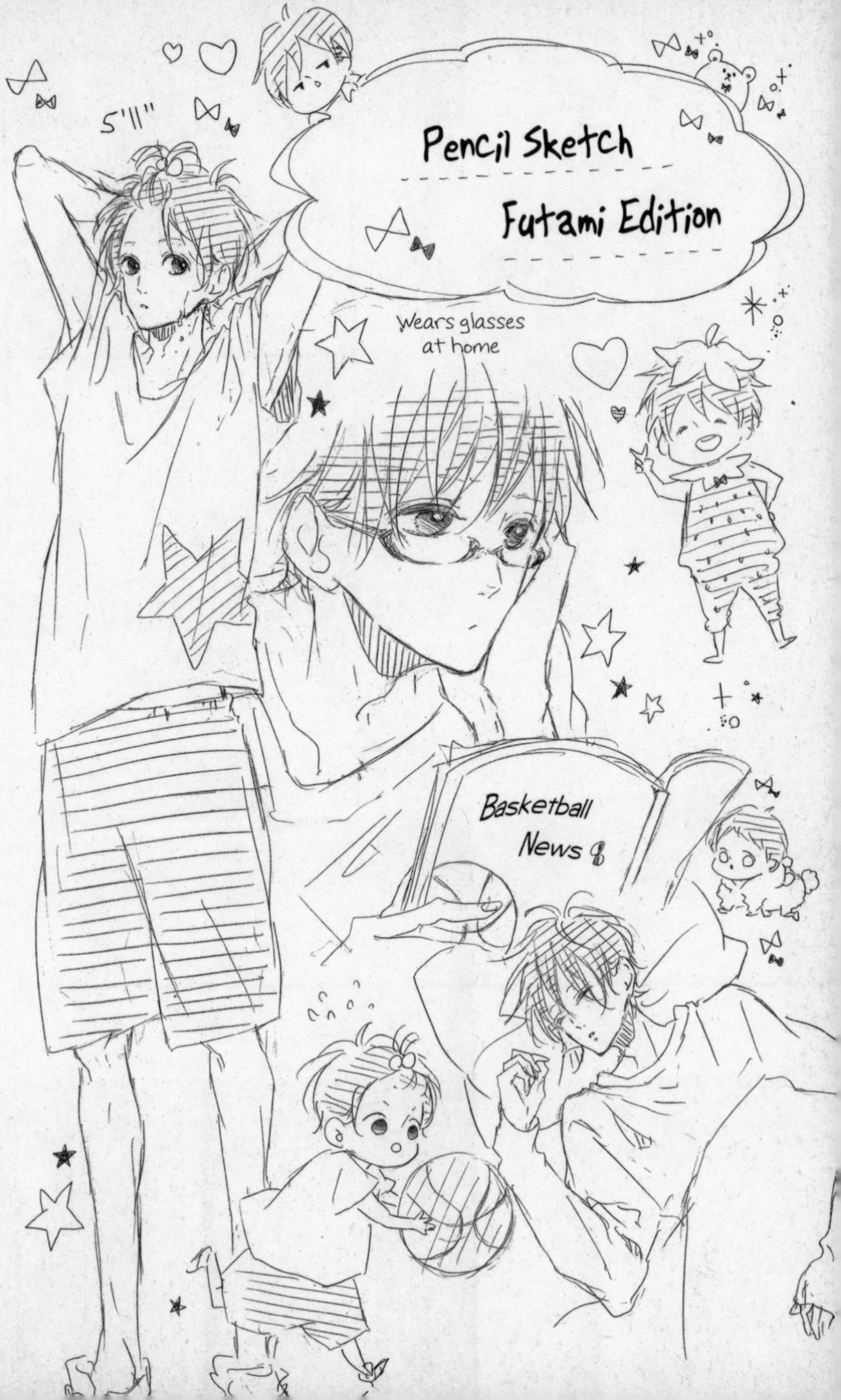
Pencil Sketch
Futami Edition
5'11"
Wears glasses at home
Basketball News

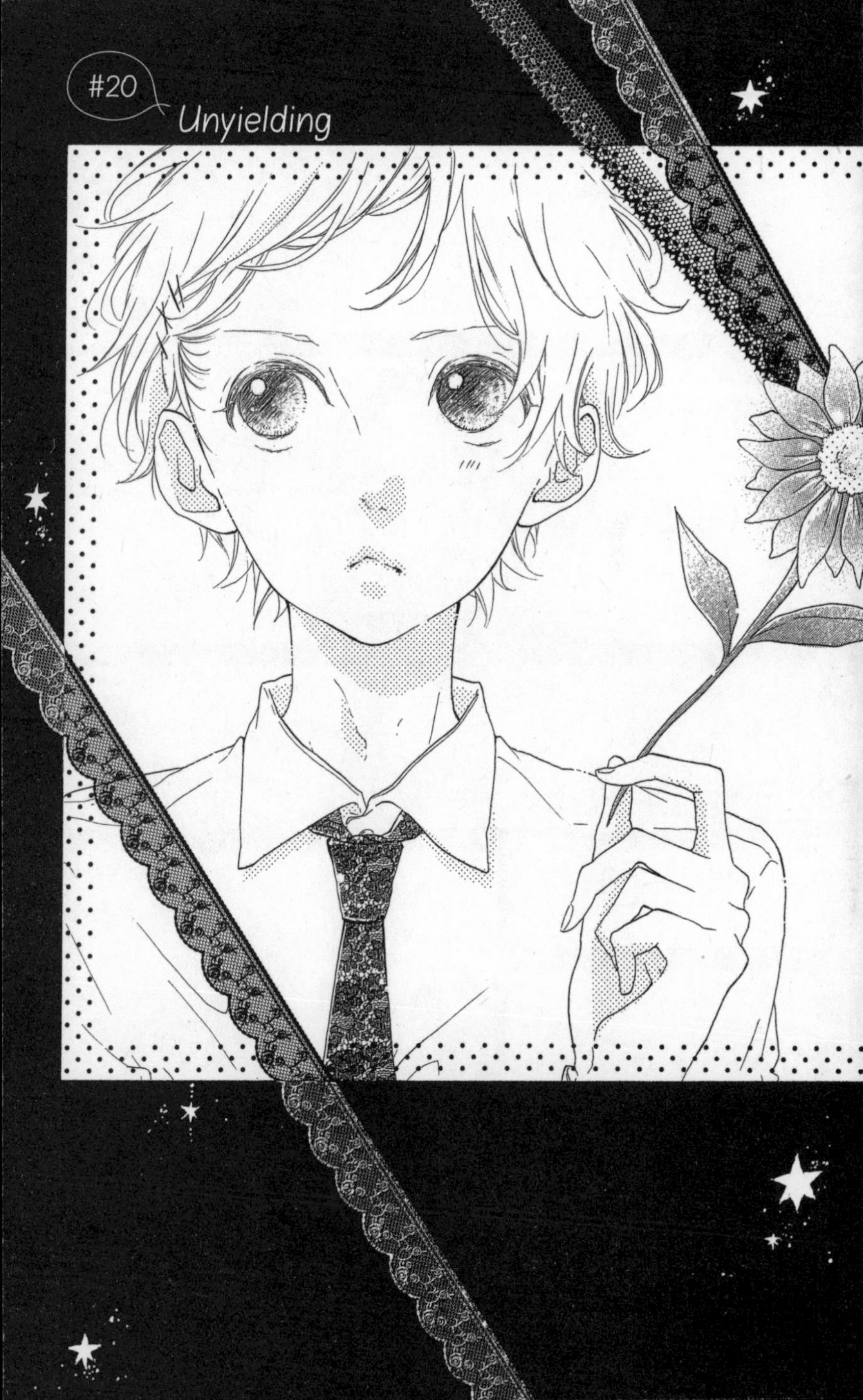
#20
Unyielding

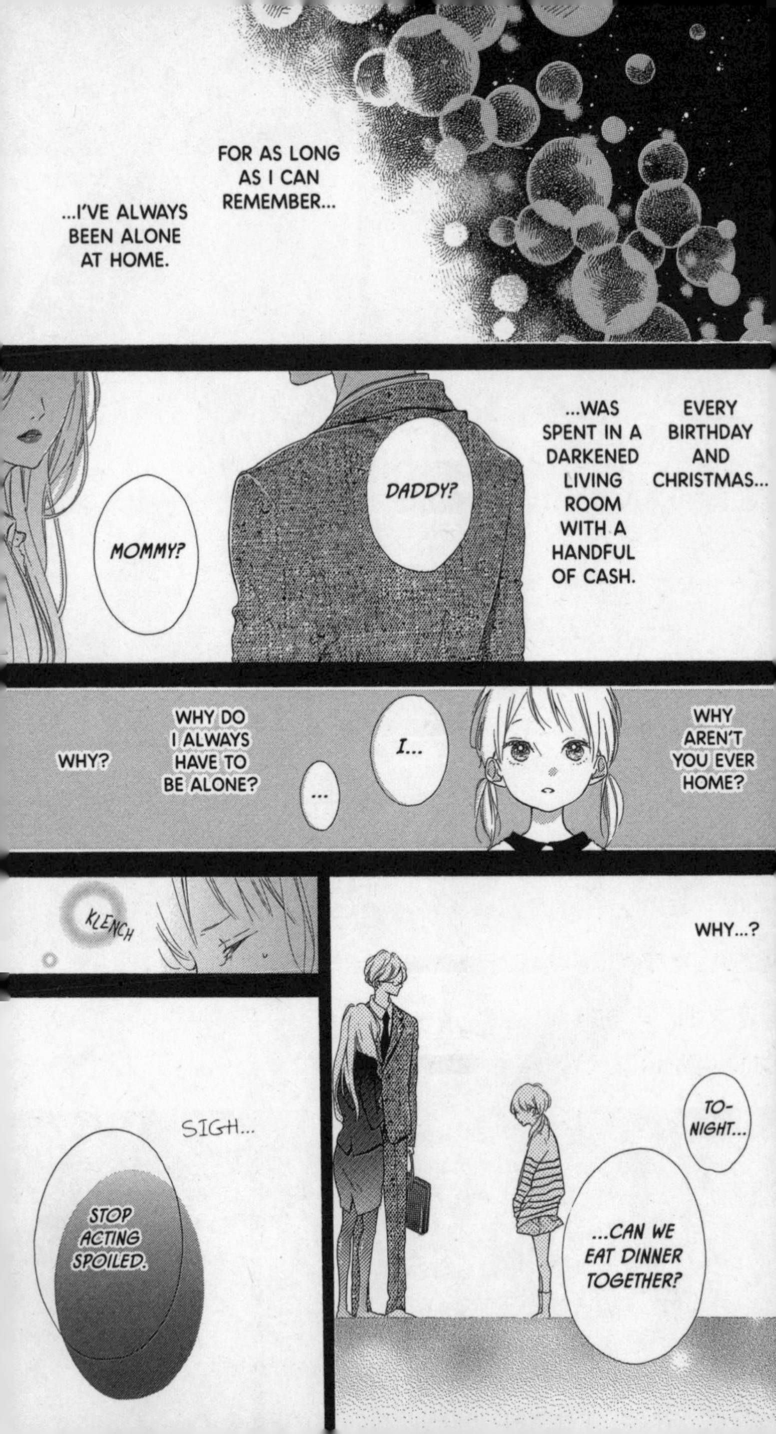

FOR AS LONG AS I CAN REMEMBER...
...I'VE ALWAYS BEEN ALONE AT HOME.
EVERY BIRTHDAY AND CHRISTMAS...
...WAS SPENT IN A DARKENED LIVING ROOM WITH A HANDFUL OF CASH.
DADDY?
MOMMY?
WHY AREN'T YOU EVER HOME?
I...
...
WHY DO I ALWAYS HAVE TO BE ALONE?
WHY?
WHY...?
TO-NIGHT...
...CAN WE EAT DINNER TOGETHER?
KLENCH
SIGH...
STOP ACTING SPOILED.

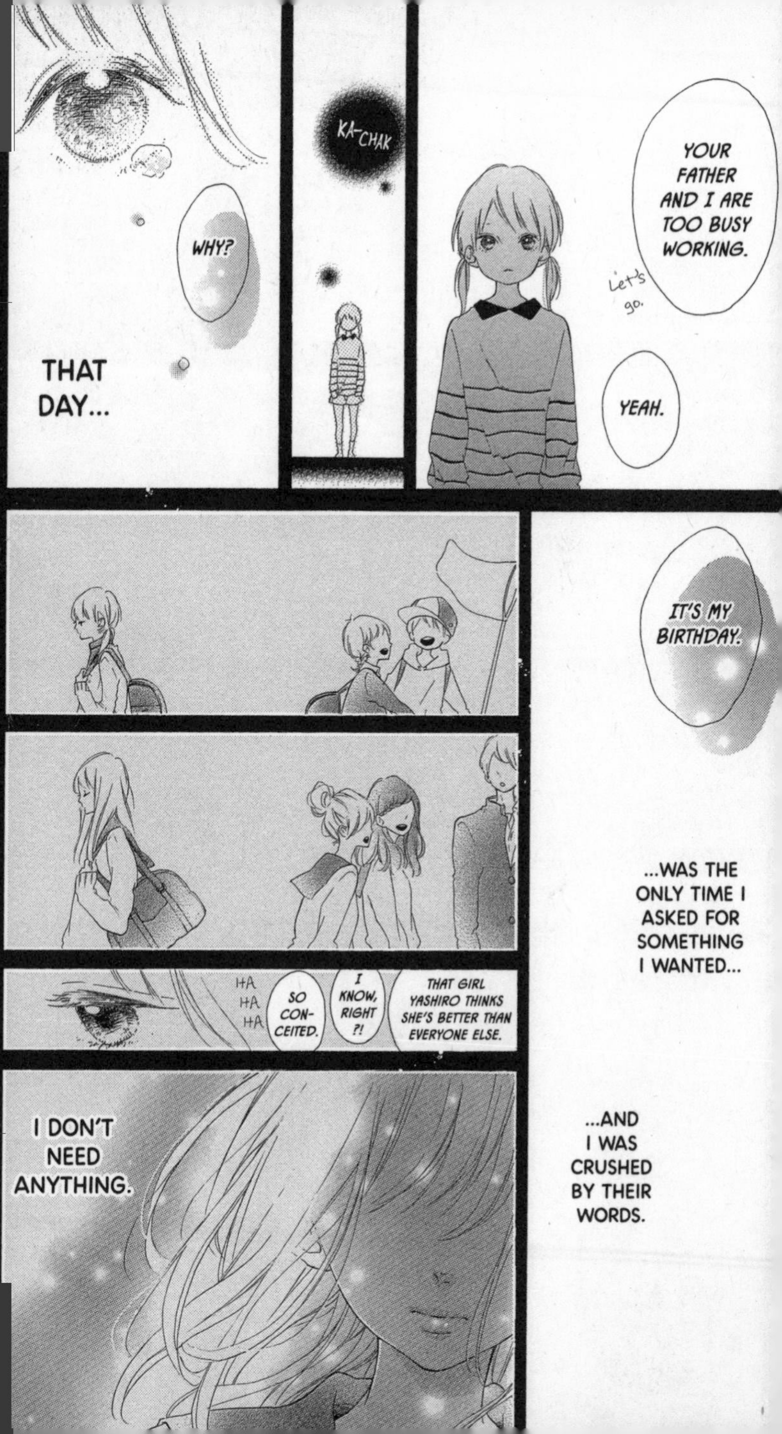

YOUR FATHER AND I ARE TOO BUSY WORKING.
Let's go.
YEAH.
KA-CHAK
WHY?
THAT DAY...
IT'S MY BIRTHDAY.
...WAS THE ONLY TIME I ASKED FOR SOMETHING I WANTED...
...AND I WAS CRUSHED BY THEIR WORDS.
THAT GIRL YASHIRO THINKS SHE'S BETTER THAN EVERYONE ELSE.
I KNOW, RIGHT?!
SO CONCEITED.
HA HA HA
I DON'T NEED ANYTHING.

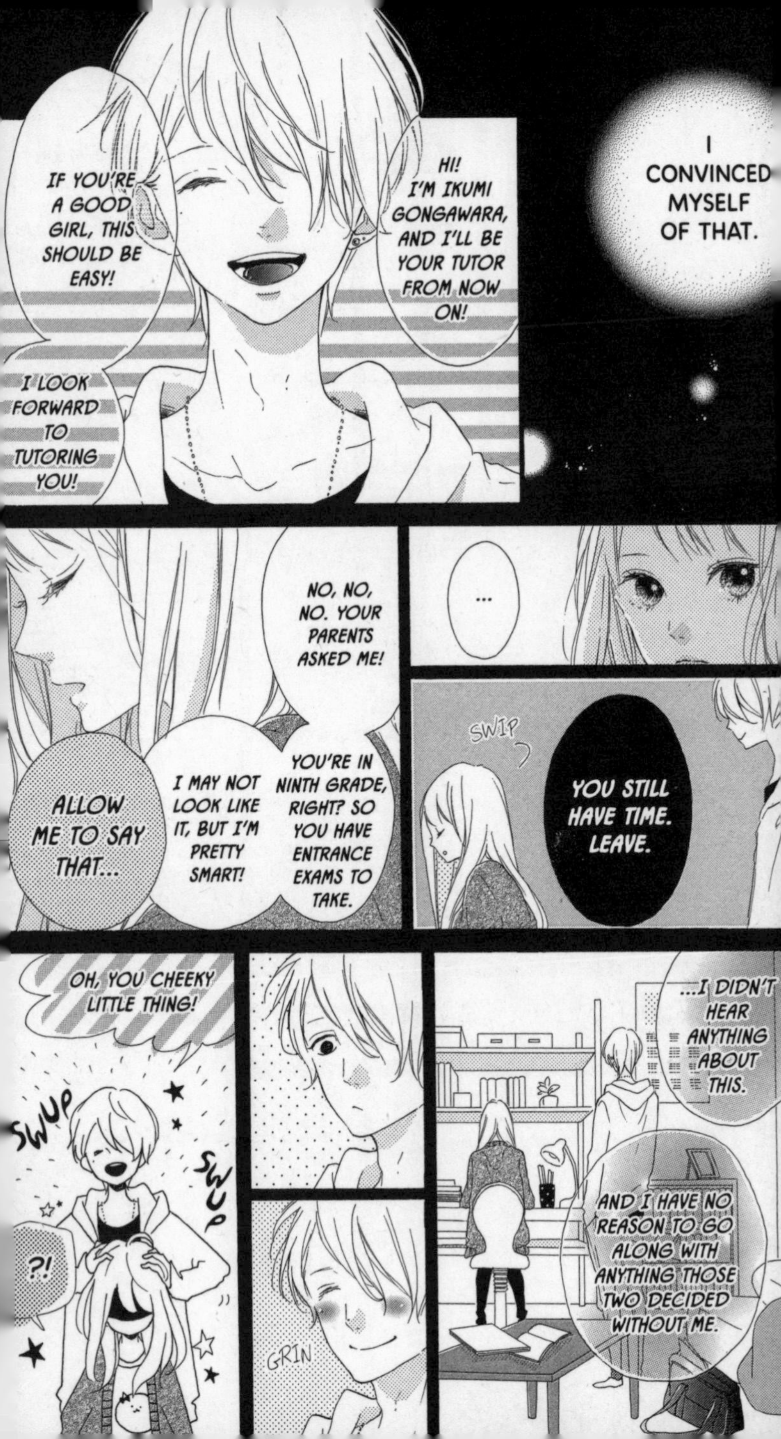
I CONVINCED MYSELF OF THAT.
HI! I'M IKUMI GONGAWARA, AND I'LL BE YOUR TUTOR FROM NOW ON!
IF YOU'RE A GOOD GIRL, THIS SHOULD BE EASY!
I LOOK FORWARD TO TUTORING YOU!
...
SWIP
YOU STILL HAVE TIME. LEAVE.
NO, NO, NO. YOUR PARENTS ASKED ME!
YOU'RE IN NINTH GRADE, RIGHT? SO YOU HAVE ENTRANCE EXAMS TO TAKE.
I MAY NOT LOOK LIKE IT, BUT I'M PRETTY SMART!
ALLOW ME TO SAY THAT...
...I DIDN'T HEAR ANYTHING ABOUT THIS.
AND I HAVE NO REASON TO GO ALONG WITH ANYTHING THOSE TWO DECIDED WITHOUT ME.
GRIN
OH, YOU CHEEKY LITTLE THING!
SWUP
SWUP
?!

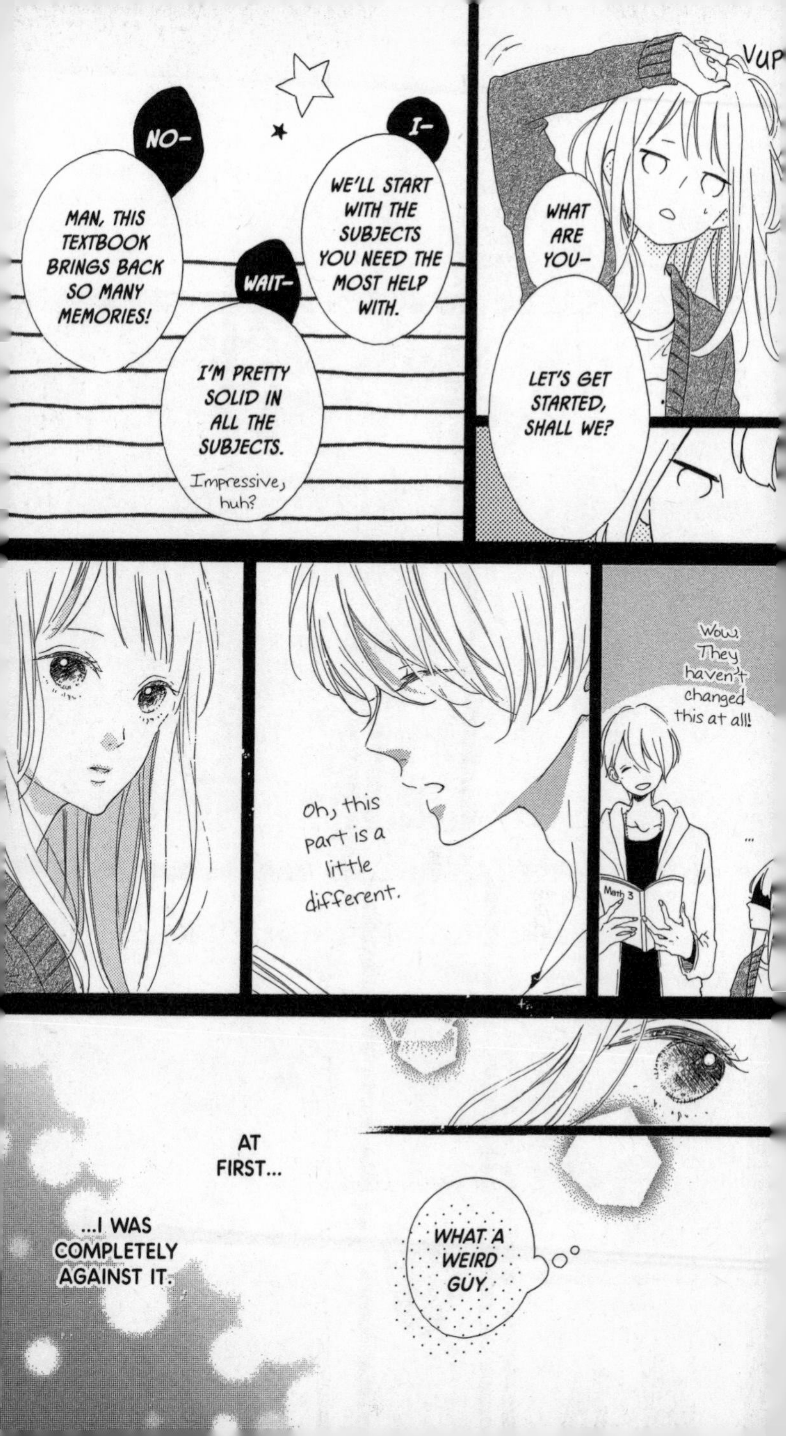
VUP
WHAT ARE YOU—
LET'S GET STARTED, SHALL WE?
I-
WE'LL START WITH THE SUBJECTS YOU NEED THE MOST HELP WITH.
NO-
MAN, THIS TEXTBOOK BRINGS BACK SO MANY MEMORIES!
WAIT-
I'M PRETTY SOLID IN ALL THE SUBJECTS.
Impressive, huh?
Wow. They haven't changed this at all!
Math 3
...
Oh, this part is a little different.
AT FIRST...
WHAT A WEIRD GUY.
...I WAS COMPLETELY AGAINST IT.

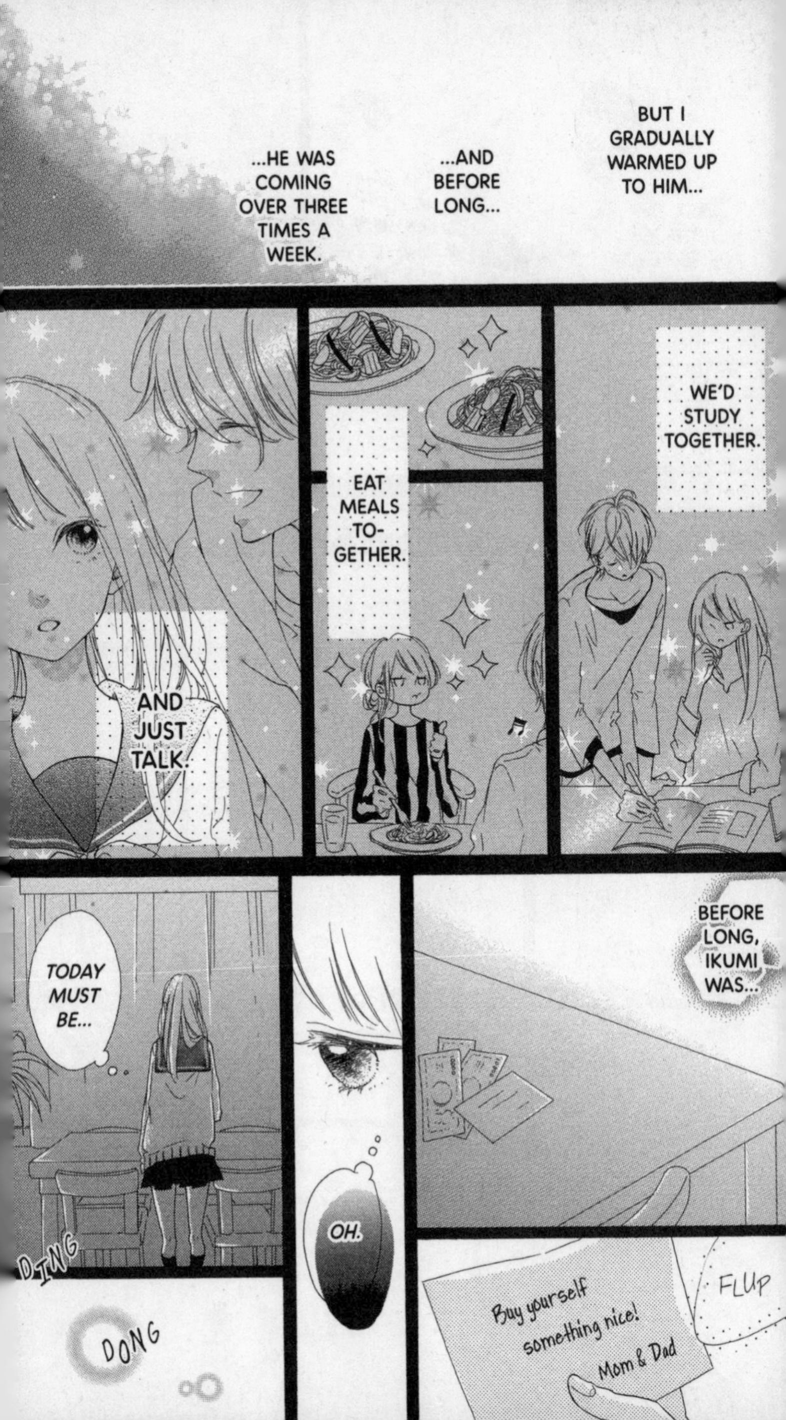
BUT I GRADUALLY WARMED UP TO HIM...
...AND BEFORE LONG...
...HE WAS COMING OVER THREE TIMES A WEEK.
WE'D STUDY TOGETHER.
EAT MEALS TO-GETHER.
AND JUST TALK.
BEFORE LONG, IKUMI WAS...
FLUP
Buy yourself something nice! Mom & Dad
OH.
TODAY MUST BE...
DING
DONG

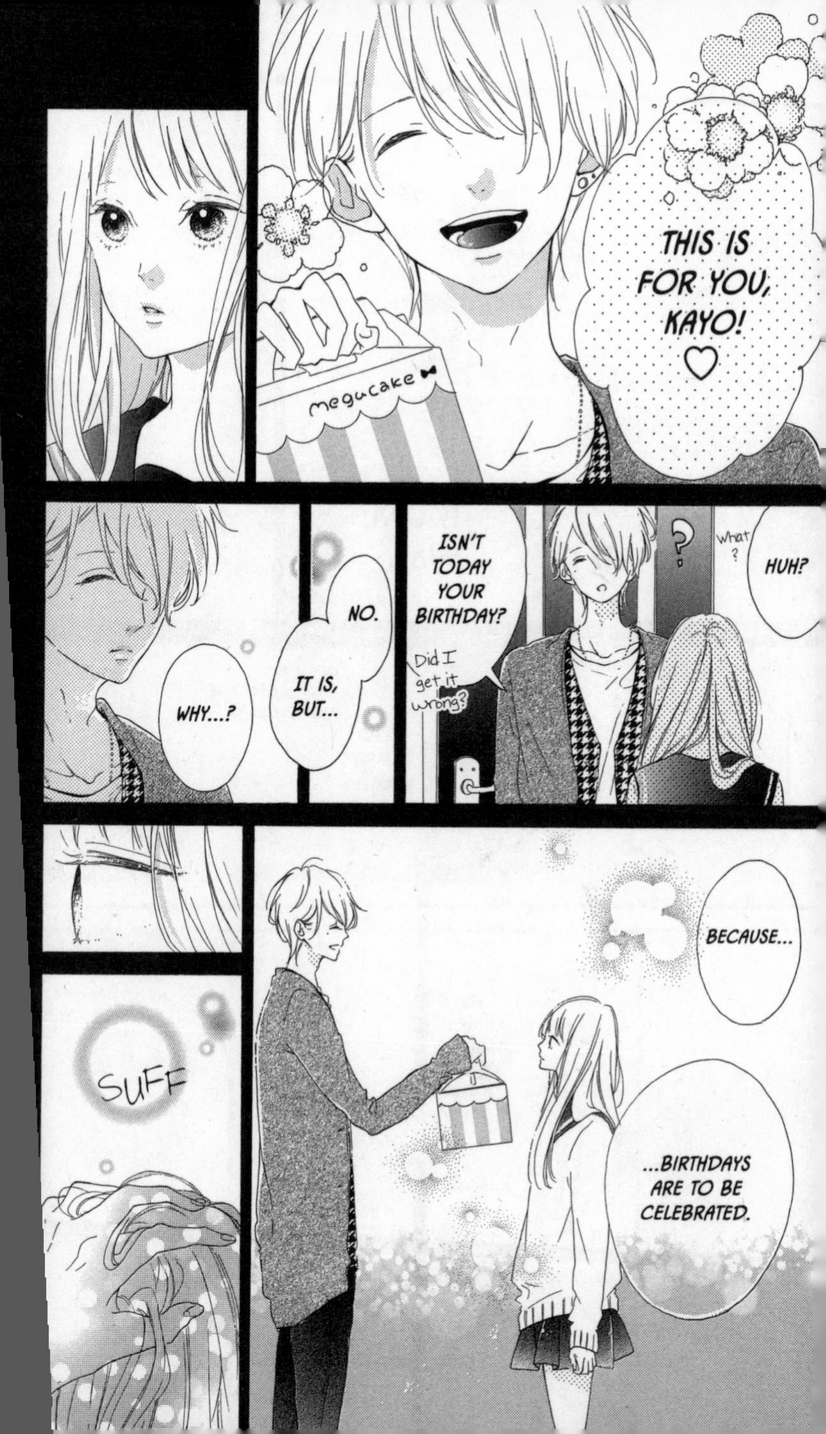
THIS IS FOR YOU, KAYO! ♡
megucake
HUH?
What?
ISN'T TODAY YOUR BIRTHDAY?
Did I get it wrong?
NO.
IT IS, BUT...
WHY...?
BECAUSE...
...BIRTHDAYS ARE TO BE CELEBRATED.
SUFF

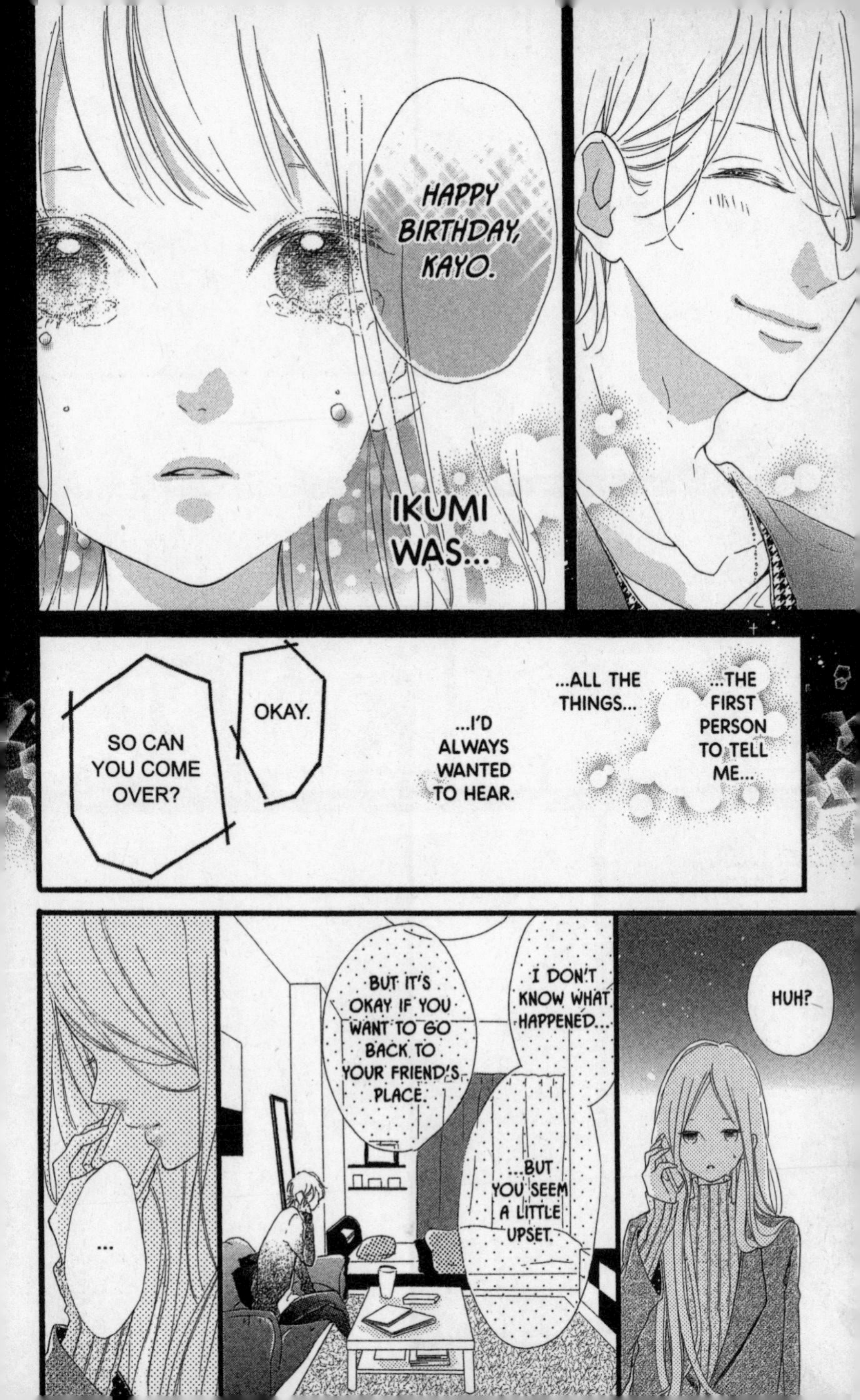
HAPPY BIRTHDAY, KAYO.
IKUMI WAS...
...THE FIRST PERSON TO TELL ME...
...ALL THE THINGS...
...I'D ALWAYS WANTED TO HEAR.
OKAY.
SO CAN YOU COME OVER?
HUH?
I DON'T KNOW WHAT HAPPENED...
...BUT YOU SEEM A LITTLE UPSET.
BUT IT'S OKAY IF YOU WANT TO GO BACK TO YOUR FRIEND'S PLACE.
...

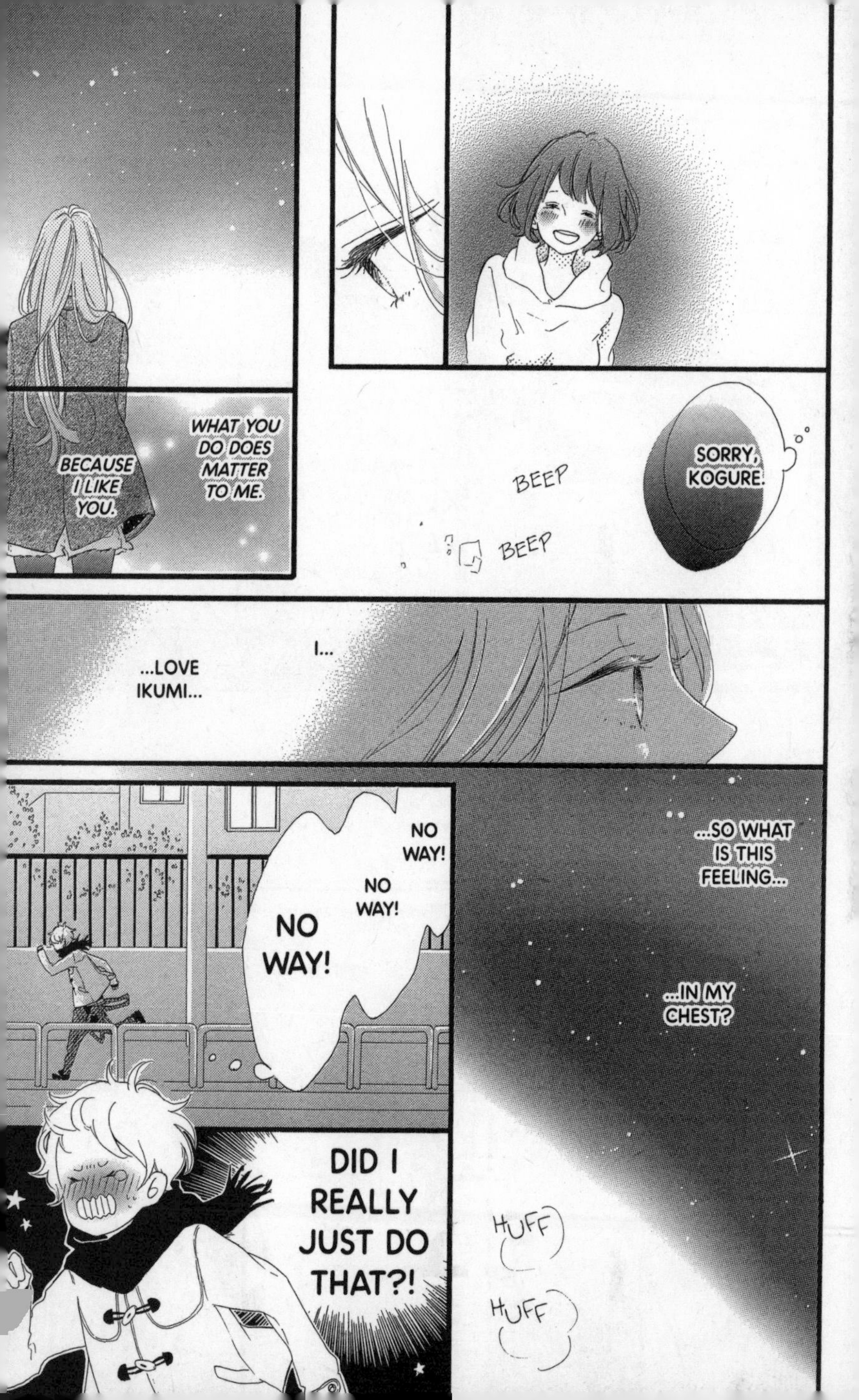
SORRY, KOGURE.
BEEP
BEEP
WHAT YOU DO DOES MATTER TO ME.
BECAUSE I LIKE YOU.
I...
...LOVE IKUMI...
...SO WHAT IS THIS FEELING...
...IN MY CHEST?
HUFF
HUFF
NO WAY!
NO WAY!
NO WAY!
DID I REALLY JUST DO THAT?!

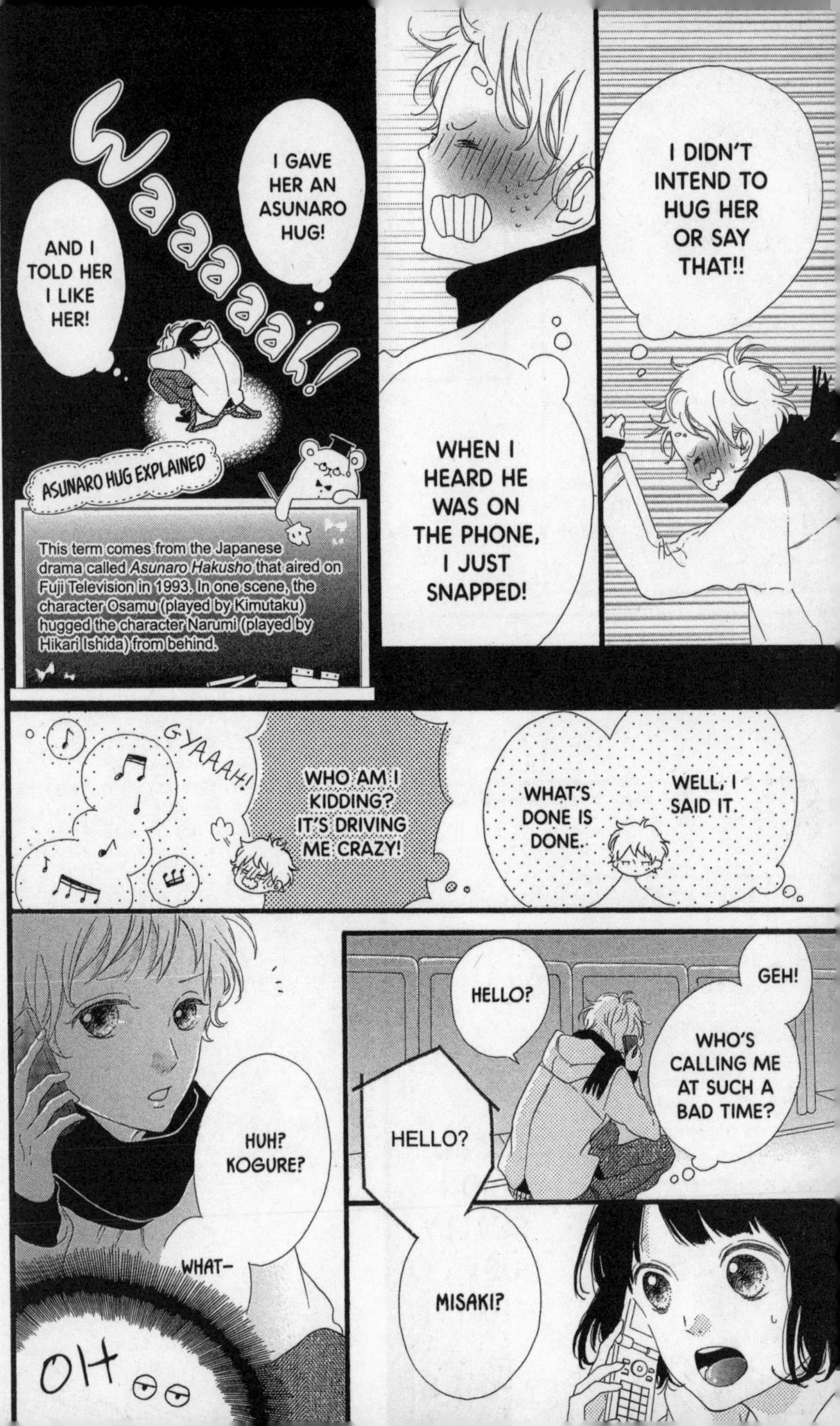
I DIDN'T INTEND TO HUG HER OR SAY THAT!!
WHEN I HEARD HE WAS ON THE PHONE, I JUST SNAPPED!
I GAVE HER AN ASUNARO HUG!
AND I TOLD HER I LIKE HER!
Waaaaah!
ASUNARO HUG EXPLAINED
This term comes from the Japanese drama called *Asunaro Hakusho* that aired on Fuji Television in 1993. In one scene, the character Osamu (played by Kimutaku) hugged the character Narumi (played by Hikari Ishida) from behind.
WELL, I SAID IT.
WHAT'S DONE IS DONE.
WHO AM I KIDDING? IT'S DRIVING ME CRAZY!
GYAAAH!
GEH!
WHO'S CALLING ME AT SUCH A BAD TIME?
HELLO?
HELLO?
MISAKI?
HUH? KOGURE?
WHAT-
OH

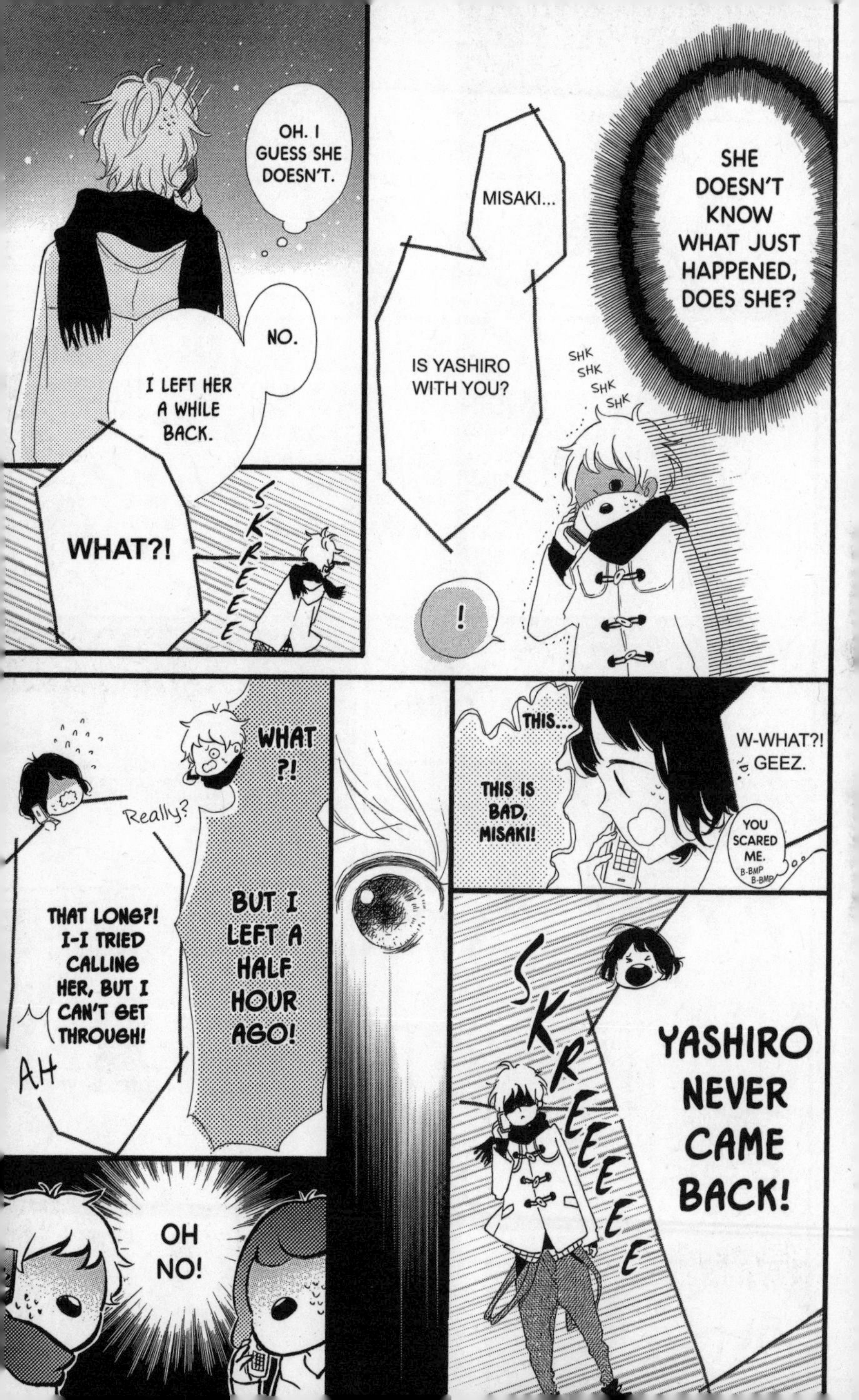
SHE DOESN'T KNOW WHAT JUST HAPPENED, DOES SHE?
SHK SHK SHK SHK
MISAKI...
IS YASHIRO WITH YOU?
!
OH. I GUESS SHE DOESN'T.
NO.
I LEFT HER A WHILE BACK.
WHAT?!
SKREEEE
W-WHAT?! GEEZ.
YOU SCARED ME.
B-BMP B-BMP
THIS...
THIS IS BAD, MISAKI!
YASHIRO NEVER CAME BACK!
SKREEEEEEE
WHAT?!
BUT I LEFT A HALF HOUR AGO!
Really?
THAT LONG?! I-I TRIED CALLING HER, BUT I CAN'T GET THROUGH!
AH
OH NO!

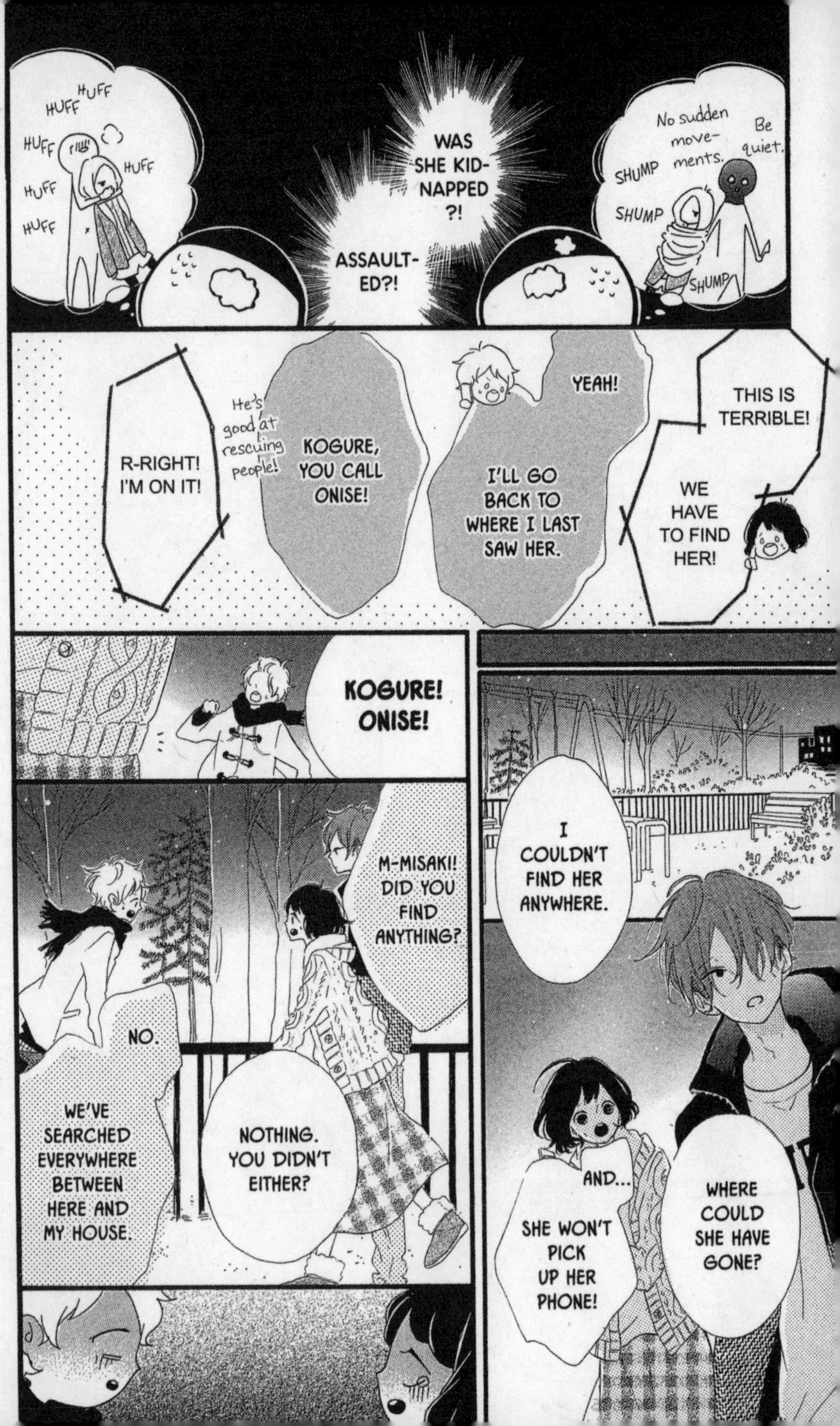
No sudden movements.
Be quiet.
SHUMP
SHUMP
SHUMP
WAS SHE KIDNAPPED?!
ASSAULTED?!
HUFF HUFF HUFF HUFF HUFF HUFF
THIS IS TERRIBLE!
WE HAVE TO FIND HER!
YEAH!
I'LL GO BACK TO WHERE I LAST SAW HER.
KOGURE, YOU CALL ONISE!
He's good at rescuing people!
R-RIGHT! I'M ON IT!
I COULDN'T FIND HER ANYWHERE.
AND...
SHE WON'T PICK UP HER PHONE!
WHERE COULD SHE HAVE GONE?
KOGURE! ONISE!
M-MISAKI! DID YOU FIND ANYTHING?
NOTHING. YOU DIDN'T EITHER?
NO.
WE'VE SEARCHED EVERYWHERE BETWEEN HERE AND MY HOUSE.

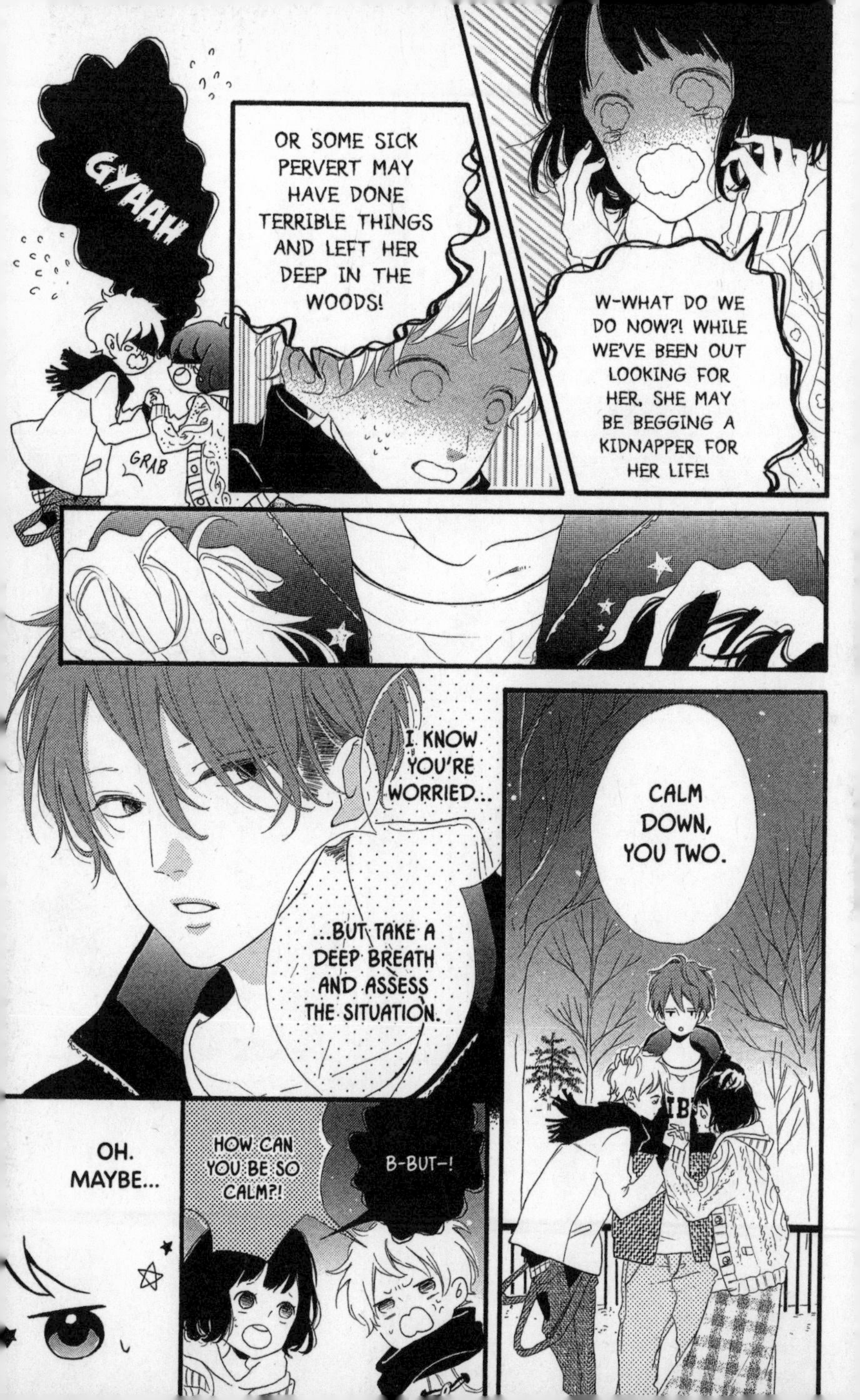
W-WHAT DO WE DO NOW?! WHILE WE'VE BEEN OUT LOOKING FOR HER, SHE MAY BE BEGGING A KIDNAPPER FOR HER LIFE!
OR SOME SICK PERVERT MAY HAVE DONE TERRIBLE THINGS AND LEFT HER DEEP IN THE WOODS!
GYAAH
GRAB
CALM DOWN, YOU TWO.
I KNOW YOU'RE WORRIED...
...BUT TAKE A DEEP BREATH AND ASSESS THE SITUATION.
B-BUT-!
HOW CAN YOU BE SO CALM?!
OH. MAYBE...

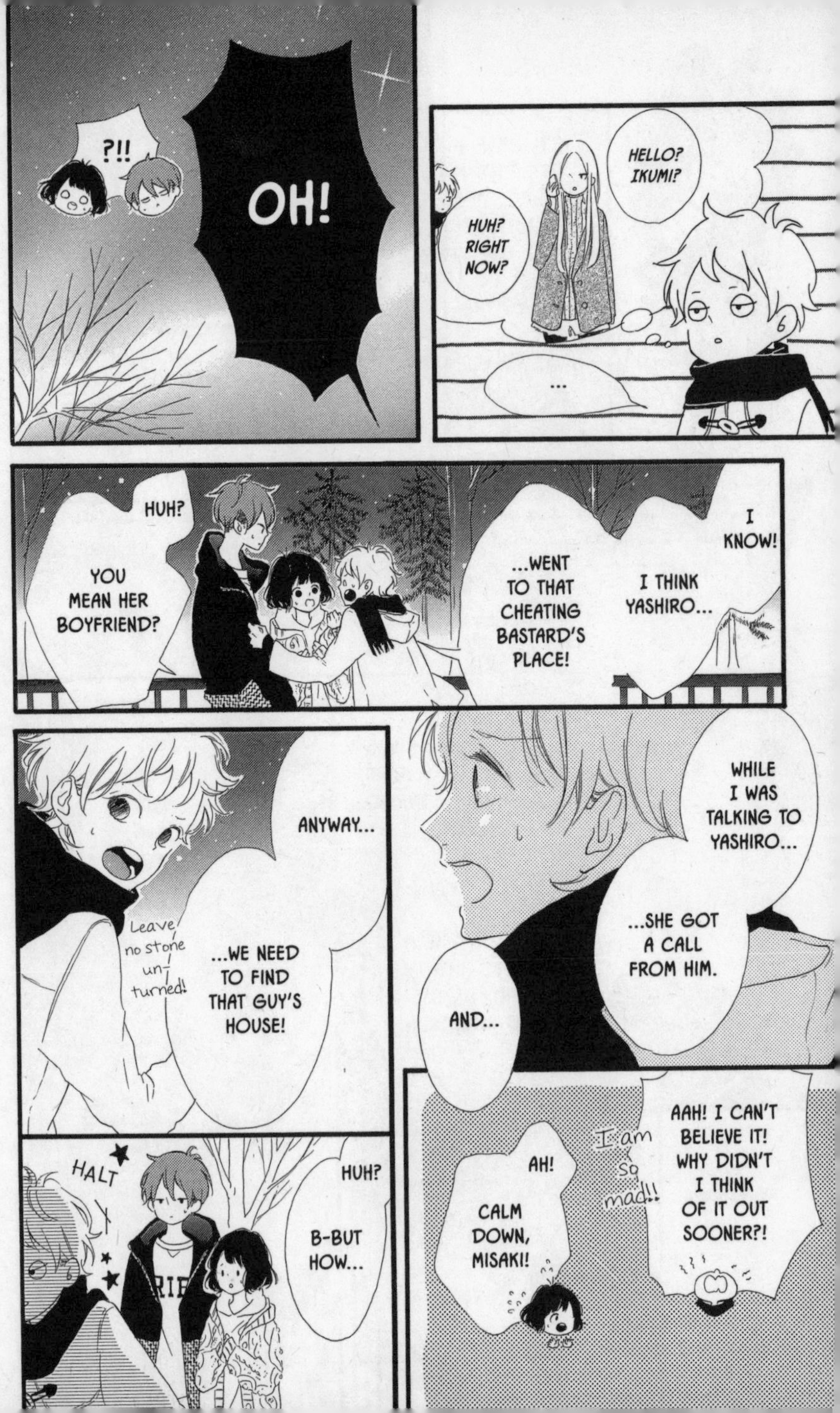
HELLO? IKUMI?
HUH? RIGHT NOW?
...
?!!
OH!
I KNOW!
I THINK YASHIRO...
...WENT TO THAT CHEATING BASTARD'S PLACE!
HUH?
YOU MEAN HER BOYFRIEND?
WHILE I WAS TALKING TO YASHIRO...
...SHE GOT A CALL FROM HIM.
AND...
AAH! I CAN'T BELIEVE IT! WHY DIDN'T I THINK OF IT OUT SOONER?!
I am so mad!!
AH!
CALM DOWN, MISAKI!
ANYWAY...
...WE NEED TO FIND THAT GUY'S HOUSE!
Leave no stone unturned!
HUH?
B-BUT HOW...
HALT

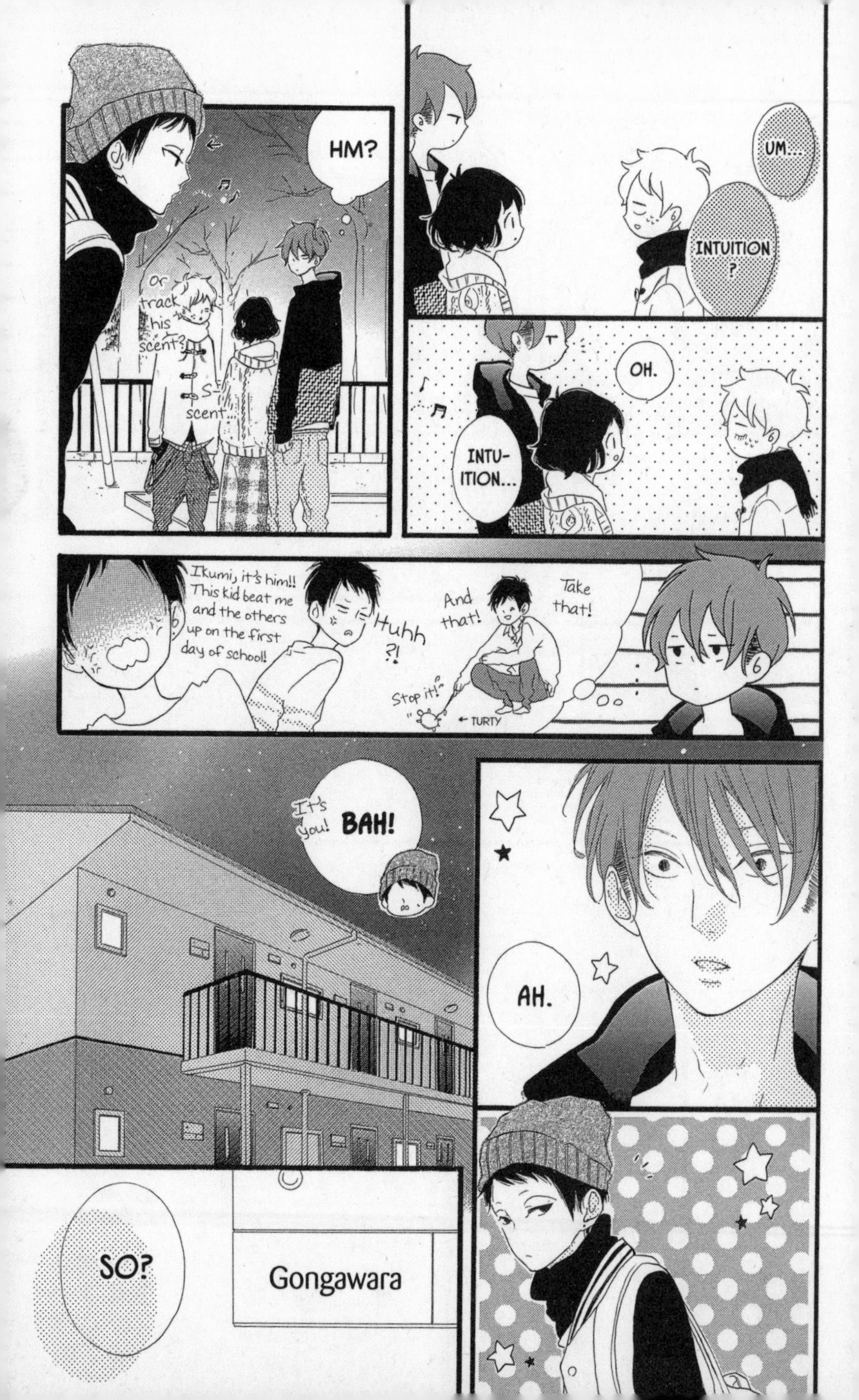

UM...
INTUITION?
OH.
INTU-ITION...
HM?
Or track his scent?
S-scent...
...
Oo
Take that!
And that!
Stop it!!
TURTY
Huhh?!
Ikumi, it's him!! This kid beat me and the others up on the first day of school!
AH.
It's you!
BAH!
Gongawara
SO?

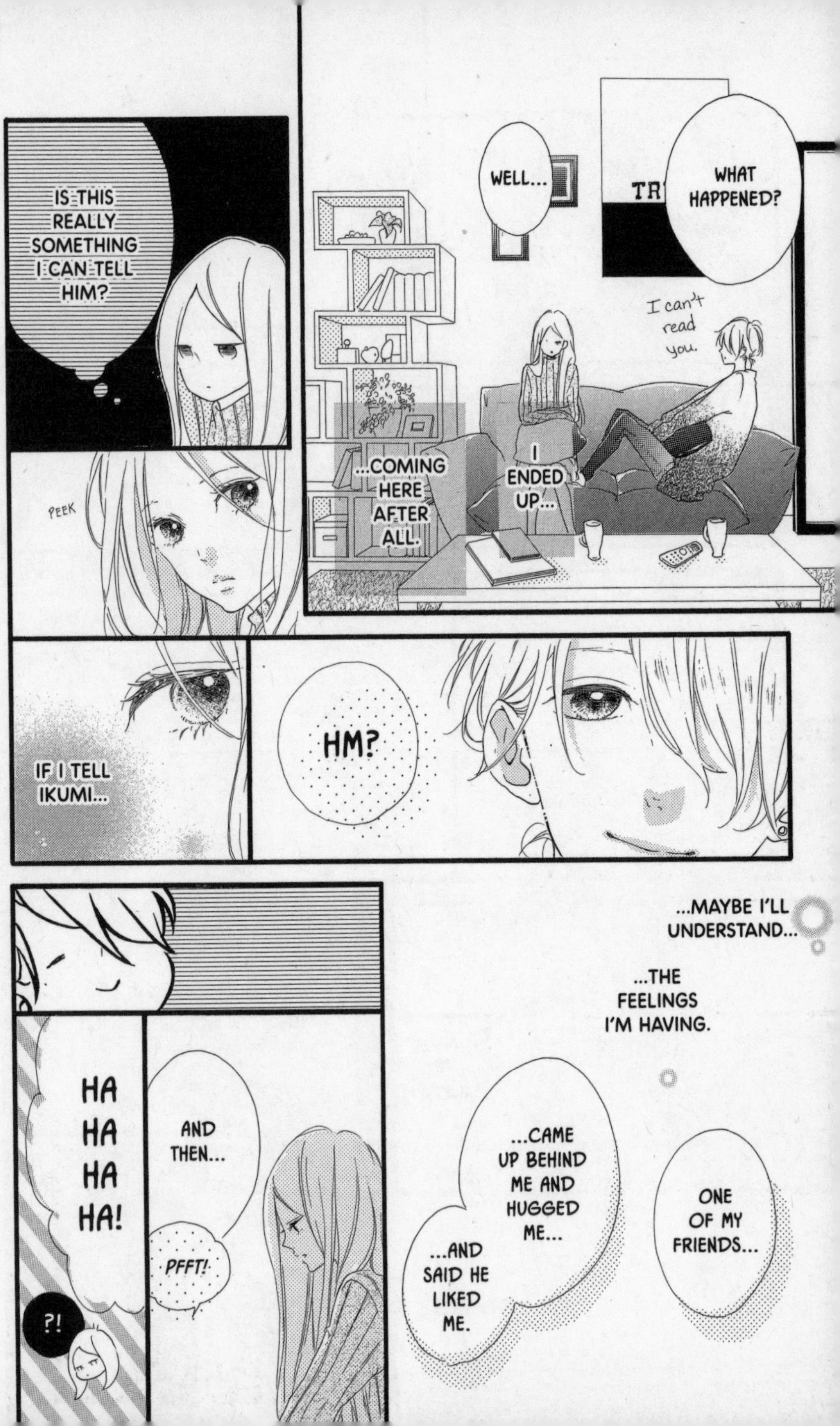
WHAT HAPPENED?
WELL...
I can't read you.
I ENDED UP...
...COMING HERE AFTER ALL.
IS THIS REALLY SOMETHING I CAN TELL HIM?
PEEK
HM?
IF I TELL IKUMI...
...MAYBE I'LL UNDERSTAND...
...THE FEELINGS I'M HAVING.
ONE OF MY FRIENDS...
...CAME UP BEHIND ME AND HUGGED ME...
...AND SAID HE LIKED ME.
AND THEN...
PFFT!
HA HA HA HA!
?!

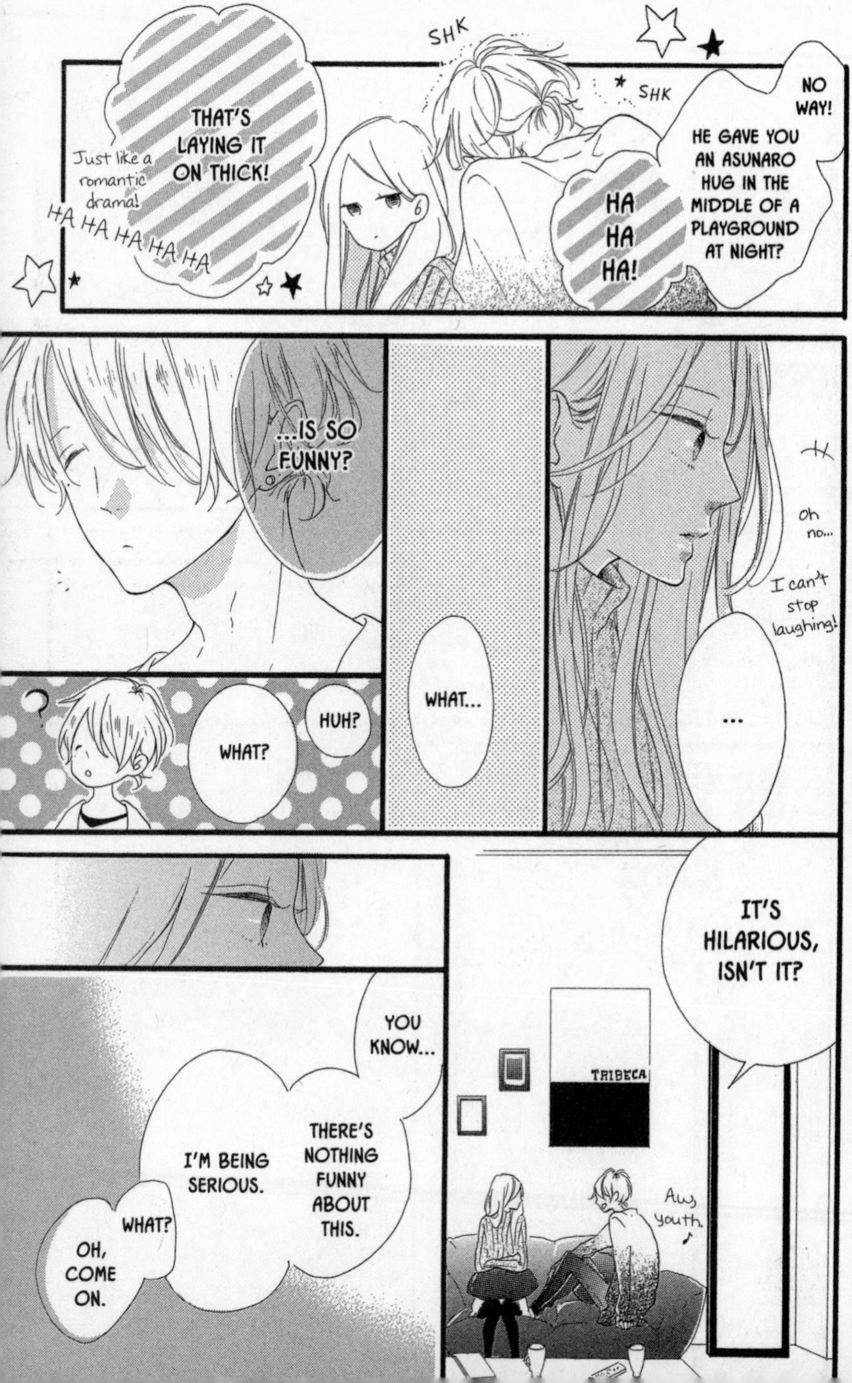
NO WAY!
HE GAVE YOU AN ASUNARO HUG IN THE MIDDLE OF A PLAYGROUND AT NIGHT?
HA HA HA!
SHK
SHK
THAT'S LAYING IT ON THICK!
Just like a romantic drama!
HA HA HA HA HA
Oh no...
I can't stop laughing!
...
WHAT...
...IS SO FUNNY?
HUH?
WHAT?
IT'S HILARIOUS, ISN'T IT?
TRIBECA
Aw, youth. ♪
YOU KNOW...
THERE'S NOTHING FUNNY ABOUT THIS.
I'M BEING SERIOUS.
WHAT?
OH, COME ON.

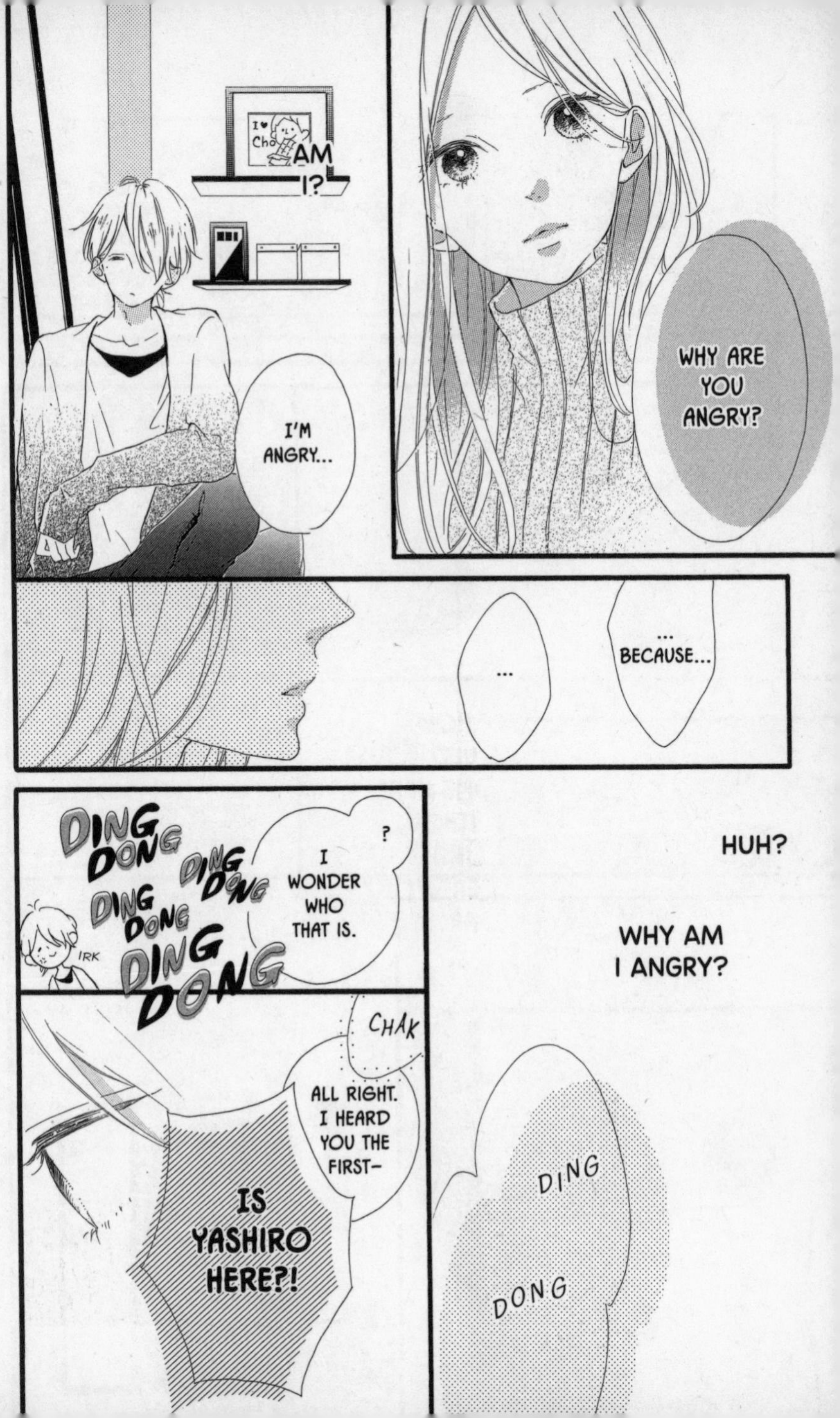
WHY ARE YOU ANGRY?
I'M ANGRY...
AM I?
... BECAUSE...
...
HUH?
WHY AM I ANGRY?
DING DONG
DING DONG DING DONG DING DONG DING DONG
I WONDER WHO THAT IS.
?
IRK
CHAK
ALL RIGHT. I HEARD YOU THE FIRST—
IS YASHIRO HERE?!

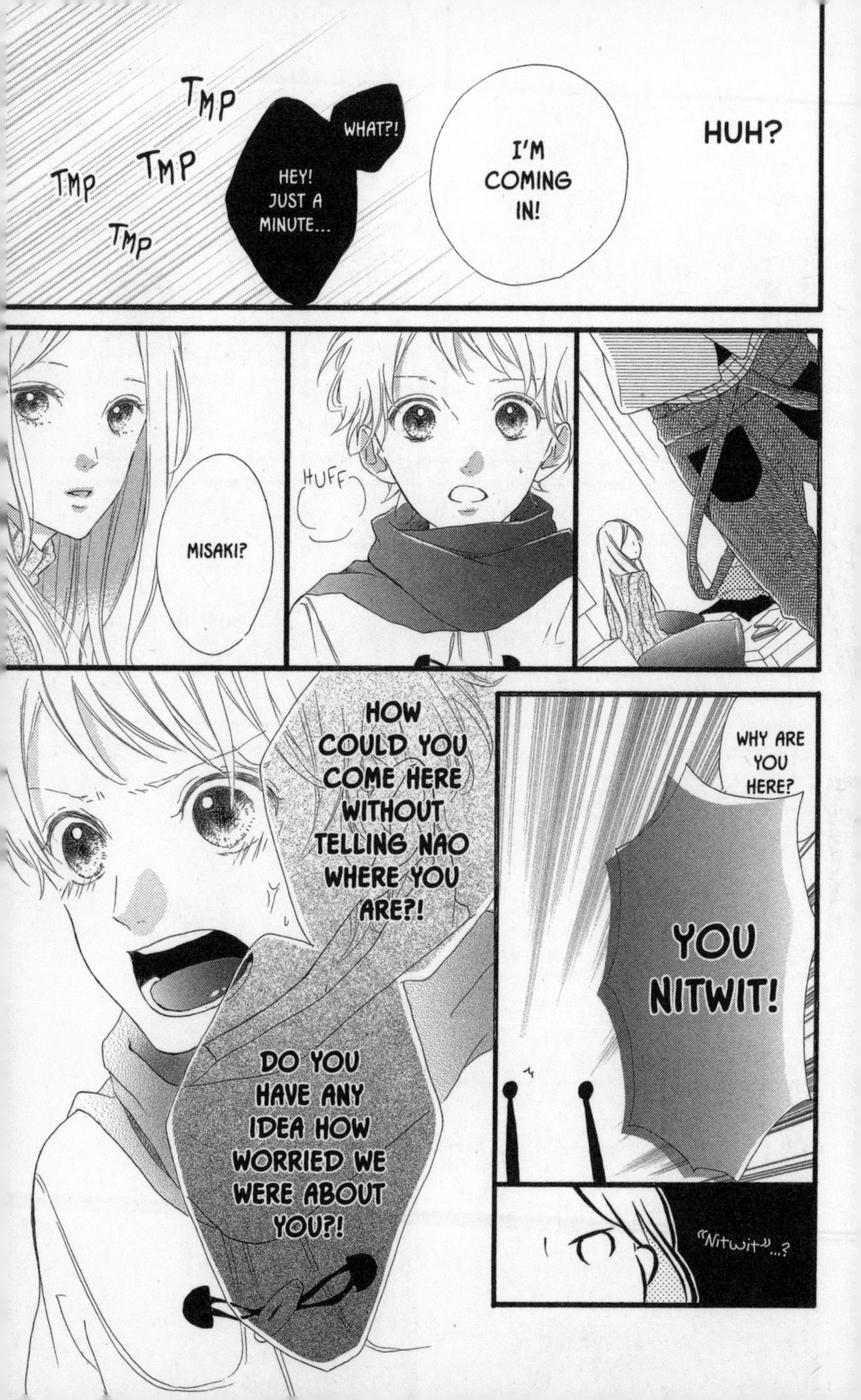
HUH?
I'M COMING IN!
WHAT?!
HEY! JUST A MINUTE...
TMP TMP TMP TMP
HUFF
MISAKI?
WHY ARE YOU HERE?
YOU NITWIT!
"Nitwit"...?
HOW COULD YOU COME HERE WITHOUT TELLING NAO WHERE YOU ARE?!
DO YOU HAVE ANY IDEA HOW WORRIED WE WERE ABOUT YOU?!

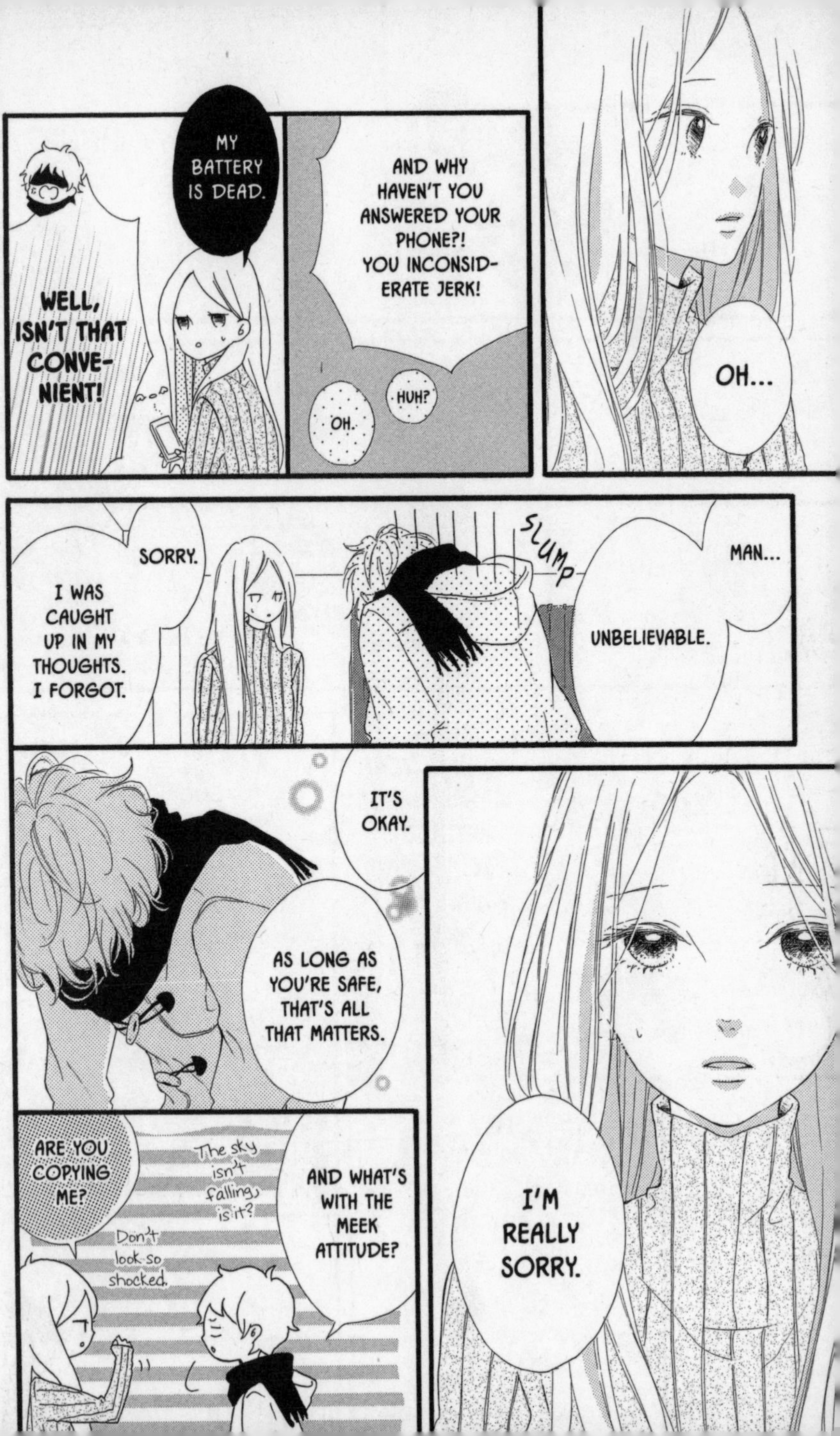
OH...
AND WHY HAVEN'T YOU ANSWERED YOUR PHONE?! YOU INCONSID-ERATE JERK!
HUH?
OH.
MY BATTERY IS DEAD.
WELL, ISN'T THAT CONVE-NIENT!
MAN... UNBELIEVABLE.
SLUMP
SORRY. I WAS CAUGHT UP IN MY THOUGHTS. I FORGOT.
I'M REALLY SORRY.
IT'S OKAY.
AS LONG AS YOU'RE SAFE, THAT'S ALL THAT MATTERS.
AND WHAT'S WITH THE MEEK ATTITUDE?
The sky isn't falling, is it?
ARE YOU COPYING ME?
Don't look so shocked.

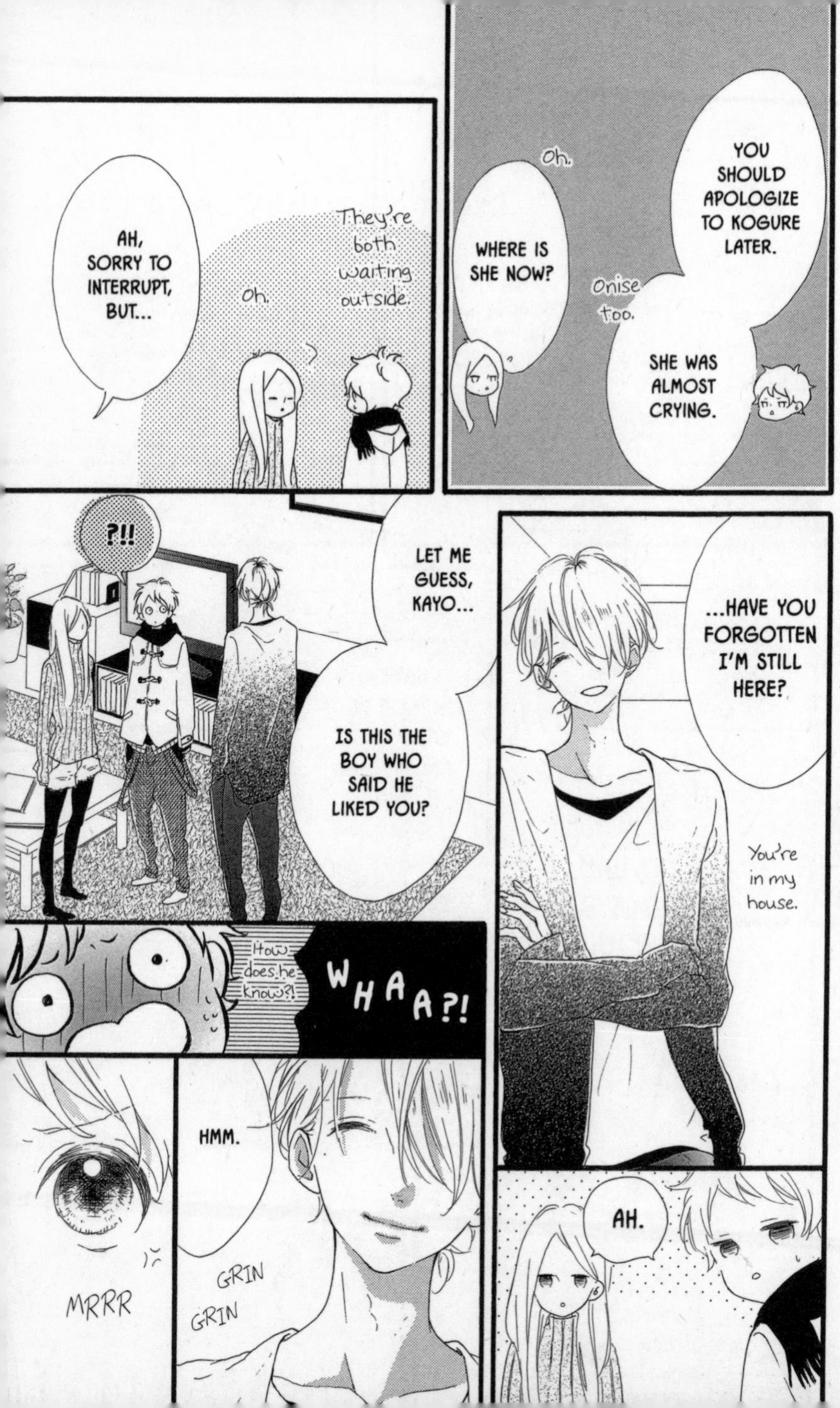
YOU SHOULD APOLOGIZE TO KOGURE LATER.
Onise too.
SHE WAS ALMOST CRYING.
Oh.
WHERE IS SHE NOW?
They're both waiting outside.
Oh.
AH, SORRY TO INTERRUPT, BUT...
...HAVE YOU FORGOTTEN I'M STILL HERE?
You're in my house.
LET ME GUESS, KAYO...
IS THIS THE BOY WHO SAID HE LIKED YOU?
?!!
WHAA?!
How does he know?!
AH.
HMM.
GRIN
GRIN
MRRR

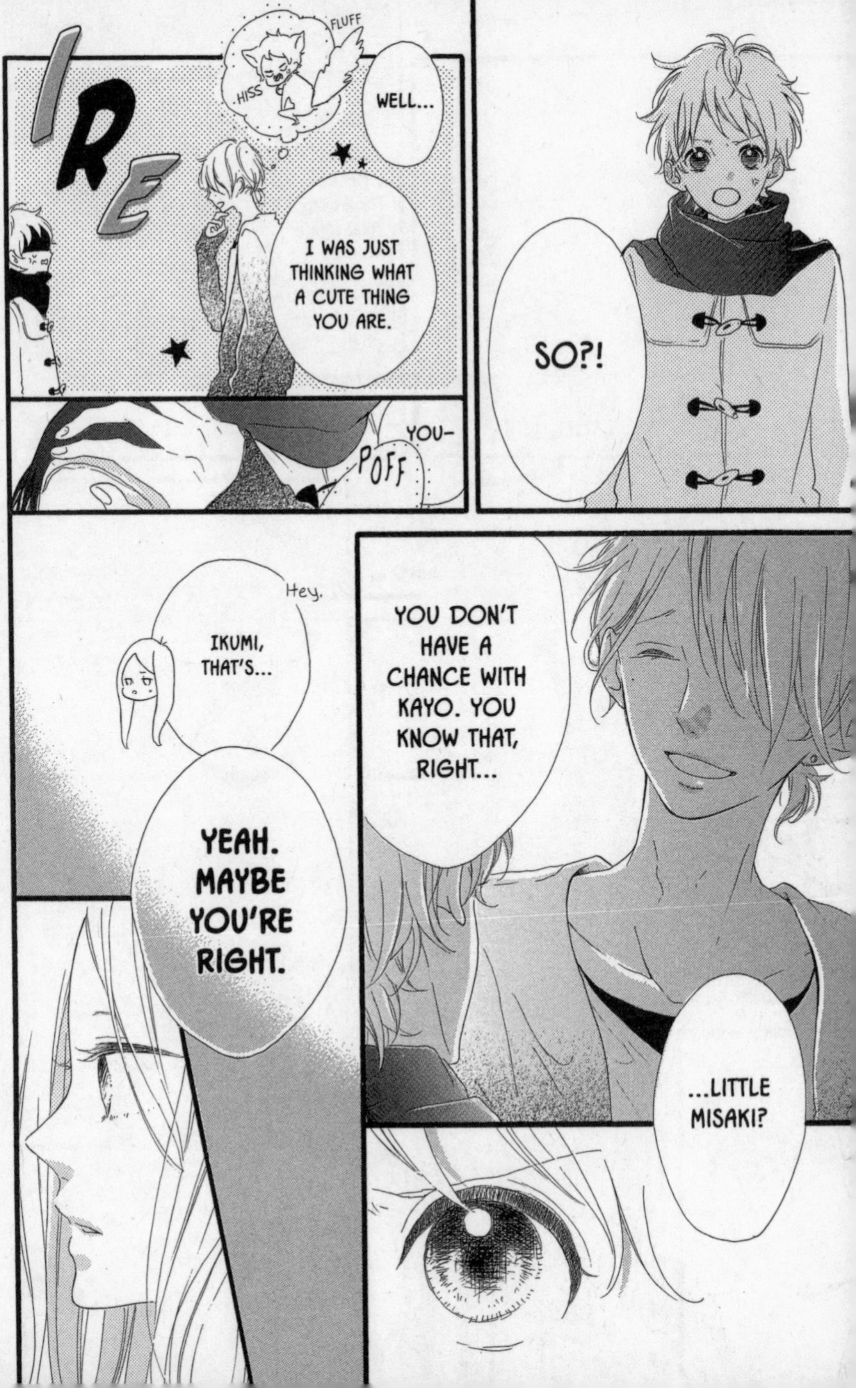
SO?!
WELL...
FLUFF
HISS
I WAS JUST THINKING WHAT A CUTE THING YOU ARE.
IRE
YOU-
POFF
YOU DON'T HAVE A CHANCE WITH KAYO. YOU KNOW THAT, RIGHT...
...LITTLE MISAKI?
Hey.
IKUMI, THAT'S...
YEAH. MAYBE YOU'RE RIGHT.

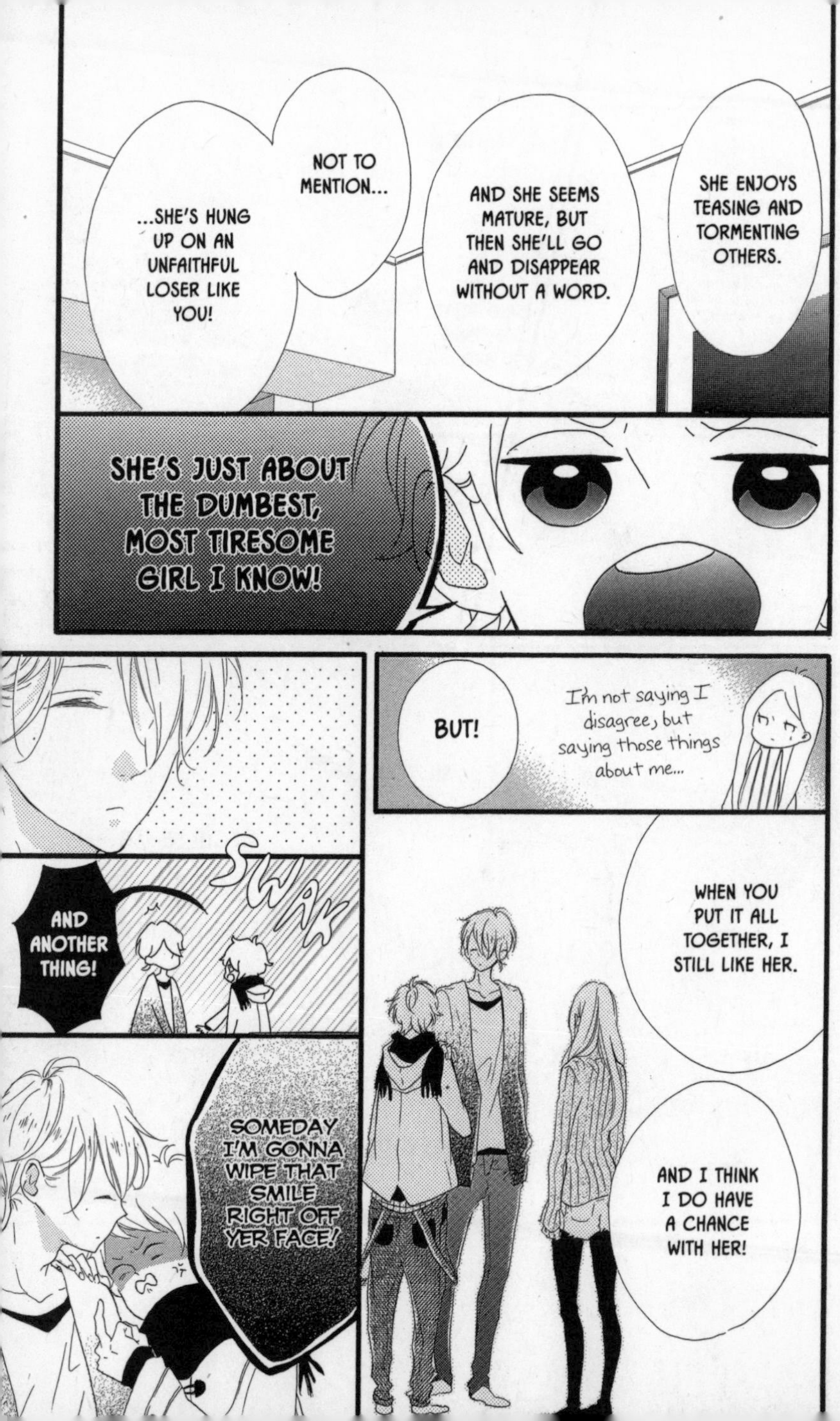
SHE ENJOYS TEASING AND TORMENTING OTHERS.
AND SHE SEEMS MATURE, BUT THEN SHE'LL GO AND DISAPPEAR WITHOUT A WORD.
NOT TO MENTION...
...SHE'S HUNG UP ON AN UNFAITHFUL LOSER LIKE YOU!
SHE'S JUST ABOUT THE DUMBEST, MOST TIRESOME GIRL I KNOW!
I'm not saying I disagree, but saying those things about me...
BUT!
WHEN YOU PUT IT ALL TOGETHER, I STILL LIKE HER.
AND I THINK I DO HAVE A CHANCE WITH HER!
SWAK
AND ANOTHER THING!
SOMEDAY I'M GONNA WIPE THAT SMILE RIGHT OFF YER FACE!

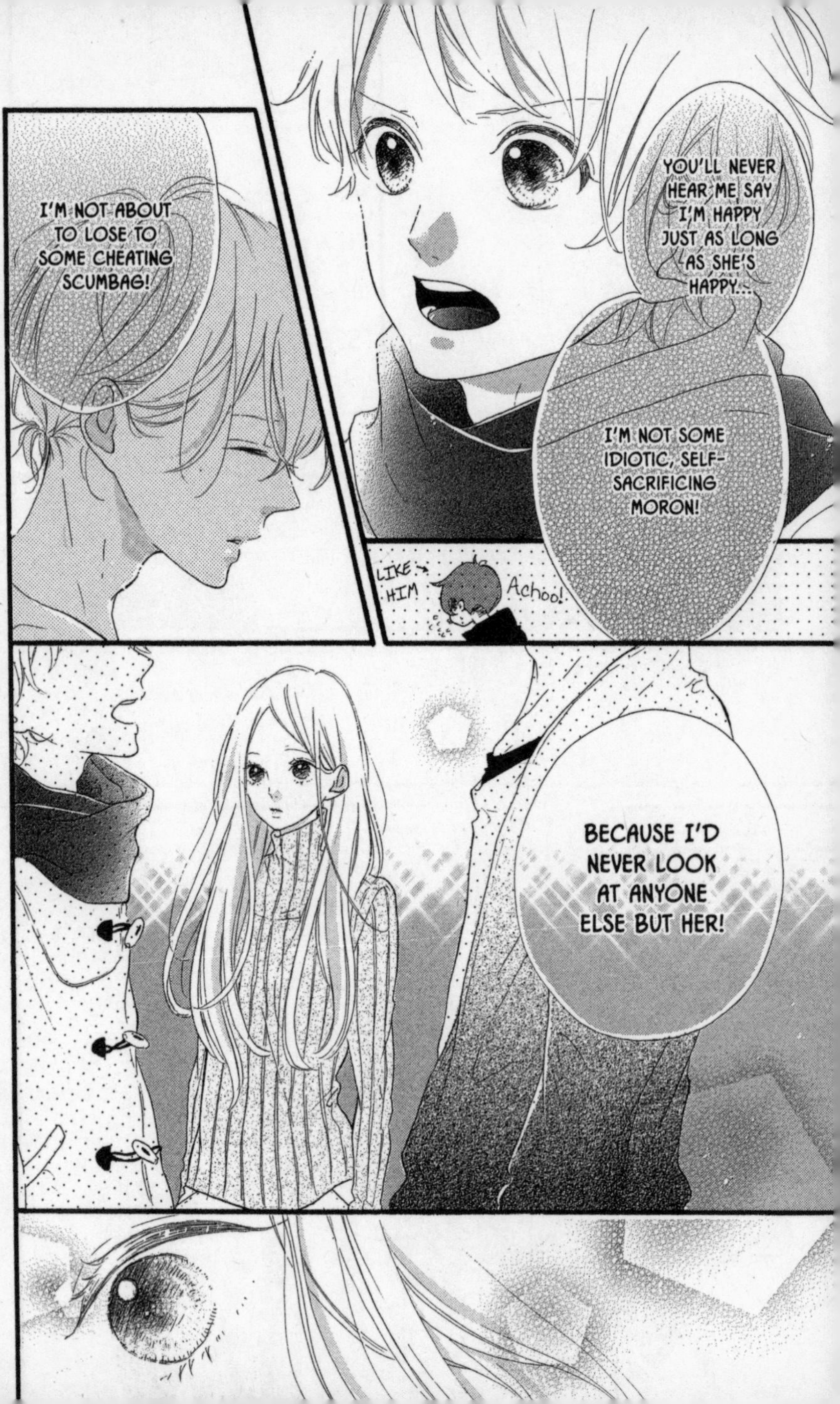
YOU'LL NEVER HEAR ME SAY I'M HAPPY JUST AS LONG AS SHE'S HAPPY...
I'M NOT SOME IDIOTIC, SELF-SACRIFICING MORON!
LIKE HIM
Achoo!
I'M NOT ABOUT TO LOSE TO SOME CHEATING SCUMBAG!
BECAUSE I'D NEVER LOOK AT ANYONE ELSE BUT HER!

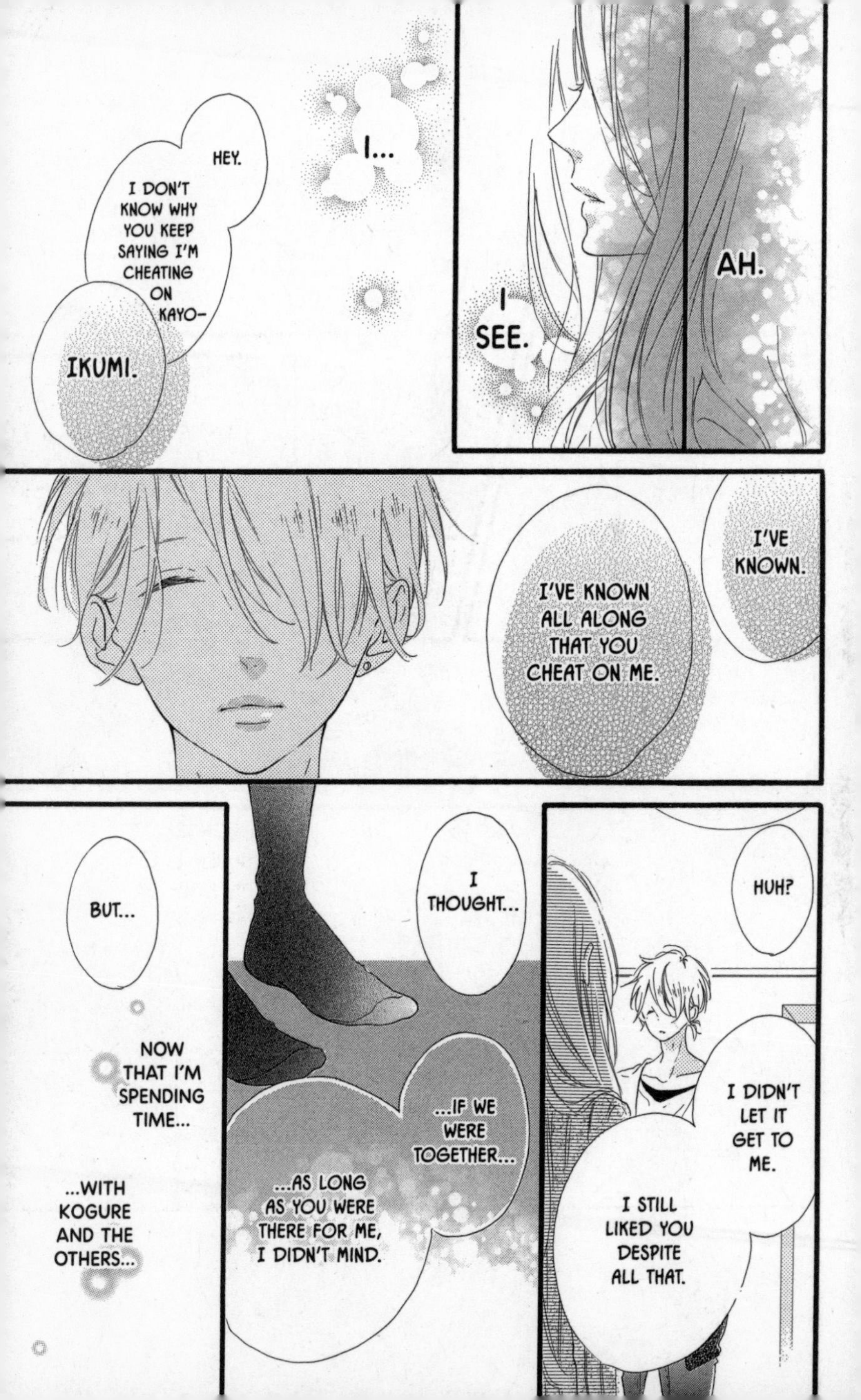
AH.
I SEE.
I...
HEY. I DON'T KNOW WHY YOU KEEP SAYING I'M CHEATING ON KAYO-
IKUMI.
I'VE KNOWN.
I'VE KNOWN ALL ALONG THAT YOU CHEAT ON ME.
HUH?
I DIDN'T LET IT GET TO ME.
I STILL LIKED YOU DESPITE ALL THAT.
I THOUGHT...
...IF WE WERE TOGETHER...
...AS LONG AS YOU WERE THERE FOR ME, I DIDN'T MIND.
BUT...
NOW THAT I'M SPENDING TIME...
...WITH KOGURE AND THE OTHERS...

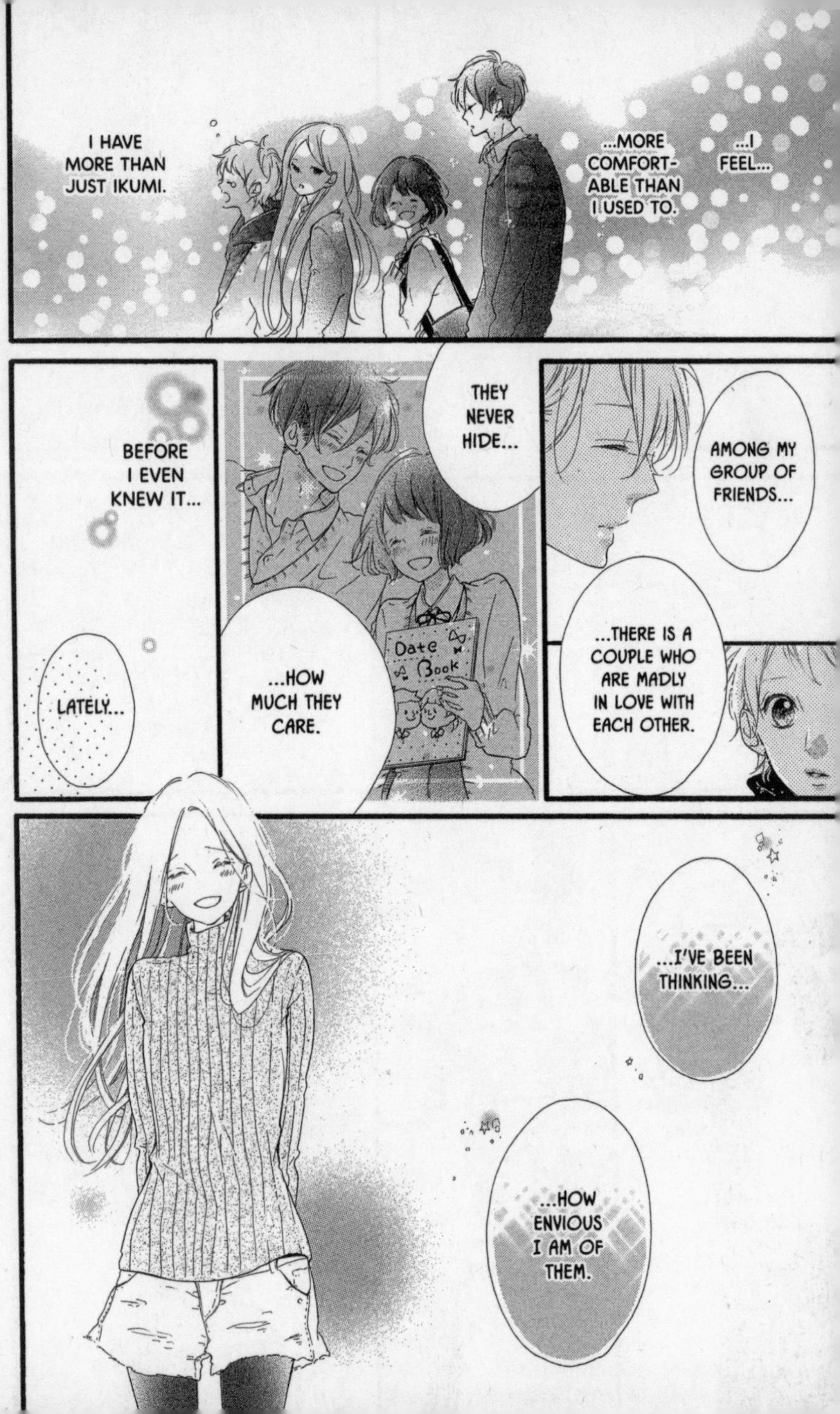
...I FEEL...
...MORE COMFORTABLE THAN I USED TO.
I HAVE MORE THAN JUST IKUMI.
AMONG MY GROUP OF FRIENDS...
...THERE IS A COUPLE WHO ARE MADLY IN LOVE WITH EACH OTHER.
THEY NEVER HIDE...
Date Book
...HOW MUCH THEY CARE.
BEFORE I EVEN KNEW IT...
LATELY...
...I'VE BEEN THINKING...
...HOW ENVIOUS I AM OF THEM.

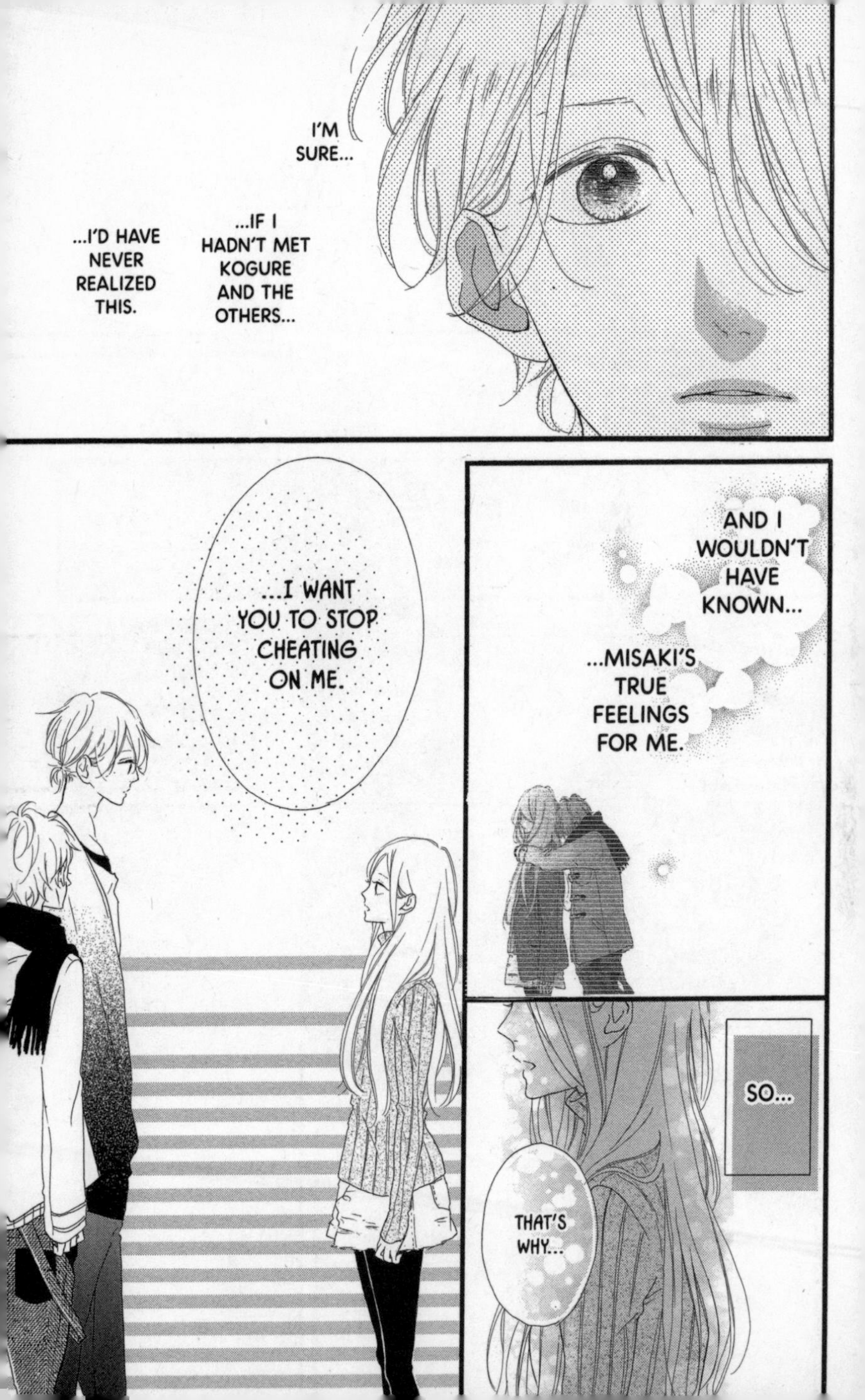
I'M SURE...
...IF I HADN'T MET KOGURE AND THE OTHERS...
...I'D HAVE NEVER REALIZED THIS.
AND I WOULDN'T HAVE KNOWN...
...MISAKI'S TRUE FEELINGS FOR ME.
SO...
THAT'S WHY...
...I WANT YOU TO STOP CHEATING ON ME.

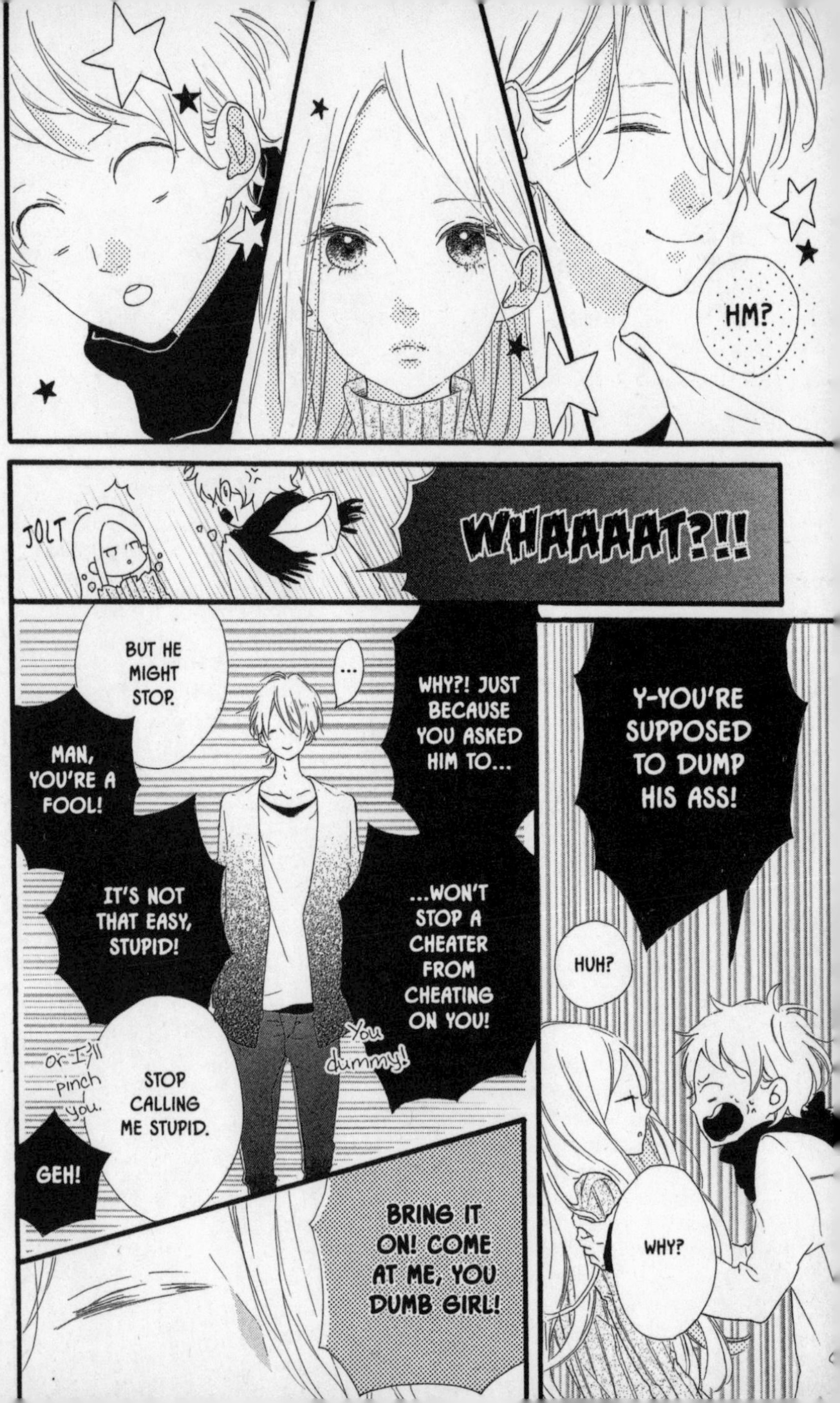
HM?
WHAAAAT?!!
JOLT
Y-YOU'RE SUPPOSED TO DUMP HIS ASS!
HUH?
WHY?
WHY?! JUST BECAUSE YOU ASKED HIM TO...
...WON'T STOP A CHEATER FROM CHEATING ON YOU!
You dummy!
...
BUT HE MIGHT STOP.
MAN, YOU'RE A FOOL!
IT'S NOT THAT EASY, STUPID!
STOP CALLING ME STUPID.
Or I'll pinch you.
GEH!
BRING IT ON! COME AT ME, YOU DUMB GIRL!

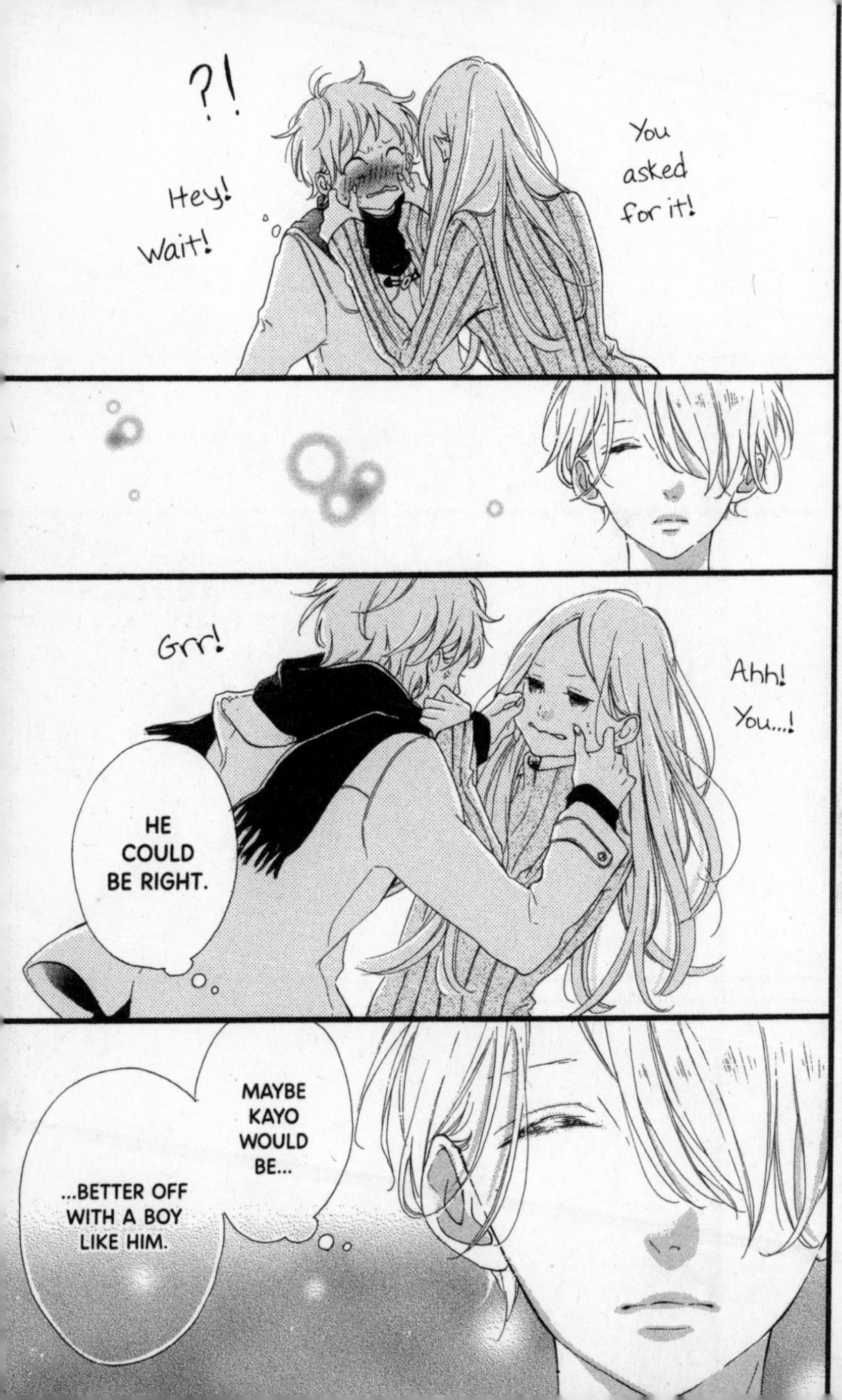
You asked for it!
?!
Hey! Wait!
Ahh! You...!
Grr!
HE COULD BE RIGHT.
MAYBE KAYO WOULD BE...
...BETTER OFF WITH A BOY LIKE HIM.

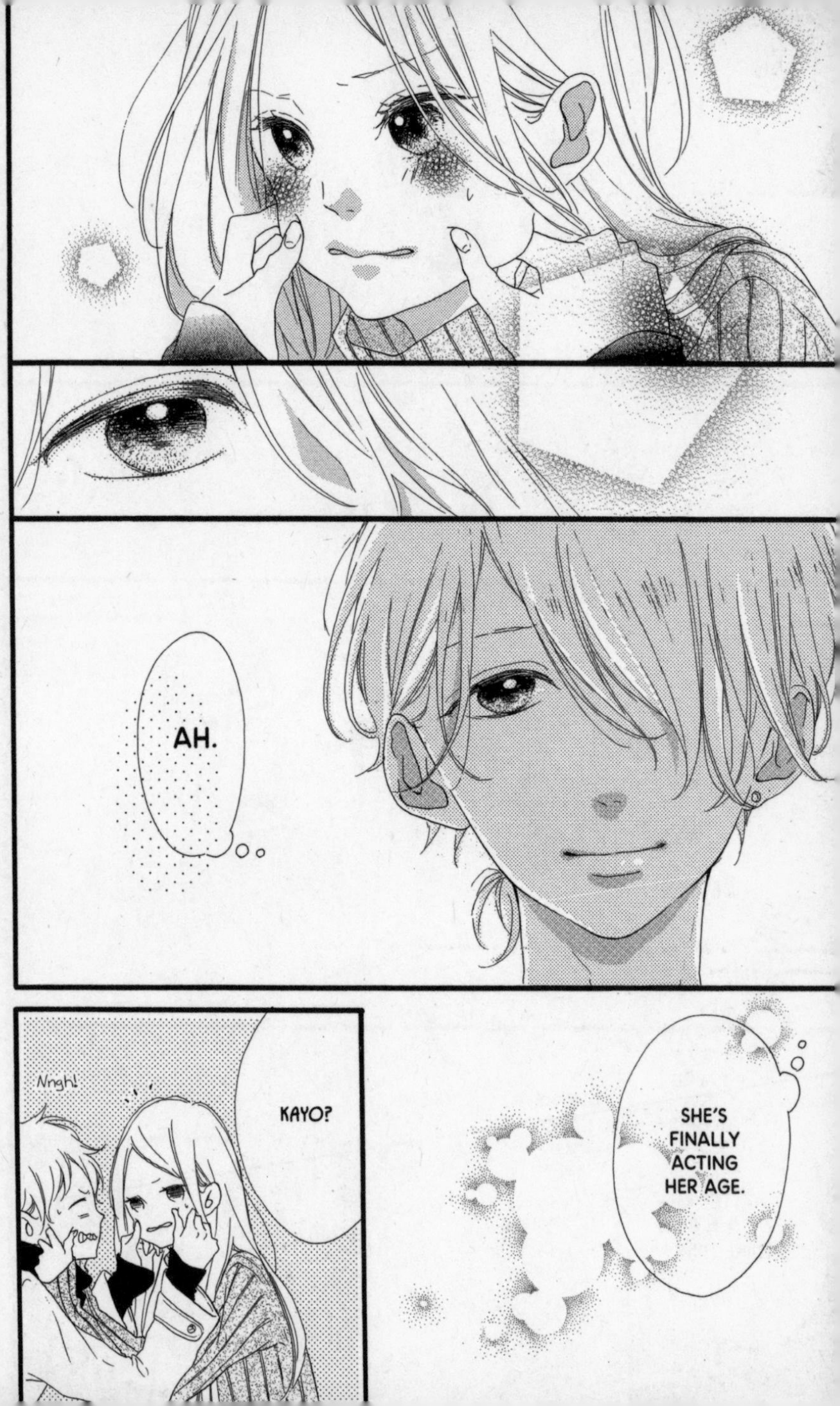
AH.
SHE'S FINALLY ACTING HER AGE.
KAYO?
Nngh!

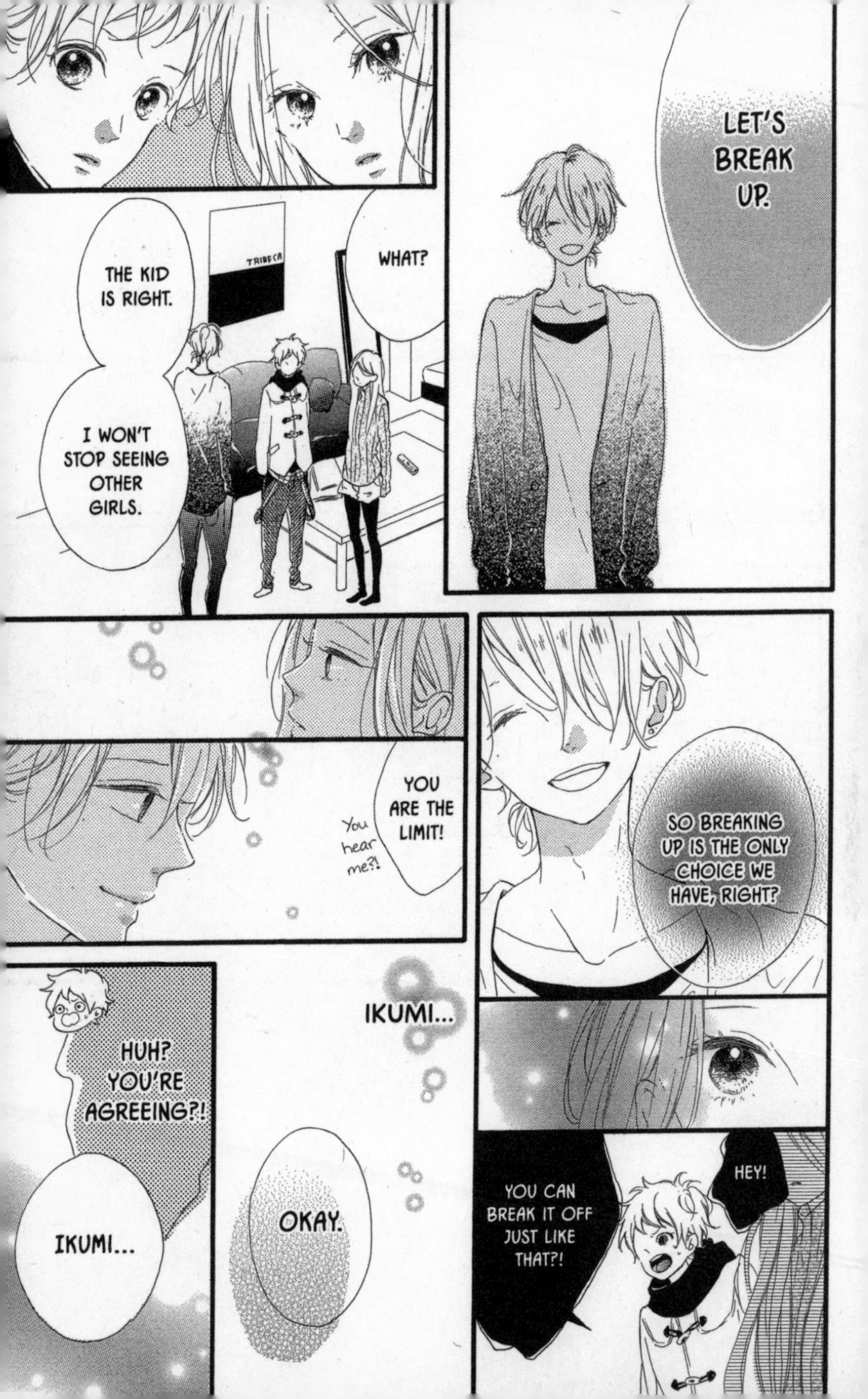

LET'S BREAK UP.
WHAT?
THE KID IS RIGHT.
I WON'T STOP SEEING OTHER GIRLS.
SO BREAKING UP IS THE ONLY CHOICE WE HAVE, RIGHT?
YOU ARE THE LIMIT!
You hear me?!
IKUMI...
HEY!
YOU CAN BREAK IT OFF JUST LIKE THAT?!
OKAY.
HUH? YOU'RE AGREEING?!
IKUMI...

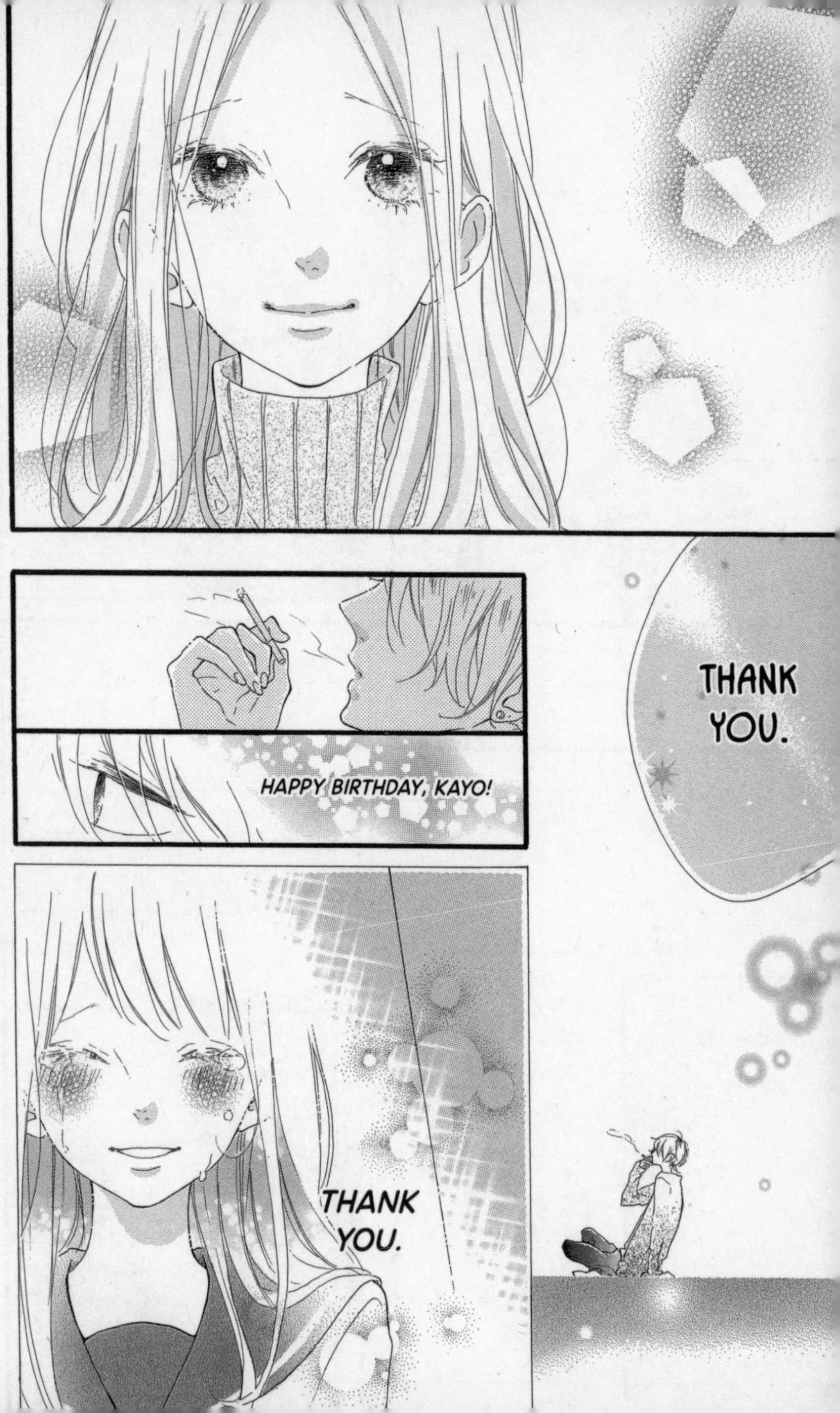
THANK YOU.
HAPPY BIRTHDAY, KAYO!
THANK YOU.

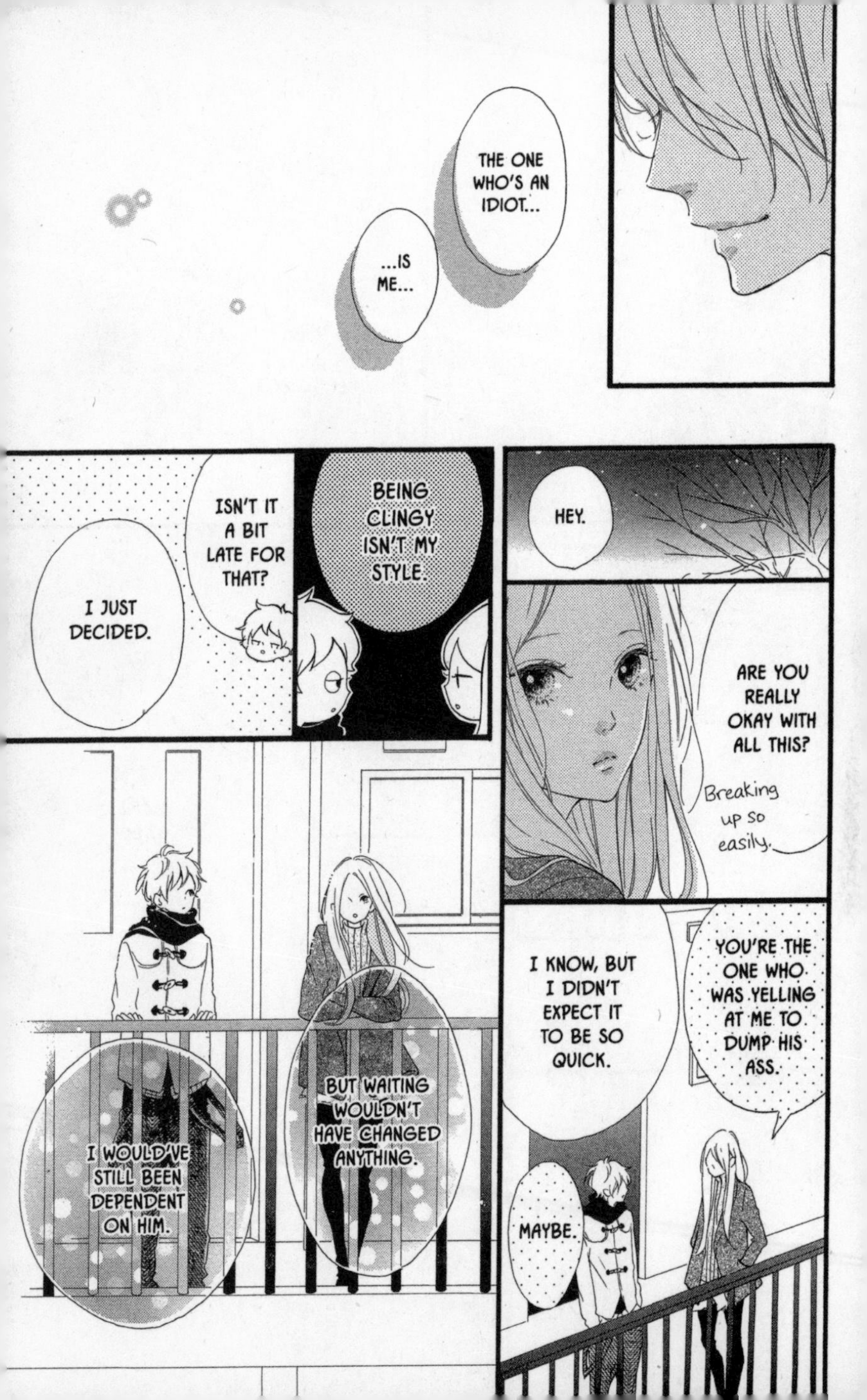
THE ONE WHO'S AN IDIOT...
...IS ME...
HEY.
ARE YOU REALLY OKAY WITH ALL THIS?
Breaking up so easily.
BEING CLINGY ISN'T MY STYLE.
ISN'T IT A BIT LATE FOR THAT?
I JUST DECIDED.
YOU'RE THE ONE WHO WAS YELLING AT ME TO DUMP HIS ASS.
I KNOW, BUT I DIDN'T EXPECT IT TO BE SO QUICK.
MAYBE.
BUT WAITING WOULDN'T HAVE CHANGED ANYTHING.
I WOULD'VE STILL BEEN DEPENDENT ON HIM.

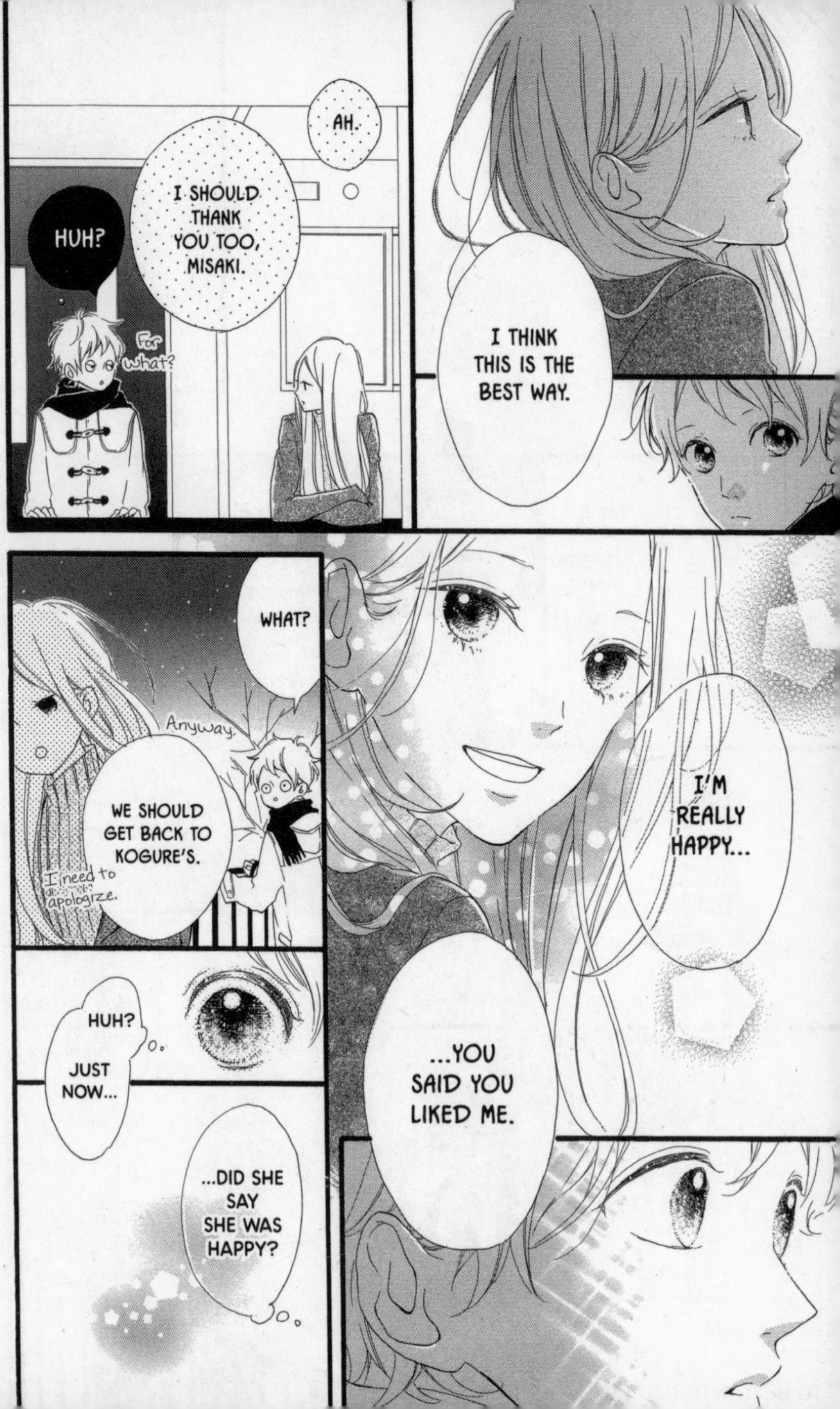

I THINK THIS IS THE BEST WAY.
AH.
I SHOULD THANK YOU TOO, MISAKI.
HUH?
For what?
I'M REALLY HAPPY...
...YOU SAID YOU LIKED ME.
WHAT?
Anyway.
WE SHOULD GET BACK TO KOGURE'S.
I need to apologize.
HUH?
JUST NOW...
...DID SHE SAY SHE WAS HAPPY?

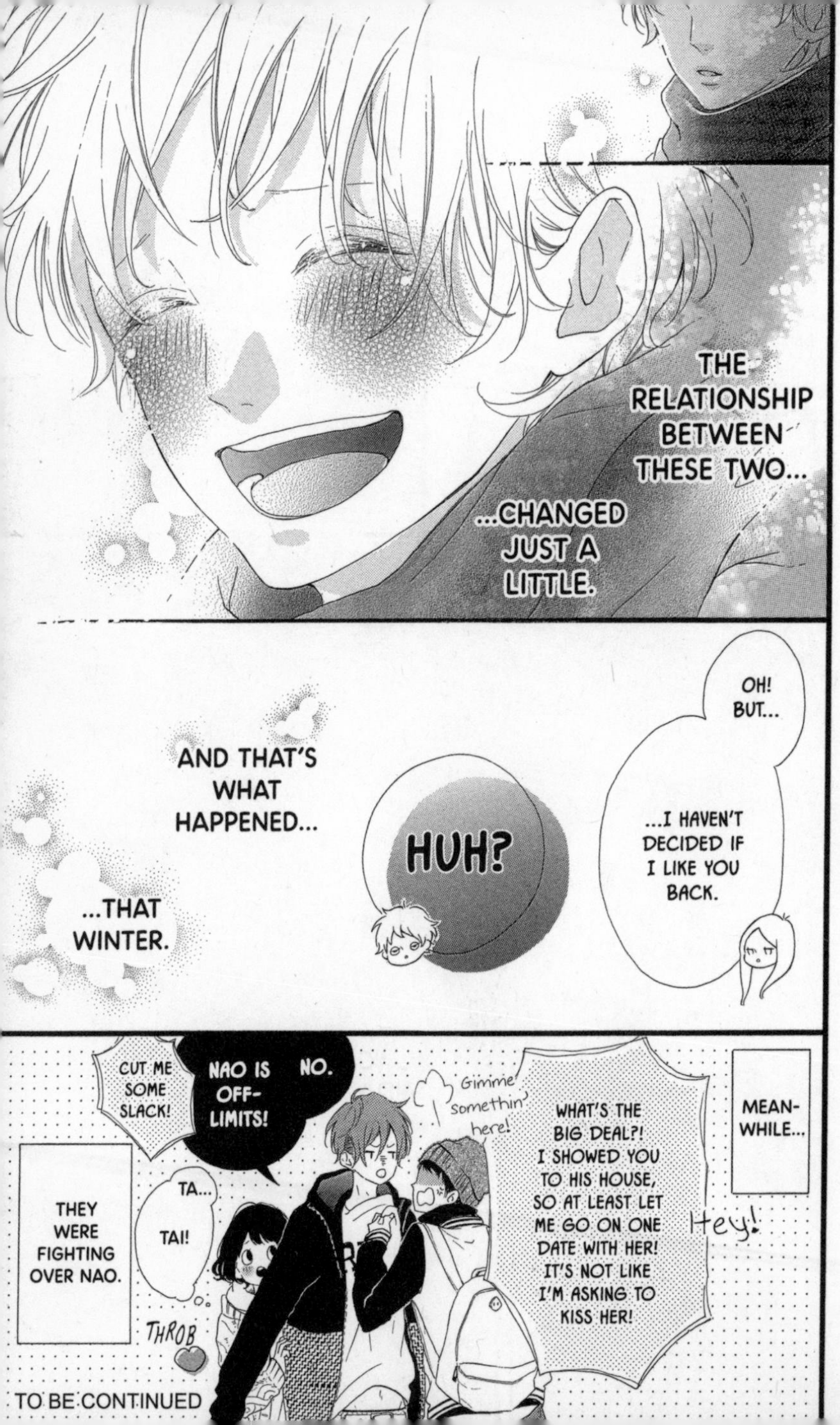
THE RELATIONSHIP BETWEEN THESE TWO...
...CHANGED JUST A LITTLE.
OH! BUT...
...I HAVEN'T DECIDED IF I LIKE YOU BACK.
HUH?
AND THAT'S WHAT HAPPENED...
...THAT WINTER.
MEAN-WHILE...
Hey!
WHAT'S THE BIG DEAL?! I SHOWED YOU TO HIS HOUSE, SO AT LEAST LET ME GO ON ONE DATE WITH HER! IT'S NOT LIKE I'M ASKING TO KISS HER!
Gimme somethin' here!
NO.
NAO IS OFF-LIMITS!
CUT ME SOME SLACK!
TA...
TAI!
THEY WERE FIGHTING OVER NAO.
THROB
TO BE CONTINUED

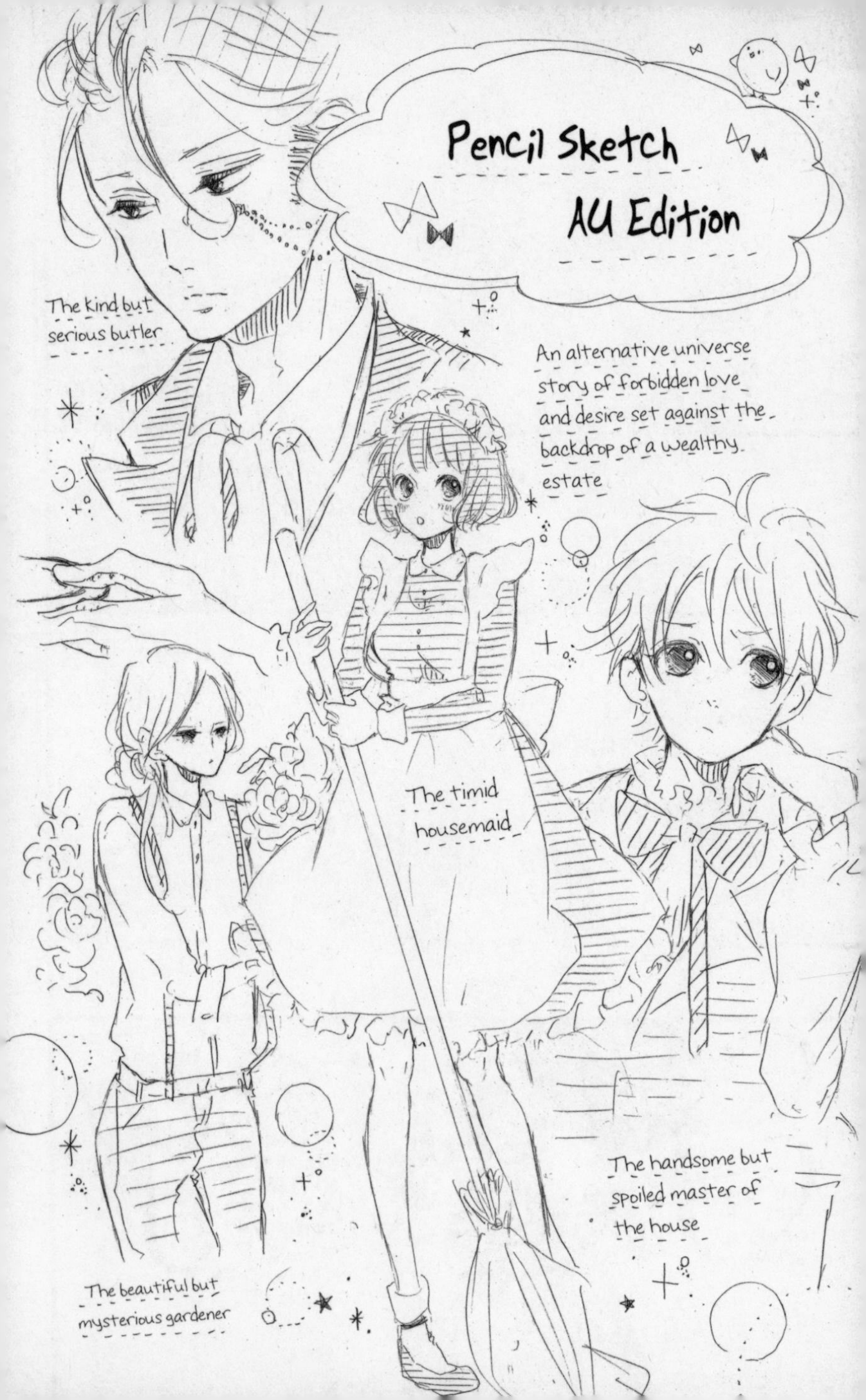

Pencil Sketch
AU Edition
The kind but serious butler
An alternative universe story of forbidden love and desire set against the backdrop of a wealthy estate
The timid housemaid
The handsome but spoiled master of the house
The beautiful but mysterious gardener

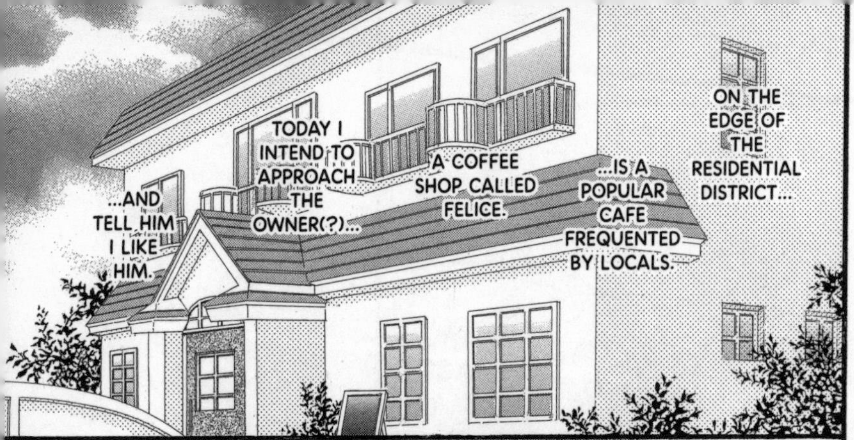
ON THE EDGE OF THE RESIDENTIAL DISTRICT...
...IS A POPULAR CAFE FREQUENTED BY LOCALS.
A COFFEE SHOP CALLED FELICE.
TODAY I INTEND TO APPROACH THE OWNER(?)...
...AND TELL HIM I LIKE HIM.

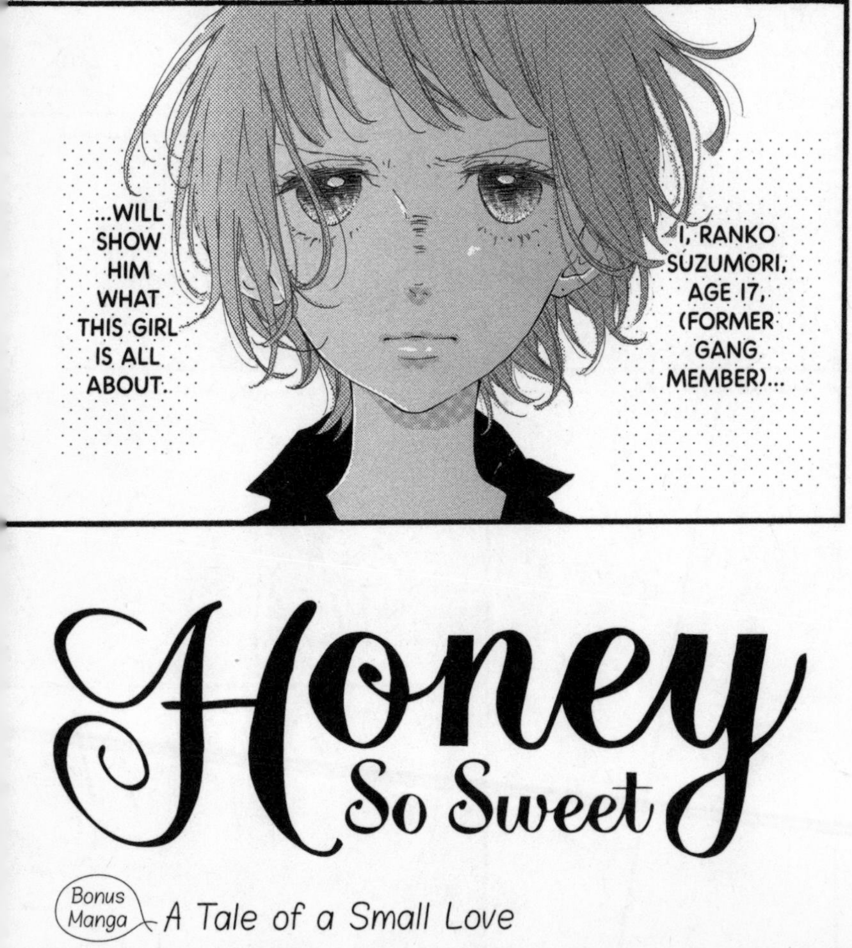
I, RANKO SUZUMORI, AGE 17, (FORMER GANG MEMBER)...
...WILL SHOW HIM WHAT THIS GIRL IS ALL ABOUT.

Honey So Sweet

Bonus Manga A Tale of a Small Love

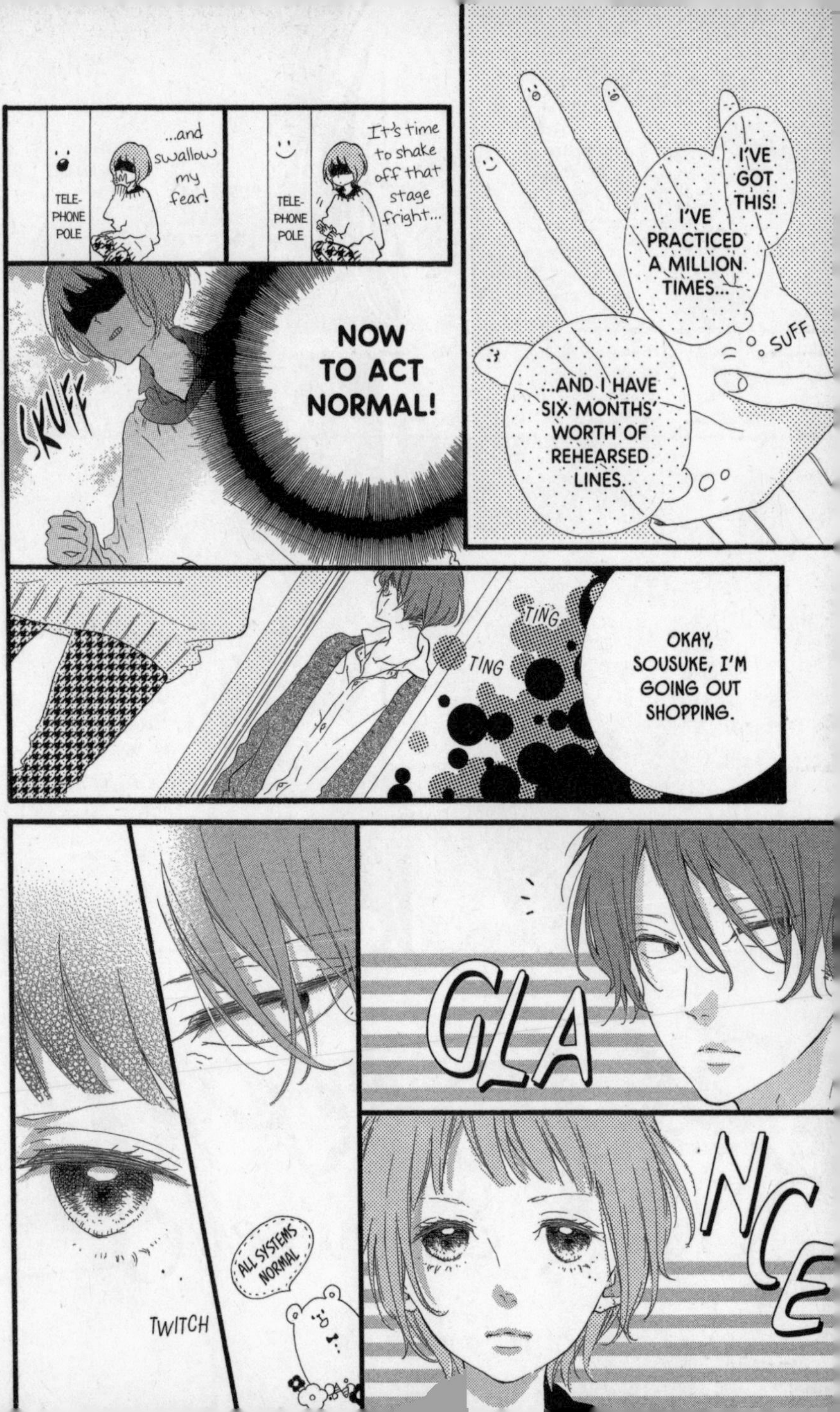
I'VE GOT THIS!
I'VE PRACTICED A MILLION TIMES...
...AND I HAVE SIX MONTHS' WORTH OF REHEARSED LINES.
SUFF
It's time to shake off that stage fright...
TELE-PHONE POLE
...and swallow my fear!
TELE-PHONE POLE
NOW TO ACT NORMAL!
SKUFF
OKAY, SOUSUKE, I'M GOING OUT SHOPPING.
TING
TING
GLA
NCE
TWITCH
ALL SYSTEMS NORMAL

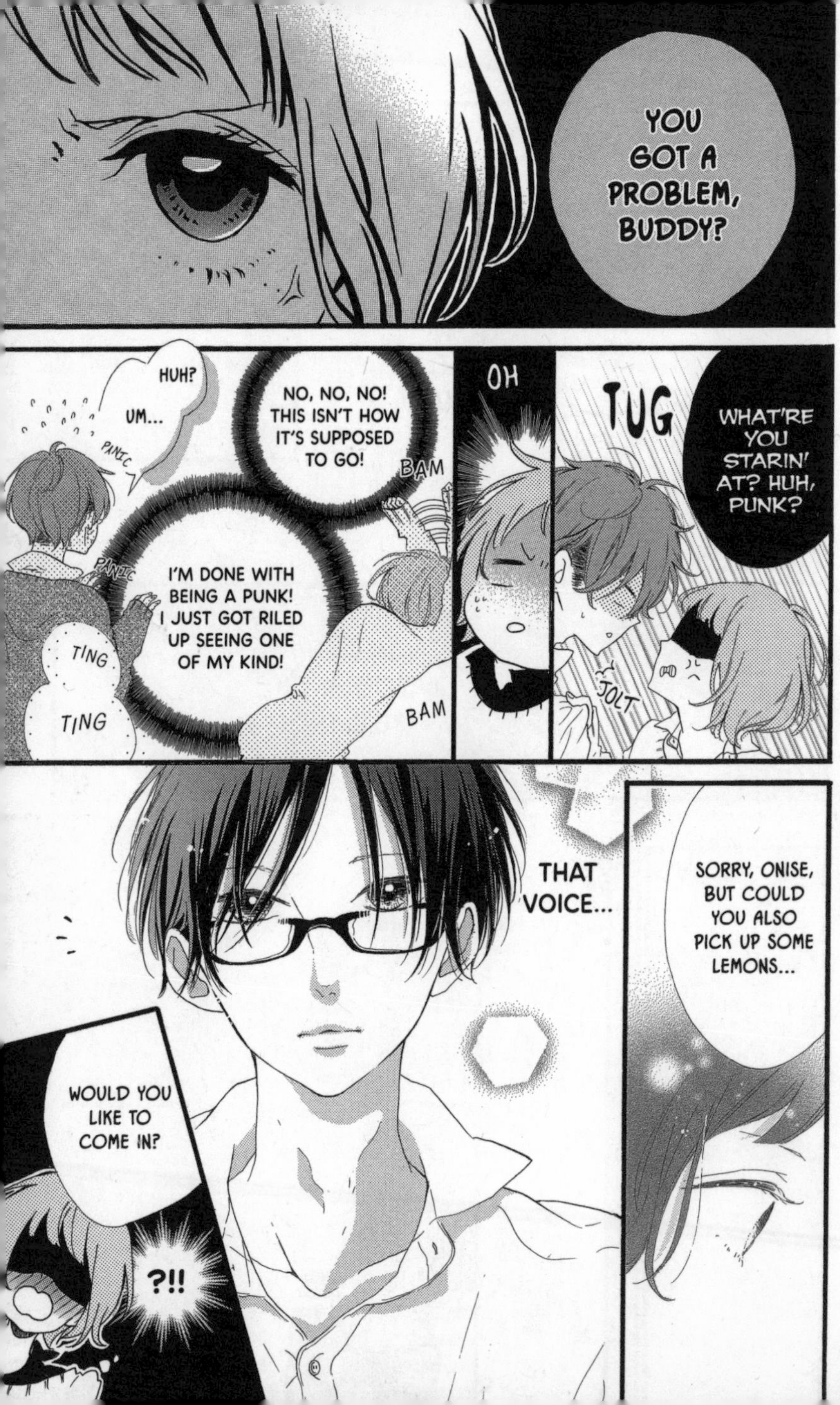
YOU GOT A PROBLEM, BUDDY?
TUG
WHAT'RE YOU STARIN' AT? HUH, PUNK?
JOLT
OH
NO, NO, NO! THIS ISN'T HOW IT'S SUPPOSED TO GO!
BAM
HUH? UM...
PANIC
I'M DONE WITH BEING A PUNK! I JUST GOT RILED UP SEEING ONE OF MY KIND!
PANIC
BAM
TING
TING
SORRY, ONISE, BUT COULD YOU ALSO PICK UP SOME LEMONS...
THAT VOICE...
WOULD YOU LIKE TO COME IN?
?!!

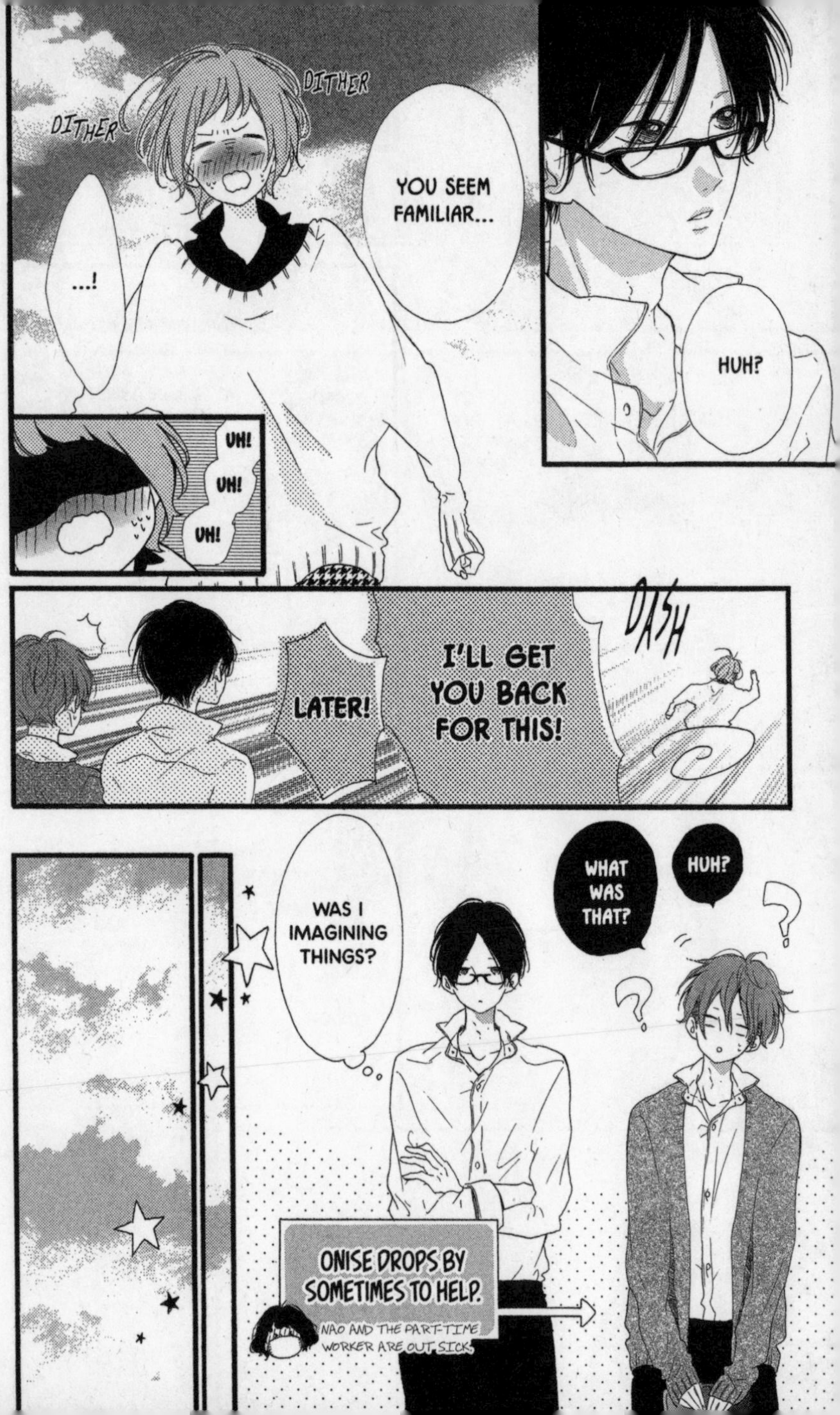
HUH?
DITHER
YOU SEEM FAMILIAR...
DITHER
...!
UH!
UH!
UH!
DASH
I'LL GET YOU BACK FOR THIS!
LATER!
HUH?
WHAT WAS THAT?
WAS I IMAGINING THINGS?
ONISE DROPS BY SOMETIMES TO HELP.
NAO AND THE PART-TIME WORKER ARE OUT SICK.

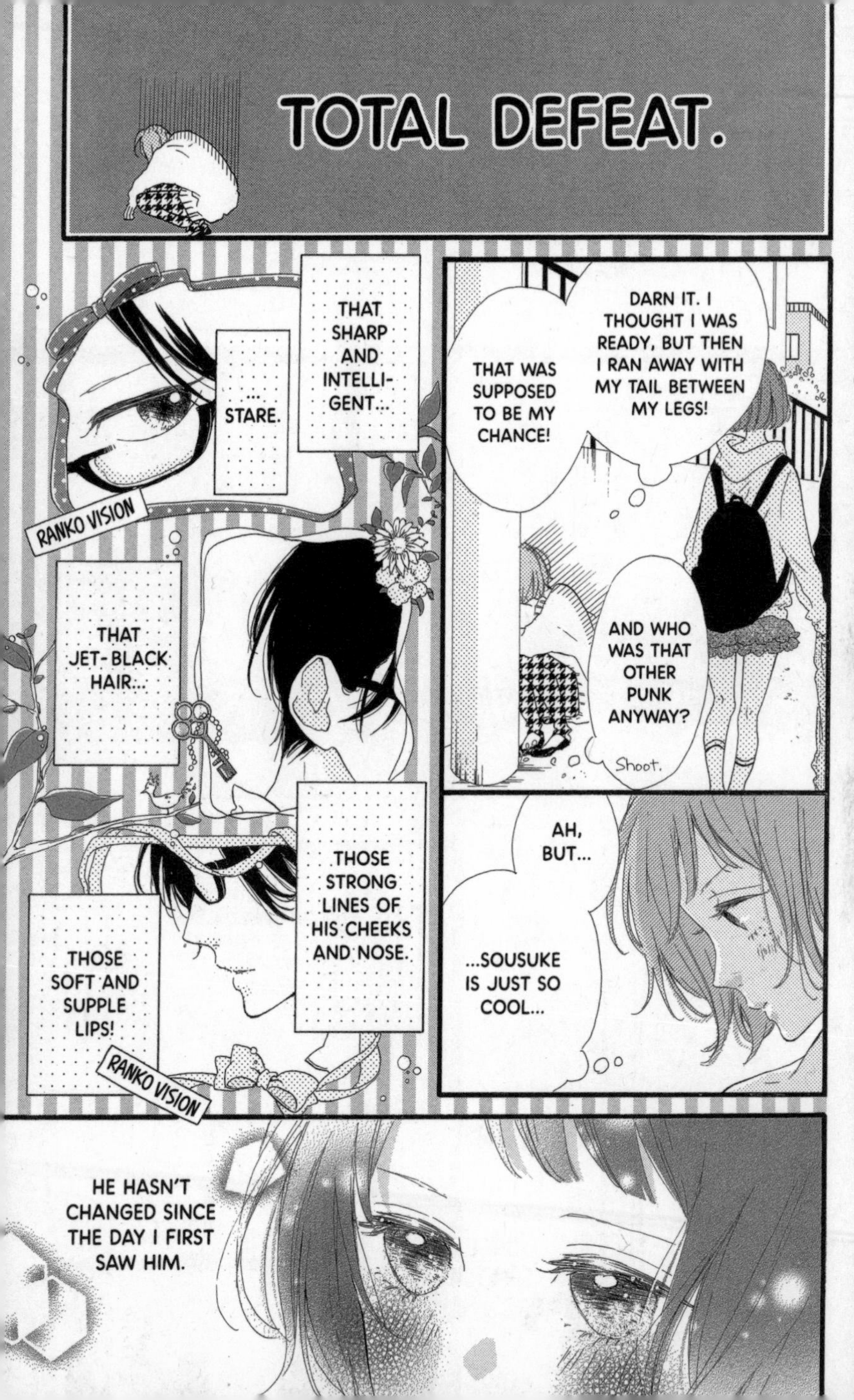
TOTAL DEFEAT.
DARN IT. I THOUGHT I WAS READY, BUT THEN I RAN AWAY WITH MY TAIL BETWEEN MY LEGS!
THAT WAS SUPPOSED TO BE MY CHANCE!
AND WHO WAS THAT OTHER PUNK ANYWAY?
Shoot.
AH, BUT...
...SOUSUKE IS JUST SO COOL...
THAT SHARP AND INTELLI-GENT...
...STARE.
RANKO VISION
THAT JET-BLACK HAIR...
THOSE STRONG LINES OF HIS CHEEKS AND NOSE.
THOSE SOFT AND SUPPLE LIPS!
RANKO VISION
HE HASN'T CHANGED SINCE THE DAY I FIRST SAW HIM.

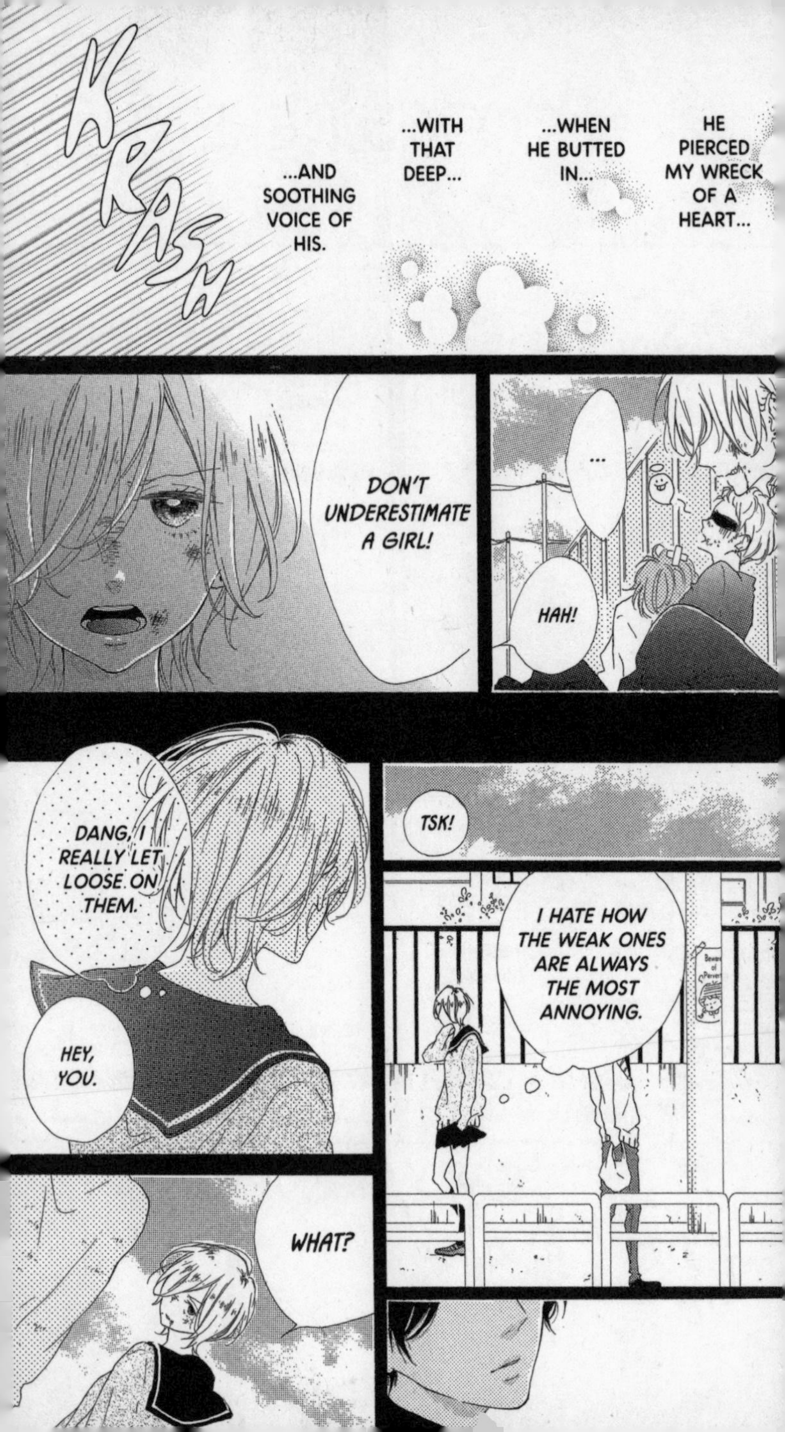
HE PIERCED MY WRECK OF A HEART...
...WHEN HE BUTTED IN...
...WITH THAT DEEP...
...AND SOOTHING VOICE OF HIS.
KRASH
...
HAH!
DON'T UNDERESTIMATE A GIRL!
TSK!
I HATE HOW THE WEAK ONES ARE ALWAYS THE MOST ANNOYING.
DANG, I REALLY LET LOOSE ON THEM.
HEY, YOU.
WHAT?

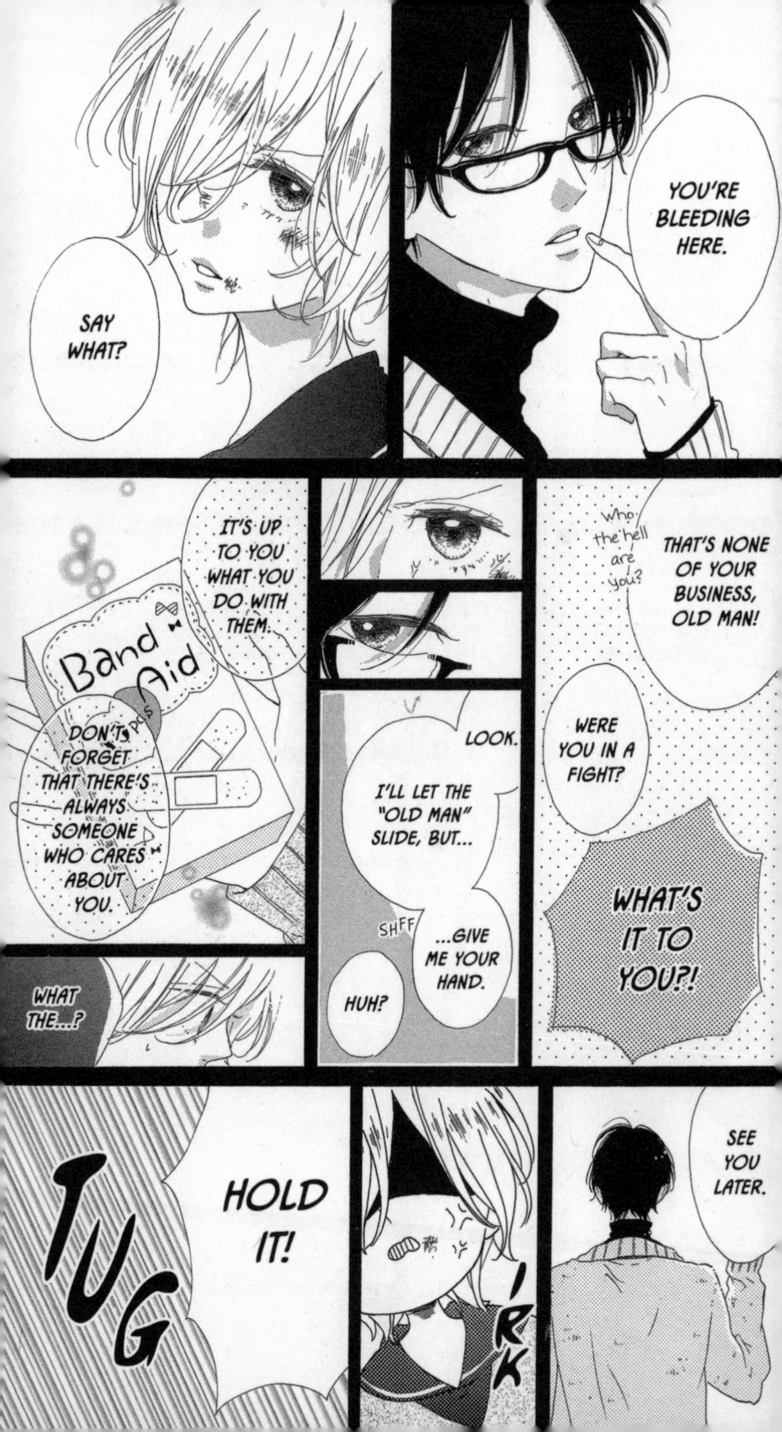
YOU'RE BLEEDING HERE.
SAY WHAT?
Who the hell are you?
THAT'S NONE OF YOUR BUSINESS, OLD MAN!
WERE YOU IN A FIGHT?
WHAT'S IT TO YOU?!
LOOK.
I'LL LET THE "OLD MAN" SLIDE, BUT...
...GIVE ME YOUR HAND.
SHFF
HUH?
IT'S UP TO YOU WHAT YOU DO WITH THEM.
Band Aid
DON'T FORGET THAT THERE'S ALWAYS SOMEONE WHO CARES ABOUT YOU.
WHAT THE...?
SEE YOU LATER.
IRK
HOLD IT!
TUG

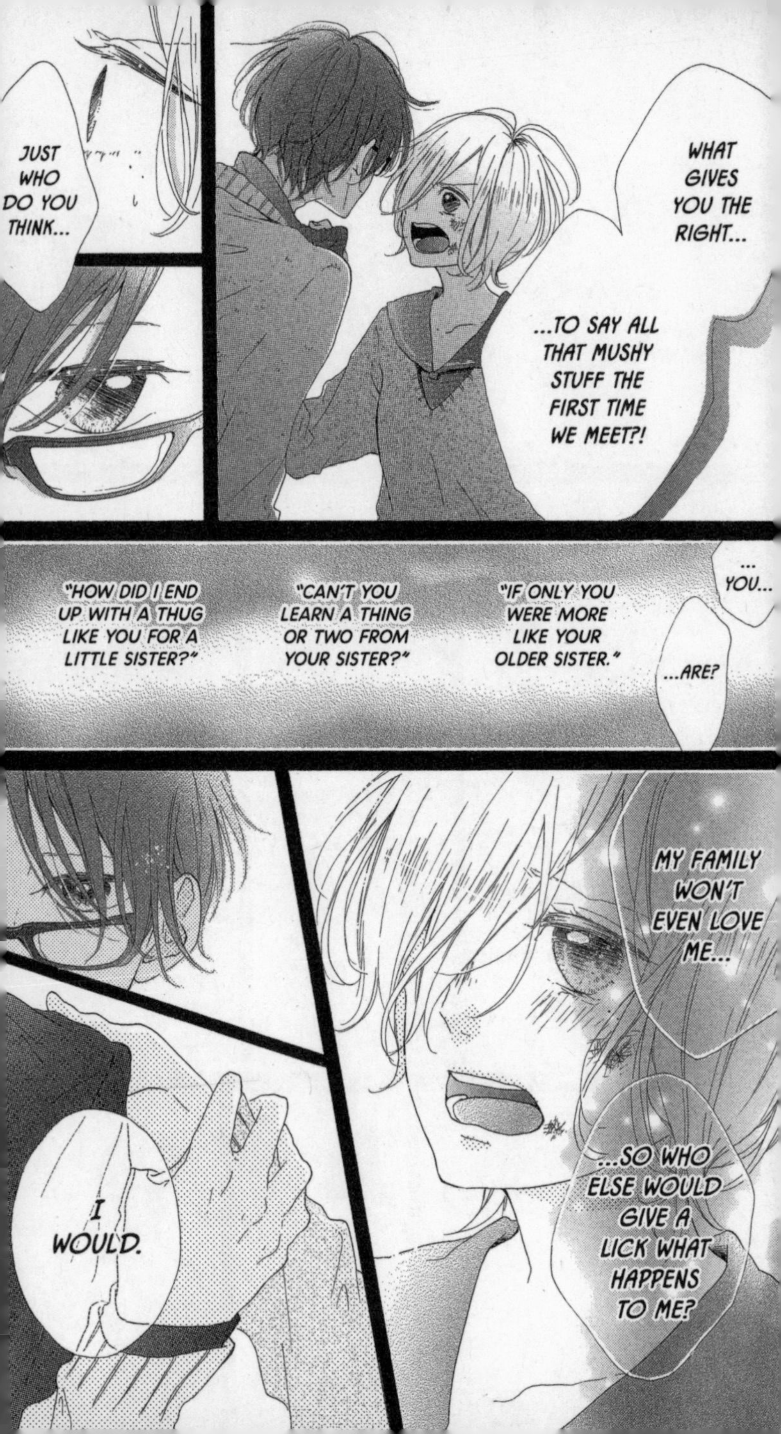
WHAT GIVES YOU THE RIGHT...
...TO SAY ALL THAT MUSHY STUFF THE FIRST TIME WE MEET?!
JUST WHO DO YOU THINK...
... YOU...
...ARE?
"IF ONLY YOU WERE MORE LIKE YOUR OLDER SISTER."
"CAN'T YOU LEARN A THING OR TWO FROM YOUR SISTER?"
"HOW DID I END UP WITH A THUG LIKE YOU FOR A LITTLE SISTER?"
MY FAMILY WON'T EVEN LOVE ME...
...SO WHO ELSE WOULD GIVE A LICK WHAT HAPPENS TO ME?
I WOULD.

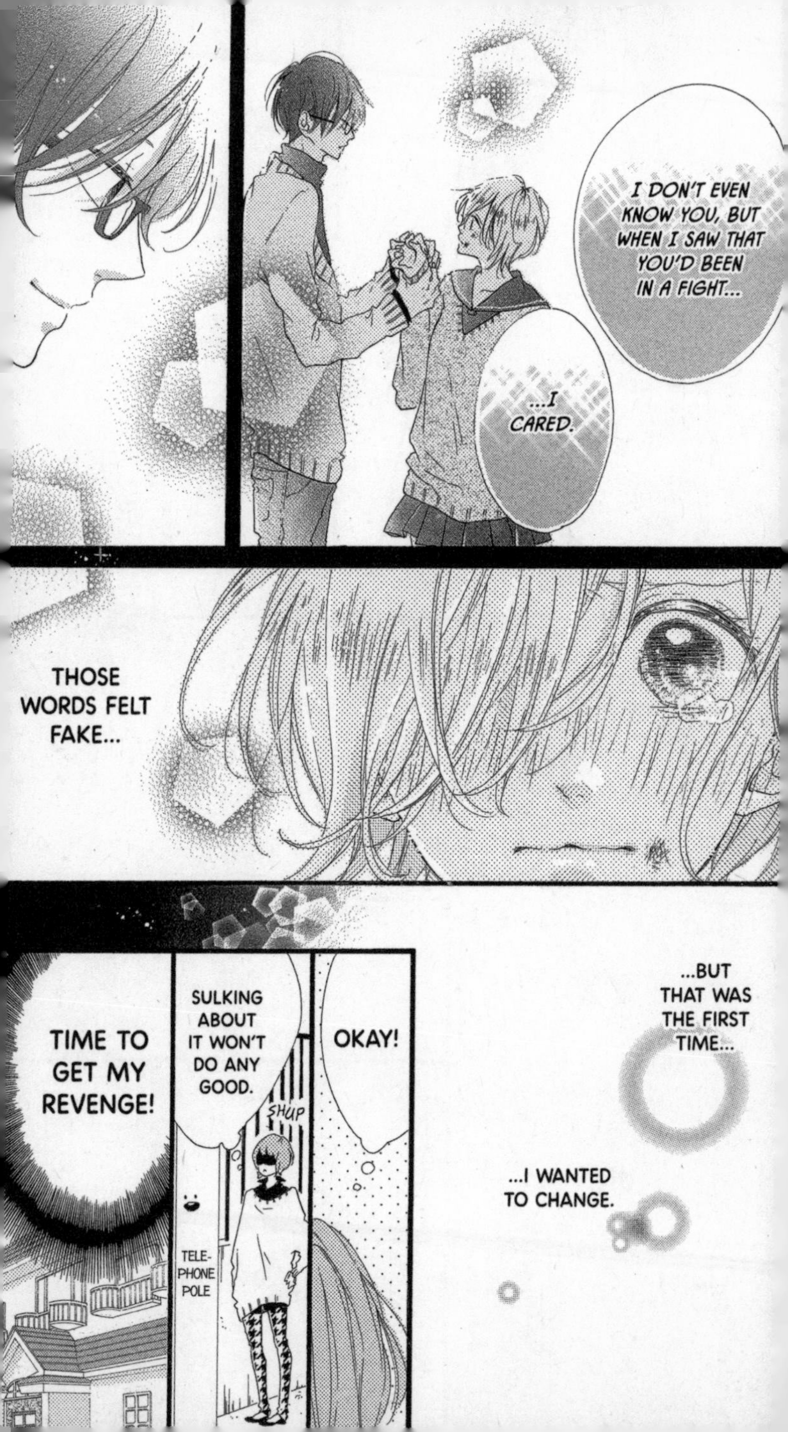
I DON'T EVEN KNOW YOU, BUT WHEN I SAW THAT YOU'D BEEN IN A FIGHT...
...I CARED.
THOSE WORDS FELT FAKE...
...BUT THAT WAS THE FIRST TIME...
...I WANTED TO CHANGE.
OKAY!
SULKING ABOUT IT WON'T DO ANY GOOD.
SHUP
TELEPHONE POLE
TIME TO GET MY REVENGE!

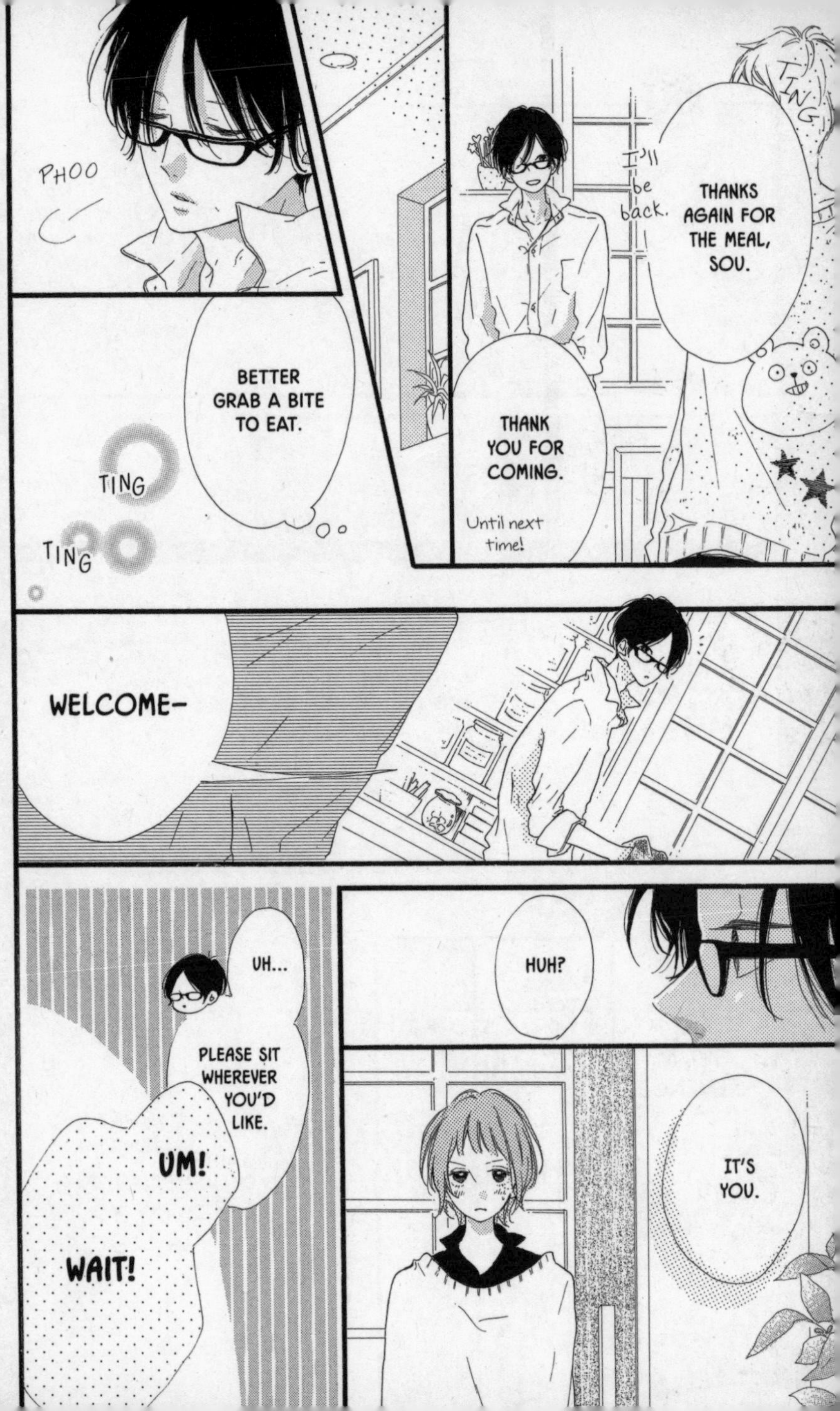
TING
THANKS AGAIN FOR THE MEAL, SOU.
I'll be back.
THANK YOU FOR COMING.
Until next time!
PHOO
BETTER GRAB A BITE TO EAT.
TING
TING
WELCOME-
HUH?
IT'S YOU.
UH...
PLEASE SIT WHEREVER YOU'D LIKE.
UM!
WAIT!

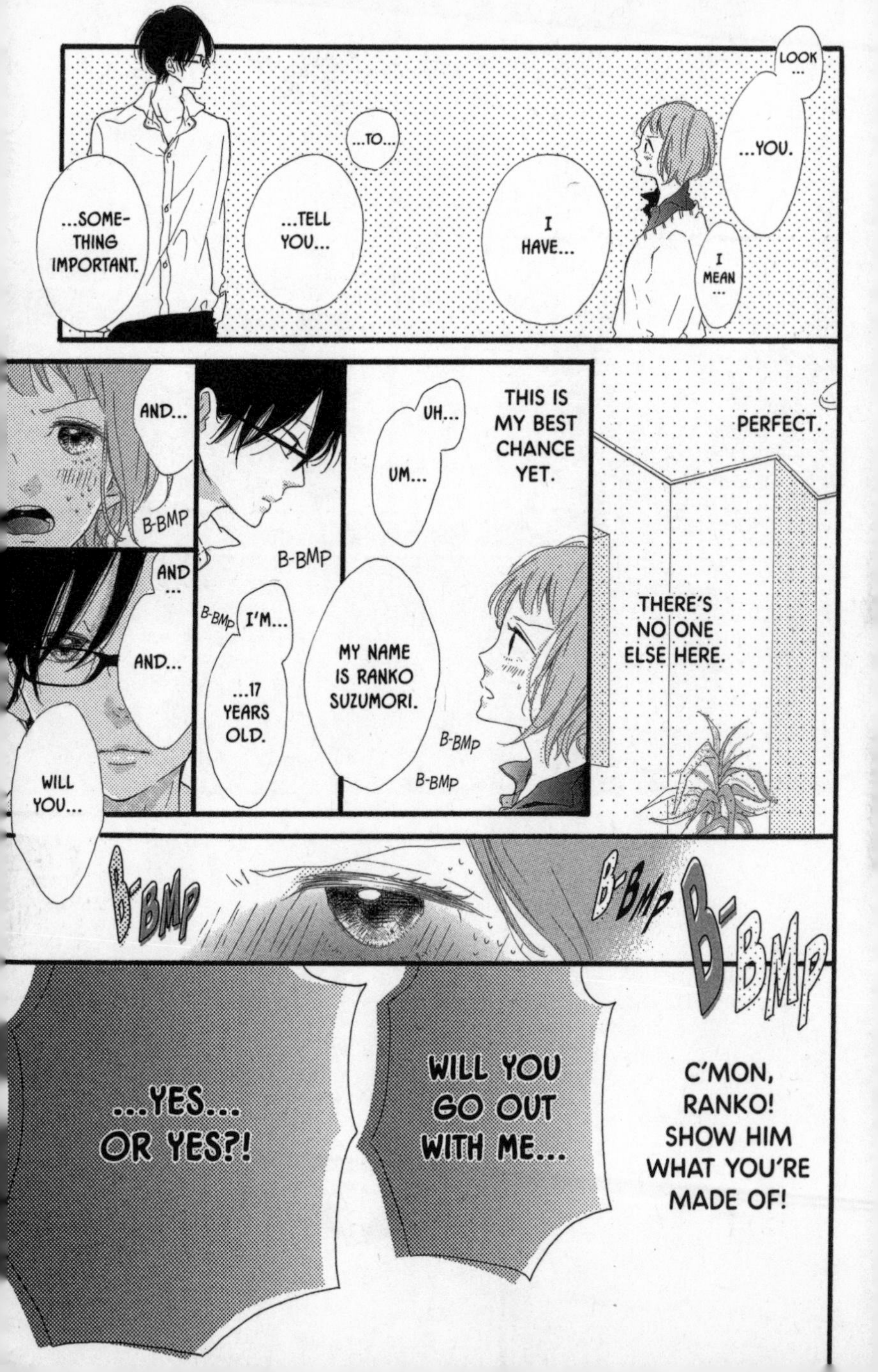
LOOK ...
...YOU.
I MEAN ...
I HAVE...
...TO...
...TELL YOU...
...SOME-THING IMPORTANT.
PERFECT.
THERE'S NO ONE ELSE HERE.
THIS IS MY BEST CHANCE YET.
UH...
UM...
MY NAME IS RANKO SUZUMORI.
B-BMP
B-BMP
B-BMP
B-BMP
I'M...
...17 YEARS OLD.
AND...
B-BMP
AND ...
AND...
WILL YOU...
B-BMP
B-BMP
B-BMP
C'MON, RANKO! SHOW HIM WHAT YOU'RE MADE OF!
WILL YOU GO OUT WITH ME...
...YES... OR YES?!

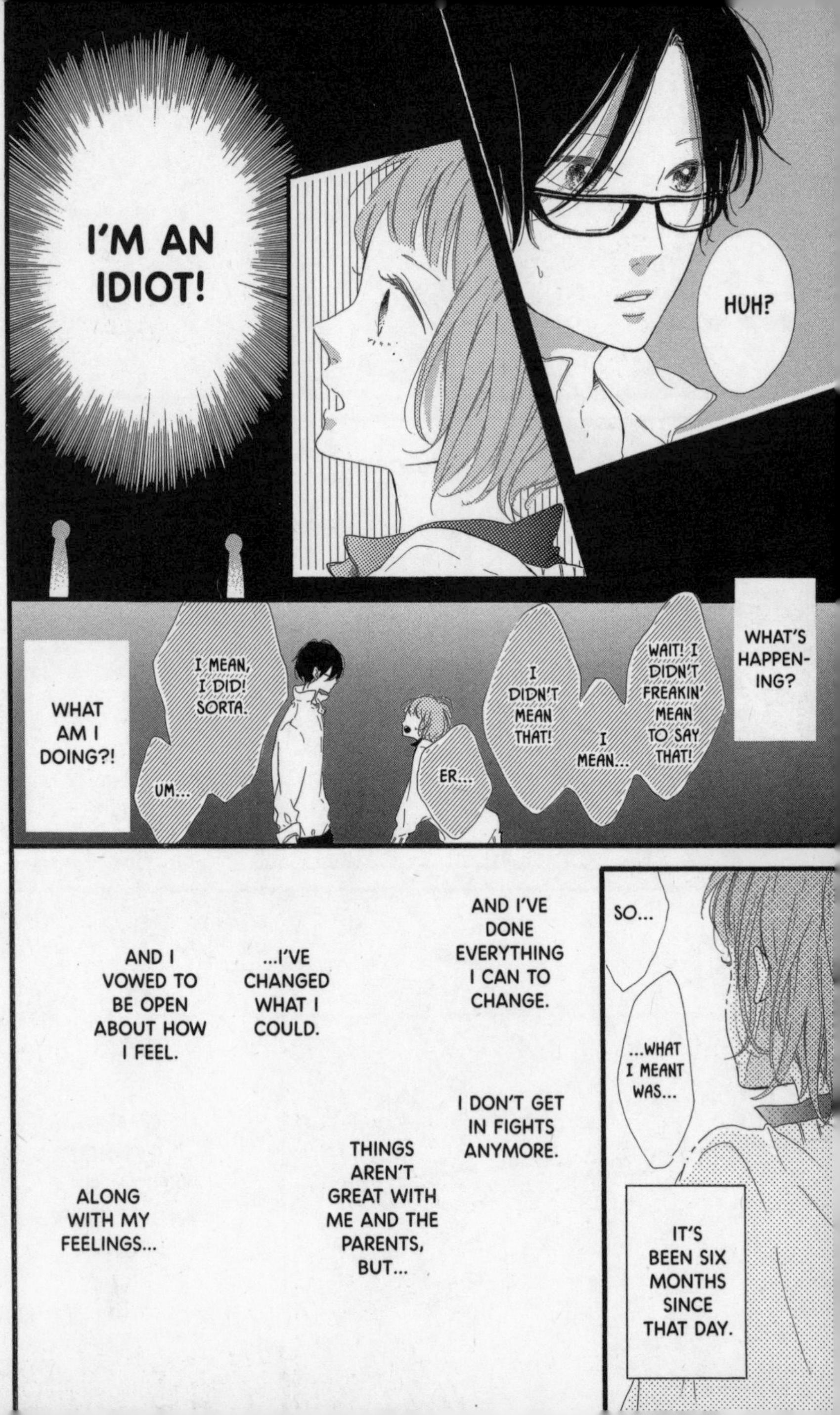
HUH?
I'M AN IDIOT!
WHAT'S HAPPENING?
WAIT! I DIDN'T FREAKIN' MEAN TO SAY THAT!
I MEAN...
I DIDN'T MEAN THAT!
ER...
I MEAN, I DID! SORTA.
UM...
WHAT AM I DOING?!
SO...
...WHAT I MEANT WAS...
IT'S BEEN SIX MONTHS SINCE THAT DAY.
AND I'VE DONE EVERYTHING I CAN TO CHANGE.
I DON'T GET IN FIGHTS ANYMORE.
THINGS AREN'T GREAT WITH ME AND THE PARENTS, BUT...
...I'VE CHANGED WHAT I COULD.
AND I VOWED TO BE OPEN ABOUT HOW I FEEL.
ALONG WITH MY FEELINGS...

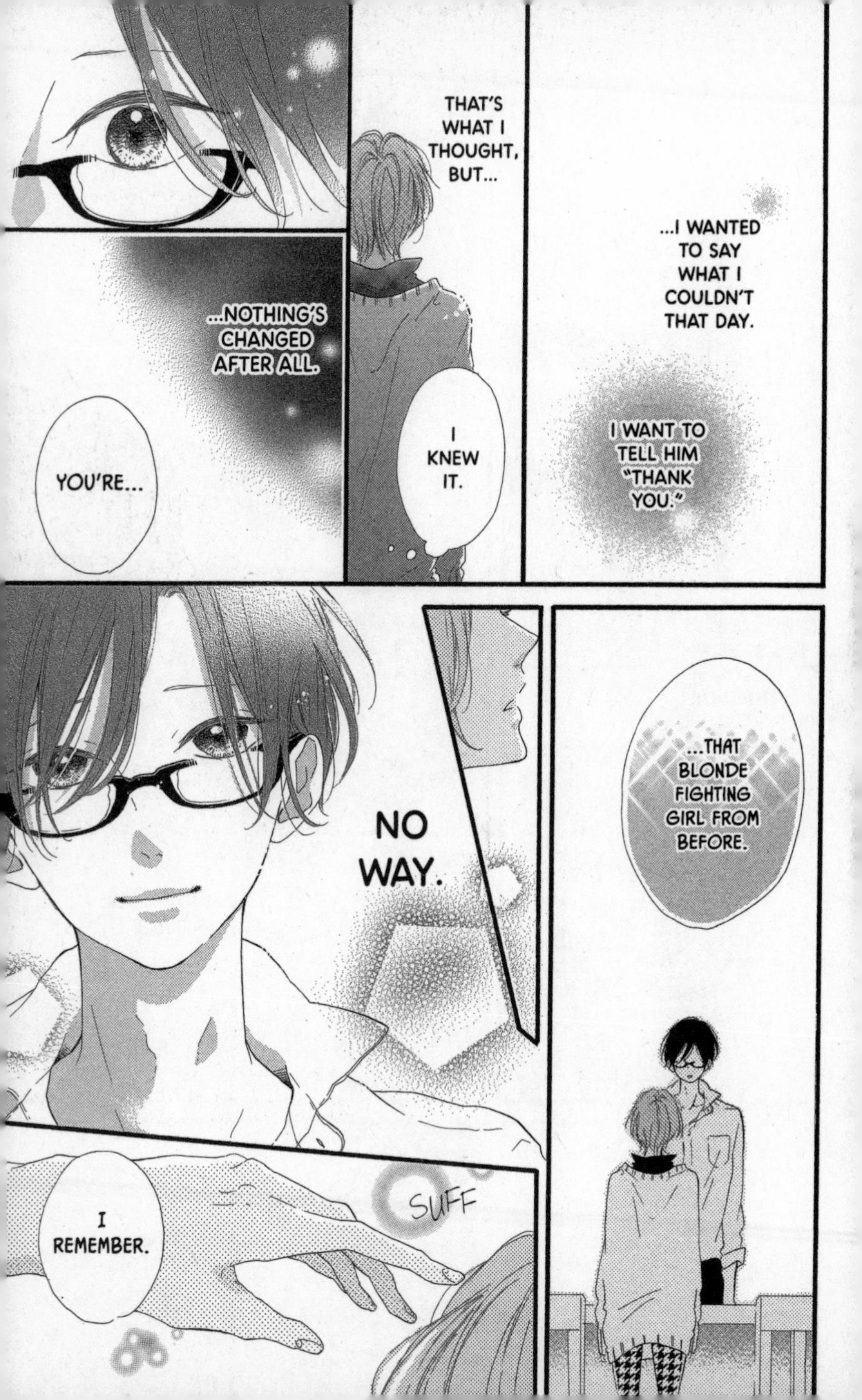
...I WANTED TO SAY WHAT I COULDN'T THAT DAY.
I WANT TO TELL HIM "THANK YOU."
THAT'S WHAT I THOUGHT, BUT...
I KNEW IT.
...NOTHING'S CHANGED AFTER ALL.
YOU'RE...
...THAT BLONDE FIGHTING GIRL FROM BEFORE.
NO WAY.
SUFF
I REMEMBER.

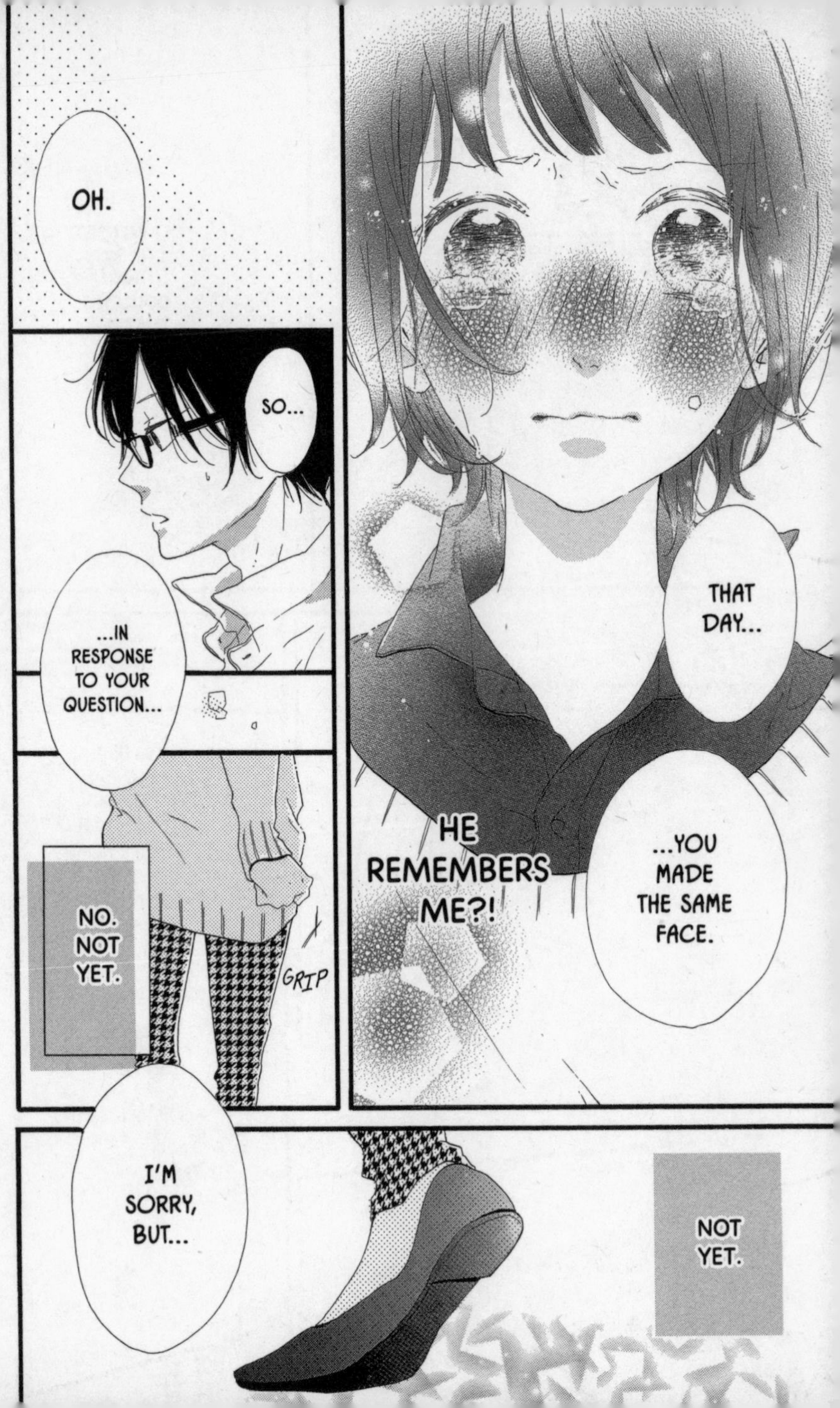
THAT DAY...
...YOU MADE THE SAME FACE.
HE REMEMBERS ME?!
OH.
SO...
...IN RESPONSE TO YOUR QUESTION...
GRIP
NO. NOT YET.
I'M SORRY, BUT...
NOT YET.

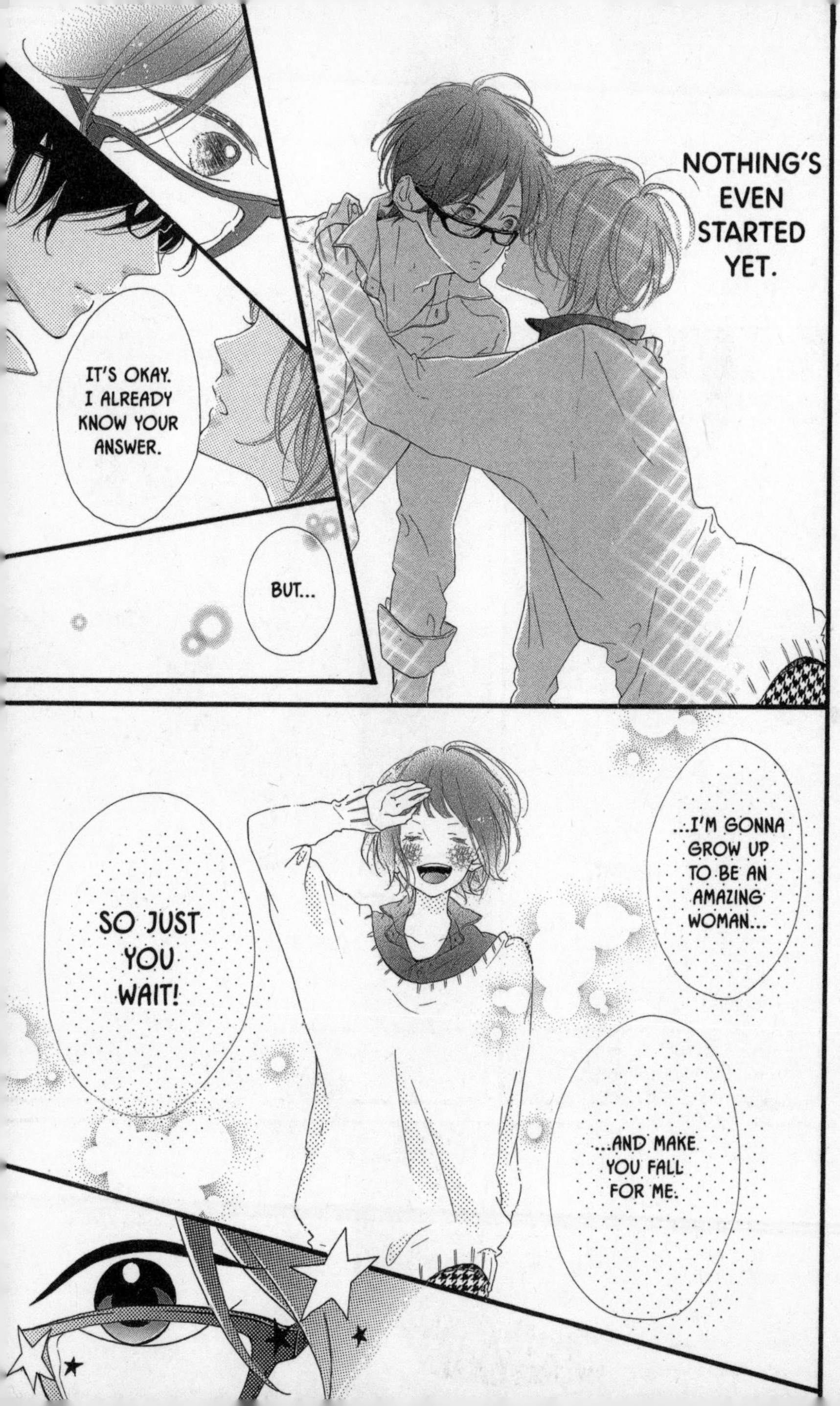
NOTHING'S EVEN STARTED YET.
IT'S OKAY. I ALREADY KNOW YOUR ANSWER.
BUT...
...I'M GONNA GROW UP TO BE AN AMAZING WOMAN...
...AND MAKE YOU FALL FOR ME.
SO JUST YOU WAIT!

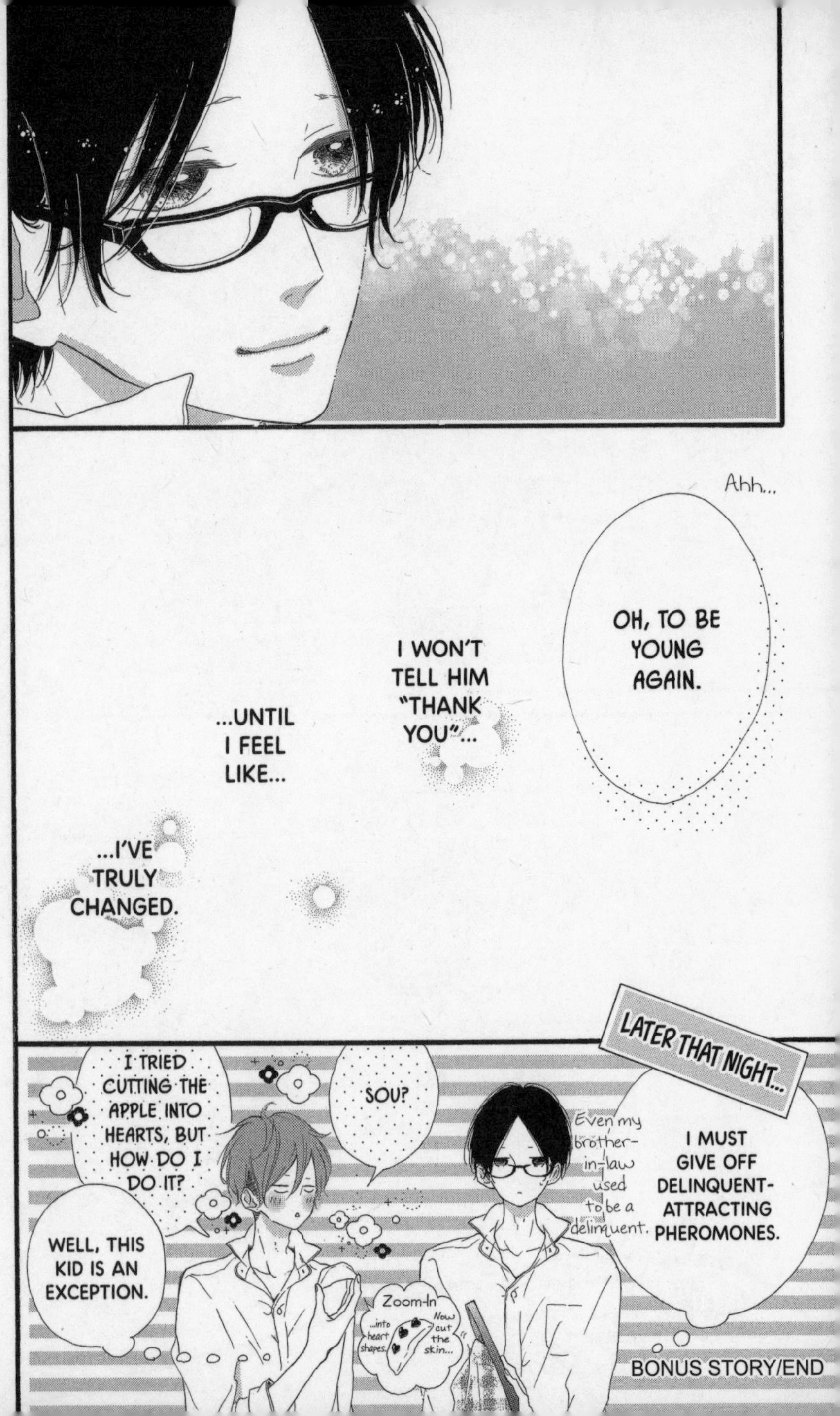
Ahh...
OH, TO BE YOUNG AGAIN.
I WON'T TELL HIM "THANK YOU"...
...UNTIL I FEEL LIKE...
...I'VE TRULY CHANGED.
LATER THAT NIGHT...
I MUST GIVE OFF DELINQUENT-ATTRACTING PHEROMONES.
Even my brother-in-law used to be a delinquent.
SOU?
I TRIED CUTTING THE APPLE INTO HEARTS, BUT HOW DO I DO IT?
WELL, THIS KID IS AN EXCEPTION.
Zoom-In
Now cut the skin...
...into heart shapes.
BONUS STORY/END

- Ranko Suzumori, high school junior, former gang member

- Defining Features: Drooping eyes and two moles

This was a special side story for *Honey So Sweet* that was published in a sister magazine! It's hard to draw Ranko's face, but she's a very unique character. ⋈ She can hold her own in a fight better than a boy! I don't think she's ever lost.

This shows that Nao and Sou are connected by both having given bandages to help delinquents. Not that Onise is a real delinquent. (*laugh*)

Bonus Manga

Sadist or Masochist

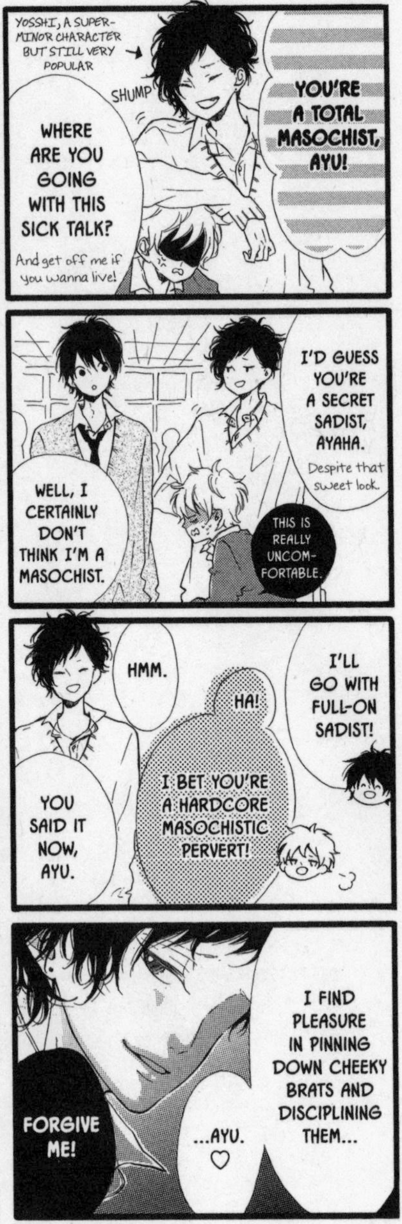
YOU'RE A TOTAL MASOCHIST, AYU!
YOSSHI, A SUPER-MINOR CHARACTER BUT STILL VERY POPULAR
SHUMP
WHERE ARE YOU GOING WITH THIS SICK TALK?
And get off me if you wanna live!
I'D GUESS YOU'RE A SECRET SADIST, AYAHA.
Despite that sweet look.
THIS IS REALLY UNCOMFORTABLE.
WELL, I CERTAINLY DON'T THINK I'M A MASOCHIST.
I'LL GO WITH FULL-ON SADIST!
HA!
HMM.
I BET YOU'RE A HARDCORE MASOCHISTIC PERVERT!
YOU SAID IT NOW, AYU.
I FIND PLEASURE IN PINNING DOWN CHEEKY BRATS AND DISCIPLINING THEM...
...AYU. ♡
FORGIVE ME!

Sadist or Masochist ②

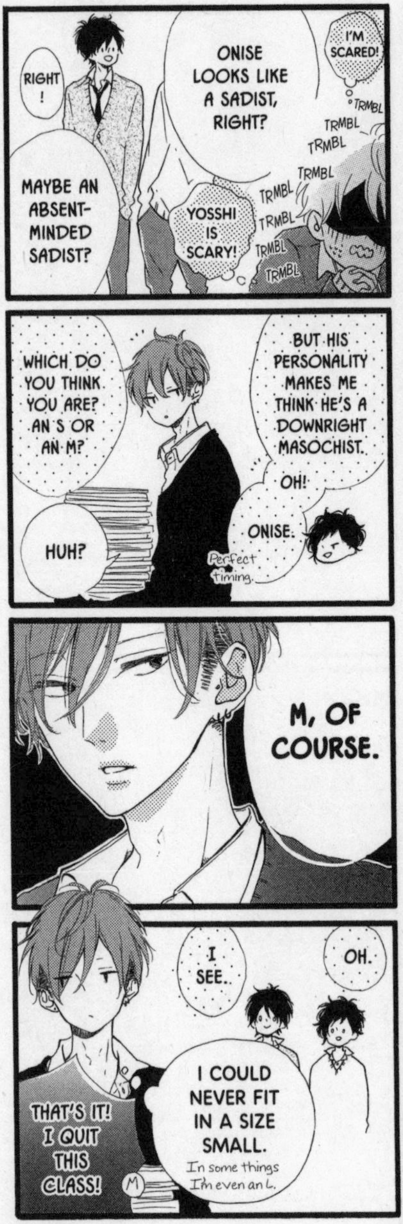
I'M SCARED!
ONISE LOOKS LIKE A SADIST, RIGHT?
RIGHT!
TRMBL TRMBL TRMBL TRMBL TRMBL TRMBL TRMBL TRMBL
YOSSHI IS SCARY!
MAYBE AN ABSENT-MINDED SADIST?
BUT HIS PERSONALITY MAKES ME THINK HE'S A DOWNRIGHT MASOCHIST.
WHICH DO YOU THINK YOU ARE? AN S OR AN M?
OH!
ONISE.
Perfect timing.
HUH?
M, OF COURSE.
OH.
I SEE.
I COULD NEVER FIT IN A SIZE SMALL.
In some things I'm even an L.
THAT'S IT! I QUIT THIS CLASS!
M

Group Messaging

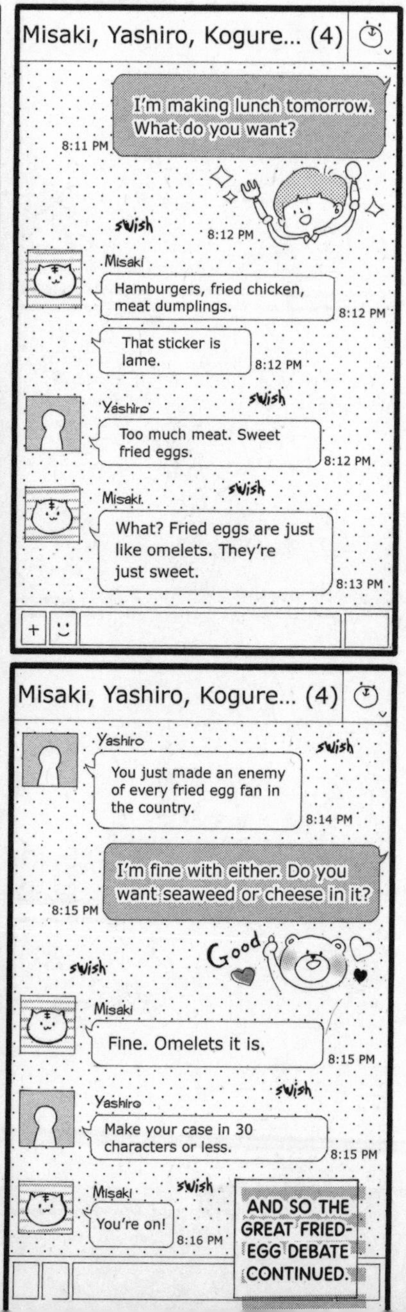
Misaki, Yashiro, Kogure... (4)
I'm making lunch tomorrow. What do you want?
8:11 PM
swish
8:12 PM
Misaki
Hamburgers, fried chicken, meat dumplings.
8:12 PM
That sticker is lame.
8:12 PM
swish
Yashiro
Too much meat. Sweet fried eggs.
8:12 PM
swish
Misaki
What? Fried eggs are just like omelets. They're just sweet.
8:13 PM
+
Misaki, Yashiro, Kogure... (4)
Yashiro
swish
You just made an enemy of every fried egg fan in the country.
8:14 PM
I'm fine with either. Do you want seaweed or cheese in it?
8:15 PM
Good
swish
Misaki
Fine. Omelets it is.
8:15 PM
swish
Yashiro
Make your case in 30 characters or less.
8:15 PM
AND SO THE GREAT FRIED-EGG DEBATE CONTINUED.
swish
Misaki
You're on!
8:16 PM

Group Text ②

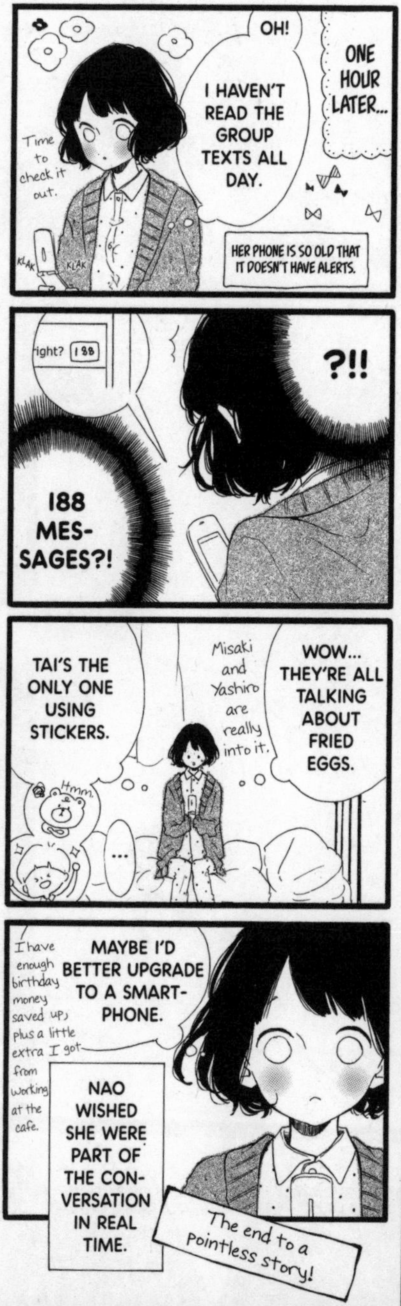
ONE HOUR LATER...
OH!
I HAVEN'T READ THE GROUP TEXTS ALL DAY.
HER PHONE IS SO OLD THAT IT DOESN'T HAVE ALERTS.
Time to check it out.
KLAK KLAK
?!!
ight? 188
188 MESSAGES?!
WOW... THEY'RE ALL TALKING ABOUT FRIED EGGS.
Misaki and Yashiro are really into it.
TAI'S THE ONLY ONE USING STICKERS.
Hmm.
...
MAYBE I'D BETTER UPGRADE TO A SMARTPHONE.
I have enough birthday money saved up, plus a little extra I got from working at the cafe.
NAO WISHED SHE WERE PART OF THE CONVERSATION IN REAL TIME.
The end to a pointless story!

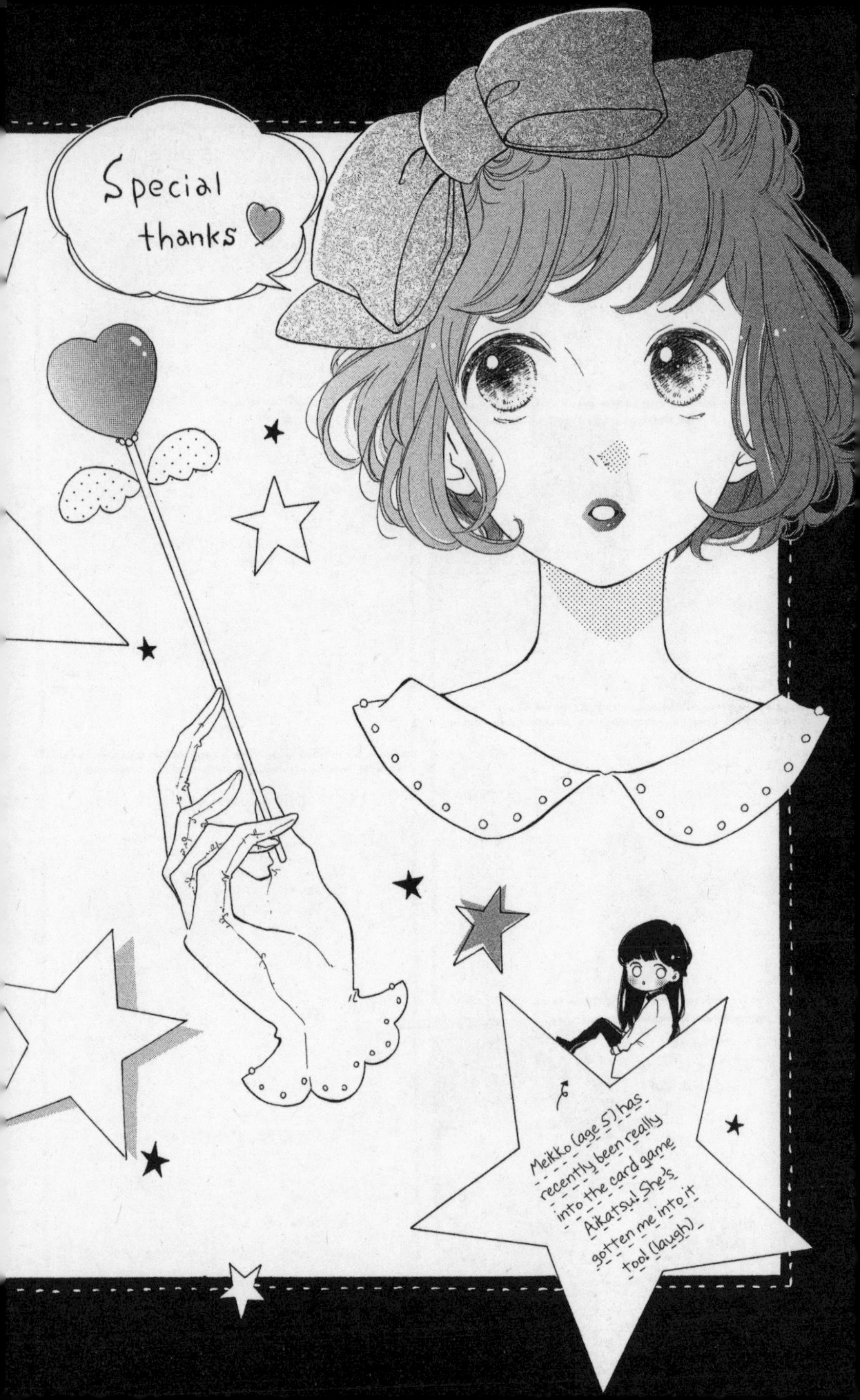
Special thanks
Meikko (age 5) has recently been really into the card game Aikatsu! She's gotten me into it too! (laugh)

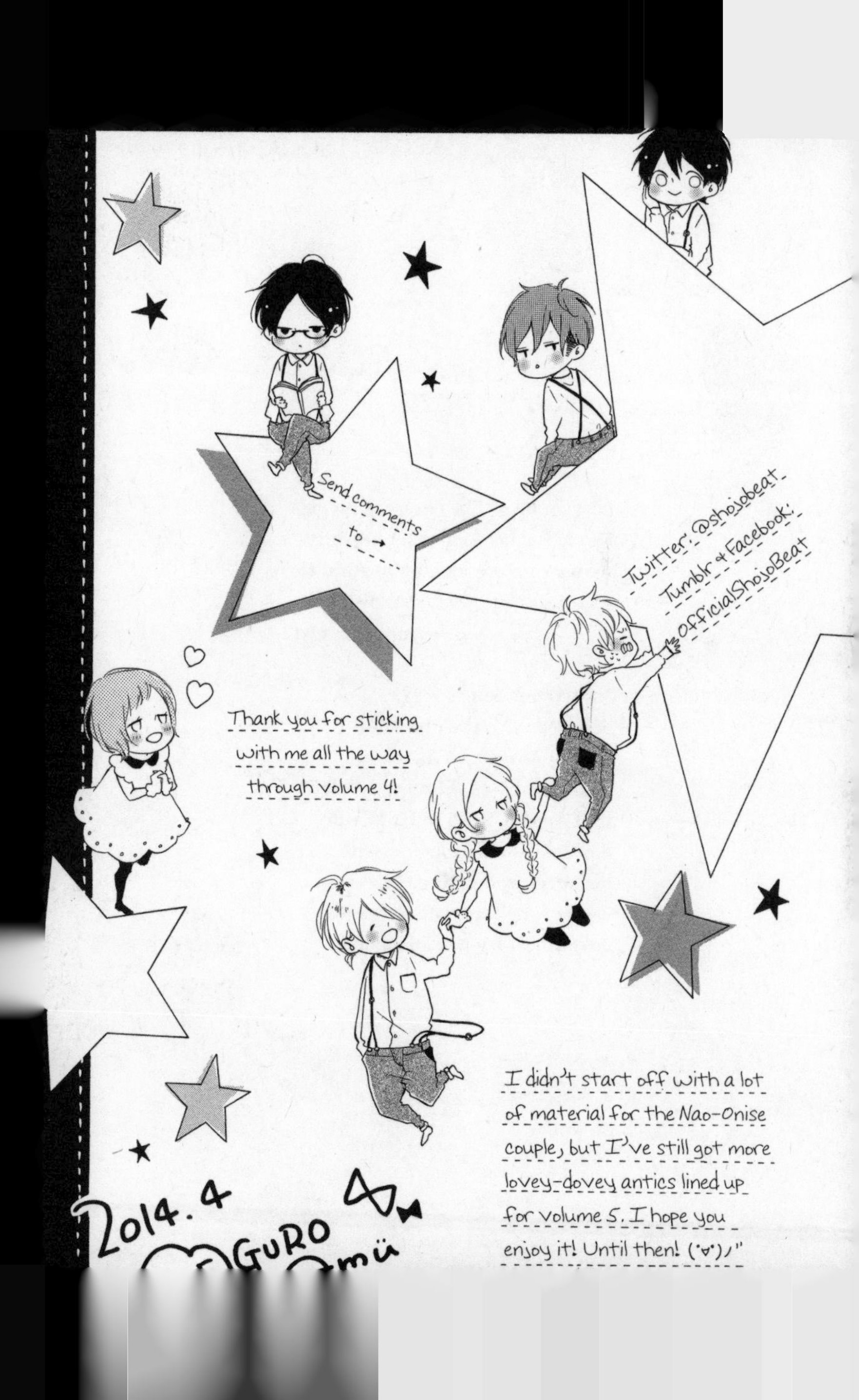
Send comments to →
Twitter: @shojobeat
Tumblr & Facebook:
OfficialShojoBeat
Thank you for sticking with me all the way through volume 4!
I didn't start off with a lot of material for the Nao-Onise couple, but I've still got more lovey-dovey antics lined up for volume 5. I hope you enjoy it! Until then! (ﾟ∀ﾟ)ﾉ"
2014.4

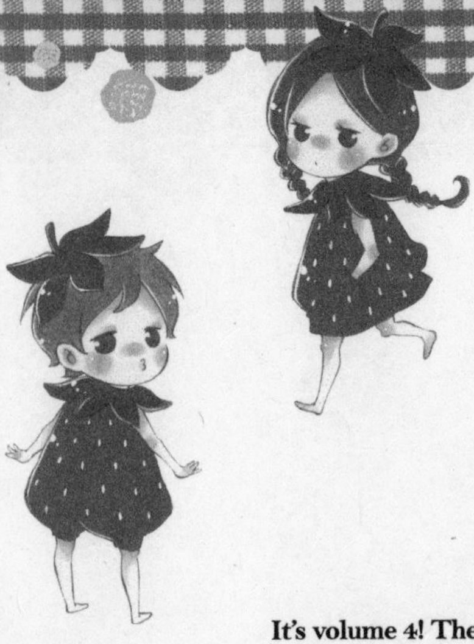

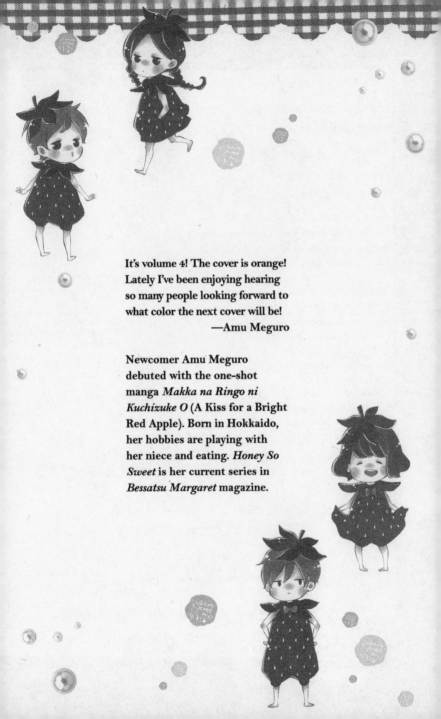

It's volume 4! The cover is orange! Lately I've been enjoying hearing so many people looking forward to what color the next cover will be!

—Amu Meguro

Newcomer Amu Meguro debuted with the one-shot manga *Makka na Ringo ni Kuchizuke O* (A Kiss for a Bright Red Apple). Born in Hokkaido, her hobbies are playing with her niece and eating. *Honey So Sweet* is her current series in *Bessatsu Margaret* magazine.

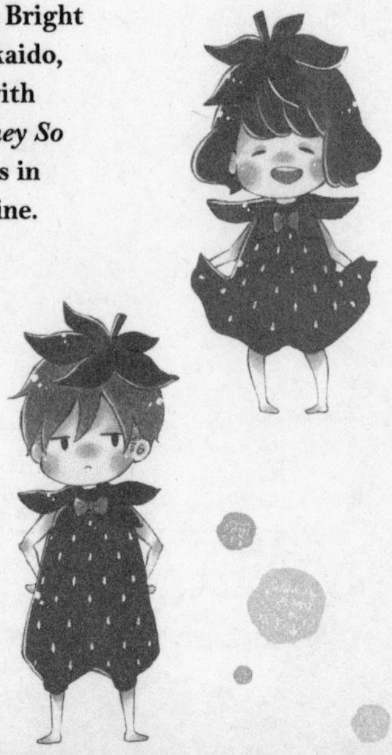

Shojo Beat Edition

Volume 4

STORY AND ART BY
Amu Meguro

Translation/Katherine Schilling
Touch-Up Art & Lettering/Inori Fukuda Trant
Design/Izumi Evers
Editor/Nancy Thistlethwaite

Printed in the U.S.A.

Published by VIZ Media, LLC
P.O. Box 77010
San Francisco, CA 94107

10 9 8 7 6 5 4 3 2 1
First printing, October 2016

 www.viz.com

 www.shojobeat.com

baya

You may be reading the wrong way!

This book reads right to left to maintain the original presentation and art of the Japanese edition, so action, sound effects and word balloons are reversed. This diagram shows how to follow the panels. Turn to the other side of the book to begin.

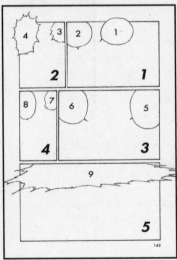